Dodd-Frank Act Stress Test 2015: Supervisory Stress Test Methodology and Results

March 2015

BOARD OF GOVERNORS OF THE FEDERAL RESERVE SYSTEM

One of the principal functions of the Federal Reserve is to regulate and supervise financial institutions, including bank holding companies (BHCs), savings and loan holding companies, state member banks, and systemically important nonbank financial institutions. Through its supervision, the Federal Reserve promotes a safe, sound, and stable banking and financial system that supports the growth and stability of the U.S. economy.[1]

To fulfill its supervisory objectives and to reorient its supervisory program in response to the lessons learned from the financial crisis, the Federal Reserve has created new frameworks and programs for the supervision of the largest and most complex financial institutions.

One of the key cross-firm programs is an annual assessment by the Federal Reserve of whether BHCs with $50 billion or more in total consolidated assets have effective capital adequacy processes and sufficient capital to absorb losses during stressful conditions, while meeting obligations to creditors and counterparties and continuing to serve as credit intermediaries. This annual assessment includes two related programs:

---

[1] Information on the Federal Reserve's regulation and supervision function, including more detail on stress testing and capital planning assessment, is available on the Federal Reserve website at www.federalreserve.gov/bankinforeg/default.htm.

- **The Comprehensive Capital Analysis and Review (CCAR)** evaluates a BHC's capital adequacy, capital adequacy process, and planned capital distributions, such as dividend payments and common stock repurchases. As part of CCAR, the Federal Reserve evaluates whether BHCs have sufficient capital to continue operations throughout times of economic and financial market stress and whether they have robust, forward-looking capital-planning processes that account for their unique risks. If the Federal Reserve objects to a BHC's capital plan, the BHC may not make any capital distribution unless the Federal Reserve indicates in writing that it does not object to the distribution.

- **Dodd-Frank Act supervisory stress testing** is a forward-looking quantitative evaluation of the impact of stressful economic and financial market conditions on BHC capital. This program serves to inform these financial companies, as well as the general public, how the institutions' capital ratios might change during a hypothetical set of adverse economic conditions as designed by the Federal Reserve. In addition to the annual supervisory stress test conducted by the Federal Reserve, each BHC is required to conduct annual company-run stress tests under the same supervisory scenarios and conduct a mid-cycle stress test under company-developed scenarios.

Contents

Executive Summary

The Dodd-Frank Wall Street Reform and Consumer Protection Act (Dodd-Frank Act) requires the Federal Reserve to conduct an annual stress test of BHCs with $50 billion or more in total consolidated assets and all nonbank financial companies designated by the Financial Stability Oversight Council (FSOC) for Federal Reserve supervision. The Board adopted rules implementing this requirement in October 2012.

For this year's stress test cycle (DFAST 2015), the Federal Reserve conducted supervisory stress tests of 31 BHCs.

This report provides

- background on Dodd-Frank Act stress testing;

- details of the adverse and severely adverse supervisory scenarios used in DFAST 2015;

- an overview of the analytical framework and methods used to generate the Federal Reserve's projections, highlighting notable changes from last year's program; and

- the results of the supervisory stress tests under adverse and severely adverse scenarios for the BHCs that participated in the DFAST 2015 program, presented both in the aggregate and for individual institutions.

The adverse and severely adverse supervisory scenarios used in DFAST 2015 feature U.S. and global recessions. In particular, the severely adverse scenario is characterized by a substantial global weakening in economic activity, including a severe recession in the United States, large reductions in asset prices, significant widening of corporate bond spreads, and a sharp increase in equity market volatility. The adverse scenario is characterized by a global weakening in economic activity and an increase in U.S. inflationary pressures that, overall, result in a rapid increase in both short- and long-term U.S. Treasury rates.

In conducting its supervisory stress tests, the Federal Reserve calculated its projections of a BHC's balance sheet, risk-weighted assets (RWAs), net income, and resulting regulatory capital ratios under these scenarios using data provided by the BHCs and a set of models developed or selected by the Federal Reserve. As compared to DFAST 2014, the Federal Reserve enhanced some of the supervisory models to incorporate more detailed data. These changes are highlighted in box 1. Specific descriptions of the supervisory models and related assumptions can be found in appendix B.

The results of the DFAST 2015 projections suggest that, in the aggregate, the 31 BHCs would experience substantial losses under both the adverse and the severely adverse scenarios.

Over the nine quarters of the planning horizon, losses at the 31 BHCs under the severely adverse scenario are projected to be $490 billion. This includes losses across loan portfolios, losses from credit impairment on securities held in the BHCs' invest-

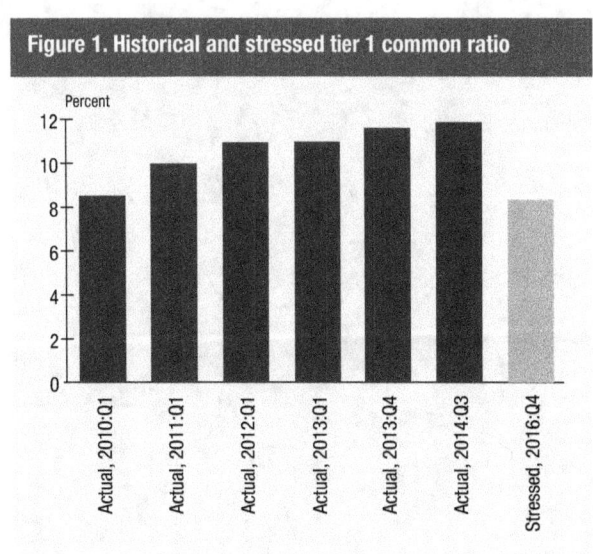

Figure 1. Historical and stressed tier 1 common ratio

ment portfolios, trading and counterparty credit losses from a global market shock, and other losses. Projected net revenue before provisions for loan and lease losses (pre-provision net revenue, or PPNR) is $310 billion, and net income before taxes is projected to be –$222 billion.

As illustrated in figure 1, in the severely adverse scenario, the aggregate tier 1 common capital ratio would fall from an actual 11.9 percent in the third quarter of 2014 to a post-stress level of 8.4 percent in the fourth quarter of 2016.

In the adverse scenario, projected losses, PPNR, and net income before taxes are $314 billion, $501 billion, and $178 billion, respectively. The aggregate tier 1 common capital ratio under the adverse scenario would fall 110 basis points to its minimum over the planning horizon of 10.8 percent before rising to 11.6 percent in the fourth quarter of 2016.

Details of the results are provided in the Supervisory Stress Test Results section of this report.

Background on Dodd-Frank Act Stress Testing

In the wake of the recent financial crisis, Congress enacted the Dodd-Frank Act.[2] Under the Dodd-Frank Act, the Federal Reserve is required to conduct an annual stress test of BHCs with total consolidated assets of $50 billion or more as well as nonbank financial companies designated by the FSOC for supervision by the Board (supervisory stress test).[3]

The Dodd-Frank Act also requires each of these "covered" companies to conduct its own stress tests and report its results to the Federal Reserve twice a year (company-run stress test).[4] The Federal Reserve first adopted rules implementing these requirements in October 2012 and most recently modified these rules in October 2014.[5]

In conducting the supervisory stress tests, the Federal Reserve projects balance sheet, RWAs, net income, and resulting post-stress capital levels and regulatory capital ratios over a nine-quarter "planning horizon," generally using a set of capital action assumptions prescribed in the Dodd-Frank Act stress test rules (see Capital Action Assumptions and Regulatory Capital Ratios). The projections are based on three supervisory macroeconomic scenarios required by the Dodd-Frank Act (baseline, adverse, and severely adverse) and created annually by the Federal Reserve.

For the "annual" company-run stress test, the BHCs use the same planning horizon, capital action assumptions, and scenarios[6] as those used in the supervisory stress test.[7] The use of common capital action assumptions and scenarios enhances the comparability of the supervisory and company-run results. The results of the company-run stress test must be submitted to the Federal Reserve. In addition, covered companies must also conduct a "mid-cycle" test and report the results to the Federal Reserve.

Together, the Dodd-Frank Act supervisory stress tests and the company-run stress tests are intended to provide company management and boards of directors, the public, and supervisors with forward-looking information to help gauge the potential effect of stressful conditions on the ability of these large banking organizations to absorb losses, while meeting obligations to creditors and other counterparties, and continuing to serve as credit intermediaries. To ensure this information is readily available, the Dodd-Frank Act requires each BHC to disclose a summary of its company-run stress test results and also requires the Federal Reserve to disclose a summary of its supervisory stress test results.[8]

---

[2] See 12 USC 5365(i)(1).

[3] The 31 BHCs that participated in the 2015 Dodd-Frank Act supervisory stress test are Ally Financial Inc.; American Express Company; Bank of America Corporation; The Bank of New York Mellon Corporation; BB&T Corporation; BBVA Compass Bancshares, Inc.; BMO Financial Corp.; Capital One Financial Corporation; Citigroup, Inc.; Citizens Financial Group, Inc.; Comerica Incorporated; Deutsche Bank Trust Corporation; Discover Financial Services; Fifth Third Bancorp; The Goldman Sachs Group, Inc.; HSBC North America Holdings Inc.; Huntington Bancshares Inc.; JPMorgan Chase & Co.; Keycorp; M&T Bank Corporation; Morgan Stanley; MUFG Americas Holdings Corporation; Northern Trust Corp.; The PNC Financial Services Group, Inc.; Regions Financial Corporation; Santander Holdings USA, Inc.; State Street Corporation; SunTrust Banks, Inc.; U.S. Bancorp; Wells Fargo & Company; and Zions Bancorporation.

[4] Under the Dodd-Frank Act, all financial companies with more than $10 billion in total consolidated assets that are supervised by a primary federal financial regulatory agency are required to conduct an annual company-run stress test. However, only the covered companies are subject to the additional mid-cycle stress test and the supervisory stress test.

[5] 12 CFR part 252, subparts E and F; see 77 FR 62378 (October 12, 2012); 79 FR 64026 (October 27, 2014); 79 FR 13498 (March 11, 2014); and 79 FR 64026 (October 27, 2014).

[6] Under the stress test rules, the Federal Reserve was required to provide the scenarios to companies no later than November 15, 2014, for DFAST 2015. See 12 CFR 252.54(b)(1).

[7] 12 CFR 252.156(b).

[8] 12 USC 5365(i)(1)(B)(v).

Supervisory Scenarios

On October 23, 2014, the Federal Reserve released the three supervisory scenarios: baseline, adverse, and severely adverse.[9] This section describes the adverse and severely adverse scenarios that were used for the projections contained in this report. These scenarios were developed using the approach described in the Board's Policy Statement on the Scenario Design Framework for Stress Testing.[10] The adverse and severely adverse scenarios are not forecasts but rather hypothetical scenarios designed to assess the strength of banking organizations and their resilience to an unfavorable economic environment.

Supervisory scenarios include trajectories for 28 variables. These include 16 variables that capture economic activity, asset prices, and interest rates in the U.S. economy and financial markets and three variables (real gross domestic product (GDP) growth, inflation, and the U.S./foreign currency exchange rate) in each of the four countries/country blocs.

Similar to last year, the Federal Reserve applied a global market shock to the trading portfolio of six BHCs with large trading and private equity exposures, and a counterparty default scenario component to eight BHCs with substantial trading, processing, or custodial operations (see Global Market Shock and Counterparty Default Components).

Severely Adverse Scenario

Figures 2 through 7 illustrate the hypothetical trajectories for some of the key variables describing U.S. economic activity and asset prices as well as global economic growth under the severely adverse scenario.

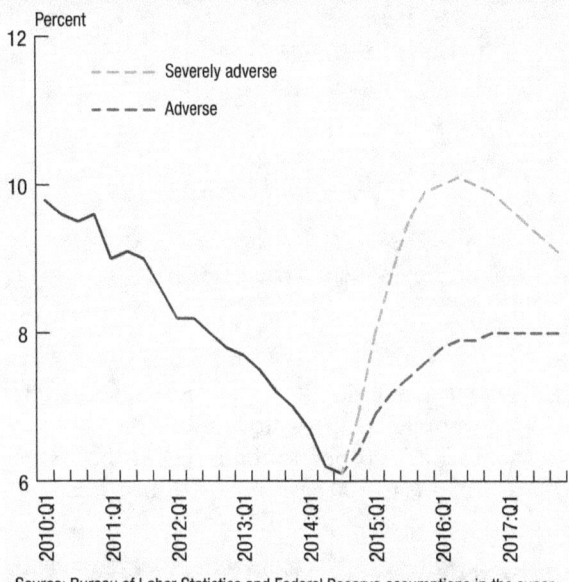

Figure 2. Unemployment rate in the severely adverse and adverse scenarios, 2010:Q1–2016:Q4

Source: Bureau of Labor Statistics and Federal Reserve assumptions in the supervisory scenarios.

The severely adverse scenario for the United States is characterized by a deep and prolonged recession in which the unemployment rate increases by 4 percentage points from its level in the third quarter of 2014, peaking at 10 percent in the middle of 2016. By the end of 2015, the level of real GDP is approximately 4.5 percent lower than its level in the third quarter of 2014; it begins to recover thereafter. Despite this decline in real activity, higher oil prices cause the annualized rate of change in the Consumer Price Index (CPI) to reach 4.3 percent in the near term, before subsequently falling back.

In response to this economic contraction—and despite the higher near-term path of CPI inflation—short-term interest rates remain near zero through 2017; long-term Treasury yields drop to 1 percent in the fourth quarter of 2014 and then edge up slowly over the remainder of the scenario period. Consistent with these developments, asset prices contract

[9] See Board of Governors of the Federal Reserve System (2014), "2015 Supervisory Scenarios for Annual Stress Tests Required under the Dodd-Frank Act Stress Testing Rules and the Capital Plan Rule" (Washington: Board of Governors, October 23), www.federalreserve.gov/newsevents/press/bcreg/bcreg20141023a1.pdf for additional information and for the details of the supervisory scenarios.

[10] 12 CFR part 252, appendix A.

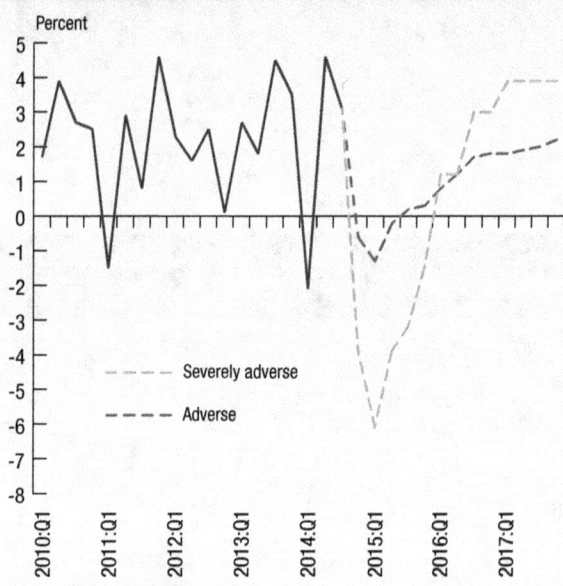

Figure 3. Real GDP growth rate in the severely adverse and adverse scenarios, 2010:Q1–2016:Q4

Source: Bureau of Economic Analysis and Federal Reserve assumptions in the supervisory scenarios.

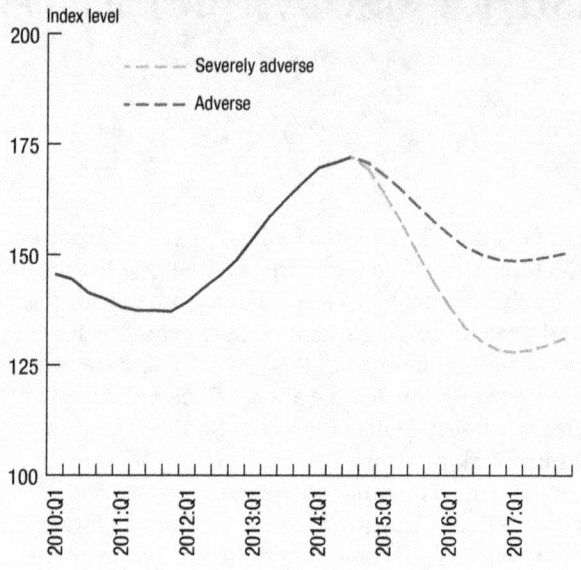

Figure 5. National House Price Index in the severely adverse and adverse scenarios, 2010:Q1–2016:Q4

Source: CoreLogic (seasonally adjusted by Federal Reserve) and Federal Reserve assumptions in the supervisory scenarios.

sharply in the scenario. Driven by an assumed decline in U.S. corporate credit quality, spreads on investment-grade corporate bonds jump from about 170 basis points to 500 basis points at their peak.

Equity prices fall approximately 60 percent from the third quarter of 2014 through the fourth quarter of 2015, and equity market volatility increases sharply. House prices decline approximately 25 percent during

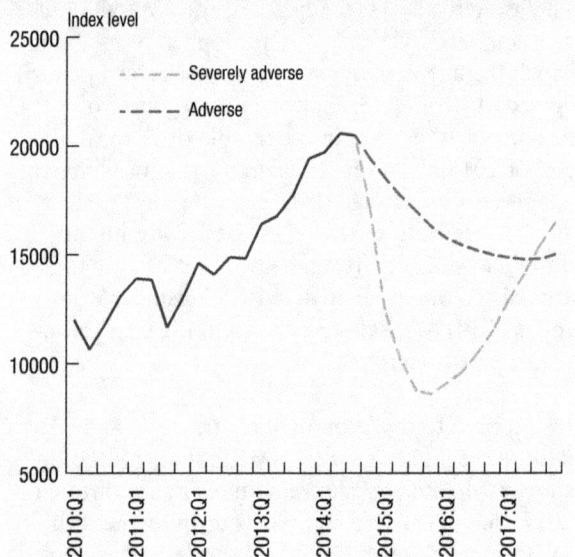

Figure 4. Dow Jones Total Stock Market Index, end of quarter in the severely adverse and adverse scenarios, 2010:Q1–2016:Q4

Source: Dow Jones and Federal Reserve assumptions in the supervisory scenarios.

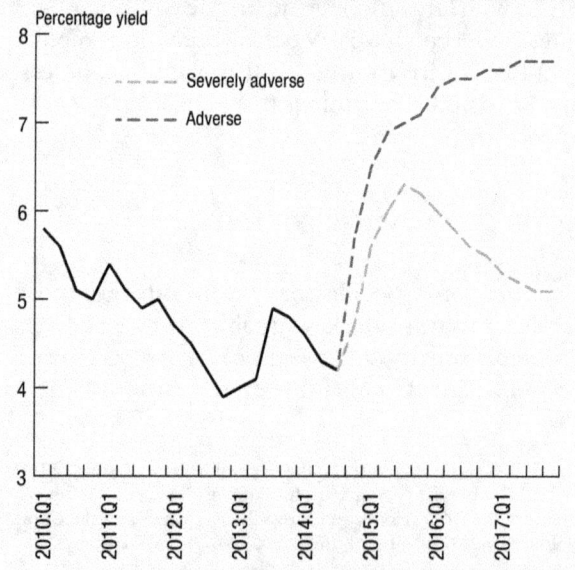

Figure 6. U.S. BBB corporate yield, quarterly average in the severely adverse and adverse scenarios, 2010:Q1–2016:Q4

Source: Merrill Lynch (adjusted by Federal Reserve using a Nelson-Siegel smoothed yield curve model) and Federal Reserve assumptions in the supervisory scenarios.

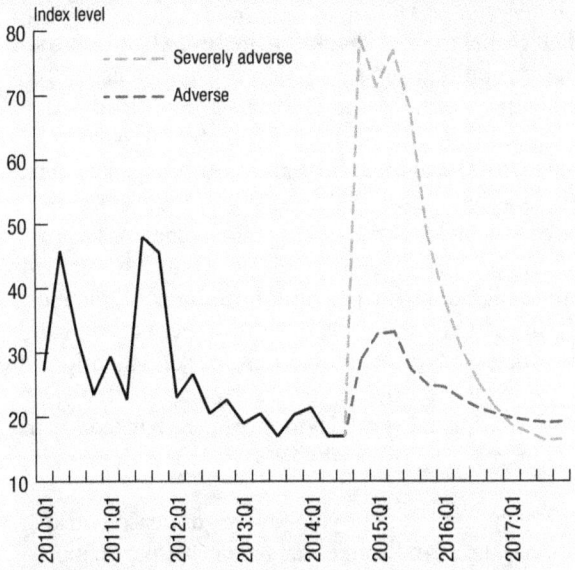

Figure 7. U.S. Market Volatility Index (VIX) in the severely adverse and adverse scenarios, 2010:Q1–2016:Q4

Index level

- - - - Severely adverse
- - - Adverse

2010:Q1 2011:Q1 2012:Q1 2013:Q1 2014:Q1 2015:Q1 2016:Q1 2017:Q1

Source: Chicago Board Options Exchange (converted to quarterly by Federal Reserve using the maximum quarterly close-of-day value) and Federal Reserve assumptions in the supervisory scenarios.

the scenario period relative to their level in the third quarter of 2014.

The international component of the severely adverse scenario features severe recessions in the euro area, the United Kingdom, and Japan, and below-trend growth in developing Asia. For economies that are heavily dependent on imported oil—including developing Asia, Japan, and the euro area—this economic weakness is exacerbated by the rise in oil prices featured in this scenario. Reflecting flight-to-safety capital flows associated with the scenario's global recession, the U.S. dollar is assumed to appreciate strongly against the euro and the currencies of developing Asia and to appreciate more modestly against the pound sterling. The dollar is assumed to depreciate modestly against the yen, also reflecting flight-to-safety capital flows.

This year's severely adverse scenario is similar to the 2014 severely adverse scenario. However, corporate credit quality is assumed to worsen even more than would be expected in a severe recession, resulting in a greater widening in corporate bond spreads, decline

in equity prices, and increase in equity market volatility than in the 2014 severely adverse scenario.

Adverse Scenario

Figures 2 through 7 illustrate the hypothetical trajectories for some of the key variables describing U.S. economic activity and asset prices as well as global economic growth under the adverse scenario. The United States experiences a mild recession that begins in the fourth quarter of 2014 and lasts through the second quarter of 2015. During this period, the level of real GDP falls approximately 0.5 percent relative to its level in the third quarter of 2014, and the unemployment rate increases to just over 7 percent. At the same time, the U.S. economy experiences a considerable rise in core inflation that results in a headline CPI inflation rate of 4 percent by the third quarter of 2015; headline inflation remains elevated thereafter. Short-term interest rates rise quickly as a result, reaching a little over 2.5 percent by the end of 2015 and 5.3 percent by the end of 2017. Longer-term Treasury yields increase by less. The recovery that begins in the second half of 2015 is quite sluggish, and the unemployment rate continues to increase, reaching 8 percent in the fourth quarter of 2016, and flattens thereafter. Equity prices fall both during and after the recession and by the end of the scenario are about 25 percent lower than in the third quarter of 2014. House prices and commercial real estate prices decline by approximately 13 and 16 percent, respectively, relative to their level in the third quarter of 2014.

Outside the United States, the adverse scenario features recessions in the euro area, the United Kingdom, and Japan and below-trend growth in developing Asia. This weakness in economic activity results in a period of deflation for some countries or country blocks. The exchange value of the dollar is little changed vis-à-vis the euro, the pound sterling, and the currencies of developing Asia. The dollar is assumed to depreciate against the yen, reflecting flight-to-safety capital flows.

This year's adverse scenario is qualitatively different from the 2014 adverse scenario. The main difference lies in the evolution of Treasury yields. The 2014 adverse scenario featured a sharp rise in long-term interest rates not accompanied by an increase in short-term interest rates and hence a steeper yield curve than in the baseline. In this year's scenario the hypothetical pick-up in U.S. inflation results in a yield curve that is higher and flatter than in the baseline.

Global Market Shock and Counterparty Default Components

The Federal Reserve applied a global market shock to the trading portfolio of six BHCs with large trading and private equity exposures.[11] In addition, the Federal Reserve applied a counterparty default component, which assumes the default of a BHC's largest counterparty under the global market shock conditions, to the same six BHCs and two other BHCs with substantial trading, processing, or custodial operations.[12] These components are an add-on to the macroeconomic conditions and financial market environment specified in the adverse and severely adverse scenarios.

The global market shock is a set of one-time, hypothetical shocks to a broad range of financial market risk factors. Generally, these shocks involve large and sudden changes in asset prices, interest rates, and spreads, reflecting general market dislocation and heightened uncertainty.[13] The Federal Reserve published the global market shock for the adverse and

severely adverse scenarios on October 30, 2014; the as-of date for the global market shock and the counterparty default is October 6, 2014.

The global market shock for the severely adverse scenario is built around a sudden sharp increase in general risk premiums and credit risk, combined with significant market illiquidity, which is associated in part with the distress of one or more large leveraged entities that rapidly sell a variety of assets into an already fragile market. Under the scenario, severe declines in the value of credit positions have immediate implications for less liquid products. While most declines are comparable to those experienced in 2008, products with favorable current market valuations are assumed to experience greater declines. Notably, option-adjusted spreads on mortgage-backed securities increase significantly.

Globally, government yield curves undergo marked shifts in level and shape due to market participants' risk aversion. The flight to quality pushes rates down across the term structure and appreciates currencies in the United States and certain European countries, while emerging markets and countries that are part of the so-called European periphery experience sharp increases in government yields. Countries that are affected by the flight to quality also experience currency appreciation. Fears of a prolonged and potentially more acute recession in Europe drive up sovereign credit default swap (CDS) spreads in a manner generally consistent with the experience of 2011.

The global market shock component for the adverse scenario is built around market shocks that are, by and large, similar in structure, but not as severe as those assumed in the severely adverse scenario. However, rates across the term structure in the United States and Europe increase, as the flight to quality mainly affects the short end of the yield curve while an aversion to long-term assets prevails. In addition, the increase in implied volatilities for equities is more subdued than what is typically associated with the level of the equity price declines in the adverse scenario.

---

[11] The six BHCs subject to the global market shock are Bank of America Corporation; Citigroup Inc.; The Goldman Sachs Group, Inc.; JPMorgan Chase & Co.; Morgan Stanley; and Wells Fargo & Co. See 12 CFR 252.54(b)(2)(i).

[12] The eight BHCs subject to the counterparty default component are Bank of America Corporation; The Bank of New York Mellon Corporation; Citigroup Inc.; The Goldman Sachs Group, Inc.; JPMorgan Chase & Co.; Morgan Stanley; State Street Corporation; and Wells Fargo & Co. See 12 CFR 252.54(b)(2)(ii).

[13] See CCAR 2015: Severely Adverse Market Shocks at www.federalreserve.gov/bankinforeg/CCAR-2015-Severely-Adverse-Market-Shocks.xlsx and CCAR 2015: Adverse Market Shocks at www.federalreserve.gov/bankinforeg/CCAR-2015-Adverse-Market-Shocks.xlsx.

Supervisory Stress Test Framework and Model Methodology

Analytical Framework

The Federal Reserve estimated the effect of the supervisory scenarios on the regulatory capital ratios of the 31 BHCs participating in DFAST 2015[14] by projecting the balance sheet, RWAs, net income, and resulting capital for each BHC over the nine-quarter planning horizon, which for DFAST 2015 begins in the fourth quarter of 2014 and ends in the fourth quarter of 2016. Projected net income, adjusted for the effect of taxes, is combined with capital action assumptions to project changes in equity capital. The approach followed is consistent with U.S. generally accepted accounting principles (GAAP) and regulatory capital rules.[15] Figure 8 illustrates the framework used to calculate changes in net income and regulatory capital.

Projected net income for the 31 BHCs is generated from projections of revenue, expenses, and various types of losses and provisions that flow into pre-tax net income, including

- pre-provision net revenue (PPNR);

- loan losses and changes in the allowance for loan and lease losses (ALLL);

- losses on loans held for sale and measured under the fair-value option;

- other-than-temporary impairment (OTTI) losses on investment securities in the available-for-sale (AFS) and held-to-maturity (HTM) portfolios;

Figure 8. Projecting net income and regulatory capital

Net interest income + noninterest income − noninterest expense
= **pre-provision net revenue (PPNR)**

Note: PPNR includes income from mortgage servicing rights and losses from operational-risk events, mortgage put-back losses, and OREO costs.

↓

PPNR + other revenue − provisions − AFS/HTM securities losses − HFS/FVO loan losses − trading and counterparty losses
= **pre-tax net income**

Note: Change in the allowance for loan and lease losses + net charge-offs = *provisions*

↓

Pre-tax net income − taxes − extraordinary items net of taxes − change in the valuation allowance
= **after-tax net income**

↓

After-tax net income − net distributions to common and preferred shareholders and other net reductions to shareholder's equity from DFAST assumptions
= **change in equity capital**

↓

Change in equity capital − deductions from regulatory capital + other additions to regulatory capital (including accumulated other comprehensive income, when applicable)
= **change in regulatory capital**

- for BHCs with large trading and private equity exposures, losses on those exposures resulting from a global market shock; and,

- for BHCs with substantial trading, processing, or custodial operations, losses from the default of their largest counterarty.

The projection of PPNR includes net interest income plus noninterest income minus noninterest expense. Consistent with U.S. GAAP, the projection of PPNR incorporates projected losses generated by operational-risk events such as fraud, computer system or other

---

[14] Certain BHCs with $50 billion in assets are not subject to the supervisory stress test this year. TD Bank US Holding Company and BancWest Corporation will be subject to Dodd-Frank Act stress testing beginning January 1, 2016. See 12 CFR 252.43(a)(3). All nonbank financial companies designated by the FSOC for supervision by the Board will be required to participate in the supervisory stress test pursuant to rule or order of the Federal Reserve Board. In 2014, the Board published a request for public comment on the application of enhanced prudential standards, including the supervisory stress test, to General Electric Capital Corporation. See 79 FR 71768 (December 3, 2014).

[15] 78 FR 62018 (October 11, 2013).

operating disruptions, and litigation-related costs; mortgage repurchase related losses; and expenses related to the disposition of foreclosed properties (other real estate owned (OREO) expenses).

Provisions for loan and lease losses equal projected loan losses for the quarter plus the amount needed for the ending ALLL to be at an appropriate level to account for projected future loan losses. The amount of provisions over and above loan losses may be negative—representing a drawdown of the ALLL (an ALLL release, increasing net income)—or positive—representing a need to build the ALLL (an additional provision, decreasing net income).

Because the loss projections follow U.S. GAAP and regulatory guidelines, they incorporate any differences in the way these guidelines recognize income and losses based on where assets are held on the BHCs' balance sheets. As a result, losses projected for similar or identical assets held in different portfolios can sometimes differ. For example, losses on loans held in accrual portfolio equal credit losses due to failure to pay obligations (cash flow losses resulting in net charge-offs). For similar loans that are held for sale, projected losses represent the change in fair value of the underlying assets in the supervisory scenario.

Following this approach, changes in both the fair value of AFS securities and OTTI losses on securities are separately projected over the nine-quarter planning horizon. Under U.S. GAAP, changes in the fair value of AFS securities are reflected in changes in accumulated other comprehensive income (AOCI) but do not flow through net income. In addition, if a security becomes OTTI, all or a portion of the difference between the fair value and amortized cost of the security must be recognized in earnings.[16] Consistent with U.S. GAAP, OTTI projections incorporate other-than-temporary differences between book value and fair value due to credit impairment but generally do not incorporate differences reflecting changes in liquidity or market conditions.

For the six BHCs subject to the global market shock, the losses on trading and private equity positions as well as the credit valuation adjustment are projected assuming an instantaneous re-pricing of these positions under the global market shock (see Global Market Shock and Counterparty Default Components). Losses from the global market shock are assumed to occur in the first quarter of the planning horizon. No subsequent recoveries on these positions are assumed, nor are there offsetting changes such as reductions in compensation or other expenses in reaction to the global market shock. In addition, incremental losses from potential defaults of obligors underlying BHCs' trading positions are projected over the planning horizon.

For the eight BHCs subject to the counterparty default component, the losses associated with the instantaneous and unexpected default of the largest counterparty across derivatives and securities financing transaction (SFT) activities are projected. These losses are assumed to occur in the first quarter of the planning horizon.

Over the planning horizon, the Federal Reserve projects quarter-end amounts for the components of the balance sheet. These projections are made under the assumption that BHCs maintain credit supply at long-run historical levels. Any new balances implied by these projections are assumed to have the same risk characteristics as those held by the BHC at the start of the planning horizon except for loan age. Where applicable, new loans are assumed to be current, and BHCs are assumed not to originate types of loans that are no longer allowed under various regulations. The Federal Reserve also incorporates material changes in a BHC's business plan, such as a planned merger, acquisition, or divestiture.[17] Only divestitures that had been completed or contractually agreed to prior to January 5, 2015, were incorporated. Once adjusted, assets are assumed to grow at the same rate as the pre-adjusted balance sheet.

Modeling Approach

The Federal Reserve's projections of revenue, expenses, and various types of losses and provisions that flow into pre-tax net income are based on data provided by the 31 BHCs participating in DFAST 2015 and on models developed or selected by Federal Reserve staff and reviewed by an independent group of Federal Reserve economists and analysts. The models are intended to capture how the balance sheet, RWAs, and net income of each BHC are affected by the macroeconomic and financial conditions described in the supervisory scenarios, given the

---

[16] A security is considered impaired when the fair value of the security falls below its amortized cost.

[17] The inclusion of the effects of such expected changes to a BHC's business plan does not—and is not intended to—express a view on the merits of such proposals and is not an approval or non-objection to such plans.

characteristics of the BHCs' loans and securities portfolios; trading, private equity, and counterparty exposures from derivatives and SFTs; business activities; and other relevant factors.[18]

Detail of model-specific methodology is provided in appendix B.

The Federal Reserve's approach to model design reflects the desire to produce supervisory stress test projections that

- are based on the same set of models and assumptions across BHCs;

- reflect an independent supervisory perspective;

- are forward-looking and may incorporate outcomes outside of historical experience; and

- are appropriately conservative and consistent with the purpose of a stress testing exercise.

With these objectives in mind, the models were developed using pooled historical data from many financial institutions and multiple data sources. As a result, the estimated parameters are the same for all BHCs and reflect the industrywide, portfolio-specific, and instrument-specific response to variation in the macroeconomic and financial market variables. This industrywide approach reflects both the challenge in estimating separate, statistically robust models for each of the 31 BHCs and the desire of the Federal Reserve not to assume that historical BHC-specific results will prevail in the future. This means that the projections made by the Federal Reserve will not necessarily match similar projections made by individual BHCs.

The Federal Reserve deviated from the industrywide modeling approach only in a very limited number of cases in which the historical data used to estimate the model were not sufficiently granular. In these cases, BHC-specific indicator variables (fixed effects) were included in the models. Additionally, in some cases, the projections of certain types of losses use sensitivities generated by the BHCs from their internal risk-measurement models.

Model Methodology and Validation

A large majority of the models used for the supervisory stress test were developed by Federal Reserve analysts and economists, but a few are third-party models.[19] Internally developed models draw on economic research and analysis as well as industry practice in modeling the effect of borrower, instrument, collateral characteristics, and macroeconomic factors on revenue, expenses, and losses. The approaches mostly build on work done by the Federal Reserve in previous stress tests. In some cases, the models represent significant refinement and advancement of earlier work, reflecting advances in modeling technique, richer and more detailed data, and longer histories of performance in both adverse and more benign economic settings (see box 1).

All models are reviewed each year by an independent model validation team composed of economists and analysts from across the Federal Reserve System with a focus on the design, estimation, and implementation of the models. Model reviewers are primarily Federal Reserve subject-matter experts who are not involved in model development and who report to a different oversight group than model developers. Additionally, control procedures surrounding the model design and implementation processes are reviewed by process control experts.

Loan losses are estimated separately for different categories of loans, based on the type of obligor (e.g., consumer or commercial and industrial), collateral (e.g., residential real estate, commercial real estate), loan structure (e.g., revolving credit lines), and accounting treatment (accrual or fair value). These categories generally follow the classifications of the Consolidated Financial Statements for Holding Companies (FR Y-9C) regulatory report, though some loss projections are made for more granular loan categories.[20]

Two general approaches are taken to model losses on the accrual loan portfolio. In the first approach, the models estimate expected losses under the macroeco-

---

[18] In some cases, the loss models estimated the effect of local-level macroeconomic data, which were projected based on their historical covariance with national variables included in the supervisory scenarios.

[19] A list of providers of the proprietary models and data used by the Federal Reserve in connection with DFAST 2015 is available in appendix B.

[20] The FR Y-9C report template is available on the Federal Reserve website at www.federalreserve.gov.

Box 1. Model Changes for DFAST 2015

Each year, the Federal Reserve has refined elements of both the substance and process of the Dodd-Frank supervisory stress tests, including the continued development and enhancement of independent supervisory models. Revisions to the Federal Reserve's supervisory stress test models generally reflect advances in modeling techniques, richer and more detailed data, and longer histories of performance in both adverse and benign economic settings. Changes in the quality of submitted data, portfolio risk characteristics, and the macroeconomic scenario are major factors that could lead to changes in the Federal Reserve's estimates. For example, this year's severely adverse scenario features a greater decline in equity prices, the somewhat greater widening of the corporate bond spread, and a sharper increase in equity market volatility than last year. These scenario features affect various elements of net income, other comprehensive income, and market risk-weighted assets.

In 2015, the Federal Reserve did not introduce significant changes to its modeling framework, and, overall, revisions to most supervisory models were relatively incremental. Changes to accrual loan loss models were generally modest and did not have a large net effect on aggregate estimates of total loan losses for the 31 participating BHCs.

The net effect of changes to models for other losses was somewhat larger, due in part to the refinement of risk factors used in selected securities models. In addition, the Federal Reserve changed two aspects of its methodology for estimating PPNR.

- Other noninterest income and expense are now modeled using a simpler approach that is designed to reduce the volatility of the results that stems from the historical volatility in the underlying income and expense items.

- Interest expense on subordinated debt is now modeled based on instrument-level informa-

tion and reflects an increase in the use of more detailed data to project PPNR.

Supervisory Capital Model Enhancement

One key enhancement the Federal Reserve has made this year is in the model it uses to project regulatory capital and capital ratios (supervisory capital model), incorporating more detailed data now available on regulatory reports regarding the Board's revised regulatory capital framework. The enhancements were made to better align the the supervisory capital model projections with the revised regulatory capital framework and related accounting guidance. The main enhancements to this model include

- differentiating AOCI items that are not subject to transition arrangements in the revised regulatory capital framework from those that are subject to transition;

- refining the calculation of future taxable income used to determine whether a deferred tax asset will be realizable in the future based on the type of deferred tax asset; and

- projecting changes in valuation allowances for net deferred tax assets based on the macroeconomic scenarios, in response to changes in the treatment of deferred tax assets in the revised regulatory capital framework.

These enhancements are possible due to data currently available on regulatory reports that allow the Federal Reserve to better differentiate between different types of deferred tax assets and AOCI. The impact of these enhancements varies across BHCs depending on the amount of AOCI items not subject to transition arrangements, projections of future taxable income, and the composition and amount of projected net deferred tax assets. The enhancements can result in higher or lower capital ratios, depending on the particular combination of such factors.

nomic scenario. These models generally involve projections of the probability of default, loss given default, and exposure at default for each loan or segment of loans in the portfolio, given conditions in the scenario. In the second approach, the models capture the historical behavior of net charge-offs relative to changes in macroeconomic and financial market variables.

Accrual loan losses are projected using detailed loan information, including borrower characteristics, collateral characteristics, characteristics of the loans or credit facilities, amounts outstanding and yet to be drawn down (for credit lines), payment history, and current payment status.

Data are collected on individual loans or credit facilities for wholesale loan, domestic retail credit card, and residential mortgage portfolios. For other domestic and international retail loans, the data are collected based on segments of the portfolio (e.g. segments defined by borrower credit score, geographic location, and loan-to-value (LTV) ratio).

Losses on retail loans for which a BHC chose the fair-value option accounting treatment and loans carried at the lower of cost or market value (i.e. loans held for sale and held for investment) are estimated over the nine quarters of the planning horizon using a duration-based approach. Losses on wholesale loans held for sale or measured under the fair-value option are estimated by revaluing each loan or commitment each quarter of the planning horizon.

Losses on securities held in the AFS and HTM portfolios are estimated using models that incorporate other-than-temporary differences between amortized cost and fair market value due to credit impairment but generally do not incorporate differences reflecting changes in liquidity or market conditions. Some securities, including U.S. Treasury and U.S. government agency obligations and U.S. government agency mortgage-backed securities, are assumed not to be at risk for the kind of credit impairment that results in OTTI charges. For securitized obligations, models estimate delinquency, default, severity, and prepayment on the underlying pool of collateral. OTTI on direct obligations such as corporate bonds is based on an assessment of the probability of default or severe credit deterioration of the security issuer or group of issuers over the planning horizon. The models use securities data collected at the individual

security (CUSIP) level, including the amortized cost, market value, and any OTTI taken on the security to date.

Losses related to the global market shock and the counterparty default components are estimated using BHC-estimated sensitivities to various market factors of trading positions, private equity, and other fair-value assets held in the trading book and the revaluations of counterparty exposures and credit valuation adjustment based on the global market shock. These estimates are based on BHCs' internal models and methodologies and are provided to the Federal Reserve by the BHCs (see Global Market Shock and Counterparty Default Components).

PPNR is projected using a series of models that relate the components of a BHC's revenues and non-credit-related expenses, expressed as a share of relevant asset or liability balances, to BHC characteristics and to macroeconomic variables. Most components are projected using data on historical revenues and operating and other non-credit-related expenses reported on the FR Y-9C report. Separate data are collected about mortgage loans that were sold or securitized but expose a BHC to potential put-back risk and the BHCs' historical losses related to operational-risk events, which are modeled separately from other components of PPNR.

The balance sheet projections are derived using a common framework for determining the effect of the scenarios on balance sheet growth, and, as noted, incorporate assumptions about credit supply that limit aggregate credit contraction. These sets of projections are based on historical data from the Federal Reserve's national flow of funds accounts, consolidated balance sheet information for each BHC, and additional data collected by the Federal Reserve.

Once pre-tax net income is determined using the above components, a consistent tax rate is applied to calculate after-tax net income.[21] After-tax net income also includes other tax effects, such as changes in the valuation allowance applied to deferred tax assets, and BHC-reported information about extraordinary

---

[21] For a discussion of the effect of changing this tax rate assumption on the post-stress tier 1 common capital ratio, see box 2 of Board of Governors of the Federal Reserve System (2013), "Dodd-Frank Act Stress Test 2013: Supervisory Stress Test Methodology and Results."

income items and income attributable to minority interests.

Data Inputs

The models are developed and executed with data collected by the Federal Reserve on regulatory reports as well as proprietary third-party industry data.

Certain projections rely on aggregate information from the *Financial Accounts of the United States* (Z.1) statistical release, which is a quarterly publication by the Federal Reserve of national flow of funds; balance sheets; and integrated macroeconomic accounts by sector, such as households and nonfinancial corporate businesses.[22] Others rely on the FR Y-9C report, which contains consolidated income statement and balance sheet information for each BHC. Additionally, FR Y-9C includes off-balance sheet items and other supporting schedules, such as the components of RWA and regulatory capital.

Most of the data used in the Federal Reserve's projections are collected through the Capital Assessments and Stress Testing (FR Y-14A/Q/M) reports, which include a set of annual, quarterly, or monthly schedules.[23] These reports collect detailed data on PPNR, loans, securities, trading and counterparty risk, and losses related to operational-risk events. Each of the 31 BHCs participating in DFAST 2015 submitted data as of September 30, 2014, through the FR Y-14M and FR Y-14Q schedules in October and November of 2014 and the FR Y-14A schedules, which also include projected data, on January 5, 2015.

BHCs were required to submit detailed loan and securities information for all material portfolios, where the portfolio is deemed to be "material" if the size of the portfolio exceeds either 5 percent of the BHC's tier 1 capital or $5 billion. The portfolio categories are defined in the FR Y-14M and Y-14Q instructions. For portfolios falling below these thresholds, the BHCs had the option to submit or not submit the detailed data. Portfolios for which the Federal Reserve did not receive detailed data were assigned a loss rate equal to a high percentile of the loss rates projected for BHCs that did submit data for that category of loan or security.

While BHCs are responsible for ensuring the completeness and accuracy of data reported on the FR Y-14, the Federal Reserve made considerable efforts to validate BHC-reported data and requested resubmissions of data where errors were identified. In certain instances, loans with insufficient or unreliable data were assigned a loss rate at or near the 90th percentile of the loss rates projected for the relevant loan segment for the BHCs that did provide reliable data. Where certain data elements were unreported, conservative values were assigned (e.g., high LTV values or low credit scores).[24] These assumptions are intended to reflect a conservative view of the risk characteristics of the portfolios, given insufficient information to make more risk-sensitive projections.

Capital Action Assumptions and Regulatory Capital Ratios

After-tax net income and AOCI are combined with prescribed capital actions to estimate components of equity capital. Changes in the equity capital components are the primary drivers in changes in capital levels and ratios over the planning horizon. In addition to the equity capital components, the calculation of capital ratios accounts for taxes and items subject to adjustment or deduction, limits the recognition of certain intangible assets, and imposes other restrictions as specified in the Board's regulatory capital rules.

The Dodd-Frank Act company-run stress test rules prescribe consistent capital action assumptions for all BHCs. In its supervisory stress tests, the Board generally followed these capital action assumptions. For the first quarter of the planning horizon, capital actions for each BHC are assumed to be the actual actions taken by the BHC during that quarter. Over the remaining eight quarters, common stock dividend payments are assumed to be the average of the first quarter of the planning horizon and the three preceding calendar quarters. Also, BHCs are assumed to pay scheduled dividend, interest, or principal payments on any other capital instrument eligible for inclusion in the numerator of a regulatory capital ratio. However, repurchases of such capital instruments and issuance of stock are assumed to be zero, except for common-stock issuance associated with

---

[22] *Financial Accounts of the United States* (Z.1) is available at www .federalreserve.gov/releases/z1/.

[23] The FR Y-14 schedules are available at www.federalreserve.gov/ apps/reportforms/default.aspx.

[24] The method of applying conservative assumptions to certain risk segments was used only in cases in which the data-related issues were isolated in such a way that the remainder of the portfolio could be readily modeled using the existing supervisory framework.

expensed employee compensation or in connection with a planned merger or acquisition.

The four regulatory capital ratios in DFAST 2015 are common equity tier 1, tier 1 risk-based capital, total risk-based capital, and tier 1 leverage. A BHC's regulatory capital ratios are calculated in accordance with the Board's regulatory capital rules using Federal Reserve projections of assets and RWAs. In 2013, the Board adopted revisions to its regulatory capital framework to address shortcomings in capital requirements that became apparent during the financial crisis.[25] The revisions to the regulatory capital framework introduce a new common equity tier 1 capital ratio, strengthen the eligibility criteria for capital, and otherwise increase the quantity and quality of capital that banking organizations are required to hold. These revisions are being phased in between 2014 and 2019. Calculations of regulatory capital for a given BHC are in accordance with the regulatory requirements that will be in effect during a particular quarter of the planning horizon for that BHC.

The applicable transition arrangements for the regulatory capital ratios vary depending on whether a BHC is an "advanced approaches BHC," which is defined as a BHC that has total consolidated assets greater than or equal to $250 billion, or total consolidated on-balance sheet foreign exposures of at least $10 billion. Specifically, advanced approaches BHCs became subject to a common equity tier 1 ratio and an increased tier 1 risk-based capital ratio in 2014, while all other BHCs became subject to these requirements beginning in 2015.[26]

Starting in 2015, the regulatory capital framework introduces a new standardized approach for calculating risk-weighted assets, which replaces the calculation of risk weights using the general risk-based capital approach set forth in the Board's capital adequacy guidelines (general risk-based capital approach).[27] For this stress test cycle, the denominator of each

BHC's regulatory capital ratios was calculated using the general risk-based capital approach for the first quarter of the planning horizon (the fourth quarter of 2014) and using the standardized approach for the remaining quarters of the planning horizon.

Notably, eight BHCs began calculating their risk-weighted assets using the advanced approaches rule in the second quarter of 2014.[28] Under the regulatory capital rules, these firms are required to meet the minimum risk-based capital ratios under both the advanced approaches rules and under the generally applicable risk-based capital rules. However, DFAST 2015 does not incorporate measures of risk-weighted assets using the advanced approaches rules.[29]

In addition to the four regulatory capital ratios, DFAST 2015 includes projections of a BHC's tier 1 common capital ratio. The tier 1 common capital ratio equals the common equity portion of tier 1 capital divided by RWAs calculated under the general risk-based capital approach.

Preserving the tier 1 common capital ratio maintains consistency with previous stress testing cycles during the phase-in of the new common equity tier 1 capital ratio. The tier 1 common capital ratio differs from the common equity tier 1 ratio in the following ways:

- For advanced approaches BHCs, most elements of AOCI flow through to common equity tier 1 but not to tier 1 common capital.

- More assets are subject to deduction from common equity tier 1 capital than from tier 1 common capital, including investments in unconsolidated financial institutions and all deferred tax assets that arise from operating losses and tax credit carryforwards.

- Beginning in 2015 (the second quarter of the planning horizon), the denominators of the two ratios use different approaches for calculating RWAs.

Table 1 shows the rules used to calculate the numerators and denominators of the capital ratios as well as the timing of implementation of these rules for advanced approaches and non-advanced approaches BHCs.

---

[25] See 12 CFR part 217.

[26] As of 2014:Q3, MUFG Americas Holdings Corporation was an advanced approaches BHC because it had opted into the advanced approaches rule, even though it did not meet the rule's numerical thresholds. In December 2014, the Board approved the MUFG's request to no longer use the advanced approaches rule, and the BHC ceased to qualify as an advanced approaches BHC. Accordingly, for all projected quarters of DFAST 2015, the BHC was treated as a non-advanced approaches BHC for purposes of calculating capital levels and ratios.

[27] 12 CFR 225, appendix A.

[28] Federal Reserve Board (2014), "Agencies Permit Certain Banking Organizations to Begin Using Advanced Approaches Framework to Determine Risk-Based Capital Requirements," press release, February 21, www.federalreserve.gov/newsevents/press/bcreg/20140221a.htm.

[29] 79 FR 13498, 13502 (March 11, 2014).

Table 1. Applicable capital ratios and calculations in the 2015 Dodd-Frank Act stress tests			
Capital ratio	Aspect of ratio	2014:Q4	2015–16
Advanced approaches BHCs			
Common equity tier 1 ratio	Capital in numerator	Revised capital framework	Revised capital framework
	Denominator	General approach RWAs	Standardized approach RWAs
Tier 1 ratio	Capital in numerator	Revised capital framework	Revised capital framework
	Denominator	General approach RWAs	Standardized approach RWAs
Total capital ratio	Capital in numerator	Revised capital framework	Revised capital framework
	Denominator	General approach RWAs	Standardized approach RWAs
Tier 1 leverage ratio	Capital in numerator	Revised capital framework	Revised capital framework
	Denominator	Average assets	Average assets
Tier 1 common ratio	Capital in numerator	Basel I-based capital	Basel I-based capital
	Denominator	General approach RWAs	General approach RWAs
Other BHCs			
Common equity tier 1 ratio	Capital in numerator	n/a	Revised capital framework
	Denominator	n/a	Standardized approach RWAs
Tier 1 ratio	Capital in numerator	Basel I-based capital	Revised capital framework
	Denominator	General approach RWAs	Standardized approach RWAs
Total capital ratio	Capital in numerator	Basel I-based capital	Revised capital framework
	Denominator	General approach RWAs	Standardized approach RWAs
Tier 1 leverage ratio	Capital in numerator	Basel I-based capital	Revised capital framework
	Denominator	Average assets	Average assets
Tier 1 common ratio	Capital in numerator	Basel I-based capital	Basel I-based capital
	Denominator	General approach RWA	General approach RWA

"Basel I-based capital" indicates that regulatory capital is calculated under the rules in place before the implementation of the revised capital framework (see 12 CFR part 225, appendix A). "Revised capital framework" indicates that regulatory capital is calculated under the revised capital framework. "General Approach RWAs" indicates that risk-weighted assets are calculated using the approach under the general risk-based capital rules (see 12 CFR part 225, appendix A), while "Standardized approach RWAs" indicates that risk-weighted assets are calculated using the standardized approach under the revised capital framework. Not applicable (n/a) indicates that the capital ratio was not calculated for that time period. An advanced approaches BHC includes any BHC that has consolidated assets greater than or equal to $250 billion or total consolidated on-balance sheet foreign exposure of at least $10 billion as of December 31, 2014. See 12 CFR 217.100(b)(1). Other BHCs include any BHC that is subject to 12 CFR 225.8 and is not an advanced approaches BHC.

Supervisory Stress Test Results

This section describes the Federal Reserve's projections of RWAs, losses, revenues, expenses, and capital positions for the 31 BHCs participating in DFAST 2015 under the severely adverse and adverse scenarios. Results are presented both in the aggregate for the 31 BHCs and for individual BHCs. The aggregate results provide a sense of the stringency of the adverse and severely adverse scenario projections and the sensitivities of losses, revenues, and capital at these BHCs as a group to the stressed economic and financial market conditions contained in those scenarios. The range of results across individual BHCs reflects differences in business focus, asset composition, revenue and expense sources, as well as differences in portfolio risk characteristics. The comprehensive results for individual BHCs are reported in appendix C.

Severely Adverse Scenario

Stressed Regulatory Capital Ratios and Risk-Weighted Assets

The projections suggest significant declines in capital ratios for nearly all the BHCs under the severely adverse scenario. In the aggregate, each of the four capital ratios calculated in the third quarter of 2014 declines over the course of the planning horizon, with year-end 2016 levels ranging from 2.9 percentage points to 5.2 percentage points lower than at the start of the planning horizon (see table 2). Table 3 presents these ratios for each of the 31 BHCs.

The changes in post-stress capital ratios vary considerably across BHCs (see figure 10). Overall, post-stress capital ratios decline from the beginning to the end of the planning horizon for all but four of the BHCs. The post-stress capital ratios incorporate Federal Reserve projections of the levels of total average assets and RWAs over the planning horizon. Declines in capital ratios in part reflect an increase in projected RWAs over the planning horizon. The increase in RWAs reflects projected asset and loan growth in

the scenario and the impact of the scenario's assumed increase in equity market volatility on market risk RWAs at firms with large trading portfolios. The shift from general approach RWA to standardized approach RWA in the first quarter of 2015 for the calculation of regulatory capital ratios resulted in a significant increase in the level of credit-related RWAs for some BHCs.

Projected Losses

The Federal Reserve projects that the 31 BHCs as a group would experience significant losses under the severely adverse scenario. In this scenario, losses are projected to be $490 billion for the 31 BHCs in the aggregate over the nine quarters of the planning horizon. These losses include

- $340 billion in accrual loan portfolio losses,

- $18 billion in OTTI and other realized securities losses,

- $103 billion in trading and/or counterparty losses at the eight BHCs with substantial trading, processing, or custodial operations, and

- $29 billion in additional losses from items such as loans booked under the fair-value option (see table 2).

The biggest sources of loss are accrual loan portfolios and trading and counterparty positions subject to the global market shock and counterparty default component. Together, these account for 90 percent of the projected losses for the 31 BHCs (figure 9).

Loan Losses

Projected losses on consumer-related lending—domestic residential mortgages, credit cards, and other consumer loans—represent 56 percent of projected loan losses and 39 percent of total projected losses for the 31 BHCs (see table 4). This is consistent with the severely adverse scenario, which features high unemployment rates and significant declines in hous-

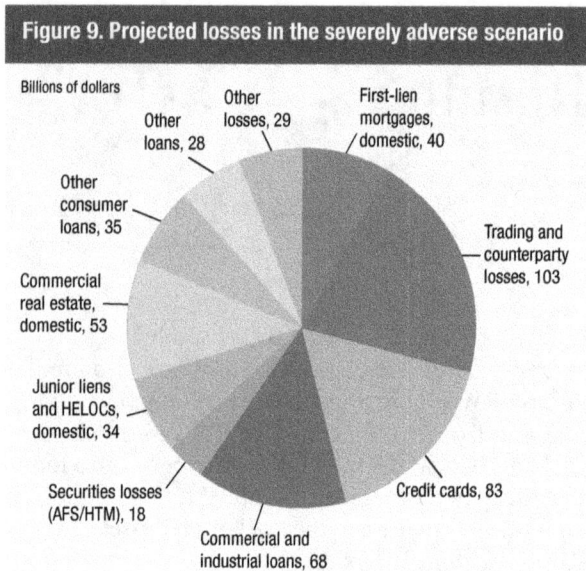

Figure 9. Projected losses in the severely adverse scenario

Billions of dollars

- Other loans, 28
- Other losses, 29
- First-lien mortgages, domestic, 40
- Other consumer loans, 35
- Trading and counterparty losses, 103
- Commercial real estate, domestic, 53
- Junior liens and HELOCs, domestic, 34
- Securities losses (AFS/HTM), 18
- Credit cards, 83
- Commercial and industrial loans, 68

ing prices. Losses on credit card loans are the single largest category of losses at $83 billion, representing 24 percent of total projected loan losses. This is followed by $74 billion of losses across domestic residential mortgage loans, including both first liens and junior liens/home equity lines of credit, and $68 billion across commercial and industrial loans.

For the 31 BHCs as a group, the nine-quarter cumulative loss rate for all accrual loan portfolios is 6.1 percent, where the loss rate is calculated as total projected loan losses over the nine quarters of the planning horizon divided by average loan balances over the horizon. This rate is lower than the overall loan loss rate in DFAST 2014, continuing a trend of declining loan loss rates under the severely adverse scenario over time, as borrower and loan characteristics have continued to improve. Still, this rate is high by historical standards and more severe than any U.S. recession since the 1930s. Total loan loss rates vary significantly across BHCs, ranging between 2.3 percent and 12.2 percent across these institutions (see figure 11).

The differences in total loan loss rates across the BHCs reflect differences in the risk characteristics of the portfolios held by each BHC with regard to both the type of lending of each portfolio and the loans within each portfolio. Loan portfolio composition matters because projected loss rates vary significantly by loan type. In the aggregate, nine-quarter cumulative loss rates vary between 2.9 percent on other loans and 13.1 percent on credit cards, reflecting both differences in typical performance of these

loans—some loan types tend to generate higher losses, though generally also higher revenue—and differences in the sensitivity of different types of lending to the severely adverse scenario. In particular, lending categories for which performance is sensitive to unemployment rates or housing prices may experience high stressed loss rates due to the considerable stress on these factors in the severely adverse scenario.

Projected loss rates on most loan categories show similar dispersion across BHCs (see figures D.1 through D.7).[30] There are significant differences across BHCs in the projected loan loss rates for similar types of loans. For example, while the median projected loss rate on domestic first-lien residential mortgages is 3.5 percent, the rates among BHCs with first-lien mortgage portfolios vary from a low of 0.9 percent to a high of 12.5 percent. Similarly, for commercial and industrial loans, the range of projected loss rates is from 3.0 percent to 14.0 percent, with a median of 4.8 percent.

Differences in projected loss rates across BHCs primarily reflect differences in loan and borrower characteristics. In addition, some BHCs have taken write-downs on portfolios of impaired loans either purchased or acquired through mergers. Losses on these loans are projected using the same loss models used for loans of the same type, and the resulting loss projections are reduced by the amount of such write-downs. For these BHCs, projected loss rates will be lower than for BHCs that hold similar loans that have not been subject to purchase-related write-downs.

Losses on Trading, Private Equity, SFT, and Derivatives Positions

The severely adverse scenario results include $103 billion in trading losses from the global market shock at the six BHCs with large trading and private-equity exposures and losses from the counterparty default component at the eight BHCs with substantial trading, processing, or custodial operations. Trading and counterparty losses range between $1 billion and $24 billion across the eight BHCs (see table 4), with the largest losses at those BHCs that were subject to

---

[30] Losses are calculated based on the exposure at default, which includes both outstanding balances and any additional draw-down of the credit line that occurs prior to default, while loss rates are calculated as a percent of average outstanding balances over the planning horizon. See appendix B for more detail on the models used to project net income and stressed capital.

both the global market shock and the counterparty default component. Even so, the relative size of losses across firms depends not on nominal portfolio size but rather on the specific risk characteristics of each BHC's trading positions, inclusive of hedges. Importantly, these projected losses are based on the trading positions and counterparty exposures held by these firms on a single date (October 6, 2014) and could have differed if they had been based on a different date.

Projected Pre-provision Net Revenue and Net Income

In the aggregate, the 31 BHCs are projected to generate $310 billion in PPNR cumulatively over the nine quarters of the planning horizon, equal to 2.1 percent of their combined average assets (see table 2). Relatively low PPNR projections reflect low levels of net interest income because of the effect of low interest rates and flattening of the yield curve in the early part of the severely adverse scenario, given the BHCs' current and projected balance sheet composition. The results also reflect low levels of noninterest income, consistent with the falling asset prices, rising equity market volatility, and sharply contracting economic activity in the severely adverse scenario. In addition, the PPNR projections incorporate expenses stemming from estimates of elevated levels of losses from operational-risk events such as fraud, employee lawsuits, litigation-related expenses, or computer system or other operating disruptions, and expenses related to put-backs of mortgages netted against actual mortgage put-back reserves reported by the BHCs.[31]

The ratio of projected cumulative PPNR to average assets varies across BHCs (see figure 12). A significant portion of this variation reflects differences in business focus across the institutions. For instance, the ratio of PPNR to assets tends to be higher at BHCs focusing on credit card lending, reflecting the higher net interest income that credit cards generally produce relative to other forms of lending.[32] Importantly, lower PPNR rates do not necessarily imply lower net income, since the same business focus and revenue risk characteristics determining differences in

PPNR across firms could also result in offsetting differences in projected losses across BHCs.

Projected PPNR and losses are the primary determinants of projected pre-tax net income. Table 4 presents projections of the components of pre-tax net income, including provisions into the ALLL and one-time income and expense and extraordinary items, under the severely adverse scenario for each of the 31 BHCs (see table 2 for aggregate). The projections are cumulative for the nine quarters of the planning horizon.

Of note, following U.S. GAAP, the net income projections incorporate loan losses indirectly through provisions, which equal projected loan losses plus the amount needed for the ALLL to be at an appropriate level at the end of each quarter. The $382 billion in total provisions includes $340 billion in net charge-offs, with the remainder being the reserve build. These amounts are cumulative over the planning horizon and mask variation in the ALLL during the course of the nine quarters. Specifically, the projected ALLL increases during the early quarters of the planning horizon, given the increased economic stress in the severely adverse scenario, and then partially retraces this increase as the economic stress abates.

The Federal Reserve's projections of pre-tax net income under the severely adverse scenario imply negative net income at most of the 31 BHCs individually and for the BHCs as a group over the nine-quarter planning horizon. Projected net income before taxes (pre-tax net income) is an aggregate net loss of $222 billion over the planning horizon for the 31 BHCs.

The ratio of pre-tax net income to average assets for each of the 31 BHCs ranges between −5.0 percent and 6.3 percent (see figure 13). Projected cumulative net income for most of the BHCs (24 of 31) is negative over the planning horizon. Differences across the firms reflect differences in the sensitivity of the various components of net income to the economic and financial market conditions in the supervisory scenarios. Projected net income for the eight BHCs subject to global market shock and/or the counterparty default component includes the effect of those additional scenario components in the adverse and severely adverse scenarios, introducing some additional variation in projected net income between these eight BHCs and the other firms participating in DFAST 2015.

---

[31] These estimates are conditional on the hypothetical adverse and severely adverse scenario and on conservative assumptions. They are not a supervisory estimate of the BHCs' current or expected legal liability.

[32] As noted, credit card lending also tends to generate relatively high loss rates, so the higher PPNR rates at these BHCs do not necessarily indicate higher profitability.

Table 2. 31 participating bank holding companies
Projected stressed capital ratios, risk-weighted assets, losses, revenues, net income before taxes, and loan losses
Federal Reserve estimates: Severely adverse scenario

Actual 2014:Q3 projected stressed capital ratios through 2016:Q4

	Actual 2014:Q3	Stressed capital ratios[1]	
		Ending	Minimum
Tier 1 common ratio (%)	11.9	8.4	8.2
Common equity tier 1 capital ratio (%)[2]	n/a	7.8	7.6
Tier 1 risk-based capital ratio (%)	13.5	8.6	8.4
Total risk-based capital ratio (%)	16.2	11.0	10.8
Tier 1 leverage ratio (%)	8.8	5.9	5.9

[1] The capital ratios are calculated using capital action assumptions provided within the Dodd-Frank Act stress testing rule. These projections represent hypothetical estimates that involve an economic outcome that is more adverse than expected. These estimates are not forecasts of expected losses, revenues, net income before taxes, or capital ratios. The minimum capital ratio presented is for the period 2014:Q4 to 2016:Q4.

[2] Advanced approaches bank holding companies (BHCs) are subject to the common equity tier 1 ratio for the third and fourth quarter of 2014. All bank holding companies are subject to the common equity tier 1 ratio for each quarter of 2015 and 2016. An advanced approaches BHC includes any BHC that has consolidated total assets greater than or equal to $250 billion or consolidated total on-balance sheet foreign exposure of at least $10 billion. See 12 CFR 217.100(b)(1). Other BHCs include any BHC that is subject to 12 CFR 225.8 and is not an advanced approaches BHC.

n/a Not applicable.

Projected loan losses, by type of loan, 2014:Q4–2016:Q4

	Billions of dollars	Portfolio loss rates (%)[1]
Loan losses	340.3	6.1
First-lien mortgages, domestic	39.7	3.6
Junior liens and HELOCs, domestic	34.0	8.0
Commercial and industrial[2]	67.8	5.4
Commercial real estate, domestic	52.8	8.6
Credit cards	82.9	13.1
Other consumer[3]	35.1	5.8
Other loans[4]	28.0	2.9

[1] Average loan balances used to calculate portfolio loss rates exclude loans held for sale and loans held for investment under the fair-value option and are calculated over nine quarters.

[2] Commercial and industrial loans include small- and medium-enterprise loans and corporate cards.

[3] Other consumer loans include student loans and automobile loans.

[4] Other loans include international real estate loans.

Actual 2014:Q3 and projected 2016:Q4 risk-weighted assets

	Actual 2014:Q3	Projected 2016:Q4	
		General approach	Standardized approach
Risk-weighted assets (billions of dollars)[1]	8,790.2	9,141.2	9,948.4

[1] For each quarter in 2014, risk-weighted assets are calculated using the general risk-based capital approach set forth in 12 CFR 225, appendix A. For each quarter in 2015 and 2016, risk-weighted assets are calculated under the Board's standardized capital risk-based approach in 12 CFR 217, subpart D, except for the risk-weighted assets used to calculate the tier 1 common ratio, which uses the general risk-based capital approach for all quarters.

Projected losses, revenue, net income and other comprehensive income through 2016:Q4

	Billions of dollars	Percent of average assets[1]
Pre-provision net revenue[2]	309.6	2.1
Other revenue[3]	0.0	
less		
Provisions	381.9	
Realized losses/gains on securities (AFS/HTM)	17.8	
Trading and counterparty losses[4]	102.7	
Other losses/gains[5]	29.3	
equals		
Net income before taxes	-222.2	-1.5
Memo items		
Other comprehensive income[6]	-12.4	
Other effects on capital	*Actual 2014:Q3*	*2016:Q4*
AOCI included in capital (billions of dollars)[7]	n/a	-27.9

[1] Average assets is the nine-quarter average of total assets.

[2] Pre-provision net revenue includes losses from operational-risk events, mortgage repurchase expenses, and other real estate owned (OREO) costs.

[3] Other revenue includes one-time income and (expense) items not included in pre-provision net revenue.

[4] Trading and counterparty losses include mark-to-market and credit valuation adjustments (CVA) losses and losses arising from the counterparty default scenario component applied to derivatives, securities lending, and repurchase agreement activities.

[5] Other losses/gains includes projected change in fair value of loans held for sale and loans held for investment measured under the fair-value option, and goodwill impairment losses.

[6] Other comprehensive income (OCI) is only calculated for advanced approaches BHCs, and other BHCs that opt into the advanced approaches treatment of AOCI.

[7] Certain AOCI items are subject to transition into projected regulatory capital. Those transitions are 20 percent included in projected regulatory capital for 2014, 40 percent included in projected regulatory capital for 2015, and 60 percent included in projected regulatory capital for 2016.

Table 3. Projected stressed capital ratios under the severely adverse scenario, 2014:Q4–2016:Q4: 31 participating bank holding companies

Bank holding company	Tier 1 common ratio (%)			Common equity tier 1 ratio (%)[1]			Tier 1 risk-based capital ratio (%)			Total-risk based capital ratio (%)			Tier 1 leverage ratio (%)		
	Actual 2014:Q3	Ending	Minimum	Actual 2014:Q3	Ending	Minimum	Actual 2014:Q3	Ending	Minimum	Actual 2014:Q3	Ending	Minimum	Actual 2014:Q3	Ending	Minimum
Ally Financial Inc.	9.7	7.9	7.9	n/a	8.0	8.0	12.7	10.1	10.1	13.5	11.6	11.6	10.9	8.8	8.8
American Express Company	13.2	15.4	12.5	13.6	15.1	13.0	13.6	15.6	13.5	15.1	17.3	15.4	11.6	13.0	11.4
Bank of America Corporation	11.3	7.4	7.1	12.0	7.2	7.1	12.8	7.9	7.8	15.8	10.4	10.4	7.9	5.1	5.1
The Bank of New York Mellon Corporation	13.9	16.0	12.6	15.1	15.1	12.6	16.3	16.1	13.6	17.0	16.5	14.2	5.8	6.0	5.2
BB&T Corporation	10.5	8.1	8.1	n/a	8.2	8.2	12.4	9.8	9.8	15.2	11.8	11.8	9.7	7.4	7.4
BBVA Compass Bancshares, Inc.	11.0	6.3	6.3	n/a	6.9	6.9	11.3	6.9	6.9	13.3	8.7	8.7	9.6	5.5	5.5
BMO Financial Corp.	11.5	9.0	9.0	n/a	7.4	7.4	11.5	7.4	7.4	15.5	10.3	10.3	8.3	5.2	5.2
Capital One Financial Corporation	12.7	9.5	9.5	12.7	9.4	9.4	13.3	10.1	10.1	15.2	11.8	11.8	10.6	7.9	7.9
Citigroup Inc.	13.4	8.2	8.2	15.1	7.1	6.8	15.1	7.1	6.8	17.7	9.5	9.2	9.0	4.7	4.6
Citizens Financial Group, Inc.	12.9	10.7	10.7	n/a	10.9	10.9	12.9	10.9	10.9	16.1	14.3	14.3	10.9	8.8	8.8
Comerica Incorporated	10.6	9.0	9.0	n/a	8.7	8.7	10.6	8.7	8.7	12.8	10.5	10.5	10.8	8.9	8.9
Deutsche Bank Trust Corporation	36.6	34.7	34.7	n/a	28.6	28.6	36.6	28.6	28.6	37.0	29.8	29.8	11.9	11.0	11.0
Discover Financial Services	14.8	15.3	13.9	n/a	14.5	13.3	15.6	15.2	14.1	17.8	16.9	15.8	13.7	13.3	12.6
Fifth Third Bancorp	9.6	7.9	7.9	n/a	7.4	7.4	10.8	8.5	8.5	14.3	11.5	11.5	9.8	7.7	7.7
The Goldman Sachs Group, Inc.	14.4	9.3	6.3	15.1	7.1	5.8	17.0	8.1	6.4	19.8	10.0	8.1	9.0	5.9	5.4
HSBC North America Holdings Inc.	14.0	8.9	8.9	16.3	8.9	8.9	17.3	10.0	10.0	26.1	14.8	14.8	9.4	6.0	6.0
Huntington Bancshares Incorporated	10.3	9.0	9.0	n/a	8.7	8.7	11.6	9.4	9.4	13.7	11.6	11.6	9.8	8.0	8.0
JPMorgan Chase & Co.	10.9	6.5	6.5	11.1	6.4	6.3	12.6	7.3	7.3	15.0	9.6	9.6	7.6	4.6	4.6
KeyCorp	11.3	9.9	9.9	n/a	9.6	9.6	12.0	9.9	9.9	14.1	12.1	12.1	11.2	9.3	9.3
M&T Bank Corporation	9.8	7.3	7.3	n/a	7.5	7.5	12.5	8.8	8.8	15.4	11.6	11.6	10.6	6.8	6.8
Morgan Stanley	15.0	8.8	6.2	15.2	8.3	6.3	17.1	8.8	6.5	19.8	11.3	8.6	8.2	4.9	4.5
MUFG Americas Holdings Corporation	12.7	8.0	8.0	12.7	8.0	8.0	12.7	8.0	8.0	14.6	10.2	10.2	11.4	7.1	7.1
Northern Trust Corporation	12.8	12.4	12.3	12.8	10.9	10.8	13.6	11.4	11.3	16.0	13.6	13.6	7.9	7.4	7.4
The PNC Financial Services Group, Inc.	11.0	9.5	9.5	11.1	8.4	8.4	12.8	9.9	9.9	16.1	12.5	12.5	11.1	8.7	8.7
Regions Financial Corporation	11.8	8.3	8.3	n/a	8.5	8.5	12.7	9.0	9.0	15.5	11.4	11.4	11.0	7.6	7.6
Santander Holdings USA, Inc.	11.0	9.4	9.4	n/a	10.3	10.3	13.1	10.7	10.7	15.0	12.5	12.5	12.3	9.6	9.6
State Street Corporation	13.7	14.1	11.8	15.0	9.7	8.1	16.7	11.2	9.7	19.1	13.1	11.6	6.4	5.4	4.8
SunTrust Banks, Inc.	9.6	8.2	8.2	n/a	8.2	8.2	10.5	9.0	9.0	12.3	10.8	10.8	9.5	7.6	7.6
U.S. Bancorp	9.5	8.6	8.5	9.7	8.2	8.1	11.3	9.6	9.6	13.6	11.7	11.7	9.4	8.1	8.0
Wells Fargo & Company	10.8	7.5	7.5	11.1	6.9	6.9	12.6	8.2	8.2	15.6	11.1	11.1	9.6	6.4	6.4
Zions Bancorporation	11.9	5.1	5.1	n/a	6.0	6.0	14.4	7.3	7.3	16.3	9.4	9.4	11.9	5.9	5.9
31 participating bank holding companies	11.9	8.4	8.2	n/a	7.8	7.6	13.5	8.6	8.4	16.2	11.0	10.8	8.8	5.9	5.9

Note: The capital ratios are calculated using capital action assumptions provided within the Dodd-Frank Act stress testing rule. These projections represent hypothetical estimates that involve an economic outcome that is more adverse than expected. These estimates are not forecasts of expected losses, revenues, net income before taxes, or capital ratios. The minimum capital ratio presented is for the period 2014:Q4 to 2016:Q4.

[1] Advanced approaches bank holding companies (BHCs) are subject to the common equity tier 1 ratio for the third and fourth quarter of 2014. All bank holding companies are subject to the common equity tier 1 ratio for each quarter of 2015 and 2016. An advanced approaches BHC includes any BHC that has consolidated total assets greater than or equal to $250 billion or consolidated total on-balance sheet foreign exposure of at least $10 billion. See 12 CFR 217.100(b)(1). Other BHCs include any BHC that is subject to 12 CFR 225.8 and is not an advanced approaches BHC.

n/a Not applicable.

Source: Federal Reserve estimates in the severely adverse scenario.

Table 4. Projected losses, revenues, net income, and other comprehensive income through 2016:Q4 under the severely adverse scenario: 31 participating bank holding companies

Billions of dollars

Bank holding company	Sum of revenues		Minus sum of provisions and losses				Equals	Memo items	Other effects on capital
	Pre-provision net revenue[1]	Other revenue[2]	Provisions	Realized losses/gains on securities (AFS/HTM)	Trading and counterparty losses[3]	Other losses/ gains[4]	Net income before taxes	Other compre-hensive income[5]	AOCI included in capital[6] (2016:Q4)
Ally Financial Inc.	4.1	0.0	6.0	0.6	0.0	0.0	-2.5	0.0	0.0
American Express Company	23.7	0.0	13.7	0.0	0.0	0.0	10.0	0.0	-1.4
Bank of America Corporation	34.4	0.0	49.1	0.9	17.6	4.1	-37.3	2.3	-1.1
The Bank of New York Mellon Corporation	11.8	0.0	1.7	0.2	0.9	1.7	7.2	-0.3	-1.0
BB&T Corporation	8.0	0.0	7.2	0.0	0.0	0.0	0.7	0.0	0.0
BBVA Compass Bancshares, Inc.	1.1	0.0	3.8	0.1	0.0	0.1	-2.8	0.0	0.0
BMO Financial Corp.	1.1	0.0	2.8	0.0	0.0	0.0	-1.7	0.0	0.0
Capital One Financial Corporation	21.7	0.0	25.9	0.1	0.0	0.1	-4.4	-0.1	-0.3
Citigroup Inc.	29.1	0.0	50.3	3.4	18.5	5.3	-48.4	-5.6	-20.5
Citizens Financial Group, Inc.	3.9	0.0	5.4	0.2	0.0	0.1	-1.8	0.0	0.0
Comerica Incorporated	1.7	0.0	2.5	0.0	0.0	0.0	-0.7	0.0	0.0
Deutsche Bank Trust Corporation	1.0	0.0	1.1	0.0	0.0	0.0	-0.1	0.0	-0.1
Discover Financial Services	12.9	0.0	10.1	0.0	0.0	0.0	2.7	0.0	0.0
Fifth Third Bancorp	4.7	0.0	5.5	0.0	0.0	0.0	-0.8	0.0	0.0
The Goldman Sachs Group, Inc.	2.4	0.0	2.8	0.0	17.0	6.8	-24.1	0.0	-0.6
HSBC North America Holdings Inc.	-0.7	0.0	7.6	0.1	0.0	0.7	-9.1	0.8	0.2
Huntington Bancshares Incorporated	2.2	0.0	2.1	0.2	0.0	0.0	-0.1	0.0	0.0
JPMorgan Chase & Co.	30.4	0.0	55.5	4.1	23.6	2.1	-54.8	-5.4	-1.3
KeyCorp	3.1	0.0	3.3	0.0	0.0	0.2	-0.4	0.0	0.0
M&T Bank Corporation	4.1	0.0	5.4	0.0	0.0	0.1	-1.4	0.0	0.0
Morgan Stanley	4.1	0.0	3.5	0.2	15.8	3.6	-19.0	0.0	-0.8
MUFG Americas Holdings Corporation	1.1	0.0	4.9	0.6	0.0	0.0	-4.4	0.0	0.0
Northern Trust Corporation	3.2	0.0	1.9	0.0	0.0	0.0	1.3	0.1	-0.1
The PNC Financial Services Group, Inc.	11.5	0.0	10.8	0.5	0.0	0.4	-0.2	-0.9	-0.3
Regions Financial Corporation	3.7	0.0	6.2	0.0	0.0	0.0	-2.6	0.0	0.0
Santander Holdings USA, Inc.	6.2	0.0	8.1	0.1	0.0	0.1	-2.1	0.0	0.0
State Street Corporation	7.0	0.0	0.8	0.9	2.0	0.0	3.3	-2.8	-1.8
SunTrust Banks, Inc.	6.2	0.0	6.6	0.0	0.0	0.7	-1.0	0.0	0.0
U.S. Bancorp	22.8	0.0	18.1	0.1	0.0	0.0	4.7	0.2	-0.2
Wells Fargo & Company	42.7	0.0	56.4	5.0	7.3	3.2	-29.3	-0.7	1.4
Zions Bancorporation	0.6	0.0	3.0	0.4	0.0	0.0	-2.9	0.0	0.0
31 participating bank holding companies	309.6	0.0	381.9	17.8	102.7	29.3	-222.2	-12.4	-27.9

Note: These projections represent hypothetical estimates that involve an economic outcome that is more adverse than expected. These estimates are not forecasts of expected losses, revenues, or net income before taxes. Estimates may not sum precisely due to rounding.

[1] Pre-provision net revenue includes losses from operational-risk events, mortgage repurchase expenses, and other real estate owned costs.

[2] Other revenue includes one-time income and (expense) items not included in pre-provision net revenue.

[3] Trading and counterparty losses include mark-to-market and credit valuation adjustments losses and losses arising from the counterparty default scenario component applied to derivatives, securities lending, and repurchase agreement activities.

[4] Other losses/gains includes projected change in fair value of loans held for sale and loans held for investment measured under the fair-value option, and goodwill impairment losses.

[5] Other comprehensive income is only calculated for advanced approaches BHCs and non-advanced approaches BHCs that have not elected to opt out of AOCI inclusion. Only those BHCs include accumulated other comprehensive income (AOCI) in calculations of regulatory capital. Other comprehensive income includes incremental unrealized losses/gains on AFS securities and on any HTM securities that have experienced other than temporary impairment.

[6] Certain AOCI items are subject to transition into projected regulatory capital. Those transitions are 20 percent included in projected regulatory capital for 2014, 40 percent included in projected regulatory capital for 2015, and 60 percent included in projected regulatory capital for 2016.

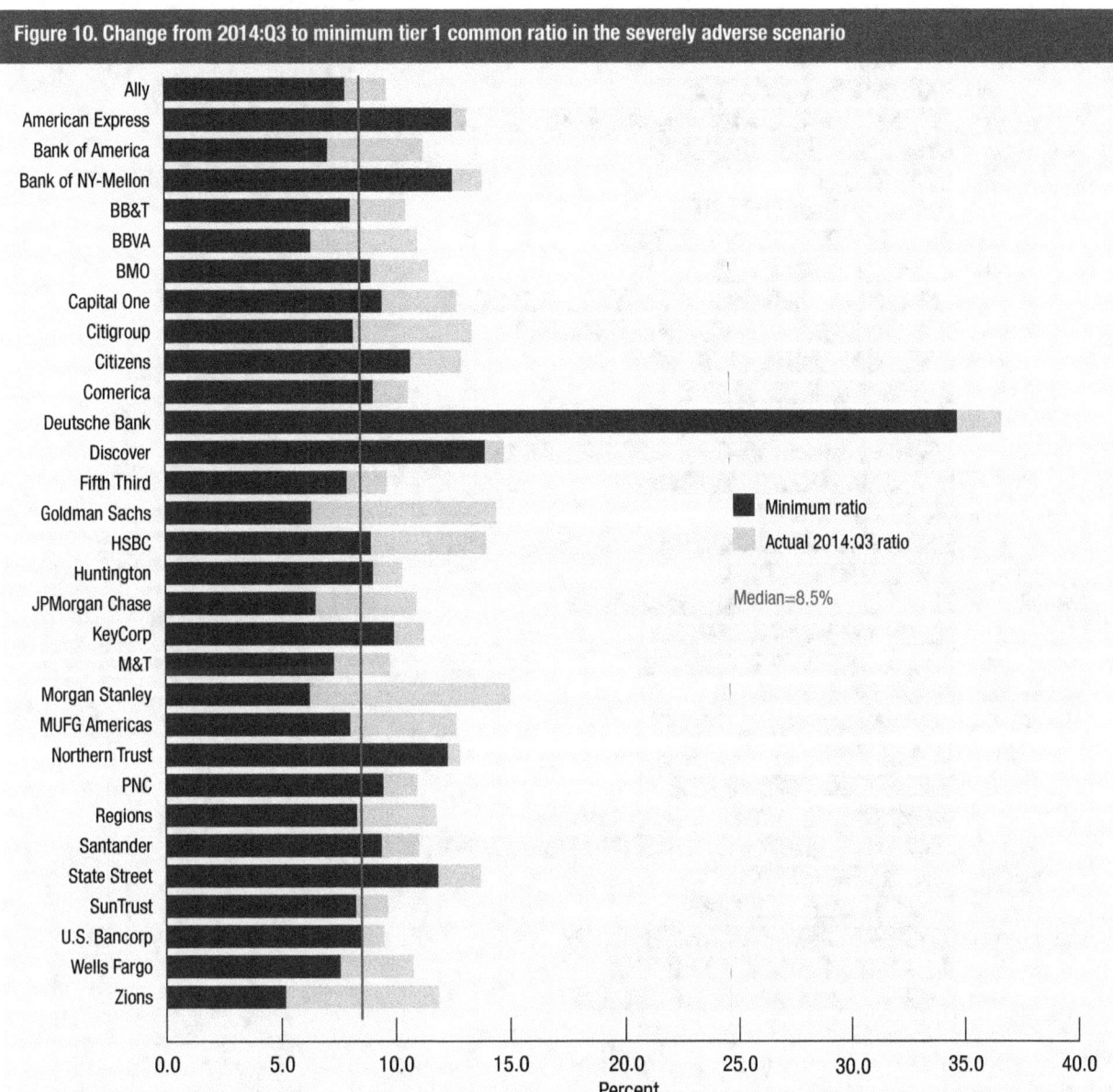

Figure 10. Change from 2014:Q3 to minimum tier 1 common ratio in the severely adverse scenario

Ally
American Express
Bank of America
Bank of NY-Mellon
BB&T
BBVA
BMO
Capital One
Citigroup
Citizens
Comerica
Deutsche Bank
Discover
Fifth Third
Goldman Sachs
HSBC
Huntington
JPMorgan Chase
KeyCorp
M&T
Morgan Stanley
MUFG Americas
Northern Trust
PNC
Regions
Santander
State Street
SunTrust
U.S. Bancorp
Wells Fargo
Zions

■ Minimum ratio
▨ Actual 2014:Q3 ratio

Median=8.5%

0.0   5.0   10.0   15.0   20.0   25.0   30.0   35.0   40.0
Percent

Note: Estimates are for the nine-quarter period from 2014:Q4–2016:Q4 as a percent of average assets.

Figure 11. Total loan loss rates in the severely adverse scenario

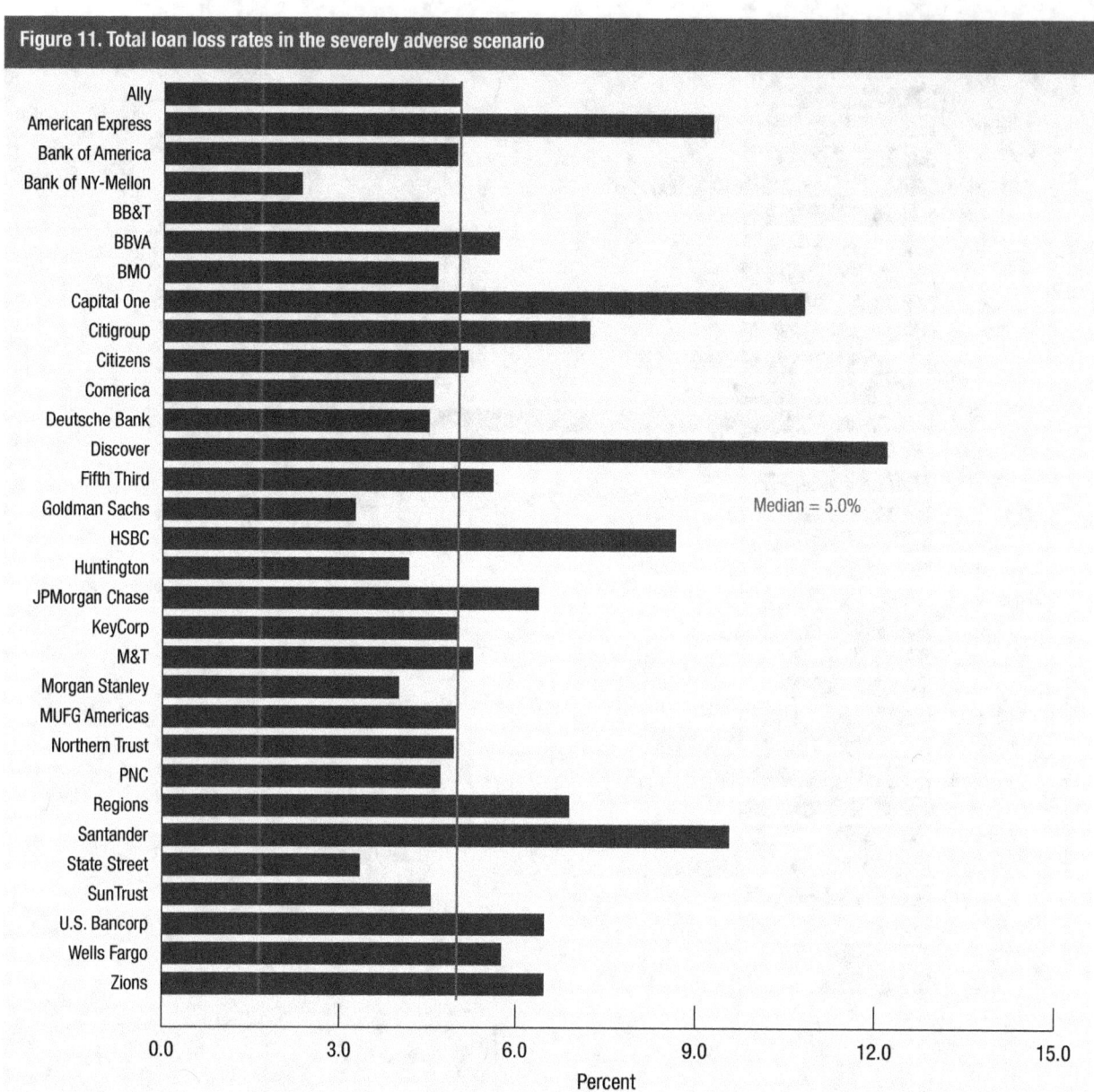

Median = 5.0%

Note: Estimates are for nine quarter period from 2014:Q4–2016:Q4 as a percent of average balances.

Table 5. Projected loan losses by type of loan for 2014:Q4–2016:Q4 under the severely adverse scenario: 31 participating bank holding companies
Billions of dollars

Bank holding company	Loan losses	First lien mortgages, domestic	Junior liens and HELOCs, domestic	Commercial and industrial	Commercial real estate, domestic[1]	Credit cards	Other consumer[2]	Other loans[3]
Ally Financial Inc.	5.1	0.3	0.2	1.6	0.2	0.0	2.8	0.0
American Express Company	10.5	0.0	0.0	3.3	0.0	7.3	0.0	0.0
Bank of America Corporation	45.7	7.1	8.2	8.0	5.1	11.7	2.2	3.3
The Bank of New York Mellon Corporation	1.4	0.2	0.0	0.1	0.2	0.0	0.3	0.6
BB&T Corporation	6.0	0.9	0.3	0.8	2.4	0.2	1.1	0.3
BBVA Compass Bancshares, Inc.	3.2	0.4	0.2	0.8	1.5	0.1	0.1	0.1
BMO Financial Corp.	2.7	0.3	0.3	0.8	0.7	0.0	0.2	0.4
Capital One Financial Corporation	22.2	0.8	0.2	1.7	1.5	14.2	3.3	0.5
Citigroup Inc.	48.3	4.4	3.5	7.4	1.0	20.9	5.9	5.1
Citizens Financial Group, Inc.	4.8	0.4	1.4	1.0	1.2	0.2	0.5	0.1
Comerica Incorporated	2.2	0.1	0.1	0.9	0.8	0.0	0.0	0.4
Deutsche Bank Trust Corporation	0.8	0.1	0.0	0.3	0.2	0.0	0.0	0.1
Discover Financial Services	8.3	0.0	0.0	0.0	0.0	6.9	1.4	0.0
Fifth Third Bancorp	5.2	0.6	0.5	1.8	1.3	0.3	0.4	0.3
The Goldman Sachs Group, Inc.	2.2	0.0	0.0	0.9	0.2	0.0	0.0	1.1
HSBC North America Holdings Inc.	8.2	4.7	1.1	1.1	0.9	0.1	0.0	0.3
Huntington Bancshares Incorporated	2.0	0.2	0.3	0.5	0.6	0.0	0.3	0.1
JPMorgan Chase & Co.	49.7	5.4	6.7	9.6	5.4	12.9	2.5	7.1
KeyCorp	3.0	0.2	0.4	0.9	0.7	0.1	0.4	0.3
M&T Bank Corporation	4.4	1.0	0.4	0.6	2.0	0.0	0.3	0.1
Morgan Stanley	2.6	0.2	0.0	0.6	0.9	0.0	0.2	0.6
MUFG Americas Holdings Corporation	3.8	0.9	0.1	0.9	1.4	0.0	0.0	0.3
Northern Trust Corporation	1.5	0.3	0.3	0.2	0.3	0.0	0.0	0.4
The PNC Financial Services Group, Inc.	9.6	0.4	0.7	3.7	3.1	0.5	0.8	0.4
Regions Financial Corporation	5.4	0.7	0.6	1.1	2.3	0.1	0.3	0.3
Santander Holdings USA, Inc.	7.2	0.4	0.3	0.6	1.6	0.0	4.2	0.1
State Street Corporation	0.6	0.0	0.0	0.1	0.1	0.0	0.0	0.5
SunTrust Banks, Inc.	6.1	1.0	1.0	1.8	1.2	0.1	0.7	0.2
U.S. Bancorp	16.2	1.4	0.9	4.9	4.4	2.7	1.2	0.8
Wells Fargo & Company	48.8	7.3	6.3	10.9	10.3	4.3	5.7	4.0
Zions Bancorporation	2.6	0.0	0.1	0.8	1.5	0.0	0.1	0.1
31 participating bank holding companies	340.3	39.7	34.0	67.8	52.8	82.9	35.1	28.0

Note: These projections represent hypothetical estimates that involve an economic outcome that is more adverse than expected. These estimates are not forecasts of expected loan losses.

[1]   Commercial and industrial loans include small and medium enterprise loans and corporate cards.

[2]   Other consumer loans include student loans and automobile loans.

[3]   Other loans include international real estate loans.

Table 6. Projected loan losses by type of loan for 2014:Q4–2016:Q4 under the severely adverse scenario: 31 participating bank holding companies

Percent of average balances[1]

Bank holding company	Loan losses	First lien mortgages, domestic	Junior liens and HELOCs, domestic	Commercial and industrial	Commercial real estate, domestic[2]	Credit cards	Other consumer[3]	Other loans[4]
Ally Financial Inc.	5.0	5.4	8.0	4.5	5.1	0.0	5.2	12.7
American Express Company	9.2	0.0	0.0	9.0	0.0	9.3	14.3	0.0
Bank of America Corporation	4.9	3.1	9.2	3.9	8.3	11.4	2.8	2.1
The Bank of New York Mellon Corporation	2.3	2.9	9.8	3.3	10.3	0.0	10.6	1.4
BB&T Corporation	4.6	2.7	3.6	4.1	7.0	13.6	6.0	2.0
BBVA Compass Bancshares, Inc.	5.7	2.9	6.8	4.6	12.5	14.4	4.0	1.5
BMO Financial Corp.	4.6	3.5	5.0	4.8	7.9	10.7	2.8	3.4
Capital One Financial Corporation	10.8	2.5	7.5	7.6	6.4	18.5	8.8	3.8
Citigroup Inc.	7.2	4.8	11.5	4.6	9.1	15.0	11.9	2.7
Citizens Financial Group, Inc.	5.1	2.8	7.2	3.9	11.3	12.5	3.4	1.9
Comerica Incorporated	4.5	2.6	4.9	3.0	7.8	0.0	7.8	6.6
Deutsche Bank Trust Corporation	4.5	3.8	9.6	9.9	7.9	0.0	2.3	1.4
Discover Financial Services	12.2	5.1	15.0	14.0	31.6	12.7	10.1	4.3
Fifth Third Bancorp	5.6	4.4	5.7	5.0	13.2	14.3	2.7	3.4
The Goldman Sachs Group, Inc.	3.2	5.1	9.3	9.8	6.1	0.0	2.7	2.0
HSBC North America Holdings Inc.	8.6	12.5	22.3	3.5	9.6	14.7	7.4	2.7
Huntington Bancshares Incorporated	4.2	2.8	4.5	4.0	7.2	14.7	3.2	2.1
JPMorgan Chase & Co.	6.4	3.8	9.7	7.5	6.7	11.0	3.7	4.1
KeyCorp	5.0	4.3	4.5	4.0	8.0	12.8	8.8	2.5
M&T Bank Corporation	5.2	3.7	6.1	3.8	7.5	14.7	6.2	2.5
Morgan Stanley	4.0	1.6	9.3	8.0	19.7	0.0	0.7	4.1
MUFG Americas Holdings Corporation	5.0	3.1	4.2	4.8	9.0	0.0	14.7	4.1
Northern Trust Corporation	4.9	3.5	13.0	4.0	8.5	0.0	13.1	3.7
The PNC Financial Services Group, Inc.	4.7	1.7	3.0	5.7	9.3	12.1	3.2	1.5
Regions Financial Corporation	6.9	4.7	6.5	4.8	14.7	13.9	5.8	2.8
Santander Holdings USA, Inc.	9.6	4.5	4.5	3.6	9.0	14.7	17.2	3.8
State Street Corporation	3.3	0.0	0.0	4.8	29.4	0.0	0.6	2.7
SunTrust Banks, Inc.	4.5	4.0	7.1	4.5	6.9	13.9	3.4	1.5
U.S. Bancorp	6.5	2.4	5.3	7.8	11.0	14.7	3.4	3.7
Wells Fargo & Company	5.8	2.9	7.9	6.7	8.3	14.8	6.6	3.4
Zions Bancorporation	6.5	0.9	4.2	6.8	8.2	14.7	11.6	4.6
31 participating bank holding companies	6.1	3.6	8.0	5.4	8.6	13.1	5.8	2.9

Note: These projections represent hypothetical estimates that involve an economic outcome that is more adverse than expected. These estimates are not forecasts of expected loan losses.

[1] Average loan balances used to calculate portfolio loss rates exclude loans held for sale and loans held for investment under the fair-value option, and are calculated over nine quarters.

[2] Commercial and industrial loans include small and medium enterprise loans and corporate cards.

[3] Other consumer loans include student loans and automobile loans.

[4] Other loans include international real estate loans.

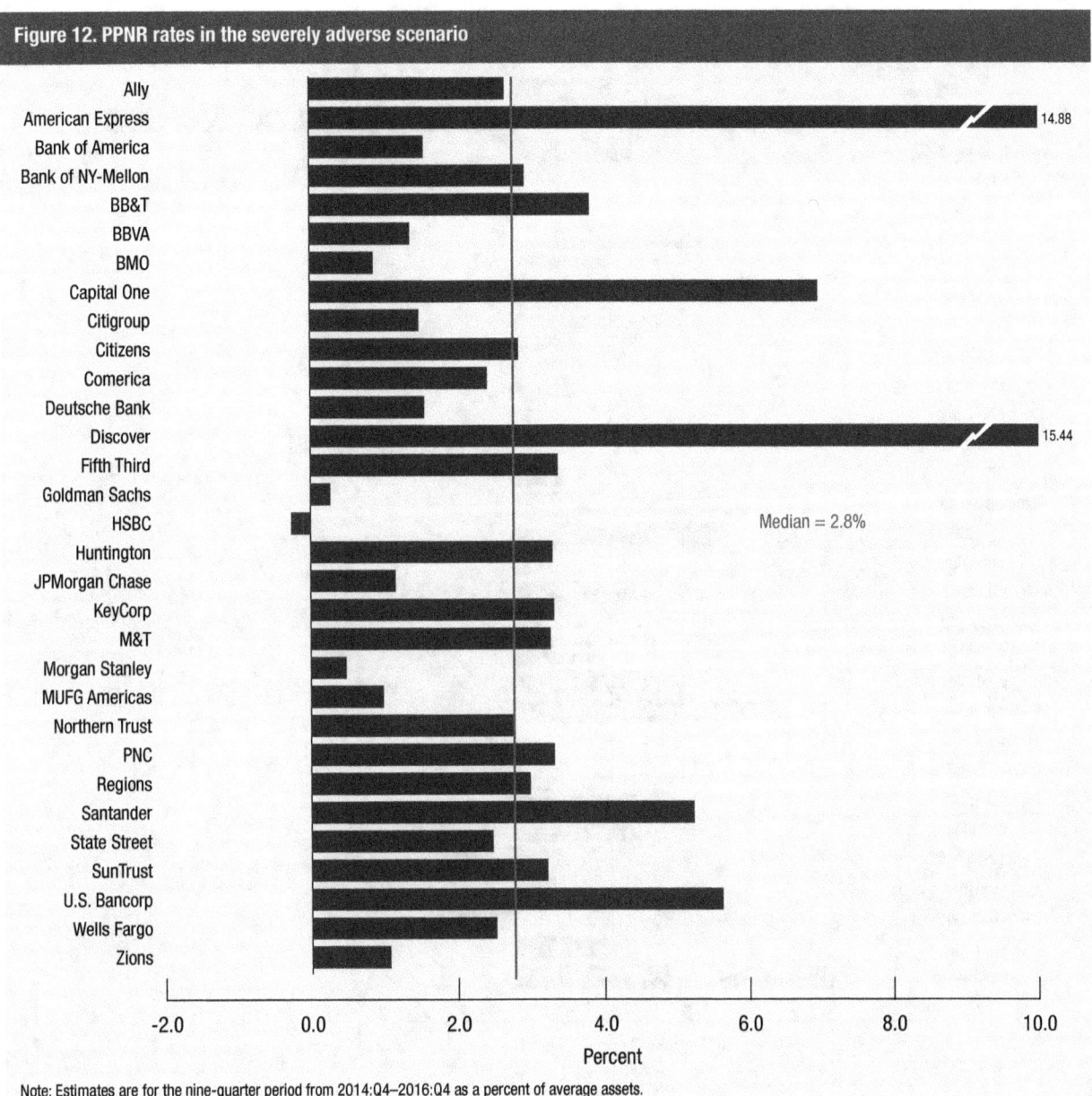

Figure 12. PPNR rates in the severely adverse scenario

Note: Estimates are for the nine-quarter period from 2014:Q4–2016:Q4 as a percent of average assets.

Figure 13. Pre-tax net income rates in the severely adverse scenario

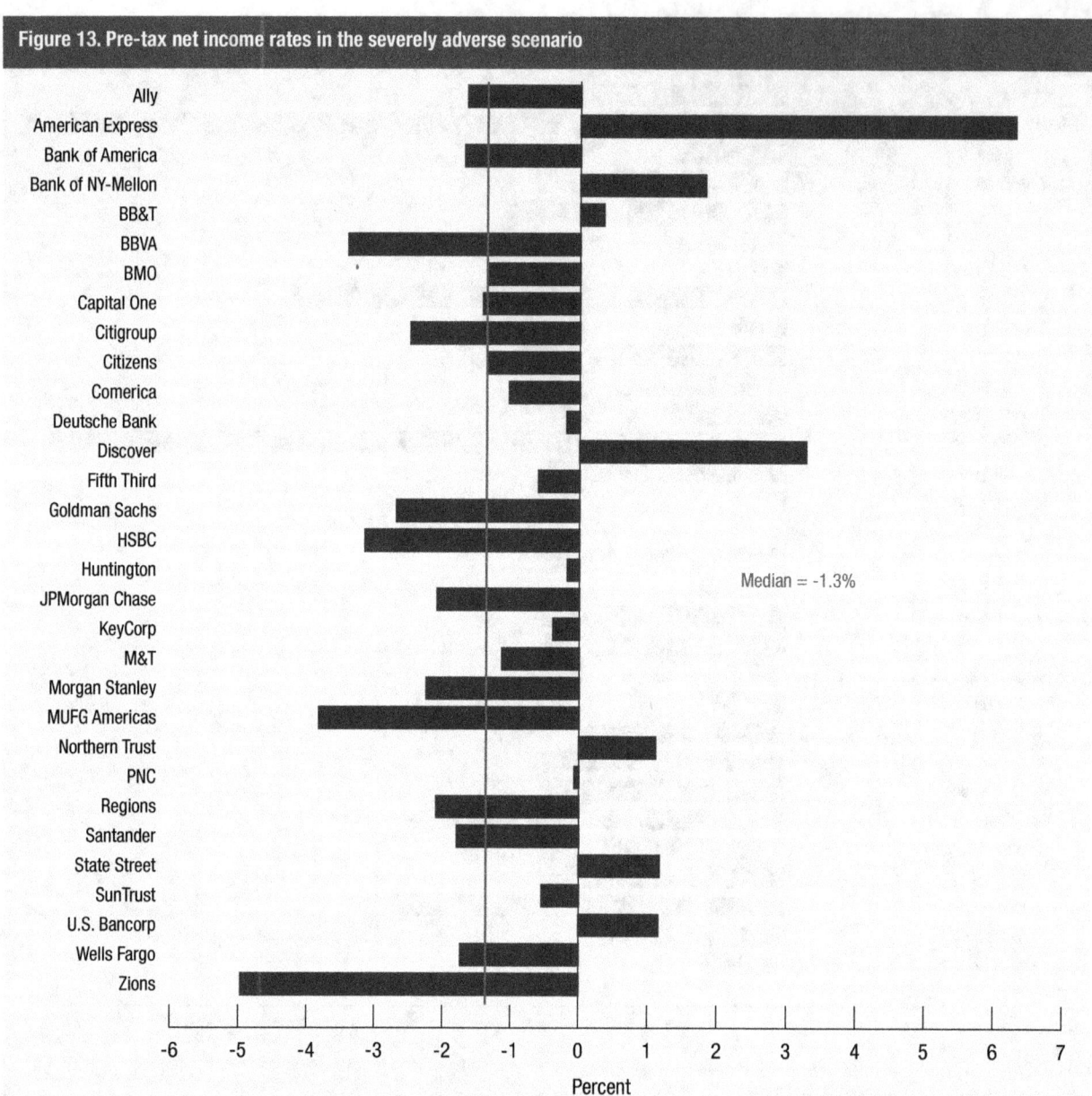

Median = -1.3%

Percent

Note: Estimates are for the nine-quarter period from 2014:Q4–2016:Q4 as a percent of average assets.

Adverse Scenario

Stressed Capital Ratios and Risk-Weighted Assets

The adverse scenario projections suggest moderate declines in aggregate capital ratios for the 31 BHCs. The aggregate tier 1 common capital ratio is projected to fall 1.1 percentage points to its minimum over the planning horizon and to be 0.3 percentage points lower at the end of the planning horizon (see table 7). In addition, at the end of the planning horizon, the tier 1 risk-based capital ratio and the total risk-based capital ratio are 2.7 and 3.2 percentage points lower than at the start of the planning horizon, respectively. The tier 1 leverage ratio is projected to decline 1.5 percentage points over the planning horizon. Finally, the common equity tier 1 capital ratio reaches a minimum of 9.5 percent before increasing to 9.8 percent at the end of the planning horizon.

The projected decreases in post-stress capital ratios are smaller than those under the severely adverse scenario, reflecting the less severe macroeconomic conditions assumed in the adverse scenario. As compared to the severely adverse scenario, the adverse scenario projections imply higher aggregate net income driven by higher PPNR and lower losses. Offsetting somewhat the effect of aggregate higher net income on capital, the adverse scenario also features more robust projected balance sheet and risk-weighted asset growth than the severely adverse scenario, which on net tends to reduce post-stress capital ratios.

Projected Losses

The Federal Reserve's projections suggest that the 31 BHCs as a group would face elevated losses under the adverse scenario, though not as large as the losses under the severely adverse scenario. In this scenario, total losses are projected to equal nearly $315 billion for the 31 BHCs over the nine-quarter planning horizon.

These losses include

- $235 billion in accrual loan losses,

- $9 billion in OTTI and other realized securities losses,

- $55 billion in losses from the global market shock and the largest counterparty default components, and

- $16 billion in additional losses from items such as loans booked under the fair-value option.

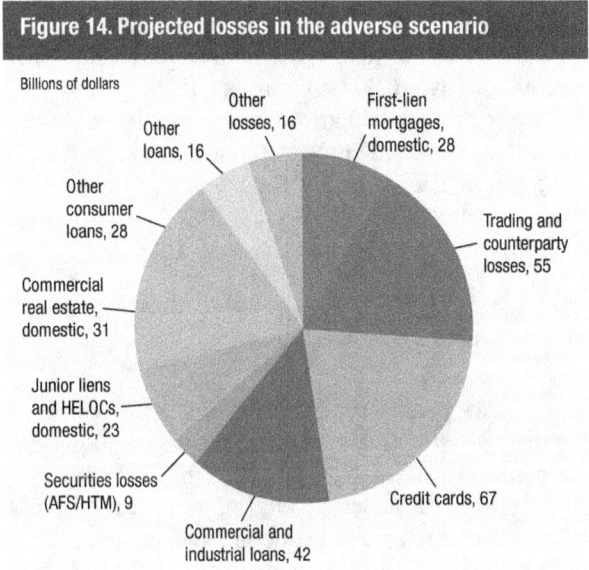

Figure 14. Projected losses in the adverse scenario

Billions of dollars

- Other losses, 16
- First-lien mortgages, domestic, 28
- Other loans, 16
- Trading and counterparty losses, 55
- Other consumer loans, 28
- Commercial real estate, domestic, 31
- Junior liens and HELOCs, domestic, 23
- Credit cards, 67
- Securities losses (AFS/HTM), 9
- Commercial and industrial loans, 42

These results are presented in aggregate (table 7) and individually for each of the 31 BHCs (appendix C). Aggregate loss amounts are lower than those projected under the severely adverse scenario, once again reflecting the relatively less stressful macroeconomic and financial market conditions assumed in the adverse scenario.

Loan Losses

As in the severely adverse scenario, the accrual loan portfolio is the largest source of losses in the adverse scenario, accounting for $235 billion of projected losses for the 31 BHCs. The lower peak unemployment rate and more moderate residential and commercial real estate price declines in the adverse scenario result in lower projected accrual loan losses on consumer and real estate-related loans. The nine-quarter loan loss rate of 4.1 percent is below the peak industry-level rate reached during the recent financial crisis but still higher than the rate during any other period since the Great Depression of the 1930s. As in the severely adverse scenario results, there is considerable diversity across firms in projected loan loss rates, both in the aggregate and by loan type (see fig-ures 16 and D.8 to D.14).

Losses on Trading, Private Equity, and Derivatives Positions

Projected losses resulting from the impact of the global market shock and the largest counterparty default on trading, private equity, and counterparty exposures for the eight BHCs with large trading, processing, or custodial operations equal $55 billion under the adverse scenario. These losses are slightly more than half those projected under the severely adverse scenario, reflecting the less severe market shocks assumed in the global market shock component of the adverse scenario.

Projected Pre-provision Net Revenue and Net Income

Aggregate PPNR is projected to equal $501 billion for the 31 BHCs under the adverse scenario, equal to 3.4 percent of average projected assets for these firms. Under the adverse scenario, projected PPNR is bolstered by high projected net interest income, driven largely by the increasing interest rates assumed in the scenario as well as by moderate loan portfolio growth over the planning horizon. As compared to the severely adverse scenario, PPNR is also strengthened by lower projected operational risk and mortgage repurchase losses, with the latter being consistent with the adverse scenario's more moderate housing price decline. As in the severely adverse scenario, projected ratios of PPNR to assets vary significantly across the 31 BHCs, reflecting differences in business focus as well as differences in sensitivities to the con-

ditions assumed in the Federal Reserve's adverse scenario (see figure 17).

In the aggregate, the 31 BHCs are projected to have cumulative pre-tax net income of $178 billion over the nine-quarter planning horizon under the adverse scenario. Twenty-seven of the BHCs are projected to have positive cumulative pre-tax net income, though about half experience at least one quarter of negative net income during the planning horizon. The higher net income, as compared to the severely adverse scenario projections, reflects the combination of higher projected PPNR and lower projected losses, especially on trading, private equity and counterparty positions, and on the accrual loan portfolio. The $244 billion in total provisions reported in table 7 includes $235 billion in net charge-offs, with the remainder being the reserve build.

While aggregate pre-tax net income under the adverse scenario is positive, it is low relative to historical standards, with an implied nine-quarter return on assets (ROA) of 1.2 percent. Projected nine-quarter ROA under the adverse scenario ranges between –0.6 and 9.3 percent for the 31 BHCs (see figure 18).

Higher long-term interest rates and wider credit spreads assumed in the scenario result in –$121 billion of other comprehensive income over the nine quarters of the planning horizon for those BHCs. Reflecting the gradual phasing-in of portions of AOCI in the revised regulatory capital framework, –$93 billion in AOCI is included in post-stress regulatory capital as of the fourth quarter of 2016.

Table 7. 31 participating bank holding companies
Projected stressed capital ratios, risk-weighted assets, losses, revenues, net income before taxes, and loan losses
Federal Reserve estimates: Adverse scenario

Actual 2014:Q3 projected stressed capital ratios through 2016:Q4

	Actual 2014:Q3	Stressed capital ratios[1]	
		Ending	Minimum
Tier 1 common ratio (%)	11.9	11.6	10.8
Common equity tier 1 capital ratio (%)[2]	n/a	9.8	9.5
Tier 1 risk-based capital ratio (%)	13.5	10.8	10.4
Total risk-based capital ratio (%)	16.2	13.0	12.8
Tier 1 leverage ratio (%)	8.8	7.3	7.2

[1] The capital ratios are calculated using capital action assumptions provided within the Dodd-Frank Act stress testing rule. These projections represent hypothetical estimates that involve an economic outcome that is more adverse than expected. These estimates are not forecasts of expected losses, revenues, net income before taxes, or capital ratios. The minimum capital ratio presented is for the period 2014:Q4 to 2016:Q4.

[2] Advanced approaches bank holding companies (BHCs) are subject to the common equity tier 1 ratio for the third and fourth quarter of 2014. All bank holding companies are subject to the common equity tier 1 ratio for each quarter of 2015 and 2016. An advanced approaches BHC includes any BHC that has consolidated total assets greater than or equal to $250 billion or consolidated total on-balance sheet foreign exposure of at least $10 billion. See 12 CFR 217.100(b)(1). Other BHCs include any BHC that is subject to 12 CFR 225.8 and is not an advanced approaches BHC.

n/a Not applicable.

Projected loan losses, by type of loan, 2014:Q4–2016:Q4

	Billions of dollars	Portfolio loss rates (%)[1]
Loan losses	234.9	4.1
First-lien mortgages, domestic	27.9	2.5
Junior liens and HELOCs, domestic	22.7	5.3
Commercial and industrial[2]	42.5	3.4
Commercial real estate, domestic	30.9	5.0
Credit cards	67.1	10.5
Other consumer[3]	27.6	4.5
Other loans[4]	16.3	1.7

[1] Average loan balances used to calculate portfolio loss rates exclude loans held for sale and loans held for investment under the fair-value option and are calculated over nine quarters.

[2] Commercial and industrial loans include small- and medium-enterprise loans and corporate cards.

[3] Other consumer loans include student loans and automobile loans.

[4] Other loans include international real estate loans.

Actual 2014:Q3 and projected 2016:Q4 risk-weighted assets

	Actual 2014:Q3	Projected 2016:Q4	
		General approach	Standardized approach
Risk-weighted assets (billions of dollars)[1]	8,790.2	9,468.8	10,262.0

[1] For each quarter in 2014, risk-weighted assets are calculated using the general risk-based capital approach set forth in 12 CFR 225, appendix A. For each quarter in 2015 and 2016, risk-weighted assets are calculated under the Board's standardized capital risk-based approach in 12 CFR 217, subpart D, except for the risk-weighted assets used to calculate the tier 1 common ratio, which uses the general risk-based capital approach for all quarters.

Projected losses, revenue, net income and other comprehensive income through 2016:Q4

	Billions of dollars	Percent of average assets[1]
Pre-provision net revenue[2]	501.3	3.4
Other revenue[3]	0.0	
less		
Provisions	244.0	
Realized losses/gains on securities (AFS/HTM)	8.6	
Trading and counterparty losses[4]	54.9	
Other losses/gains[5]	16.0	
equals		
Net income before taxes	177.8	1.2
Memo items		
Other comprehensive income[6]	-120.5	
Other effects on capital	Actual 2014:Q3	2016:Q4
AOCI included in capital (billions of dollars)[7]	n/a	-92.7

[1] Average assets is the nine-quarter average of total assets.

[2] Pre-provision net revenue includes losses from operational-risk events, mortgage repurchase expenses, and other real estate owned (OREO) costs.

[3] Other revenue includes one-time income and (expense) items not included in pre-provision net revenue.

[4] Trading and counterparty losses include mark-to-market and credit valuation adjustments (CVA) losses and losses arising from the counterparty default scenario component applied to derivatives, securities lending, and repurchase agreement activities.

[5] Other losses/gains includes projected change in fair value of loans held for sale and loans held for investment measured under the fair-value option, and goodwill impairment losses.

[6] Other comprehensive income (OCI) is only calculated for advanced approaches BHCs, and other BHCs that opt into the advanced approaches treatment of AOCI.

[7] Certain AOCI items are subject to transition into projected regulatory capital. Those transitions are 20 percent included in projected regulatory capital for 2014, 40 percent included in projected regulatory capital for 2015, and 60 percent included in projected regulatory capital for 2016.

Table 8. Projected stressed capital ratios under the adverse scenario, 2014:Q4–2016:Q4: 31 participating bank holding companies

Bank holding company	Tier 1 common ratio (%)			Common equity tier 1 ratio (%)[1]			Tier 1 risk-based capital ratio (%)			Total-risk based capital ratio (%)			Tier 1 leverage ratio (%)		
	Actual 2014:Q3	Ending	Minimum	Actual 2014:Q3	Ending	Minimum	Actual 2014:Q3	Ending	Minimum	Actual 2014:Q3	Ending	Minimum	Actual 2014:Q3	Ending	Minimum
Ally Financial Inc.	9.7	9.5	9.3	n/a	9.4	9.4	12.7	11.6	11.6	13.5	13.0	13.0	10.9	9.9	9.9
American Express Company	13.2	17.4	12.8	13.6	17.1	13.4	13.6	17.6	14.0	15.1	19.3	15.8	11.6	14.4	11.6
Bank of America Corporation	11.3	11.5	10.0	12.0	8.5	8.0	12.8	9.7	9.1	15.8	11.8	11.5	7.9	6.2	5.9
The Bank of New York Mellon Corporation	13.9	19.6	13.3	15.1	16.1	12.7	16.3	17.1	13.9	17.0	17.4	14.3	5.8	6.3	5.2
BB&T Corporation	10.5	9.4	8.9	n/a	9.7	9.3	12.4	11.2	10.9	15.2	13.3	13.1	9.7	8.5	8.3
BBVA Compass Bancshares, Inc.	11.0	9.5	9.5	n/a	10.0	10.0	11.3	10.0	10.0	13.3	11.7	11.7	9.6	7.8	7.8
BMO Financial Corp.	11.5	12.4	11.5	n/a	11.5	10.5	11.5	11.5	10.5	15.5	13.9	13.9	8.3	7.9	7.4
Capital One Financial Corporation	12.7	11.5	11.5	12.7	10.4	10.4	13.3	11.1	11.1	15.2	12.8	12.8	10.6	8.5	8.5
Citigroup Inc.	13.4	12.5	11.5	15.1	9.4	9.3	15.1	9.6	9.4	17.7	11.8	11.7	9.0	6.2	6.1
Citizens Financial Group, Inc.	12.9	12.3	12.1	n/a	12.5	12.3	12.9	12.5	12.3	16.1	15.9	15.8	10.9	10.0	9.9
Comerica Incorporated	10.6	10.9	10.4	n/a	10.7	10.1	10.6	10.7	10.1	12.8	11.9	11.8	10.8	10.7	10.4
Deutsche Bank Trust Corporation	36.6	40.6	36.3	n/a	33.8	30.2	36.6	33.8	30.2	37.0	34.6	30.6	11.9	12.8	11.8
Discover Financial Services	14.8	16.8	14.3	n/a	16.1	14.1	15.6	16.8	14.9	17.8	18.4	16.7	13.7	14.4	13.0
Fifth Third Bancorp	9.6	9.7	9.3	n/a	9.3	9.0	10.8	10.3	10.1	14.3	12.6	12.6	9.8	9.2	9.1
The Goldman Sachs Group, Inc.	14.4	13.8	12.2	15.1	10.2	9.2	17.0	11.4	10.5	19.8	13.2	12.4	9.0	8.1	7.8
HSBC North America Holdings Inc.	14.0	14.4	13.9	16.3	11.3	11.1	17.3	12.7	12.5	26.1	16.6	16.6	9.4	7.6	7.5
Huntington Bancshares Incorporated	10.3	10.1	10.0	n/a	9.8	9.7	11.6	10.5	10.4	13.7	12.4	12.4	9.8	8.8	8.8
JPMorgan Chase & Co.	10.9	10.1	9.6	11.1	9.1	8.8	12.6	10.3	10.0	15.0	12.1	12.1	7.6	6.3	6.3
KeyCorp	11.3	11.3	10.8	n/a	10.9	10.5	12.0	11.2	10.9	14.1	13.1	12.9	11.2	10.4	10.2
M&T Bank Corporation	9.8	9.4	9.3	n/a	9.7	9.5	12.5	11.0	10.9	15.4	13.7	13.7	10.6	8.3	8.3
Morgan Stanley	15.0	14.0	12.2	15.2	11.9	10.7	17.1	13.1	11.9	19.8	15.5	14.4	8.2	7.0	6.7
MUFG Americas Holdings Corporation	12.7	11.3	11.3	12.7	11.4	11.4	12.7	11.4	11.4	14.6	13.3	13.3	11.4	9.8	9.8
Northern Trust Corporation	12.8	14.3	12.5	12.8	11.7	10.9	13.6	12.2	11.5	16.0	14.0	13.5	7.9	7.8	7.4
The PNC Financial Services Group, Inc.	11.0	11.2	10.7	11.1	9.8	9.5	12.8	11.1	10.9	16.1	13.5	13.5	11.1	9.7	9.6
Regions Financial Corporation	11.8	10.7	10.6	n/a	10.7	10.7	12.7	11.4	11.4	15.5	13.8	13.7	11.0	9.5	9.5
Santander Holdings USA, Inc.	11.0	11.5	11.5	n/a	12.2	12.2	13.1	13.0	13.0	15.0	14.9	14.9	12.3	11.5	11.5
State Street Corporation	13.7	17.3	12.7	15.0	10.0	8.7	16.7	11.5	10.3	19.1	13.3	12.0	6.4	5.5	5.0
SunTrust Banks, Inc.	9.6	10.0	9.4	n/a	10.3	9.8	10.5	11.1	10.7	12.3	12.8	12.4	9.5	9.2	9.0
U.S. Bancorp	9.5	10.5	9.3	9.7	9.4	8.8	11.3	10.8	10.3	13.6	12.9	12.4	9.4	8.9	8.6
Wells Fargo & Company	10.8	9.9	9.7	11.1	8.4	8.4	12.6	9.7	9.6	15.6	12.3	12.3	9.6	7.4	7.4
Zions Bancorporation	11.9	10.4	10.4	n/a	10.3	10.3	14.4	12.3	12.3	16.3	14.4	14.4	11.9	9.8	9.8
31 participating bank holding companies	11.9	11.6	10.8	n/a	9.8	9.5	13.5	10.8	10.4	16.2	13.0	12.8	8.8	7.3	7.2

Note: The capital ratios are calculated using capital action assumptions provided within the Dodd-Frank Act stress testing rule. These projections represent hypothetical estimates that involve an economic outcome that is more adverse than expected. These estimates are not forecasts of expected losses, revenues, net income before taxes, or capital ratios. The minimum capital ratio presented is for the period 2014:Q4 to 2016:Q4.

[1] Advanced approaches bank holding companies (BHCs) are subject to the common equity tier 1 ratio for the third and fourth quarter of 2014. All bank holding companies are subject to the common equity tier 1 ratio for each quarter of 2015 and 2016. An advanced approaches BHC includes any BHC that has consolidated total assets greater than or equal to $250 billion or consolidated total on-balance sheet foreign exposure of at least $10 billion. See 12 CFR 217.100(b)(1). Other BHCs include any BHC that is subject to 12 CFR 225.8 and is not an advanced approaches BHC.

n/a Not applicable.

Source: Federal Reserve estimates in the severely adverse scenario.

Table 9. Projected losses, revenues, net income, and other comprehensive income through 2016:Q4 under the adverse scenario: 31 participating bank holding companies

Billions of dollars

Bank holding company	Sum of revenues		Minus sum of provisions and losses				Equals	Memo items	Other effects on capital
	Pre-provision net revenue[1]	Other revenue[2]	Provisions	Realized losses/gains on securities (AFS/HTM)	Trading and counterparty losses[3]	Other losses/ gains[4]	Net income before taxes	Other compre-hensive income[5]	AOCI included in capital[6] (2016:Q4)
Ally Financial Inc.	4.5	0.0	4.1	0.2	0.0	0.0	0.1	0.0	0.0
American Express Company	25.9	0.0	10.8	0.0	0.0	0.0	15.1	-0.3	-1.6
Bank of America Corporation	61.6	0.0	29.2	0.5	9.1	2.2	20.6	-26.0	-18.0
The Bank of New York Mellon Corporation	19.4	0.0	1.1	0.1	0.7	0.9	16.6	-6.1	-4.5
BB&T Corporation	9.7	0.0	4.5	0.0	0.0	0.0	5.2	0.0	0.0
BBVA Compass Bancshares, Inc.	1.8	0.0	2.2	0.0	0.0	0.0	-0.4	0.0	0.0
BMO Financial Corp.	2.4	0.0	1.5	0.0	0.0	0.0	0.9	0.0	0.0
Capital One Financial Corporation	23.1	0.0	20.1	0.0	0.0	0.1	2.9	-2.5	-1.8
Citigroup Inc.	50.9	0.0	34.8	2.0	10.1	3.5	0.5	-20.2	-29.3
Citizens Financial Group, Inc.	4.8	0.0	3.4	0.0	0.0	0.0	1.4	0.0	0.0
Comerica Incorporated	2.8	0.0	1.2	0.0	0.0	0.0	1.6	0.0	0.0
Deutsche Bank Trust Corporation	2.8	0.0	0.7	0.0	0.0	0.0	2.2	0.0	-0.1
Discover Financial Services	13.5	0.0	8.5	0.0	0.0	0.0	5.0	0.0	0.0
Fifth Third Bancorp	6.3	0.0	3.3	0.0	0.0	0.0	3.0	0.0	0.0
The Goldman Sachs Group, Inc.	19.0	0.0	1.7	0.0	9.9	3.4	4.1	0.0	-0.6
HSBC North America Holdings Inc.	4.5	0.0	4.9	0.0	0.0	0.3	-0.7	-2.3	-1.7
Huntington Bancshares Incorporated	2.5	0.0	1.4	0.1	0.0	0.0	1.0	0.0	0.0
JPMorgan Chase & Co.	70.5	0.0	33.7	2.3	12.2	1.1	21.2	-22.8	-11.7
KeyCorp	4.1	0.0	2.0	0.0	0.0	0.2	2.0	0.0	0.0
M&T Bank Corporation	5.3	0.0	3.5	0.0	0.0	0.0	1.8	0.0	0.0
Morgan Stanley	16.6	0.0	2.0	0.1	8.1	1.7	4.7	-3.7	-3.1
MUFG Americas Holdings Corporation	2.2	0.0	2.6	0.3	0.0	0.0	-0.7	0.0	0.0
Northern Trust Corporation	4.8	0.0	1.1	0.0	0.0	0.0	3.7	-1.0	-0.8
The PNC Financial Services Group, Inc.	15.8	0.0	6.0	0.2	0.0	0.3	9.3	-3.4	-1.8
Regions Financial Corporation	4.9	0.0	3.9	0.0	0.0	0.0	1.0	0.0	0.0
Santander Holdings USA, Inc.	6.6	0.0	5.4	0.1	0.0	0.0	1.1	0.0	0.0
State Street Corporation	10.9	0.0	0.5	0.4	0.8	0.0	9.2	-6.5	-4.1
SunTrust Banks, Inc.	8.7	0.0	4.1	0.0	0.0	0.3	4.4	0.0	0.0
U.S. Bancorp	27.1	0.0	11.3	0.0	0.0	0.0	15.8	-3.7	-2.5
Wells Fargo & Company	66.5	0.0	33.2	2.1	4.0	1.7	25.5	-21.9	-11.3
Zions Bancorporation	1.5	0.0	1.6	0.1	0.0	0.0	-0.2	0.0	0.0
31 participating bank holding companies	501.3	0.0	244.0	8.6	54.9	16.0	177.8	-120.5	-92.7

Note: These projections represent hypothetical estimates that involve an economic outcome that is more adverse than expected. These estimates are not forecasts of expected losses, revenues, or net income before taxes. Estimates may not sum precisely due to rounding.

[1]   Pre-provision net revenue includes losses from operational-risk events, mortgage repurchase expenses, and other real estate owned costs.

[2]   Other revenue includes one-time income and (expense) items not included in pre-provision net revenue.

[3]   Trading and counterparty losses include mark-to-market and credit valuation adjustments losses and losses arising from the counterparty default scenario component applied to derivatives, securities lending, and repurchase agreement activities.

[4]   Other losses/gains includes projected change in fair value of loans held for sale and loans held for investment measured under the fair-value option, and goodwill impairment losses.

[5]   Other comprehensive income is only calculated for advanced approaches BHCs and non-advanced approaches BHCs that have not elected to opt out of AOCI inclusion. Only those BHCs include accumulated other comprehensive income (AOCI) in calculations of regulatory capital. Other comprehensive income includes incremental unrealized losses/gains on AFS securities and on any HTM securities that have experienced other than temporary impairment.

[6]   Certain AOCI items are subject to transition into projected regulatory capital. Those transitions are 20 percent included in projected regulatory capital for 2014, 40 percent included in projected regulatory capital for 2015, and 60 percent included in projected regulatory capital for 2016.

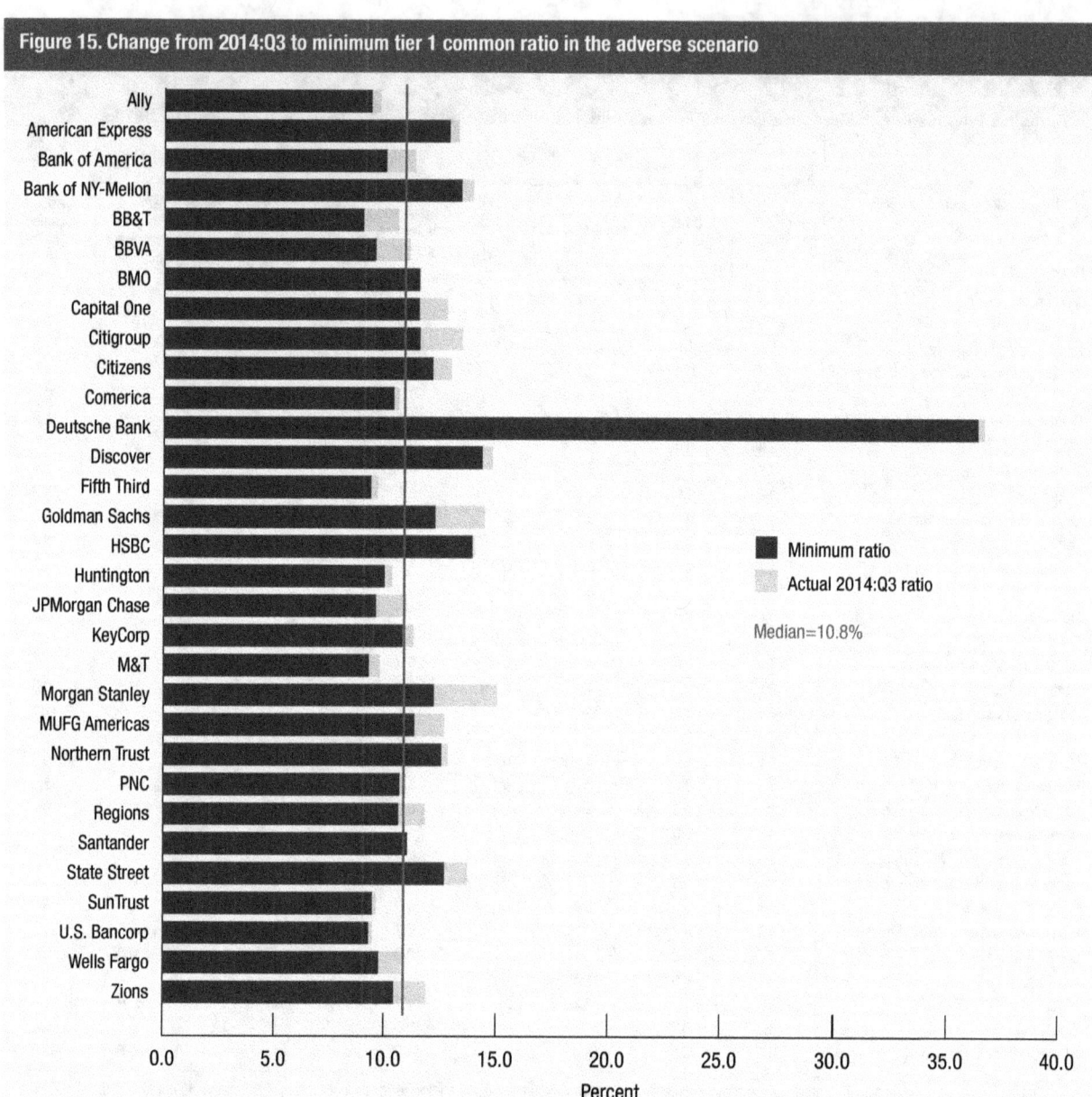

Figure 15. Change from 2014:Q3 to minimum tier 1 common ratio in the adverse scenario

Legend:
- Minimum ratio
- Actual 2014:Q3 ratio
- Median=10.8%

Note: Estimates are for the nine-quarter period from 2014:Q4–2016:Q4 as a percent of average balances.

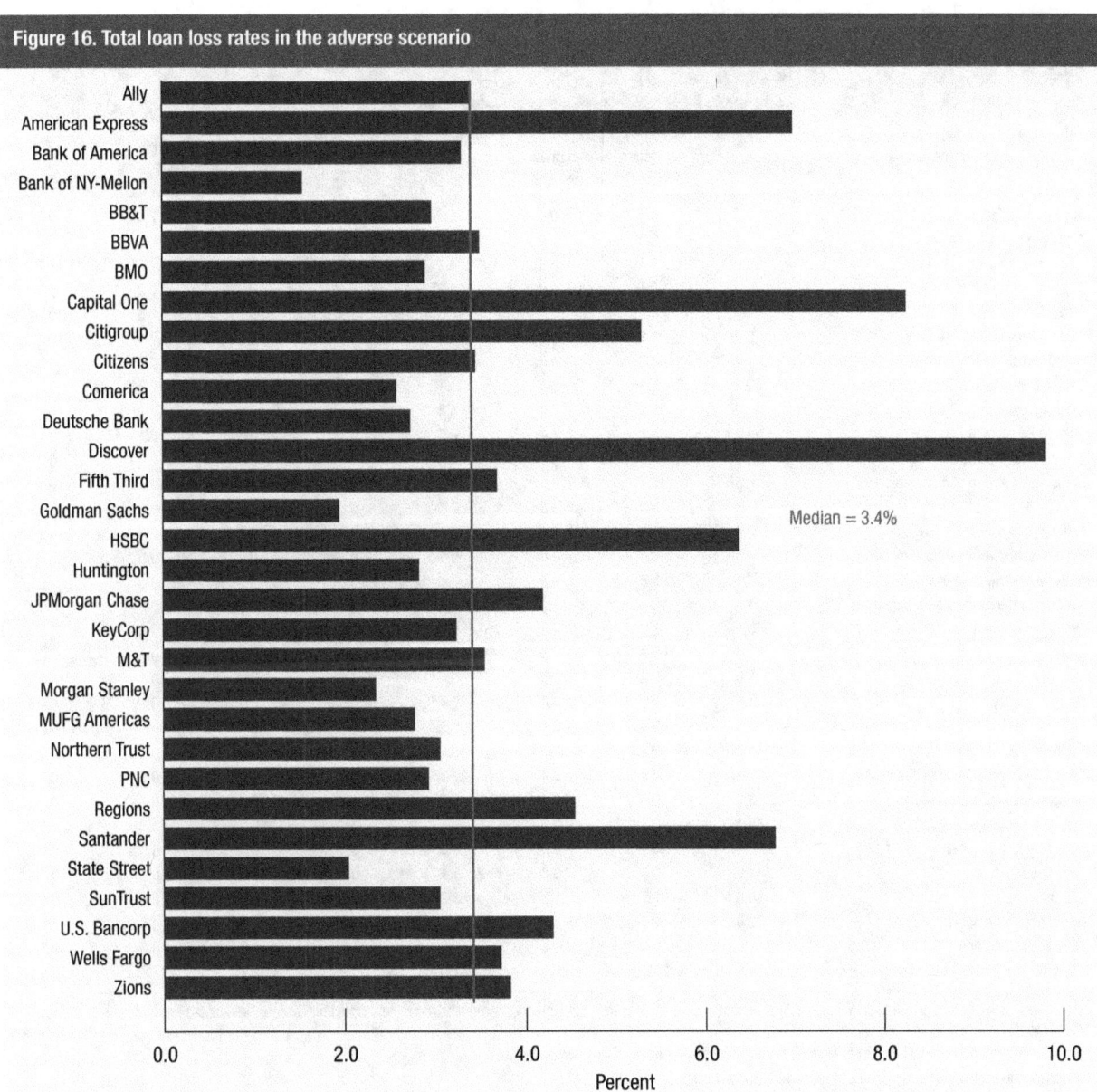

Figure 16. Total loan loss rates in the adverse scenario

Median = 3.4%

Percent

Note: Estimates are for the nine-quarter period from 2014:Q4–2016:Q4 as a percent of average balances.

Table 10. Projected loan losses by type of loan for 2014:Q4–2016:Q4 under the adverse scenario: 31 participating bank holding companies

Billions of dollars

Bank holding company	Loan losses	First lien mortgages, domestic	Junior liens and HELOCs, domestic	Commercial and industrial	Commercial real estate, domestic[1]	Credit cards	Other consumer[2]	Other loans[3]
Ally Financial Inc.	3.5	0.2	0.1	1.0	0.1	0.0	2.0	0.0
American Express Company	8.1	0.0	0.0	2.4	0.0	5.7	0.0	0.0
Bank of America Corporation	31.0	4.9	5.4	4.7	2.9	9.4	1.7	2.0
The Bank of New York Mellon Corporation	0.9	0.1	0.0	0.0	0.1	0.0	0.2	0.4
BB&T Corporation	3.9	0.7	0.2	0.5	1.4	0.2	0.8	0.2
BBVA Compass Bancshares, Inc.	2.0	0.3	0.1	0.5	0.9	0.1	0.1	0.1
BMO Financial Corp.	1.7	0.2	0.2	0.5	0.4	0.0	0.2	0.2
Capital One Financial Corporation	17.2	0.5	0.1	1.1	0.9	11.8	2.5	0.3
Citigroup Inc.	36.0	3.0	2.3	4.8	0.5	17.0	5.2	3.1
Citizens Financial Group, Inc.	3.3	0.3	1.1	0.6	0.7	0.2	0.4	0.1
Comerica Incorporated	1.3	0.0	0.1	0.5	0.5	0.0	0.0	0.2
Deutsche Bank Trust Corporation	0.5	0.1	0.0	0.2	0.1	0.0	0.0	0.1
Discover Financial Services	6.8	0.0	0.0	0.0	0.0	5.6	1.2	0.0
Fifth Third Bancorp	3.4	0.5	0.4	1.1	0.8	0.3	0.3	0.2
The Goldman Sachs Group, Inc.	1.4	0.0	0.0	0.5	0.1	0.0	0.0	0.7
HSBC North America Holdings Inc.	6.1	3.8	0.9	0.6	0.5	0.1	0.0	0.2
Huntington Bancshares Incorporated	1.4	0.2	0.2	0.3	0.4	0.0	0.2	0.0
JPMorgan Chase & Co.	33.1	3.6	4.2	5.9	3.0	10.3	2.0	4.0
KeyCorp	2.0	0.2	0.3	0.5	0.5	0.1	0.3	0.2
M&T Bank Corporation	3.0	0.8	0.3	0.4	1.3	0.0	0.2	0.0
Morgan Stanley	1.5	0.2	0.0	0.4	0.5	0.0	0.1	0.4
MUFG Americas Holdings Corporation	2.1	0.6	0.1	0.5	0.8	0.0	0.0	0.2
Northern Trust Corporation	1.0	0.2	0.2	0.1	0.2	0.0	0.0	0.2
The PNC Financial Services Group, Inc.	6.1	0.3	0.4	2.3	1.8	0.4	0.6	0.3
Regions Financial Corporation	3.6	0.6	0.4	0.6	1.4	0.1	0.2	0.2
Santander Holdings USA, Inc.	5.1	0.3	0.2	0.4	1.0	0.0	3.3	0.0
State Street Corporation	0.4	0.0	0.0	0.0	0.1	0.0	0.0	0.3
SunTrust Banks, Inc.	4.2	0.8	0.8	1.1	0.7	0.1	0.5	0.1
U.S. Bancorp	10.8	1.0	0.6	3.2	2.5	2.2	0.8	0.5
Wells Fargo & Company	32.0	4.5	4.0	7.2	6.0	3.5	4.5	2.3
Zions Bancorporation	1.6	0.0	0.1	0.5	0.8	0.0	0.0	0.1
31 participating bank holding companies	234.9	27.9	22.7	42.5	30.9	67.1	27.6	16.3

Note: These projections represent hypothetical estimates that involve an economic outcome that is more adverse than expected. These estimates are not forecasts of expected loan losses.

[1]   Commercial and industrial loans include small and medium enterprise loans and corporate cards.

[2]   Other consumer loans include student loans and automobile loans.

[3]   Other loans include international real estate loans.

Table 11. Projected loan losses by type of loan for 2014:Q4–2016:Q4 under the adverse scenario: 31 participating bank holding companies

Percent of average balances[1]

Bank holding company	Loan losses	First lien mortgages, domestic	Junior liens and HELOCs, domestic	Commercial and industrial	Commercial real estate, domestic[2]	Credit cards	Other consumer[3]	Other loans[4]
Ally Financial Inc.	3.4	4.3	5.3	2.8	2.8	0.0	3.7	7.1
American Express Company	7.0	0.0	0.0	6.5	0.0	7.2	12.2	0.0
Bank of America Corporation	3.3	2.1	5.9	2.3	4.7	9.0	2.0	1.2
The Bank of New York Mellon Corporation	1.5	2.1	6.3	2.0	5.9	0.0	8.6	0.9
BB&T Corporation	3.0	1.9	2.3	2.6	4.2	10.8	4.2	1.2
BBVA Compass Bancshares, Inc.	3.5	2.0	5.2	2.8	7.2	11.9	3.0	0.9
BMO Financial Corp.	2.9	2.7	3.0	2.8	4.9	8.5	2.2	1.9
Capital One Financial Corporation	8.3	1.5	5.6	5.0	3.9	15.1	6.5	2.0
Citigroup Inc.	5.3	3.3	7.3	3.0	5.1	12.1	10.3	1.6
Citizens Financial Group, Inc.	3.5	1.9	5.5	2.3	6.6	10.3	2.7	1.0
Comerica Incorporated	2.6	1.8	3.1	1.7	4.4	0.0	6.4	3.4
Deutsche Bank Trust Corporation	2.7	2.8	6.0	5.6	4.5	0.0	2.0	0.8
Discover Financial Services	9.8	3.9	12.9	10.6	18.3	10.1	8.7	2.3
Fifth Third Bancorp	3.7	3.7	4.3	3.0	7.8	10.9	2.0	2.2
The Goldman Sachs Group, Inc.	1.9	3.8	5.6	5.5	3.5	0.0	2.3	1.3
HSBC North America Holdings Inc.	6.4	10.0	19.2	1.9	5.3	11.9	6.4	1.5
Huntington Bancshares Incorporated	2.8	2.2	3.4	2.5	4.5	11.9	2.4	1.2
JPMorgan Chase & Co.	4.2	2.5	6.0	4.6	3.6	8.7	3.0	2.3
KeyCorp	3.2	3.4	3.3	2.2	4.8	10.1	7.1	1.5
M&T Bank Corporation	3.6	2.8	4.7	2.5	4.6	11.9	4.3	1.4
Morgan Stanley	2.3	1.0	5.6	4.4	10.8	0.0	0.7	2.4
MUFG Americas Holdings Corporation	2.8	1.9	1.8	2.7	4.9	0.0	11.9	2.2
Northern Trust Corporation	3.1	2.6	9.1	2.2	5.0	0.0	10.4	2.0
The PNC Financial Services Group, Inc.	2.9	1.0	1.8	3.4	5.5	9.5	2.6	0.9
Regions Financial Corporation	4.5	4.0	4.8	2.8	8.9	11.0	4.4	1.7
Santander Holdings USA, Inc.	6.8	3.6	3.2	2.2	5.3	11.9	13.2	2.2
State Street Corporation	2.0	0.0	0.0	2.6	17.0	0.0	0.6	1.7
SunTrust Banks, Inc.	3.1	3.3	5.5	2.5	4.1	10.7	2.5	0.9
U.S. Bancorp	4.3	1.8	3.5	5.0	6.4	11.8	2.5	2.2
Wells Fargo & Company	3.7	1.8	5.0	4.3	4.8	12.0	5.1	1.9
Zions Bancorporation	3.8	0.4	2.6	4.2	4.7	11.9	9.3	2.7
31 participating bank holding companies	4.1	2.5	5.3	3.4	5.0	10.5	4.5	1.7

Note: These projections represent hypothetical estimates that involve an economic outcome that is more adverse than expected. These estimates are not forecasts of expected loan losses.

[1] Average loan balances used to calculate portfolio loss rates exclude loans held for sale and loans held for investment under the fair-value option, and are calculated over nine quarters.

[2] Commercial and industrial loans include small and medium enterprise loans and corporate cards.

[3] Other consumer loans include student loans and automobile loans.

[4] Other loans include international real estate loans.

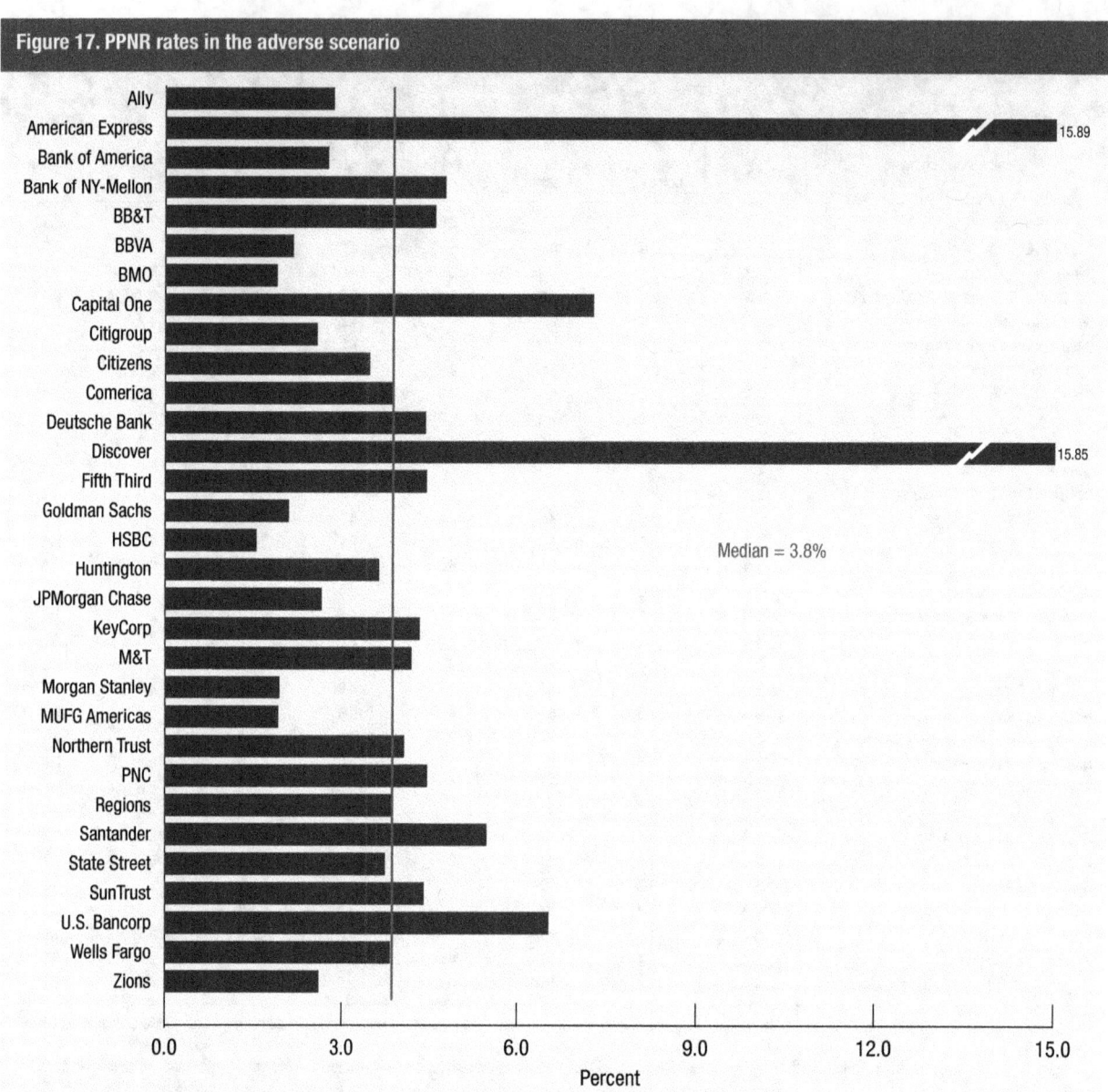

Figure 17. PPNR rates in the adverse scenario

Median = 3.8%

American Express — 15.89

Discover — 15.85

Percent

Note: Estimates are for the nine-quarter period from 2014:Q4–2016:Q4 as a percent of average assets.

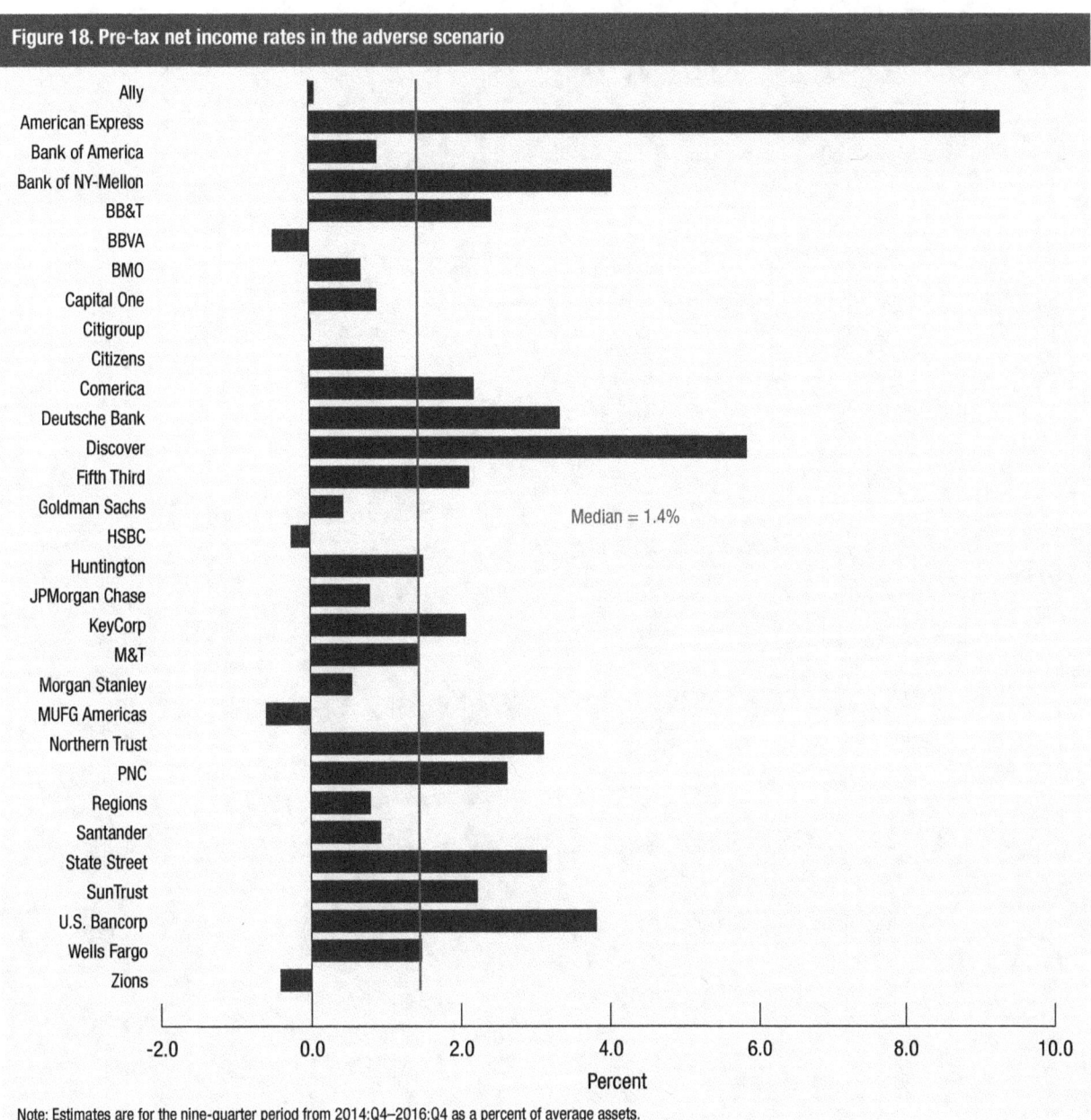

Figure 18. Pre-tax net income rates in the adverse scenario

Median = 1.4%

Percent

Note: Estimates are for the nine-quarter period from 2014:Q4–2016:Q4 as a percent of average assets.

Appendix A: Supervisory Scenarios

This appendix includes the adverse and severely adverse scenarios provided by the Federal Reserve.

It is important to note that the adverse and severely adverse scenarios are not forecasts but rather are

hypothetical scenarios designed to assess the strength of banking organizations and their resilience to adverse economic environments.

Table A.1. Supervisory severely adverse scenario: Domestic
Percent unless otherwise indicated

Date	Real GDP growth	Nominal GDP growth	Real dispo-sable income growth	Nominal dispo-sable income growth	Un-employ-ment rate	CPI inflation rate	3-month Treasury rate	5-year Treasury yield	10-year Treasury yield	BBB corporate yield	Mortgage rate	Prime rate	Dow Jones Total Stock Market Index	House Price Index	Com-mercial Real Estate Price Index	Market Volatility Index
2001:Q1	-1.1	1.4	3.5	6.3	4.2	3.9	4.8	4.9	5.3	7.4	7.0	8.6	10645.9	113.2	139.5	32.8
2001:Q2	2.1	5.1	-0.3	1.6	4.4	2.8	3.7	4.9	5.5	7.5	7.1	7.3	11407.2	115.2	138.6	34.7
2001:Q3	-1.3	0.0	9.8	10.1	4.8	1.1	3.2	4.6	5.3	7.3	7.0	6.6	9563.0	117.5	141.0	43.7
2001:Q4	1.1	2.3	-4.9	-4.6	5.5	-0.3	1.9	4.2	5.1	7.2	6.8	5.2	10707.7	119.8	135.6	35.3
2002:Q1	3.7	5.1	10.1	10.9	5.7	1.3	1.7	4.5	5.4	7.6	7.0	4.8	10775.7	122.1	137.4	26.1
2002:Q2	2.2	3.8	2.0	5.2	5.8	3.2	1.7	4.5	5.4	7.6	6.8	4.8	9384.0	125.4	135.8	28.4
2002:Q3	2.0	3.8	-0.5	1.5	5.7	2.2	1.6	3.4	4.5	7.3	6.3	4.8	7773.6	128.7	138.7	45.1
2002:Q4	0.3	2.4	1.9	3.8	5.9	2.4	1.3	3.1	4.3	7.0	6.1	4.5	8343.2	131.3	142.5	42.6
2003:Q1	2.1	4.6	1.1	4.0	5.9	4.2	1.2	2.9	4.2	6.5	5.8	4.3	8051.9	134.1	147.9	34.7
2003:Q2	3.8	5.1	5.9	6.3	6.1	-0.7	1.0	2.6	3.8	5.7	5.5	4.2	9342.4	137.0	149.2	29.1
2003:Q3	6.9	9.3	6.7	9.3	6.1	3.0	0.9	3.1	4.4	6.0	6.0	4.0	9649.7	141.1	147.3	22.7
2003:Q4	4.8	6.8	1.6	3.3	5.8	1.5	0.9	3.2	4.4	5.8	5.9	4.0	10799.6	146.0	145.7	21.1
2004:Q1	2.3	5.9	2.9	6.1	5.7	3.4	0.9	3.0	4.1	5.5	5.6	4.0	11039.4	151.8	152.9	21.6
2004:Q2	3.0	6.6	4.0	7.0	5.6	3.2	1.1	3.7	4.7	6.1	6.2	4.0	11144.6	158.0	160.4	20.0
2004:Q3	3.7	6.3	2.1	4.5	5.4	2.6	1.5	3.5	4.4	5.8	5.9	4.4	10893.8	163.4	171.8	19.3
2004:Q4	3.5	6.4	5.1	8.5	5.4	4.4	2.0	3.5	4.3	5.4	5.7	4.9	11951.5	169.4	175.8	16.6
2005:Q1	4.3	8.3	-3.8	-1.8	5.3	2.0	2.5	3.9	4.4	5.4	5.8	5.4	11637.3	177.6	175.8	14.6
2005:Q2	2.1	5.1	3.2	6.0	5.1	2.7	2.9	3.9	4.2	5.5	5.7	5.9	11856.7	185.0	182.3	17.7
2005:Q3	3.4	7.3	2.1	6.6	5.0	6.2	3.4	4.0	4.3	5.5	5.8	6.4	12282.9	190.8	187.1	14.2
2005:Q4	2.3	5.4	3.4	6.6	5.0	3.8	3.8	4.4	4.6	5.9	6.2	7.0	12497.2	195.5	195.4	16.5
2006:Q1	4.9	8.2	9.5	11.5	4.7	2.1	4.4	4.6	4.7	6.0	6.2	7.4	13121.6	198.7	200.0	14.6
2006:Q2	1.2	4.5	0.6	3.7	4.6	3.7	4.7	5.0	5.2	6.5	6.6	7.9	12808.9	197.8	209.0	23.8
2006:Q3	0.4	3.2	1.2	4.1	4.6	3.8	4.9	4.8	5.0	6.4	6.6	8.3	13322.5	196.5	218.6	18.6
2006:Q4	3.2	4.6	5.3	4.6	4.4	-1.6	4.9	4.6	4.7	6.1	6.2	8.3	14215.8	196.5	217.3	12.7
2007:Q1	0.2	4.8	2.6	6.5	4.5	4.0	5.0	4.6	4.8	6.1	6.2	8.3	14354.0	194.0	227.1	19.6
2007:Q2	3.1	5.4	0.8	4.0	4.5	4.6	4.7	4.7	4.9	6.3	6.4	8.3	15163.1	189.1	236.4	18.9
2007:Q3	2.7	4.2	1.1	3.4	4.7	2.6	4.3	4.5	4.8	6.5	6.6	8.2	15317.8	183.6	249.1	30.8
2007:Q4	1.4	3.2	0.3	4.4	4.8	5.0	3.4	3.8	4.4	6.4	6.2	7.5	14753.6	178.1	251.5	31.1
2008:Q1	-2.7	-0.5	2.9	6.5	5.0	4.4	2.1	2.8	3.9	6.5	5.9	6.2	13284.1	171.2	239.9	32.2
2008:Q2	2.0	4.0	8.7	13.3	5.3	5.3	1.6	3.2	4.1	6.8	6.1	5.1	13016.4	163.9	223.9	24.1
2008:Q3	-1.9	0.8	-8.9	-5.1	6.0	6.3	1.5	3.1	4.1	7.2	6.3	5.0	11826.0	157.3	233.4	46.7
2008:Q4	-8.2	-7.7	2.6	-3.2	6.9	-8.9	0.3	2.2	3.7	9.4	5.8	4.1	9056.7	149.2	222.5	80.9

(continued on next page)

Table A.1.—*continued*

Date	Real GDP growth	Nominal GDP growth	Real disposable income growth	Nominal disposable income growth	Un-employ-ment rate	CPI inflation rate	3-month Treasury rate	5-year Treasury yield	10-year Treasury yield	BBB corporate yield	Mortgage rate	Prime rate	Dow Jones Total Stock Market Index	House Price Index	Com-mercial Real Estate Price Index	Market Volatility Index
2009:Q1	-5.4	-4.5	-0.8	-3.0	8.3	-2.7	0.2	1.9	3.2	9.0	5.1	3.3	8044.2	143.1	208.9	56.7
2009:Q2	-0.5	-1.2	2.9	4.7	9.3	2.1	0.2	2.3	3.7	8.2	5.0	3.3	9342.8	142.9	178.5	42.3
2009:Q3	1.3	1.2	-4.3	-1.9	9.6	3.5	0.2	2.5	3.8	6.8	5.1	3.3	10812.8	144.1	154.0	31.3
2009:Q4	3.9	5.2	-0.5	2.2	9.9	3.2	0.1	2.3	3.7	6.1	4.9	3.3	11385.1	145.0	155.2	30.7
2010:Q1	1.7	3.2	0.4	1.8	9.8	0.6	0.1	2.4	3.9	5.8	5.0	3.3	12032.5	145.5	149.8	27.3
2010:Q2	3.9	5.8	5.3	5.8	9.6	0.0	0.1	2.3	3.6	5.6	4.9	3.3	10645.8	144.4	164.5	45.8
2010:Q3	2.7	4.6	2.0	3.2	9.5	1.2	0.2	1.6	2.9	5.1	4.4	3.3	11814.0	141.3	166.9	32.9
2010:Q4	2.5	4.7	2.8	5.0	9.6	3.1	0.1	1.5	3.0	5.0	4.4	3.3	13131.5	140.0	172.7	23.5
2011:Q1	-1.5	0.2	5.0	8.2	9.0	4.2	0.1	2.1	3.5	5.4	4.8	3.3	13908.5	138.1	179.6	29.4
2011:Q2	2.9	6.0	-0.6	3.5	9.1	5.0	0.0	1.8	3.3	5.1	4.7	3.3	13843.5	137.3	177.0	22.7
2011:Q3	0.8	3.3	2.1	4.3	9.0	2.6	0.0	1.1	2.5	4.9	4.3	3.3	11676.5	137.3	177.0	48.0
2011:Q4	4.6	5.2	0.2	1.6	8.6	1.6	0.0	1.0	2.1	5.0	4.0	3.3	13019.3	137.1	188.4	45.5
2012:Q1	2.3	4.4	6.8	9.1	8.2	2.1	0.1	0.9	2.1	4.7	3.9	3.3	14627.5	139.3	188.2	23.0
2012:Q2	1.6	3.5	2.3	3.7	8.2	1.4	0.1	0.8	1.8	4.5	3.8	3.3	14100.2	142.5	189.4	26.7
2012:Q3	2.5	4.4	-0.4	0.9	8.0	1.7	0.1	0.7	1.6	4.2	3.6	3.3	14894.7	145.4	196.6	20.5
2012:Q4	0.1	1.6	11.8	13.8	7.8	2.4	0.1	0.7	1.7	3.9	3.4	3.3	14834.9	148.9	198.3	22.7
2013:Q1	2.7	4.2	-12.6	-11.7	7.7	1.2	0.1	0.8	1.9	4.0	3.5	3.3	16396.2	153.8	203.2	19.0
2013:Q2	1.8	2.9	3.8	4.3	7.5	0.4	0.1	0.9	2.0	4.1	3.7	3.3	16771.3	158.7	212.4	20.5
2013:Q3	4.5	6.2	2.0	3.7	7.2	2.2	0.0	1.5	2.7	4.9	4.4	3.3	17718.3	162.6	222.8	17.0
2013:Q4	3.5	5.0	0.2	1.2	7.0	1.1	0.1	1.4	2.8	4.8	4.3	3.3	19413.2	166.4	229.2	20.3
2014:Q1	-2.1	-0.8	3.4	4.8	6.7	1.9	0.0	1.6	2.8	4.6	4.4	3.3	19711.2	169.7	227.6	21.4
2014:Q2	4.6	6.8	4.4	6.8	6.2	3.0	0.0	1.7	2.7	4.3	4.2	3.3	20568.7	170.8	233.0	17.0
2014:Q3	3.1	3.8	2.7	3.6	6.1	1.1	0.0	1.7	2.5	4.2	4.1	3.3	20458.8	172.1	236.0	17.0
2014:Q4	-3.9	-2.8	-3.0	-0.1	6.9	4.3	0.1	0.4	0.9	4.7	4.2	3.3	17133.5	169.5	238.9	79.0
2015:Q1	-6.1	-4.7	-4.4	-2.3	8.0	3.0	0.1	0.4	1.0	5.6	4.6	3.3	12498.5	164.0	230.2	71.3
2015:Q2	-3.9	-2.4	-3.4	-2.2	8.8	1.7	0.1	0.4	1.2	6.0	4.8	3.3	10190.1	157.6	213.6	76.9
2015:Q3	-3.2	-1.7	-2.4	-1.4	9.5	1.3	0.1	0.4	1.3	6.3	5.0	3.3	8770.7	150.7	195.1	68.1
2015:Q4	-1.5	0.0	-1.5	-0.7	9.9	1.1	0.1	0.4	1.5	6.2	5.0	3.2	8606.3	144.3	177.6	48.1
2016:Q1	1.2	2.4	0.2	1.5	10.0	1.6	0.1	0.5	1.5	6.0	4.9	3.2	9087.3	138.4	164.4	38.4
2016:Q2	1.2	2.5	0.4	1.8	10.1	1.9	0.1	0.6	1.6	5.8	4.8	3.2	9607.2	133.4	157.4	30.7
2016:Q3	3.0	4.4	1.2	2.8	10.0	2.0	0.1	0.8	1.8	5.6	4.8	3.2	10480.7	130.4	154.4	25.5
2016:Q4	3.0	4.3	1.8	3.3	9.9	1.9	0.1	0.9	1.9	5.5	4.7	3.2	11521.4	128.4	154.6	21.6
2017:Q1	3.9	5.2	2.7	4.2	9.7	1.9	0.1	1.1	2.0	5.3	4.7	3.2	12894.7	127.9	156.1	18.7
2017:Q2	3.9	5.2	2.8	4.1	9.5	1.7	0.1	1.2	2.1	5.2	4.7	3.2	14079.2	128.4	159.6	17.6
2017:Q3	3.9	5.1	2.9	4.2	9.3	1.6	0.1	1.3	2.2	5.1	4.7	3.2	15430.3	129.5	164.0	16.4
2017:Q4	3.9	5.1	3.0	4.3	9.1	1.6	0.1	1.5	2.3	5.1	4.7	3.2	16487.6	131.0	169.1	16.5

Note: Refer to Notes Regarding Scenario Variables for more information on variables.

Table A.2. Supervisory severely adverse scenario: International
Percent unless otherwise indicated

Date	Euro area real GDP growth	Euro area inflation	Euro area bilateral dollar exchange rate (USD/euro)	Developing Asia real GDP growth	Developing Asia inflation	Developing Asia bilateral dollar exchange rate (F/USD, index)	Japan real GDP growth	Japan inflation	Japan bilateral dollar exchange rate (yen/USD)	U.K. real GDP growth	U.K. inflation	U.K. bilateral dollar exchange rate (USD/pound)
2001:Q1	3.7	1.1	0.879	4.0	1.6	106.0	2.6	-1.2	125.5	4.6	0.1	1.419
2001:Q2	0.3	4.1	0.847	5.9	2.0	106.1	-0.7	-0.3	124.7	3.1	3.1	1.408
2001:Q3	0.3	1.4	0.910	4.9	1.2	106.4	-4.3	-1.1	119.2	2.1	1.0	1.469
2001:Q4	0.6	1.7	0.890	7.7	0.1	106.8	-0.5	-1.4	131.0	1.3	0.0	1.454
2002:Q1	0.7	3.0	0.872	6.8	0.3	107.3	-0.9	-2.7	132.7	1.8	1.9	1.425
2002:Q2	2.1	2.0	0.986	9.0	1.1	104.7	4.3	1.7	119.9	3.3	0.9	1.525
2002:Q3	1.4	1.6	0.988	5.5	1.4	105.5	2.6	-0.7	121.7	3.6	1.4	1.570
2002:Q4	0.3	2.4	1.049	6.2	0.9	104.4	1.5	-0.4	118.8	3.7	1.9	1.610
2003:Q1	-0.9	3.3	1.090	7.0	3.5	105.5	-2.2	-1.6	118.1	3.9	1.6	1.579
2003:Q2	0.3	0.3	1.150	2.6	1.1	104.0	5.2	1.7	119.9	5.7	0.3	1.653
2003:Q3	2.1	2.2	1.165	13.4	0.0	102.6	1.7	-0.7	111.4	5.2	1.7	1.662
2003:Q4	3.1	2.2	1.260	11.8	5.7	103.3	4.2	-0.6	107.1	4.1	1.7	1.784
2004:Q1	1.9	2.3	1.229	5.1	4.0	101.4	3.8	-0.9	104.2	1.3	1.3	1.840
2004:Q2	2.2	2.4	1.218	6.1	4.1	102.7	0.3	1.1	109.4	1.2	1.0	1.813
2004:Q3	1.4	2.0	1.242	8.6	4.0	102.7	0.6	0.1	110.2	0.5	1.1	1.809
2004:Q4	1.5	2.4	1.354	7.9	0.8	98.9	-1.1	1.7	102.7	1.6	2.4	1.916
2005:Q1	0.4	1.5	1.297	7.9	2.9	98.6	0.8	-2.7	107.2	2.9	2.6	1.889
2005:Q2	2.8	2.2	1.210	7.6	1.5	98.9	5.3	-1.2	110.9	4.2	1.9	1.793
2005:Q3	2.9	3.2	1.206	9.5	2.3	98.5	1.4	-1.3	113.3	4.2	2.7	1.770
2005:Q4	2.5	2.5	1.184	10.5	1.8	98.1	0.7	0.7	117.9	5.5	1.4	1.719
2006:Q1	3.4	1.7	1.214	12.2	2.3	96.7	1.8	1.3	117.5	2.4	1.9	1.739
2006:Q2	4.8	2.5	1.278	7.8	3.2	96.6	1.7	-0.1	114.5	2.0	3.0	1.849
2006:Q3	2.5	2.0	1.269	8.8	2.1	96.2	-0.3	0.5	118.0	0.7	3.3	1.872
2006:Q4	4.4	0.9	1.320	10.7	3.7	94.5	5.2	-0.4	119.0	3.0	2.6	1.959
2007:Q1	3.2	2.2	1.337	14.8	3.6	93.9	4.1	-0.2	117.6	3.1	2.6	1.969
2007:Q2	2.3	2.3	1.352	10.1	4.9	91.9	0.5	0.0	123.4	2.4	1.6	2.006
2007:Q3	2.0	2.1	1.422	8.8	7.5	90.6	-1.5	0.1	115.0	3.4	0.3	2.039
2007:Q4	1.9	4.9	1.460	10.8	6.1	89.4	3.5	2.2	111.7	1.9	4.0	1.984
2008:Q1	2.7	4.2	1.581	8.2	8.1	88.0	2.7	1.3	99.9	1.3	3.7	1.986
2008:Q2	-1.6	3.2	1.575	7.6	6.3	88.6	-4.7	1.6	106.2	-0.9	5.6	1.991
2008:Q3	-2.3	3.2	1.408	4.2	2.9	91.4	-4.1	3.6	105.9	-6.5	5.9	1.780
2008:Q4	-7.1	-1.4	1.392	0.7	-0.9	92.2	-12.5	-2.2	90.8	-8.6	0.6	1.462
2009:Q1	-10.8	-1.1	1.326	3.3	-1.6	94.4	-15.0	-3.6	99.2	-7.0	-0.1	1.430
2009:Q2	-1.1	0.0	1.402	15.4	2.3	92.3	7.1	-1.7	96.4	-1.0	2.0	1.645
2009:Q3	1.3	1.1	1.463	12.5	4.0	91.3	0.2	-1.2	89.5	0.8	3.7	1.600
2009:Q4	1.8	1.6	1.433	8.3	5.2	90.7	7.1	-1.6	93.1	1.6	3.1	1.617
2010:Q1	2.0	1.7	1.353	9.2	4.3	89.8	6.1	0.8	93.4	2.1	4.0	1.519
2010:Q2	4.1	2.0	1.229	9.3	3.4	91.0	4.4	-1.0	88.5	4.0	3.0	1.495
2010:Q3	1.3	1.7	1.360	8.7	3.9	88.4	5.8	-1.9	83.5	2.6	2.5	1.573
2010:Q4	2.1	2.6	1.327	8.4	7.8	87.4	-2.2	1.1	81.7	0.1	4.0	1.539
2011:Q1	3.7	3.6	1.418	9.2	6.5	86.4	-6.9	-0.4	82.8	2.2	6.6	1.605
2011:Q2	0.1	3.2	1.452	7.1	5.8	85.3	-2.7	-0.4	80.6	0.9	4.5	1.607
2011:Q3	0.0	1.5	1.345	6.9	5.7	87.4	10.8	0.4	77.0	2.8	4.0	1.562
2011:Q4	-1.1	3.4	1.297	6.3	3.0	87.2	0.6	-0.8	77.0	-0.1	3.3	1.554
2012:Q1	-0.4	2.6	1.333	5.8	3.0	86.3	4.1	1.8	82.4	0.3	1.9	1.599
2012:Q2	-1.0	2.4	1.267	6.0	3.9	88.0	-2.2	-0.7	79.8	-0.7	1.9	1.569
2012:Q3	-0.4	1.8	1.286	6.5	2.3	86.2	-2.7	-1.7	77.9	3.4	2.7	1.613
2012:Q4	-1.9	2.3	1.319	7.5	3.7	85.9	-0.5	-0.1	86.6	-1.3	3.9	1.626
2013:Q1	-1.3	0.8	1.282	5.4	4.1	86.2	5.1	0.0	94.2	2.1	2.5	1.519
2013:Q2	1.3	0.7	1.301	6.1	3.0	87.1	3.4	0.8	99.2	2.7	1.8	1.521
2013:Q3	0.6	1.6	1.354	7.7	3.5	86.5	1.8	3.0	98.3	3.5	2.7	1.618

(continued on next page)

Table A.2.—*continued*

Date	Euro area real GDP growth	Euro area inflation	Euro area bilateral dollar exchange rate (USD/euro)	Developing Asia real GDP growth	Developing Asia inflation	Developing Asia bilateral dollar exchange rate (F/USD, index)	Japan real GDP growth	Japan inflation	Japan bilateral dollar exchange rate (yen/USD)	U.K. real GDP growth	U.K. inflation	U.K. bilateral dollar exchange rate (USD/pound)
2013:Q4	1.0	0.1	1.378	6.9	4.0	85.6	-0.5	1.9	105.3	2.5	1.3	1.657
2014:Q1	1.2	0.2	1.378	5.1	1.4	86.7	6.0	0.4	103.0	3.0	1.2	1.668
2014:Q2	0.3	0.4	1.369	6.9	2.8	86.4	-7.1	9.4	101.3	3.7	1.8	1.711
2014:Q3	1.0	0.6	1.263	6.5	3.1	86.9	1.0	1.6	109.7	2.9	1.6	1.622
2014:Q4	-8.8	3.8	1.112	-3.2	11.9	98.0	-9.4	0.3	101.4	-4.0	1.5	1.572
2015:Q1	-6.5	0.7	1.110	0.8	3.7	97.7	-10.6	-2.0	101.2	-4.2	-0.4	1.575
2015:Q2	-3.6	-0.7	1.103	4.1	0.1	97.5	-8.5	-3.3	101.7	-3.2	-1.3	1.571
2015:Q3	-1.5	-1.1	1.094	5.8	-1.1	97.2	-6.4	-3.3	102.6	-2.0	-1.3	1.564
2015:Q4	-0.1	-1.1	1.084	6.6	-1.2	96.7	-4.4	-2.7	103.4	-0.8	-0.9	1.558
2016:Q1	1.0	-0.3	1.088	6.8	0.4	94.7	-2.5	-1.5	103.4	0.3	0.0	1.559
2016:Q2	1.7	0.2	1.095	6.6	1.3	92.6	-1.0	-0.7	103.1	1.3	0.6	1.560
2016:Q3	2.1	0.5	1.105	6.5	1.8	90.7	0.2	-0.2	102.9	2.1	1.0	1.559
2016:Q4	2.2	0.5	1.114	6.4	1.8	89.2	1.1	-0.1	102.9	2.6	1.2	1.555
2017:Q1	2.2	0.6	1.125	6.3	1.9	88.4	1.7	0.0	103.0	3.0	1.4	1.552
2017:Q2	2.2	0.5	1.135	6.3	1.7	87.9	2.1	0.0	103.1	3.1	1.4	1.552
2017:Q3	2.0	0.5	1.143	6.4	1.7	87.5	2.3	0.1	103.1	3.2	1.4	1.552
2017:Q4	1.9	0.6	1.152	6.4	1.9	87.2	2.4	0.4	102.9	3.1	1.5	1.552

Note: Refer to Notes Regarding Scenario Variables for more information on variables.

Table A.3. Supervisory adverse scenario: Domestic
Percent unless otherwise indicated

Date	Real GDP growth	Nominal GDP growth	Real disposable income growth	Nominal disposable income growth	Un-employ-ment rate	CPI inflation rate	3-month Treasury rate	5-year Treasury yield	10-year Treasury yield	BBB corporate yield	Mortgage rate	Prime rate	Level			
													Dow Jones Total Stock Market Index	House Price Index	Commercial Real Estate Price Index	Market Volatility Index
2001:Q1	-1.1	1.4	3.5	6.3	4.2	3.9	4.8	4.9	5.3	7.4	7.0	8.6	10645.9	113.2	139.5	32.8
2001:Q2	2.1	5.1	-0.3	1.6	4.4	2.8	3.7	4.9	5.5	7.5	7.1	7.3	11407.2	115.2	138.6	34.7
2001:Q3	-1.3	0.0	9.8	10.1	4.8	1.1	3.2	4.6	5.3	7.3	7.0	6.6	9563.0	117.5	141.0	43.7
2001:Q4	1.1	2.3	-4.9	-4.6	5.5	-0.3	1.9	4.2	5.1	7.2	6.8	5.2	10707.7	119.8	135.6	35.3
2002:Q1	3.7	5.1	10.1	10.9	5.7	1.3	1.7	4.5	5.4	7.6	7.0	4.8	10775.7	122.1	137.4	26.1
2002:Q2	2.2	3.8	2.0	5.2	5.8	3.2	1.7	4.5	5.4	7.6	6.8	4.8	9384.0	125.4	135.8	28.4
2002:Q3	2.0	3.8	-0.5	1.5	5.7	2.2	1.6	3.4	4.5	7.3	6.3	4.8	7773.6	128.7	138.7	45.1
2002:Q4	0.3	2.4	1.9	3.8	5.9	2.4	1.3	3.1	4.3	7.0	6.1	4.5	8343.2	131.3	142.5	42.6
2003:Q1	2.1	4.6	1.1	4.0	5.9	4.2	1.2	2.9	4.2	6.5	5.8	4.3	8051.9	134.1	147.9	34.7
2003:Q2	3.8	5.1	5.9	6.3	6.1	-0.7	1.0	2.6	3.8	5.7	5.5	4.2	9342.4	137.0	149.2	29.1
2003:Q3	6.9	9.3	6.7	9.3	6.1	3.0	0.9	3.1	4.4	6.0	6.0	4.0	9649.7	141.1	147.3	22.7
2003:Q4	4.8	6.8	1.6	3.3	5.8	1.5	0.9	3.2	4.4	5.8	5.9	4.0	10799.6	146.0	145.7	21.1
2004:Q1	2.3	5.9	2.9	6.1	5.7	3.4	0.9	3.0	4.1	5.5	5.6	4.0	11039.4	151.8	152.9	21.6
2004:Q2	3.0	6.6	4.0	7.0	5.6	3.2	1.1	3.7	4.7	6.1	6.2	4.0	11144.6	158.0	160.4	20.0
2004:Q3	3.7	6.3	2.1	4.5	5.4	2.6	1.5	3.5	4.4	5.8	5.9	4.4	10893.8	163.4	171.8	19.3
2004:Q4	3.5	6.4	5.1	8.5	5.4	4.4	2.0	3.5	4.3	5.4	5.7	4.9	11951.5	169.4	175.8	16.6
2005:Q1	4.3	8.3	-3.8	-1.8	5.3	2.0	2.5	3.9	4.4	5.4	5.8	5.4	11637.3	177.6	175.8	14.6
2005:Q2	2.1	5.1	3.2	6.0	5.1	2.7	2.9	3.9	4.2	5.5	5.7	5.9	11856.7	185.0	182.3	17.7
2005:Q3	3.4	7.3	2.1	6.6	5.0	6.2	3.4	4.0	4.3	5.5	5.8	6.4	12282.9	190.8	187.1	14.2
2005:Q4	2.3	5.4	3.4	6.6	5.0	3.8	3.8	4.4	4.6	5.9	6.2	7.0	12497.2	195.5	195.4	16.5
2006:Q1	4.9	8.2	9.5	11.5	4.7	2.1	4.4	4.6	4.7	6.0	6.2	7.4	13121.6	198.7	200.0	14.6
2006:Q2	1.2	4.5	0.6	3.7	4.6	3.7	4.7	5.0	5.2	6.5	6.6	7.9	12808.9	197.8	209.0	23.8
2006:Q3	0.4	3.2	1.2	4.1	4.6	3.8	4.9	4.8	5.0	6.4	6.6	8.3	13322.5	196.5	218.6	18.6
2006:Q4	3.2	4.6	5.3	4.6	4.4	-1.6	4.9	4.6	4.7	6.1	6.2	8.3	14215.8	196.5	217.3	12.7
2007:Q1	0.2	4.8	2.6	6.5	4.5	4.0	5.0	4.6	4.8	6.1	6.2	8.3	14354.0	194.0	227.1	19.6
2007:Q2	3.1	5.4	0.8	4.0	4.5	4.6	4.7	4.7	4.9	6.3	6.4	8.3	15163.1	189.1	236.4	18.9
2007:Q3	2.7	4.2	1.1	3.4	4.7	2.6	4.3	4.5	4.8	6.5	6.6	8.2	15317.8	183.6	249.1	30.8
2007:Q4	1.4	3.2	0.3	4.4	4.8	5.0	3.4	3.8	4.4	6.4	6.2	7.5	14753.6	178.1	251.5	31.1
2008:Q1	-2.7	-0.5	2.9	6.5	5.0	4.4	2.1	2.8	3.9	6.5	5.9	6.2	13284.1	171.2	239.9	32.2
2008:Q2	2.0	4.0	8.7	13.3	5.3	5.3	1.6	3.2	4.1	6.8	6.1	5.1	13016.4	163.9	223.9	24.1
2008:Q3	-1.9	0.8	-8.9	-5.1	6.0	6.3	1.5	3.1	4.1	7.2	6.3	5.0	11826.0	157.3	233.4	46.7
2008:Q4	-8.2	-7.7	2.6	-3.2	6.9	-8.9	0.3	2.2	3.7	9.4	5.8	4.1	9056.7	149.2	222.5	80.9
2009:Q1	-5.4	-4.5	-0.8	-3.0	8.3	-2.7	0.2	1.9	3.2	9.0	5.1	3.3	8044.2	143.1	208.9	56.7
2009:Q2	-0.5	-1.2	2.9	4.7	9.3	2.1	0.2	2.3	3.7	8.2	5.0	3.3	9342.8	142.9	178.5	42.3
2009:Q3	1.3	1.2	-4.3	-1.9	9.6	3.5	0.2	2.5	3.8	6.8	5.1	3.3	10812.8	144.1	154.0	31.3
2009:Q4	3.9	5.2	-0.5	2.2	9.9	3.2	0.1	2.3	3.7	6.1	4.9	3.3	11385.1	145.0	155.2	30.7
2010:Q1	1.7	3.2	0.4	1.8	9.8	0.6	0.1	2.4	3.9	5.8	5.0	3.3	12032.5	145.5	149.8	27.3
2010:Q2	3.9	5.8	5.3	5.8	9.6	0.0	0.1	2.3	3.6	5.6	4.9	3.3	10645.8	144.4	164.5	45.8
2010:Q3	2.7	4.6	2.0	3.2	9.5	1.2	0.2	1.6	2.9	5.1	4.4	3.3	11814.0	141.3	166.9	32.9
2010:Q4	2.5	4.7	2.8	5.0	9.6	3.1	0.1	1.5	3.0	5.0	4.4	3.3	13131.5	140.0	172.7	23.5
2011:Q1	-1.5	0.2	5.0	8.2	9.0	4.2	0.1	2.1	3.5	5.4	4.8	3.3	13908.5	138.1	179.6	29.4
2011:Q2	2.9	6.0	-0.6	3.5	9.1	5.0	0.0	1.8	3.3	5.1	4.7	3.3	13843.5	137.3	177.0	22.7
2011:Q3	0.8	3.3	2.1	4.3	9.0	2.6	0.0	1.1	2.5	4.9	4.3	3.3	11676.5	137.3	177.0	48.0
2011:Q4	4.6	5.2	0.2	1.6	8.6	1.6	0.0	1.0	2.1	5.0	4.0	3.3	13019.3	137.1	188.4	45.5
2012:Q1	2.3	4.4	6.8	9.1	8.2	2.1	0.1	0.9	2.1	4.7	3.9	3.3	14627.5	139.3	188.2	23.0
2012:Q2	1.6	3.5	2.3	3.7	8.2	1.4	0.1	0.8	1.8	4.5	3.8	3.3	14100.2	142.5	189.4	26.7
2012:Q3	2.5	4.4	-0.4	0.9	8.0	1.7	0.1	0.7	1.6	4.2	3.6	3.3	14894.7	145.4	196.6	20.5
2012:Q4	0.1	1.6	11.8	13.8	7.8	2.4	0.1	0.7	1.7	3.9	3.4	3.3	14834.9	148.9	198.3	22.7
2013:Q1	2.7	4.2	-12.6	-11.7	7.7	1.2	0.1	0.8	1.9	4.0	3.5	3.3	16396.2	153.8	203.2	19.0
2013:Q2	1.8	2.9	3.8	4.3	7.5	0.4	0.1	0.9	2.0	4.1	3.7	3.3	16771.3	158.7	212.4	20.5
2013:Q3	4.5	6.2	2.0	3.7	7.2	2.2	0.0	1.5	2.7	4.9	4.4	3.3	17718.3	162.6	222.8	17.0

(continued on next page)

Table A.3.—*continued*

Date	Real GDP growth	Nominal GDP growth	Real disposable income growth	Nominal disposable income growth	Un-employment rate	CPI inflation rate	3-month Treasury rate	5-year Treasury yield	10-year Treasury yield	BBB corporate yield	Mortgage rate	Prime rate	Dow Jones Total Stock Market Index	House Price Index	Com-mercial Real Estate Price Index	Market Volatility Index
													Level			
2013:Q4	3.5	5.0	0.2	1.2	7.0	1.1	0.1	1.4	2.8	4.8	4.3	3.3	19413.2	166.4	229.2	20.3
2014:Q1	-2.1	-0.8	3.4	4.8	6.7	1.9	0.0	1.6	2.8	4.6	4.4	3.3	19711.2	169.7	227.6	21.4
2014:Q2	4.6	6.8	4.4	6.8	6.2	3.0	0.0	1.7	2.7	4.3	4.2	3.3	20568.7	170.8	233.0	17.0
2014:Q3	3.1	3.8	2.7	3.6	6.1	1.1	0.0	1.7	2.5	4.2	4.1	3.3	20458.8	172.1	236.0	17.0
2014:Q4	-0.6	1.1	0.0	2.0	6.4	2.5	0.7	2.6	3.3	5.7	5.1	3.9	19418.4	170.8	238.9	28.9
2015:Q1	-1.3	0.9	-0.4	2.2	6.9	3.0	1.2	2.9	3.7	6.5	5.7	4.3	18508.7	168.0	235.3	32.9
2015:Q2	-0.2	2.8	-0.3	2.7	7.2	3.5	1.6	3.3	4.0	6.9	6.1	4.7	17689.2	164.8	228.1	33.2
2015:Q3	0.2	3.8	-0.1	3.5	7.4	4.0	2.1	3.7	4.3	7.0	6.3	5.2	16983.8	161.2	220.8	27.3
2015:Q4	0.3	4.1	0.0	3.6	7.6	4.0	2.6	4.0	4.6	7.1	6.6	5.7	16257.8	157.7	214.8	24.9
2016:Q1	0.8	4.3	1.0	4.7	7.8	4.0	3.1	4.3	4.8	7.4	6.8	6.2	15737.3	154.5	207.7	24.6
2016:Q2	1.2	4.9	1.1	4.8	7.9	4.0	3.6	4.5	5.0	7.5	7.0	6.7	15430.8	151.7	202.9	22.8
2016:Q3	1.7	5.4	1.4	5.1	7.9	4.0	4.0	4.8	5.2	7.5	7.1	7.1	15188.2	150.0	199.6	21.4
2016:Q4	1.8	5.4	1.5	5.2	8.0	4.0	4.4	5.0	5.4	7.6	7.3	7.5	14992.3	148.9	197.7	20.5
2017:Q1	1.8	5.4	1.8	5.5	8.0	4.0	4.7	5.2	5.5	7.6	7.4	7.8	14866.4	148.6	196.6	19.8
2017:Q2	1.9	5.5	1.6	5.2	8.0	3.9	5.0	5.3	5.7	7.7	7.5	8.0	14791.4	148.9	196.5	19.4
2017:Q3	2.0	5.5	1.6	5.1	8.0	3.8	5.2	5.5	5.8	7.7	7.6	8.2	14807.1	149.5	196.6	19.1
2017:Q4	2.2	5.5	1.7	5.1	8.0	3.6	5.3	5.5	5.8	7.7	7.6	8.4	15005.9	150.3	197.1	19.2

Note: Refer to Notes Regarding Scenario Variables for more information on variables.

Table A.4. Supervisory adverse scenario: International
Percent unless otherwise indicated

Date	Euro area real GDP growth	Euro area inflation	Euro area bilateral dollar exchange rate (USD/euro)	Developing Asia real GDP growth	Developing Asia inflation	Developing Asia bilateral dollar exchange rate (F/USD, index)	Japan real GDP growth	Japan inflation	Japan bilateral dollar exchange rate (yen/USD)	U.K. real GDP growth	U.K. inflation	U.K. bilateral dollar exchange rate (USD/pound)
2001:Q1	3.7	1.1	0.879	4.0	1.6	106.0	2.6	-1.2	125.5	4.6	0.1	1.419
2001:Q2	0.3	4.1	0.847	5.9	2.0	106.1	-0.7	-0.3	124.7	3.1	3.1	1.408
2001:Q3	0.3	1.4	0.910	4.9	1.2	106.4	-4.3	-1.1	119.2	2.1	1.0	1.469
2001:Q4	0.6	1.7	0.890	7.7	0.1	106.8	-0.5	-1.4	131.0	1.3	0.0	1.454
2002:Q1	0.7	3.0	0.872	6.8	0.3	107.3	-0.9	-2.7	132.7	1.8	1.9	1.425
2002:Q2	2.1	2.0	0.986	9.0	1.1	104.7	4.3	1.7	119.9	3.3	0.9	1.525
2002:Q3	1.4	1.6	0.988	5.5	1.4	105.5	2.6	-0.7	121.7	3.6	1.4	1.570
2002:Q4	0.3	2.4	1.049	6.2	0.9	104.4	1.5	-0.4	118.8	3.7	1.9	1.610
2003:Q1	-0.9	3.3	1.090	7.0	3.5	105.5	-2.2	-1.6	118.1	3.9	1.6	1.579
2003:Q2	0.3	0.3	1.150	2.6	1.1	104.0	5.2	1.7	119.9	5.7	0.3	1.653
2003:Q3	2.1	2.2	1.165	13.4	0.0	102.6	1.7	-0.7	111.4	5.2	1.7	1.662
2003:Q4	3.1	2.2	1.260	11.8	5.7	103.3	4.2	-0.6	107.1	4.1	1.7	1.784
2004:Q1	1.9	2.3	1.229	5.1	4.0	101.4	3.8	-0.9	104.2	1.3	1.3	1.840
2004:Q2	2.2	2.4	1.218	6.1	4.1	102.7	0.3	1.1	109.4	1.2	1.0	1.813
2004:Q3	1.4	2.0	1.242	8.6	4.0	102.7	0.6	0.1	110.2	0.5	1.1	1.809
2004:Q4	1.5	2.4	1.354	7.9	0.8	98.9	-1.1	1.7	102.7	1.6	2.4	1.916
2005:Q1	0.4	1.5	1.297	7.9	2.9	98.6	0.8	-2.7	107.2	2.9	2.6	1.889
2005:Q2	2.8	2.2	1.210	7.6	1.5	98.9	5.3	-1.2	110.9	4.2	1.9	1.793
2005:Q3	2.9	3.2	1.206	9.5	2.3	98.5	1.4	-1.3	113.3	4.2	2.7	1.770
2005:Q4	2.5	2.5	1.184	10.5	1.8	98.1	0.7	0.7	117.9	5.5	1.4	1.719
2006:Q1	3.4	1.7	1.214	12.2	2.3	96.7	1.8	1.3	117.5	2.4	1.9	1.739
2006:Q2	4.8	2.5	1.278	7.8	3.2	96.6	1.7	-0.1	114.5	2.0	3.0	1.849
2006:Q3	2.5	2.0	1.269	8.8	2.1	96.2	-0.3	0.5	118.0	0.7	3.3	1.872
2006:Q4	4.4	0.9	1.320	10.7	3.7	94.5	5.2	-0.4	119.0	3.0	2.6	1.959
2007:Q1	3.2	2.2	1.337	14.8	3.6	93.9	4.1	-0.2	117.6	3.1	2.6	1.969
2007:Q2	2.3	2.3	1.352	10.1	4.9	91.9	0.5	0.0	123.4	2.4	1.6	2.006
2007:Q3	2.0	2.1	1.422	8.8	7.5	90.6	-1.5	0.1	115.0	3.4	0.3	2.039
2007:Q4	1.9	4.9	1.460	10.8	6.1	89.4	3.5	2.2	111.7	1.9	4.0	1.984
2008:Q1	2.7	4.2	1.581	8.2	8.1	88.0	2.7	1.3	99.9	1.3	3.7	1.986
2008:Q2	-1.6	3.2	1.575	7.6	6.3	88.6	-4.7	1.6	106.2	-0.9	5.6	1.991
2008:Q3	-2.3	3.2	1.408	4.2	2.9	91.4	-4.1	3.6	105.9	-6.5	5.9	1.780
2008:Q4	-7.1	-1.4	1.392	0.7	-0.9	92.2	-12.5	-2.2	90.8	-8.6	0.6	1.462
2009:Q1	-10.8	-1.1	1.326	3.3	-1.6	94.4	-15.0	-3.6	99.2	-7.0	-0.1	1.430
2009:Q2	-1.1	0.0	1.402	15.4	2.3	92.3	7.1	-1.7	96.4	-1.0	2.0	1.645
2009:Q3	1.3	1.1	1.463	12.5	4.0	91.3	0.2	-1.2	89.5	0.8	3.7	1.600
2009:Q4	1.8	1.6	1.433	8.3	5.2	90.7	7.1	-1.6	93.1	1.6	3.1	1.617
2010:Q1	2.0	1.7	1.353	9.2	4.3	89.8	6.1	0.8	93.4	2.1	4.0	1.519
2010:Q2	4.1	2.0	1.229	9.3	3.4	91.0	4.4	-1.0	88.5	4.0	3.0	1.495
2010:Q3	1.3	1.7	1.360	8.7	3.9	88.4	5.8	-1.9	83.5	2.6	2.5	1.573
2010:Q4	2.1	2.6	1.327	8.4	7.8	87.4	-2.2	1.1	81.7	0.1	4.0	1.539
2011:Q1	3.7	3.6	1.418	9.2	6.5	86.4	-6.9	-0.4	82.8	2.2	6.6	1.605
2011:Q2	0.1	3.2	1.452	7.1	5.8	85.3	-2.7	-0.4	80.6	0.9	4.5	1.607
2011:Q3	0.0	1.5	1.345	6.9	5.7	87.4	10.8	0.4	77.0	2.8	4.0	1.562
2011:Q4	-1.1	3.4	1.297	6.3	3.0	87.2	0.6	-0.8	77.0	-0.1	3.3	1.554
2012:Q1	-0.4	2.6	1.333	5.8	3.0	86.3	4.1	1.8	82.4	0.3	1.9	1.599
2012:Q2	-1.0	2.4	1.267	6.0	3.9	88.0	-2.2	-0.7	79.8	-0.7	1.9	1.569
2012:Q3	-0.4	1.8	1.286	6.5	2.3	86.2	-2.7	-1.7	77.9	3.4	2.7	1.613
2012:Q4	-1.9	2.3	1.319	7.5	3.7	85.9	-0.5	-0.1	86.6	-1.3	3.9	1.626
2013:Q1	-1.3	0.8	1.282	5.4	4.1	86.2	5.1	0.0	94.2	2.1	2.5	1.519
2013:Q2	1.3	0.7	1.301	6.1	3.0	87.1	3.4	0.8	99.2	2.7	1.8	1.521
2013:Q3	0.6	1.6	1.354	7.7	3.5	86.5	1.8	3.0	98.3	3.5	2.7	1.618
2013:Q4	1.0	0.1	1.378	6.9	4.0	85.6	-0.5	1.9	105.3	2.5	1.3	1.657

(continued on next page)

Table A.4.—*continued*

Date	Euro area real GDP growth	Euro area inflation	Euro area bilateral dollar exchange rate (USD/euro)	Developing Asia real GDP growth	Developing Asia inflation	Developing Asia bilateral dollar exchange rate (F/USD, index)	Japan real GDP growth	Japan inflation	Japan bilateral dollar exchange rate (yen/USD)	U.K. real GDP growth	U.K. inflation	U.K. bilateral dollar exchange rate (USD/pound)
2014:Q1	1.2	0.2	1.378	5.1	1.4	86.7	6.0	0.4	103.0	3.0	1.2	1.668
2014:Q2	0.3	0.4	1.369	6.9	2.8	86.4	-7.1	9.4	101.3	3.7	1.8	1.711
2014:Q3	1.0	0.6	1.263	6.5	3.1	86.9	1.0	1.6	109.7	2.9	1.6	1.622
2014:Q4	-4.1	-0.4	1.265	2.0	1.6	89.3	-4.6	-1.6	97.6	-1.6	0.1	1.680
2015:Q1	-3.3	-0.4	1.257	3.9	1.3	89.3	-6.0	-1.4	97.7	-1.7	0.1	1.676
2015:Q2	-1.7	-0.4	1.243	5.3	1.1	89.0	-5.0	-1.6	98.4	-0.9	0.1	1.668
2015:Q3	-0.5	-0.1	1.226	6.1	1.1	88.7	-3.7	-1.2	99.5	-0.1	0.3	1.656
2015:Q4	0.4	0.1	1.210	6.4	1.4	88.2	-2.5	-0.7	100.5	0.6	0.6	1.645
2016:Q1	1.1	0.4	1.209	6.5	1.6	86.8	-1.4	-0.2	100.7	1.2	0.9	1.641
2016:Q2	1.6	0.6	1.212	6.5	1.9	85.5	-0.5	0.3	100.6	1.7	1.2	1.638
2016:Q3	1.9	0.8	1.217	6.5	2.1	84.2	0.2	0.5	100.3	2.2	1.4	1.636
2016:Q4	2.1	0.9	1.222	6.5	2.2	82.9	0.7	0.6	100.2	2.5	1.6	1.633
2017:Q1	2.1	1.0	1.229	6.5	2.3	82.4	1.2	0.5	99.9	2.7	1.6	1.634
2017:Q2	2.1	1.1	1.236	6.5	2.4	81.9	1.4	0.6	99.6	2.8	1.7	1.634
2017:Q3	2.0	1.1	1.242	6.5	2.5	81.6	1.6	0.7	99.5	2.8	1.8	1.634
2017:Q4	2.0	1.2	1.248	6.6	2.6	81.3	1.7	0.9	99.3	2.8	1.8	1.635

Note: Refer to Notes Regarding Scenario Variables for more information on variables.

Data Notes

Sources for data through the third quarter of 2014 (as released through October 22, 2014). The third-quarter-2014 values of variables marked with an asterisk (*) are projected.

*U.S. real GDP growth: Percent change in real gross domestic product at an annualized rate, Bureau of Economic Analysis.

*U.S. nominal GDP growth: Percent change in nominal gross domestic product at an annualized rate, Bureau of Economic Analysis.

*U.S. real disposable income growth: Percent change in nominal disposable personal income divided by the price index for personal consumption expenditures at an annualized rate, Bureau of Economic Analysis.

*U.S. nominal disposable income growth: Percent change in nominal disposable personal income at an annualized rate, Bureau of Economic Analysis.

U.S. unemployment rate: Quarterly average of monthly data, Bureau of Labor Statistics.

U.S. CPI inflation: Percent change in the Consumer Price Index at an annualized rate, Bureau of Labor Statistics.

U.S. 3-month Treasury rate: Quarterly average of 3-month Treasury bill secondary market rate on a discount basis, H.15 Release, Selected Interest Rates, Federal Reserve Board.

U.S. 5-year Treasury yield: Quarterly average of the yield on 5-year U.S. Treasury bonds, constructed for FRB/US model by Federal Reserve staff based on the Svensson smoothed term structure model; see Lars E. O. Svensson (1995), "Estimating Forward Interest Rates with the Extended Nelson-Siegel Method," *Quarterly Review*, no. 3, Sveriges Riksbank, pp. 13–26.

U.S. 10-year Treasury yield: Quarterly average of the yield on 10-year U.S. Treasury bonds, constructed for FRB/US model by Federal Reserve staff based on the Svensson smoothed term structure model; see id.

U.S. BBB corporate yield: Quarterly average of the yield on 10-year BBB-rated corporate bonds, constructed for FRB/US model by Federal Reserve staff using a Nelson-Siegel smoothed yield curve model; see Charles R. Nelson and Andrew F. Siegel (1987), "Parsimonious Modeling of Yield Curves," *Journal of Business*, vol. 60, pp. 473–89. Data prior to 1997 is based on the WARGA database. Data after 1997 is based on the Merrill Lynch database.

U.S. mortgage rate: Quarterly average of weekly series for the interest rate of a conventional, conforming, 30-year fixed rate mortgage, obtained from the Primary Mortgage Market Survey of the Federal Home Loan Mortgage Corporation.

U.S. prime rate: Quarterly average of monthly series, H.15 Release, Selected Interest Rates, Federal Reserve Board.

U.S. Dow Jones Total Stock Market (Float Cap) Index: End of quarter value, Dow Jones.

*U.S. House Price Index: CoreLogic, index level, seasonally adjusted by Federal Reserve staff.

*U.S. Commercial Real Estate Price Index: From the Financial Accounts of the United States, Federal Reserve Board (Z.1 release); the series corresponds to the data for price indexes: Commercial Real Estate Price Index (series FL075035503.Q divided by 1,000).

U.S. Market Volatility Index (VIX): Chicago Board Options Exchange, converted to quarterly by using the maximum close-of-day value in any quarter.

*Euro area real GDP growth: Staff calculations based on Statistical Office of the European Communities via Haver, extended back using ECB Area Wide Model dataset (ECB Working Paper series no. 42).

Euro area inflation: Staff calculations based on Statistical Office of the European Community via Haver.

*Developing Asia real GDP growth: Staff calculations based on Bank of Korea via Haver; Chinese National Bureau of Statistics via CEIC; Indian Central Statistical Organization via CEIC; Census and Statistics Department of Hong Kong via CEIC; and Taiwan Directorate-General of Budget, Accounting, and Statistics via CEIC.

*Developing Asia inflation: Staff calculations based on Chinese National Bureau of Statistics via CEIC; Indian Ministry of Statistics and Programme Implementation via Haver; Labour Bureau of India via CEIC; National Statistical Office of Korea via CEIC; Census and Statistic Department of Hong Kong via CEIC; and Taiwan Directorate-General of Budget, Accounting, and Statistics via CEIC.

*Japan real GDP growth: Cabinet Office via Haver.

Japan inflation: Ministry of Internal Affairs and Communications via Haver.

U.K. real GDP growth: Office for National Statistics via Haver.

U.K. inflation: Staff calculations based on Office for National Statistics (uses Retail Price Index to extend series back to 1960) via Haver.

*Exchange rates: Bloomberg.

Appendix B: Models to Project Net Income and Stressed Capital

This appendix describes the models used to project stressed capital ratios and pre-tax net income and its components for the 31 bank holding companies (BHCs) subject to DFAST 2015.[33] The models fall into five broad categories:

1. Models to project losses on loans held in the accrual loan portfolio. Loans in the accrual loan portfolio are those measured under accrual accounting, rather than fair-value accounting.

2. Models to project other types of losses, including those from changes in fair value on loans held for sale or measured under the fair-value option; losses on securities, trading, and counterparty exposures; losses related to operational-risk events; and mortgage repurchase/put-back losses.

3. Models to project the components of pre-provision net revenue (PPNR) (revenues and non-credit-related expenses).

4. Models to project balance sheet items and risk-weighted assets (RWA).

5. The model to project capital ratios, given projections of pre-tax net income, assumptions for determining provisions into the allowance for loan and lease losses (ALLL), and prescribed capital actions.

A majority of the models described here were refined incrementally over the past year. However, the Federal Reserve enhanced its methods for estimating PPNR and regulatory capital and capital ratios (see box 1).

Losses on the Accrual Loan Portfolio

More than a dozen individual models are used to project losses on loans held in the accrual loan portfolio. The individual loan types modeled can broadly be divided into wholesale loans, such as commercial and industrial (C&I) loans and commercial real estate (CRE) loans, and retail loans, including various types of residential mortgages, credit cards, student loans, auto loans, small business loans, and other consumer lending. In some cases, these major categories comprise several subcategories, each with its own loss projection model, but the models within a subcategory are similar in structure and approach. The models project losses using detailed loan portfolio data provided by the BHCs on the Capital Assessments and Stress Testing (FR Y-14) report.

Two general approaches are taken to model losses on the accrual loan portfolio. In the first approach—an approach broadly used for DFAST 2015—the models estimate expected losses under the macroeconomic scenario; that is, they project the probability of default (PD), loss given default (LGD), and exposure at default (EAD) for each quarter of the planning horizon. Expected losses in quarter t are the product of these three components:

$$Loss_t = PD_t * LGD_t * EAD_t$$

PD is generally modeled as part of a transition process in which loans move from one payment status to another (e.g., from current to delinquent) in response to economic conditions. Default is the last possible

---

[33] In connection with DFAST 2015, and in addition to the models developed and data collected by the Federal Reserve, the Federal Reserve used proprietary models or data licensed from the following providers: Andrew Davidson & Co., Inc.; Bank of America Corporation; BlackRock Financial Management, Inc.; Bloomberg Finance L.P.; CB Richard Ellis, Inc.; CoreLogic Inc.; CoStar Group, Inc.; Equifax Information Services LLC; Kenneth French; Intex Solutions, Inc.; McDash Analytics, LLC, a wholly owned subsidiary of Lender Processing Services, Inc.; Markit Group; Moody's Analytics, Inc.; Moody's Investors Service, Inc.; Mergent, Inc.; Morningstar, Inc.; MSCI, Inc.; StataCorp LP; the Organisation for Economic Co-operation and Development; and Standard & Poor's Financial Services LLC. In addition, with respect to the global market shock component of the adverse and severely adverse scenarios, the Federal Reserve used proprietary data licensed from the following providers: Bank of America Corporation; Barclays Bank PLC; Bloomberg Finance L.P.; CoreLogic, Inc.; Intex Solutions, Inc.; JPMorgan Chase & Co.; Lender Processing Services, Inc.; Markit Group; Moody's Investors Service, Inc.; New York University; and Standard & Poor's Financial Services LLC.

transition, and PD represents the likelihood that a loan will default during a given period. The number of payment statuses and the transition paths modeled differ by loan type.

LGD is typically defined as a percentage of EAD and is based on historical data. For some loan types, LGD is modeled as a function of borrower, collateral, or loan characteristics and the macroeconomic variables from the supervisory scenarios. For other loan types, LGD is assumed to be a fixed percentage for all loans in a category. Finally, the approach to EAD varies by loan type and depends on whether the outstanding loan amount can change between the current period and the period in which the loan defaults (e.g., for lines of credit).

In the second approach, the models capture the historical behavior of net charge-offs relative to changes in macroeconomic and financial market variables and loan portfolio characteristics.

The loss models primarily focus on losses arising from loans in the accrual loan portfolio as of September 30, 2014. The loss projections also incorporate losses on loans originated after the planning horizon begins. These incremental loan balances are calculated based on the Federal Reserve's projections of loan balances over the planning horizon. These balances are assumed to have the same risk characteristics as those of the loan portfolio as of September 30, 2014, with the exception of loan age in the retail and CRE portfolios, where seasoning is incorporated. Where applicable, new loans are assumed to be current, and BHCs are assumed not to originate types of loans that are no longer allowed under various regulations. This is a simple, but generally conservative, assumption. Loss projections also incorporate losses on loans acquired through mergers or purchase after the planning horizon begins. Additional information provided by the BHCs about the size and composition of acquired loan portfolios was used to estimate losses on acquired portfolios.

Loss projections generated by the models are adjusted to take account of purchase accounting treatment, which recognizes discounts on impaired loans acquired during mergers and any other write-downs already taken on loans held in the accrual loan portfolio. This latter adjustment ensures that losses related to these loans are not double counted in the projections.

Wholesale Lending: Corporate Loans

Losses stemming from default on corporate loans are projected at the loan level using an expected loss modeling framework. Corporate loans consist of a number of different categories of loans, as defined by the Consolidated Financial Statements for Holding Companies—FR Y-9C report (FR Y-9C). The largest group of these loans include C&I loans, which are generally defined as loans to corporate or commercial borrowers with more than $1 million in committed balances that are "graded" using a BHC's corporate loan rating process.[34]

The PD for a C&I loan is projected over the planning horizon by first calculating the loan's PD at the beginning of the planning horizon and then projecting it forward using an equation that relates historical changes in PD to changes in the macroeconomic environment. The PD as of September 30, 2014, is calculated for every C&I loan in a BHC's portfolio using detailed, loan-level information submitted by the BHC. For publicly traded borrowers, a borrower-specific PD, based on the expected default frequency, is used. For other borrowers, the PD is estimated based on the BHC's internal credit rating, which is converted to a standardized rating scale. Loans that are 90 days past due, in non-accrual status, or that have a Financial Accounting Standards Board Accounting Standards Codification Subtopic 310-10 (ASC 310-10) reserve as of September 30, 2014, are assigned a PD of 100 percent.

Quarterly changes in the PD after the third quarter of 2014 are projected over the planning horizon using a series of equations that relate historical changes in the average PD as a function of changes in macroeconomic variables, including changes in real gross domestic product (GDP), the unemployment rate, and the spread on BBB-rated corporate bonds. The equations are estimated separately by borrower industries, credit quality categories, and countries.

The LGD for a C&I loan at the beginning of the planning horizon is determined by the line of business, seniority of lien (if secured), country, and ASC 310-10 reserve, if applicable. The LGD is then pro-

---

[34] All definitions of loan categories and default in this appendix are definitions used for the purposes of the supervisory stress test models and do not necessarily align with general industry definitions or classifications.

jected forward by relating the change in the LGD to changes in the PD. In the model, the PD is used as a proxy for economic conditions, and, by construct, increases in PD generally lead to higher LGDs.

The EAD for C&I loans equals the sum of the funded balance and a portion of the unfunded commitment, which reflects the amount that is likely to be drawn down by the borrower in the event of default. This drawdown amount was estimated based on the historical drawdown experience for defaulted U.S. syndicated revolving lines of credit that are in the Shared National Credit (SNC) database.[35] In the case of closed-end C&I loans, the funded balance and the corresponding EAD equals the outstanding balance. The EAD for standby letters of credit and trade finance credit are conservatively assumed to equal the total commitment.

Other corporate loans that are similar in some respects to C&I loans are modeled using the same framework. These loans include owner-occupied CRE loans, capital equipment leases, loans to depositories, and other loans.[36] Projected losses on owner-occupied CRE loans are disclosed in total CRE losses, while projected losses for the remaining other corporate loans are disclosed in the other loans category.

Wholesale Lending: CRE Mortgages

CRE mortgages are loans collateralized by domestic and international multifamily or nonfarm, nonresidential properties, and construction and land development loans (C&LD), as defined by the FR Y-9C report. Losses stemming from default on CRE mortgages are projected at the loan level using an expected-loss modeling framework.

The PD model for CRE mortgages is a hazard model of the probability that a loan transitions from current to default status, given the characteristics of the loan as well as macroeconomic variables such as house prices and CRE vacancy rates, at both the geographic market and national level. Once defaulted,

the model assumes the loan does not re-perform; the effect of re-performance on the estimated loan loss is captured in the LGD model. A CRE mortgage loan is considered in default if it is 90 days past due, in non-accrual status, has an ASC 310-10 reserve, or had a very low internal credit rating at the most recent time its maturity was extended. The PD model also incorporates a nonlinear increase in PD as the loan maturity nears. The effect of loan maturity on the PD is estimated to be different for income-producing and C&LD loans, and is estimated separately for each loan type using historical Capital Assessments and Stress Testing (FR Y-14Q) data. However, the effect of other loan characteristics and the macroeconomic variables is assumed to be the same for income-producing properties and C&LD loans and is estimated using a single model for both types of loans using historical commercial mortgage-backed security data.

The LGD for CRE mortgages is estimated using FR Y-14Q data on ASC 310-10 reserves. The model first estimates the probability that a defaulted loan will have losses as a function of loan characteristics and macroeconomic variables, and then, using loans with losses, estimates the loss on the CRE mortgage as a function of the expected probability of loss, characteristics of the loan, and macroeconomic variables. Finally, the EAD for CRE mortgages is assumed to equal the loan's full committed balance for both income producing and C&LD loans. As was the case with closed-end C&I loans, for amortizing income-producing loans the EAD equals the outstanding balance.

Retail Lending: Residential Mortgages

Residential mortgages held in BHC portfolios include first and junior liens—both closed-end loans and revolving credits—that are secured by one- to four-family residential real estate as defined by the FR Y-9C report. Losses stemming from default on residential mortgages are projected at the loan level using an expected-loss modeling framework.[37]

The PD model for first-lien residential mortgages estimates the probability that a loan transitions to different payment statuses, including current, delinquent, default, and paid off. Separate PD models are estimated for three types of closed-end, first-lien

---

[35] SNCs have commitments of greater than $20 million and are held by three or more regulated participating entities. For additional information, see "Shared National Credit Program," Board of Governors, www.federalreserve.gov/bankinforeg/snc.htm.

[36] The corporate loan category also includes loans that are dissimilar from typical corporate loans, such as securities lending and farmland loans, which are generally a small share of BHC portfolios. For these loans, a conservative and uniform loss rate based on analysis of historical data was assigned.

[37] To predict losses on new originations over the planning horizon, newly originated loans are assumed to have the same risk characteristics as the existing portfolio, with the exception of the loan age and delinquency status.

mortgages: fixed-rate, adjustable-rate, and option adjustable-rate mortgages. The PD model specification varies somewhat by loan type; however, in general, each model estimates the probability that a loan transitions from one payment state to another (e.g., from current to delinquent or from delinquent to default) over a single quarter, given the characteristics of the loan, borrower, and underlying property as well as macroeconomic variables such as local house prices, the statewide unemployment rate, and interest rates.[38]

Origination vintage effects are also included in the estimation in part to capture unobserved characteristics of loan quality. The historical data used to estimate this model are industrywide, loan-level data from many banks and mortgage loan originators. These estimated PD models are used to simulate default for each loan reported by each BHC under the supervisory scenarios. Loans that are 180 days or more past due as of September 30, 2014, are considered in default and are assigned a PD of 100 percent.

The LGD for residential mortgages is estimated using two models. One model estimates the amount of time that elapses between default and real estate owned (REO) disposition (timeline model), while the other relates characteristics of the defaulted loan, such as the property value at default, to one component of losses net of recoveries—the proceeds from the sale of the property net of foreclosure expenses (loss model).[39]

These net proceeds are calculated from historical data on loan balances, servicer advances, and losses from defaulted loans in private-label, residential mortgage-backed securities (RMBS). These RMBS data are also used to estimate the LGD loss model separately for prime jumbo loans, subprime, and alt-A loans.[40]

Finally, using the elapsed time between default and REO disposition estimated in the timeline model,

total estimated losses are allocated into credit losses on the defaulted loans, which are fully written down at the time of default, or net losses arising from the eventual sale of the underlying property (other real estate owned—or OREO—expenses), which flow through PPNR. House price changes from the time of default to foreclosure completion (REO acquisition) are captured in LGD, while house price changes after foreclosure completion and before sale of the property are captured in OREO expenses. The LGD for loans already in default as of September 30, 2014, includes further home price declines through the point of foreclosure.

Home equity loans (HELs) are junior-lien, closed-end loans, and home equity lines of credit (HELOCs) are revolving open-end loans extended under lines of credit, both secured by one- to four-family residential real estate as defined by the FR Y-9C report. Losses stemming from default on HELs and HELOCs are projected at the loan level in an expected loss framework that is similar to first-lien mortgages, with a few differences.

For second-lien HELs and HELOCs that are current as of September 30, 2014, but are behind a seriously delinquent first-lien, the model assumes elevated default rates under the supervisory scenarios. In addition, most HELOC contracts require only payment of interest on the outstanding line balance during the period when the line can be drawn upon (draw period). When the line reaches the end of its draw period (end-of-draw), the outstanding line balance either becomes immediately payable or converts to a fully amortizing loan. HELOCs that reach the end-of-draw period are assumed to prepay at a higher rate just prior to end-of-draw and to default at a higher rate just after end-of-draw than HELOCs that are still in their draw period.

The LGD for HELs and HELOCs is estimated using data from private-label mortgage-backed securities, using the same models used for closed-end first-lien, but the estimated total mortgage losses for properties with a defaulted HEL or HELOC are allocated based on the lien position. Finally, for HELOCs, EAD is conservatively assumed to equal the credit limit.

Retail Lending: Credit Cards

Credit cards include both general purpose and private-label credit cards, as well as charge cards, as defined by the FR Y-9C report. Credit card loans extended to individuals are included in retail credit

---

[38] The effects of loan modification and evolving modification practices are captured in the probability that a delinquent loan transitions back to current status (re-performing loans).

[39] Other components of losses net of recoveries are calculated directly from available data. Private mortgage insurance is not incorporated into the LGD models. Industry data suggest that insurance coverage on portfolio loans is infrequent and cancellation or nullification of guarantees was a common occurrence during the recent downturn.

[40] The differences between characteristics of mortgages in RMBS and mortgages in bank portfolios, such as loan-to-value (LTV) ratio, are controlled for by including various risk characteristics in the LGD model, such as original LTV ratio, credit score, and credit quality segment (prime, alt-A, and subprime).

cards, while credit cards loans extended to businesses and corporations are included in other retail lending and are modeled separately. Losses stemming from defaults on credit cards are projected at the loan level using an expected-loss modeling framework.

The PD model for credit cards estimates the probability that a loan transitions from delinquency status to default status, given the characteristics of the account and borrower as well as macroeconomic variables such as unemployment. When an account defaults, it is assumed to be closed and does not return to current status. Credit card loans are considered in default when they are 120 days past due. Because the relationship between the PD and its determinants can vary with the initial status of the account, separate transition models are estimated for accounts that are current and active, current and inactive accounts, and delinquent accounts. In addition, because this relationship can also vary with time horizons, separate transition models are estimated for short-, medium-, and long-term horizons. The historical data used to estimate this model are industry-wide, loan-level data from many banks, and separate models were estimated for bank cards and charge cards. The PD model is used to forecast the PD for each loan reported by each BHC in the Capital Assessments and Stress Testing (FR Y-14M) report.

The LGD for credit cards is assumed to be a fixed percentage and is calculated separately for bank cards and charge cards based on historical industry data on LGD during the most recent economic downturn. The EAD for credit cards equals the sum of the amount outstanding on the account and a portion of the credit line, which reflects the amount that is likely to be drawn down by the borrower between the beginning of the planning horizon and the time of default. This drawdown amount is estimated as a function of account and borrower characteristics. Because this relationship can vary with the initial status of the account and time to default, separate models are estimated for current and delinquent accounts and for accounts with short-, medium-, and long-term transition to default. For accounts that are current, separate models were also estimated for different credit-line-size segments.

Retail Lending: Auto

Auto loans are consumer loans extended for the purpose of purchasing new and used automobiles and light motor vehicles as defined by the FR Y-9C report. Losses stemming from default in auto retail

loan portfolios are projected at the portfolio segment level using an expected loss framework.

The PD model for auto loans estimates the probability that a loan transitions from either a current or delinquent status to default status, given the characteristics of the loan and borrower as well as macroeconomic variables such as house prices and the unemployment rate (which, in some cases, are interacted with loan and borrower characteristics to allow for greater sensitivity to stressful conditions in high-risk segments). Default on auto loans is defined based on either the payment status (120 days past due), actions of the borrower (bankruptcy), or the lender (repossession). Because the relationship between the PD and its determinants can vary with the initial status of the account, separate transition models are estimated for accounts that are current and delinquent accounts. The historical data used to estimate this model are loan-level, credit bureau data.

The LGD for auto loans is estimated given the characteristics of the loan as well as macroeconomic variables. The historical data used to estimate this model are pooled, segment-level data provided by the BHCs on the FR Y-14Q reports. The EAD for auto loans is based on the typical pattern of amortization of loans that ultimately defaulted in historical credit bureau data. The estimated EAD model captures the average amortization by loan age for current and delinquent loans over nine quarters.

Retail Lending: Other Retail Lending

Other retail lending includes the small business loan portfolio, the other consumer loan portfolio, the student loan portfolio, the business and corporate credit card portfolio, and international retail portfolio. Losses due to default on other retail lending are forecast by modeling net charge-off rates as a function of portfolio risk characteristics and macroeconomic variables. This model is then used to predict future charge-offs consistent with the macroeconomic variables provided in the supervisory scenarios.[41] The predicted net charge-off rate is applied to balances projected by the Federal Reserve to estimate projected losses. Default is defined as 90 days or more past due for domestic and international other consumer loans and 120 days or more past due for student loans, small business loans, corporate cards, and

---

[41] An exception is made for the government-guaranteed portion of BHCs' student loan portfolios, to which an assumed monthly PD of 1.5 percent and LGD of 3 percent is applied.

international retail portfolios. The net charge-off rate is modeled in a system of equations that also includes the delinquency rate and the default rate. In general, each rate is modeled in an autoregressive specification that also includes the rate in the previous delinquency state, characteristics of the underlying loans, macroeconomic variables and, in some cases, seasonal factors. The models are specified to implicitly capture roll-rate dynamics. In some cases, the characteristics of the underlying loans, such as dummy variables for each segment of credit score at origination, are also interacted with the macroeconomic variables to capture differences in sensitivities across risk segments to changes in the macroeconomic environment. Each retail product type is modeled separately and, for each product type, economic theory and the institutional characteristics of the product guide the inclusion and lag structure of the macroeconomic variables in the model.

Because of data limitations and the relatively small size of these portfolios, the net charge-off rate for each loan type is modeled using industry-wide, monthly data at the segment level. For most portfolios, these data are collected on the FR Y-14Q Retail schedule, which segments each portfolio by characteristics such as borrower credit score; loan vintage; type of facility (e.g., installment versus revolving); and, for international portfolios, geographic region.[42]

Charge-off rates are projected by applying the estimated system of equations to each segment of the BHC's loan portfolio as of September 30, 2014. The portfolio level charge-off rate equals the dollar-weighted average of the segment-level charge-off rates.[43] These projected charge-off rates are applied to the balances projected by the Federal Reserve to calculate portfolio losses.

Loan-Loss Provisions for the Accrual Loan Portfolio

Losses on the accrual loan portfolio flow into net income through provisions for loan and lease losses.

Provisions for loan and lease losses equal projected loan losses for the quarter plus the amount needed for the ALLL to be at an appropriate level at the end of the quarter, which is a function of projected future loan losses. The appropriate level of ALLL at the end of a given quarter is generally assumed to be the amount needed to cover projected loan losses over the next four quarters.[44] Because this calculation of ALLL is based on projected losses under the adverse or severely adverse scenarios, it may differ from a BHC's actual level of ALLL at the beginning of the planning horizon, which is based on the BHC's assessment of future losses in the current economic environment. Any difference between these two measures of ALLL is smoothed into the provisions projection over the nine quarters of the planning horizon. Because projected loan losses include off-balance sheet commitments, the BHC's allowance at the beginning of the planning horizon for credit losses on off-balance sheet exposures (as reported on the FR Y-9C report) is subtracted from the provisions projection in equal amounts each quarter.

Other Losses

Loans Held for Sale or Measured under the Fair-Value Option

Certain loans are not accounted for on an accrual basis. Loans to which the fair-value option (FVO) is applied are valued as mark-to-market assets. Loans under the held-for-sale (HFS) and some loans under the held-for-investment (HFI) accounting classifications are carried at the lower of cost or market value. FVO, HFS, and HFI loan portfolios are identified by the BHCs and reported on the FR Y-14Q report. Losses related to FVO, HFS, and HFI loans are recognized in the income statement at the time of the devaluation.

Losses are estimated by applying the macroeconomic scenario to loans held in portfolio under FVO, HFS, and HFI accounting. Losses on C&I and CRE loans and commitments are estimated by revaluing each loan or commitment each quarter using a stressed discount yield (and spread for floating rate loans). The initial discount yield is based on the loan or commitment's initial fair value, settlement date, maturity date, and interest rate for fixed rate loans

---

[42] Business and corporate credit card portfolio data, which previously were collected on the FR Y-14Q Retail schedule, are now collected at the loan level on the FR Y-14M Credit Card schedule and subsequently aggregated to the segment level.

[43] The dollar weights used are based on the distribution reported during the previous observation period. This method assumes that the distribution of loans across risk segments, other than delinquency status segments, remains constant over the projection period.

[44] For loan types modeled in a charge-off framework, the appropriate level of ALLL was adjusted to reflect the difference in timing between the recognition of expected losses and that of charge-offs.

and the fair value, settlement date, maturity date, and interest rate spread for floating rate loans. Quarterly movements in the discount yield over the planning horizon are assumed to equal the stressed change in corporate bond yields of the same credit rating and maturity, adjusted for potential changes in credit ratings. The models estimate changes in the fair value of the loan in a given scenario on a committed-balance basis. Gains on FVO loan hedges were modeled using a similar methodology as one used for comparable assets in the trading portfolio, using the FVO-specific sensitivities reported by the BHC, and were netted from estimated losses on the FVO loans.

Losses on retail loans held under FVO, HFS, and HFI accounting are estimated over the nine quarters of the planning horizon using a duration-based approach. This approach uses balances on these loans reported on the FR Y-14Q report, estimates of portfolio-weighted duration, and quarterly changes in stressed spreads from the macroeconomic scenario. Estimates are calculated separately by vintage and loan type. No losses are assumed for residential mortgage loans under forward contract with the government-sponsored enterprises (GSEs).

In addition, under the revised regulatory capital rules, the difference between the amortized cost (accounting for any OTTI charges) and fair value of AFS securities as well as HTM securities that have taken OTTI is phased into the calculation of tier 1 capital for advanced approaches BHCs.[45] To address this issue, a separate fair-value model is used to project quarterly changes in the prices of AFS securities under the supervisory scenarios, as described below.

Securities in the Available-for-Sale and Held-to-Maturity Portfolios

If a security becomes OTTI, then all or a portion of the difference between the fair value and amortized cost of the security must be recognized in earnings.[46] Losses on OTTI securities are projected using a suite of models reflecting differences in the basic structure of the securities (i.e., securitized versus direct obligation) and differences in underlying collateral and obligor type.

The OTTI models are designed to incorporate other-than-temporary differences between amortized cost and fair market value due to credit impairment but not differences reflecting changes in liquidity or market conditions unless the firm will be required to sell the security. Some AFS/HTM securities, including U.S. Treasury and U.S. government agency obligations and U.S. government agency or GSE mortgage-backed securities, are assumed not to be at risk for the kind of credit impairment that results in OTTI charges. The remaining securities can be grouped into three basic categories: securitizations, where the value of the security depends on the value of an underlying pool of collateral; direct debt obligations, such as corporate and sovereign bonds, where the value of the security depends primarily on the credit quality of the issuer; and equity securities.[47]

For securitized obligations, credit and prepayment models estimate delinquency, default, severity, and prepayment vectors on the underlying pool of collateral under the supervisory scenarios. Where feasible, these projections incorporate detailed information on the underlying collateral characteristics for each individual security, derived from commercial databases that contain collateral and security structure information. Delinquency, default, severity, and prepayment vectors are projected either using econometric models developed by the Federal Reserve or third-party models used by Federal Reserve analysts that are designed to project these estimates in stressed economic environments. The models used vary with the type of underlying collateral but generally estimate the relationship between the collateral's performance vectors and economic variables, such as the unemployment rate and house prices. These vectors are then applied to a cash flow engine that captures the specific structure of each security (e.g., tranche, subordination, and payment rules) to calculate the present value of the cash flows (intrinsic value) for that security. If the projected intrinsic value is less than amortized cost, then the security is considered

---

[45] An advanced approaches BHC includes any BHC that has consolidated assets greater than or equal to $250 billion or total consolidated on-balance sheet foreign exposure of at least $10 billion as of December 31, 2014. The advanced approaches BHCs in DFAST 2015 are American Express Company; Bank of America Corporation; The Bank of New York Mellon Corporation; Capital One Financial Corporation; Citigroup, Inc.; The Goldman Sachs Group, Inc.; HSBC North America Holdings, Inc.; JPMorgan Chase & Co.; Morgan Stanley; Northern Trust Corporation; The PNC Financial Services Group, Inc.; State Street Corporation; U.S. Bancorp; and Wells Fargo & Co. Non-advanced approaches BHCs may elect to opt out of including AOCI in capital. For DFAST 2015, all other BHCs (other than Deutsche Bank Trust Corporation) opted out of including AOCI in capital. For DBTC, the Federal Reserve included AOCI in its capital calculations.

[46] A security is considered impaired when the fair value of the security falls below its amortized cost.

[47] Equities are also held in the AFS portfolios, although in small amounts. Losses on these positions under each scenario are calculated based on projected equity price changes.

to be other than temporarily impaired, and OTTI is calculated as the difference between amortized cost and intrinsic value.

For direct obligations, the predominant approach is to assess the PD or severe credit deterioration for each security issuer or group of security issuers over the planning horizon. PD is either modeled directly or inferred by modeling changes in expected frequency of default or CDS spreads for the bonds in question. A security is considered other than temporarily impaired if the projected value of the PD or CDS spread crosses a predetermined threshold level—generally the level consistent with a CCC/Caa rating—at any point during the planning horizon. LGD on these securities is based on historical data on bond recovery rates. OTTI is calculated as the difference between the bond's amortized cost and its projected recovery value under the supervisory scenarios.

For certain securitized obligations with smaller levels of exposure and municipal bonds, the OTTI is estimated as a fraction of projected unrealized losses on the security from the fair-value model.

After a security is written down as OTTI, the difference between its original value and the post-OTTI value is assumed to be invested in securities with the same risk characteristics. Increases projected by the Federal Reserve in a BHC's securities portfolio after September 30, 2014, are assumed to be in short-term, riskless assets, and no OTTI charges are assigned to these securities.

In addition, under the revised regulatory capital rules, the difference between the amortized cost (accounting for any OTTI charges) and fair value of AFS securities as well as non-credit-loss OTTI on HTM securities is phased into the calculation of tier 1 capital for advanced approaches BHCs.[48] To

address this issue, a separate fair-value model is used to project quarterly changes in the prices of AFS and HTM securities under the supervisory scenarios, as described below.

In order to project fair-value changes for AFS securities, each security is re-priced using one of three methods depending on the asset class of the security—a duration-based approach, generic revaluation, or model-based revaluation.

- Duration-based approach—The duration-based approach is taken for all AFS securities except Treasury securities and agency RMBS. This approach approximates the quarterly price path for a security over a nine-quarter planning horizon using projected changes in the security's yield and its initial interest rate and spread durations. The yields used in the approximation vary over the projection period with changes in Treasury yields and the securities' option-adjusted spread. Separate yield projections were estimated for securities in different asset classes and with different credit ratings and maturities.

- Generic revaluation—U.S. Treasury securities are directly re-priced using a simple present-value calculation that incorporates the timing and amount of contractual cash flows and quarterly Treasury yields from the macroeconomic scenario.

- Model-based revaluation—Agency RMBS are revalued using a security-specific pricing model to capture the effect of embedded options on the cash flows of each security.

Trading and Private Equity

Total potential mark-to-market losses stemming from trading positions under a stressed market environment can be broken into two primary types. The first type of loss arises from a decrease in the market value of trading positions, regardless of the default of credit instruments (e.g., loans or bonds) or the BHC's counterparties. The second type is the loss associated with the risk of default—both the risk of the default of obligors and the counterparty credit risk associated with changes in counterparty exposures as well as the deterioration of counterparties' creditworthiness under stressed market conditions, which adversely affects the riskiness of positively valued trading positions. The models used to project losses on trading positions under the global market shock account for both sources of potential losses, generally relying on information provided by firms

---

[48] An advanced approaches BHC includes any BHC that has consolidated assets greater than or equal to $250 billion or total consolidated on-balance sheet foreign exposure of at least $10 billion as of December 31, 2014. The advanced approaches BHCs in DFAST 2015 are: American Express Company; Bank of America Corporation; The Bank of New York Mellon Corporation; Capital One Financial Corporation; Citigroup, Inc.; The Goldman Sachs Group, Inc.; HSBC North America Holdings, Inc.; JPMorgan Chase & Co.; Morgan Stanley; Northern Trust Corporation; The PNC Financial Services Group, Inc.; State Street Corporation; U.S. Bancorp; and Wells Fargo & Co. Non-advanced approaches BHCs may elect to opt out of including AOCI in capital. For DFAST 2015, Deutsche Bank & Trust Co. did not opt out of including AOCI, and so the Federal Reserve included AOCI in their capital calculations.

on estimated sensitivities of their exposures to specific risk-factor shocks. Because positions in the trading account are marked to market on a daily basis, the approach used to generate loss projections on trading positions is intended to capture the market-value effect of the global market shock. Losses on trading positions as a result of a global market shock were estimated only for the six BHCs with large trading operations, since trading operations determine risk and performance to a larger extent at these firms than at any other BHCs participating in DFAST 2015.

Losses on trading positions, such as equities, foreign exchange, interest rates, commodities, credit products, private equity, and other fair-value assets arising from the global market shock are calculated using position values or the BHCs' own estimates of the sensitivity of the position values to changes in a wide range of market rates, prices, spreads, and volatilities. Trading losses are calculated by multiplying these sensitivities by the risk-factor changes included in the global market shock developed by the Federal Reserve or by interpolating the change in position values from BHC-supplied profit/(loss) grids. These shocks are assumed to be instantaneous and no additional hedging, recovery in value, or changes in positions are incorporated into the loss calculation.

Losses in the global market shock include losses from credit valuation adjustments (CVA) and trading incremental default risk (IDR) of the six BHCs with large trading positions. CVAs are adjustments above and beyond the mark-to-market valuation of the BHCs' trading portfolios that capture changes in the risk that a counterparty to derivatives transaction or other trading position will default on its obligations. Using detailed data provided by the six trading BHCs on the FR Y-14Q Counterparty schedule, each trading firm's baseline and stressed CVA for each counterparty is calculated as a function of unstressed and stressed values of exposure, PD, and LGD. CVA losses equal the difference between the baseline and the stressed CVAs.

In addition to CVA and other mark-to-market losses on trading positions, default risk of credit instruments in the trading book is captured through IDR. IDR estimates the potential additional loss stemming from the default of issuers in excess of the mark-to-market losses in the trading book. IDR estimates the losses from jump-to-default in the tail of the distribution of defaults, where the tail percentile is calibrated to the severity of the macroeconomic scenario.

The IDR models estimate losses from jump-to-default for various exposure types, including single-name, index and index-tranche, and securitizations, at different levels of granularity depending on exposure type. The loss estimates are based on simulation models of issuer-level defaults. The IDR loss models rely on position and exposure data provided by the firms. IDR losses occur over nine quarters.

Largest Counterparty Default

To estimate losses from the default of counterparties to derivatives and securities financing agreements, the Federal Reserve applied a counterparty default scenario component to the eight BHCs that have substantial trading or custodial operations. The loss is based on the assumed instantaneous and unexpected default of a BHC's largest counterparty, defined as the counterparty that would produce the largest total net stressed loss if it were to default on all of its derivative and securities financing agreements. Net stressed loss was estimated using net stressed current exposure (CE), which is derived by applying the global market shock to the unstressed positions as well as any collateral posted or received. For derivative agreements, applicable CDS hedges and CVA were netted from the net stressed current exposure. A recovery rate of 10 percent was assumed for both net stressed CE and applicable CDS hedges.

Similar to the global market shock component, the loss associated with the counterparty default component occurs in the first quarter of the projection and is an add-on to the macroeconomic conditions and financial market environment in the supervisory scenarios. Certain sovereign entities (Canada, France, Germany, Italy, Japan, the United Kingdom, and the United States) and designated clearing counterparties were excluded when selecting the largest counterparty.

Losses Related to Operational-Risk Events

Losses related to operational-risk events are a component of PPNR and include losses stemming from events such as fraud, employee lawsuits, or computer system or other operating disruptions. Operational-risk loss estimates include historically based loss estimates, based on the average of three approaches, and estimates of potential costs from unfavorable litigation outcomes, which reflect elevated litigation risk and the associated increase in legal reserves observed in recent years. In all three models—a panel regression model, a loss distribution approach, and a historical simulation approach—projections of operational-risk-related losses for the 31 BHCs are modeled for each of seven operational-risk categories identified in the Board's advanced approaches rule.[49] All three models are based on historical operational-loss data submitted by the BHCs on the FR Y-14Q report.

In the panel regression model, projections of losses related to operational-risk events are the product of two primary components: loss frequency and loss severity. The expected loss frequency is the estimated number of operational-loss events in the supervisory scenario, while loss severity is the estimated loss per event in each category. Loss frequency is modeled as a function of macroeconomic variables and BHC-specific characteristics. Macroeconomic variables, such as the real GDP growth rate, stock market return and volatility, credit spread, and the unemployment rate, are included directly in the panel regression model and/or used to project certain firm-specific characteristics. Loss is projected as a product of projected loss frequency from the panel regression model and loss severity, which equals the average historical dollar loss per event in each operational-risk category. Total losses related to operational-risk events equal losses summed across operational-risk categories. Because the relationship between the frequency of operational-risk events and macroeconomic conditions varies across the categories, separate models were estimated for each category.[50]

In the loss distribution approach model, losses at different percentiles of simulated, annualized loss distributions are used as a proxy for the expected losses related to operational risk conditional on the macroeconomic scenarios. The loss frequency is assumed to follow a Poisson distribution, in which the estimated intensity parameter of the Poisson distribution is specific to each event type and BHC. A loss severity distribution is also fit to each event type for each BHC.[51] The distribution of aggregate annual losses is simulated, and the macroeconomic scenario is implicitly incorporated in the results through the percentile choice, which was based on analysis of historical loss data for all BHCs taken together. The approach used to choose the percentile for each scenario essentially targets the total loss forecast for all BHCs and allows the loss distribution approach to split this loss among the individual BHCs and event types. Loss forecasts for an individual BHC are the sum of the BHCs' loss estimates for each event type.

In the third approach—the historical simulation approach—the distribution of aggregate annual losses are simulated by repeatedly drawing the annual event frequency from the same distribution used in the loss distribution approach, but the severity of those events was drawn from historical realized loss data rather than an estimated loss severity distribution. Losses from the same percentile of the distribution as in the loss distribution approach are used to approximate the supervisory scenarios.

Mortgage Repurchase Losses

Mortgage repurchase expenses are a component of PPNR and are related to litigation, or to demands by mortgage investors to repurchase loans deemed to have breached representations and warranties, or to loans insured by the U.S. government for which coverage could be denied if loan defects are identified. Mortgage repurchase losses for loans sold with representations and warranties liability are estimated in two parts.

The first part is to estimate credit losses for all loans sold by a BHC that have outstanding representations and warranties liability, including loans sold as whole loans, into private-label securities (PLS) or to a GSE (Fannie Mae and Freddie Mac) or loans insured by the government. This part takes into account both losses recognized to date and future losses projected over the remaining lifetime of the loans.

The second part is to estimate the share of this credit loss that may be ultimately put back to the selling BHC (whether through contractual repurchase, a settlement agreement, or litigation loss).

---

[49] The seven operational-loss event type categories identified in the Federal Reserve's advanced approaches rule are internal fraud; external fraud; employment practices and workplace safety; clients, products, and business practices; damage to physical assets; business disruption and system failures; and execution, delivery, and process management. See 12 CFR 217.101(b).

[50] Operational-risk losses due to damage to physical assets, and business disruption and system failure, employment practices, and workplace safety are not expected to be dependent on the macroeconomic environment and therefore were set equal to each BHC's average nine-quarter operational-risk loss in that category. External fraud losses of firms focused on credit card activities were modeled using each BHC's average quarterly losses during the period from the beginning of the financial crisis in the third quarter of 2007 through the second quarter of 2009.

[51] Multiple candidate specifications for the distribution were fit to the data, and the final specification was chosen based on a number of criteria, including a measure of goodness-of-fit.

Future credit loss rates for mortgages (grouped by vintage and investor type) are projected using industrywide data and models that incorporate the house price assumptions in the supervisory scenario.[52] For GSE loans, industrywide credit loss rates are adjusted to reflect the relative credit performance of loans sold by each BHC and are applied to the BHC's outstanding balances. These estimates are based on vintage-level data on original and current unpaid balances, current delinquency status, and losses recognized to date.

The share of past and future credit losses likely to be ultimately put back to the selling BHCs (the put-back rate) is estimated separately for each investor type.

- **Whole loans and loans sold into PLS**—The estimated put-back rate is based on information from recent settlement activities in the banking industry and incorporates adjustments for supervisory assessments of BHC-specific put-back risk.

- **Government-insured loans**—The estimated put-back rate is also based on information from recent settlement activities.

- **GSE loans**—The estimated put-back rate is based on historical information on the repurchases of loans sold to Fannie Mae or Freddie Mac, with consideration given to the relative seasoning of each vintage and the time interval between default and demand.

Mortgage repurchase expenses are netted against actual mortgage put-back reserves as reported by the BHCs.

Pre-provision Net Revenue

PPNR is forecast with a mix of structural models using granular data on individual positions: autoregressive models that relate the components of a BHC's revenues and non-credit-related expenses, expressed as a share of relevant asset or liability balances, to BHC characteristics and to macroeconomic variables; and simple models based on recent firm-level performance.

Autoregressive models are estimated using historical, merger-adjusted data from the FR Y-9C report. Separate models are estimated for 22 different components of PPNR, including eight components of interest income, five components of interest expense, five components of noninterest non-trading income, three components of noninterest expenses, and trading revenue.

When choosing the level of detail at which to model the components of PPNR, consideration is given both to the BHCs' business models and the ability to accurately model small components of revenue. Movements in PPNR stemming from operational-risk events, mortgage repurchases, or OREO are modeled in separate frameworks, described earlier in this document.

The PPNR model estimates and projections are adjusted where appropriate to avoid double counting movements associated with these items. In addition, gains or losses associated with debt valuation adjustments (DVA) for firms' own liabilities are removed from the historical PPNR data series used to estimate the model, and, as a result, PPNR projections do not include DVA gains or losses under the supervisory scenarios.

The autoregressive model specifications vary somewhat by PPNR component. But, in general, each component is related to characteristics of the BHCs, including, in some cases, total assets, asset composition, funding sources, and liabilities. In some PPNR components, these measures of BHC portfolio and business activity do not adequately capture the significant variation across BHCs, so BHC-specific controls are included in the models for these components. Macroeconomic variables used to project PPNR include yields on Treasury securities, corporate bond yields, mortgage rates, real GDP, and stock market price movements and volatility. The specific macroeconomic variables differ across equations based on statistical predictive power and economic interpretation.

Trading revenues are volatile because they include both changes in the market value of trading assets and fees from market-making activities. Forecasts of PPNR from trading activities at the six BHCs subject to the global market shock are modeled in the aggregate and then allocated to each BHC based on a measure of the BHC's market share. In addition, because forecasts of trading revenues are intended to include the effect of the relevant macroeconomic

---

[52] The data used to model credit losses for government-insured loans and loans sold to GSEs were loans randomly selected from an industry database. The data used to model credit losses for loans sold into private-label securities and as whole loans were loans in proxy deals chosen based on the dealer, issuer, and originator information contained in the database.

variables and to exclude the effect of the global market shock, net trading revenue is modeled using a median regression approach to lessen the influence of extreme movements in trading revenue associated with the recent financial crisis. Trading revenues for the remaining BHCs are modeled in a framework similar to that of other PPNR components.

For other volatile components of PPNR, we follow alternative approaches to the autoregressive model. For example, some noninterest income and noninterest expense components that are highly volatile quarter-to-quarter but do not exhibit a clear cyclical pattern are modeled as a constant forecast ratio to reflect a most recent eight-quarter median performance. Finally, the forecast of interest expenses on subordinated debt is based on security-level information and takes into account differences across firms in their maturity schedule and debt pricing in each of the supervisory scenarios.

Balance Sheet Items and Risk-Weighted Assets

The BHC balance sheet is projected based on a model that relates industrywide loan and non-loan asset growth to each other and to broader economic variables including a proxy for loan supply. The model allows for both long-run relationships between the industry aggregates and macroeconomic variables, as well as short-term dynamics that cause deviations from these relationships. It is estimated using aggregate data from the Federal Reserve's Financial Accounts of the United States (Z.1) and the Bureau of Economic Analysis's National Income and Product Accounts.

Industry loan and asset growth rates are projected over the planning horizon using the macroeconomic variables prescribed in the supervisory scenario. Over this horizon, each BHC is assumed to maintain a constant share of the industry's total assets, total loans, and total trading assets. In addition, each BHC is assumed to maintain a constant mix within their loan and trading asset categories. These assumptions are applied as follows:

- Each category of loans at a BHC is assumed to grow at the projected rate of total loans in the industry.

- Each category of trading assets at a BHC is assumed to grow as a function of both the pro-

jected rate of total assets and the projected market value of trading assets in the industry.

- All other assets of a BHC, including securities, are assumed to grow at the projected rate of non-loan assets in the industry.

- A BHC's cash holdings is the residual category, and its level is set such that the sum of cash and noncash assets grows at the projected rate of total assets.

- Growth in securities is assumed to be in short-term, riskless assets.

Balance sheet projections incorporated expected changes to a BHC's business plan, such as mergers, acquisition, and divestitures, that are likely to have a material impact on the its capital adequacy and funding profile.

BHC-submitted data were used to adjust the projected balance sheet in the quarter when the change was expected to occur. Once adjusted, assets were assumed to grow at the same rate as the pre-adjusted balance sheet. Only divestitures that were either completed or contractually agreed upon before January 5, 2015, were incorporated.

Estimating RWA under the two different regulatory capital regimes in place over the planning horizon requires the calculation of four RWA components: market risk-weighted assets (MRWA) and credit RWA as computed under both the general approach that was in effect as of October 1, 2014, and the standardized approach of the revised regulatory capital framework.

For asset categories subject to the market risk rule, the seven components of MRWA are value at risk (VaR), stressed VaR (SVaR), incremental risk charge, correlation trading, non-modeled securitization, specific risk charge, and other risk charge.

VaR and the incremental risk charge are updated using the estimated volatility of the trading portfolio, which is a function of stock market volatility in the supervisory scenarios, and the projected change in trading assets. The remaining categories are assumed to evolve according to projections of a BHC's trading assets.

For all asset categories not subject to the market risk rule, generalized risk weights are imputed from FR Y-9C report data. These weights are held fixed throughout the forecast horizon to reflect an assumption that the credit portfolio's underlying risk features remain constant throughout the horizon. In computing standardized RWA, we apply the generalized RWA growth path to the standardized RWA as-of date value reported by the BHCs. Estimates of the additional capital requirements for past-due exposures under the standardized approach are consistent with the estimated loss forecast for that exposure.

Equity Capital and Regulatory Capital

The final modeling step translates the projections of revenues, expenses, losses, provisions, balances, and RWAs from the models described above into estimates of tier 1 common and regulatory capital for each BHC under the supervisory scenarios. The supervisory projections of total losses and revenues are combined to estimate taxable income.

A consistent tax rate across all BHCs is applied to taxable income to calculate after-tax net income over the projection period.[53] The consistent tax rate is also used to generate projections of deferred tax assets (DTAs) from temporary timing differences and net operating losses. A valuation allowance is estimated to determine whether a BHC will have sufficient taxable income in the future to realize the DTAs, with changes in the valuation allowance factored into after-tax net income. Finally, projected after-tax income incorporates each BHC's reported one-time revenue and expense items and adjusts for income attributable to minority interests. Projected after-tax net income, combined with common capital action assumptions, are used to project quarter-by-quarter changes in equity capital components.[54]

The quarterly change in the components of equity capital equals projected after-tax net income minus capital distributions (dividends and any other actions that disperse equity), plus any employee compensation-related issuance or other corporate actions that increase equity, plus other reported changes in equity capital such as other comprehensive income, where applicable, and changes incident to business combinations.

Projected changes in equity capital components determine changes in equity capital (for tier 1 common and regulatory capital ratios) and common equity tier 1 capital before adjustments and deductions (for regulatory capital ratios), which in turn drive changes in tier 1 common and regulatory capital. Tier 1 common capital is calculated using the definition of capital in the Board's prior capital adequacy guidelines.[55] Regulatory capital is calculated consistent with the requirements that are in effect during the projected quarter of the planning horizon.[56] The definition of regulatory capital changes throughout the planning horizon in accordance with the transition arrangements in the revised regulatory capital framework.[57]

Projected capital levels are calculated using the applicable capital rules to incorporate, as appropriate, projected levels of non-common capital and certain items that are subject to adjustment or deduction in capital. Some items, such as DVA, goodwill, and intangible assets (other than mortgage and non-mortgage servicing assets), and components of accumulated other comprehensive income (AOCI) other than unrealized gains (losses) on AFS securities, are assumed to remain constant at their starting value over the planning horizon. For other items, BHC projections were factored into capital calculations. Those items include the reported path of additional tier 1 and tier 2 capital and significant investments in the capital of unconsolidated financial institutions in the form of common stock. The Federal Reserve also included the effects of certain planned mergers,

[53] For a discussion of the effect of changing this tax rate assumption on the post-stress tier 1 common ratio, see box 2 of Board of Governors of the Federal Reserve System (2012), "Dodd-Frank Act Stress Test 2013: Supervisory Stress Test Methodology and Results."

[54] The Federal Reserve used the following capital action assumptions in projecting post-stress capital levels and ratios: (1) for the fourth quarter of 2014, each company's actual capital actions as of the end of that quarter; (2) for each quarter from the first quarter of 2015 through the end of 2016, each company's projections of capital included: (i) common stock dividends equal to the quarterly average dollar amount of common stock dividends that the company paid in the previous year (that is, from first through the fourth quarter of 2014); (ii) payments on any other instrument that is eligible for inclusion in the numerator of a regulatory capital ratio equal to the stated dividend, interest, or principal due on such instrument during the quarter; and

(iii) an assumption of no redemption, repurchase, or issuance of any capital instrument that is eligible for inclusion in the numerator of a regulatory capital ratio, except for common stock issuances associated with expensed employee compensation and planned mergers. These assumptions are generally consistent with the capital action assumptions BHCs are required to use in their Dodd-Frank Act company-run stress tests. See 12 CFR 252.56(b)(2).

[55] 12 CFR part 225, appendix A.

[56] See 79 FR 13498 (March 11, 2014).

[57] See 12 CFR part 217.

acquisitions, or divestitures in its projections of capital and the components of capital.

The projections of capital levels are combined with Federal Reserve projections of average total assets and risk-weighted assets to calculate capital ratios after adjusting for capital deductions. The tier 1 common ratio is calculated based on the general approach for calculating risk-weighted assets in all quarters of the planning horizon. All other risk-based capital ratios incorporate the general approach for calculating risk-weighted assets in projections of the first quarter of the planning horizon (fourth quarter 2014) and the standardized approach for calculating risk-weighted assets in projections of the following eight quarters of the planning horizon (first quarter 2015 through fourth quarter 2016). Projected capital levels and ratios are not adjusted to account for any differences between projected and actual performance of the BHCs during the time the supervisory stress test results were being produced in the fourth quarter of 2014 and the first quarter of 2015.

Appendix C: BHC-Specific Results

Tables begin on next page.

Table C.1.A. Ally Financial Inc.
Projected stressed capital ratios, risk-weighted assets, losses, revenues, net income before taxes, and loan losses
Federal Reserve estimates: Severely adverse scenario

Actual 2014:Q3 projected stressed capital ratios through 2016:Q4

	Actual 2014:Q3	Stressed capital ratios[1]	
		Ending	Minimum
Tier 1 common ratio (%)	9.7	7.9	7.9
Common equity tier 1 capital ratio (%)[2]	n/a	8.0	8.0
Tier 1 risk-based capital ratio (%)	12.7	10.1	10.1
Total risk-based capital ratio (%)	13.5	11.6	11.6
Tier 1 leverage ratio (%)	10.9	8.8	8.8

[1] The capital ratios are calculated using capital action assumptions provided within the Dodd-Frank Act stress testing rule. These projections represent hypothetical estimates that involve an economic outcome that is more adverse than expected. These estimates are not forecasts of expected losses, revenues, net income before taxes, or capital ratios. The minimum capital ratio presented is for the period 2014:Q4 to 2016:Q4.

[2] Advanced approaches bank holding companies (BHCs) are subject to the common equity tier 1 ratio for the third and fourth quarter of 2014. All bank holding companies are subject to the common equity tier 1 ratio for each quarter of 2015 and 2016. An advanced approaches BHC includes any BHC that has consolidated total assets greater than or equal to $250 billion or consolidated total on-balance sheet foreign exposure of at least $10 billion. See 12 CFR 217.100(b)(1). Other BHCs include any BHC that is subject to 12 CFR 225.8 and is not an advanced approaches BHC.

n/a Not applicable.

Projected loan losses, by type of loan, 2014:Q4–2016:Q4

	Billions of dollars	Portfolio loss rates (%)[1]
Loan losses	5.1	5.0
First-lien mortgages, domestic	0.3	5.4
Junior liens and HELOCs, domestic	0.2	8.0
Commercial and industrial[2]	1.6	4.5
Commercial real estate, domestic	0.2	5.1
Credit cards	0.0	0.0
Other consumer[3]	2.8	5.2
Other loans[4]	0.0	12.7

[1] Average loan balances used to calculate portfolio loss rates exclude loans held for sale and loans held for investment under the fair-value option and are calculated over nine quarters.

[2] Commercial and industrial loans include small- and medium-enterprise loans and corporate cards.

[3] Other consumer loans include student loans and automobile loans.

[4] Other loans include international real estate loans.

Actual 2014:Q3 and projected 2016:Q4 risk-weighted assets

	Actual 2014:Q3	Projected 2016:Q4	
		General approach	Standardized approach
Risk-weighted assets (billions of dollars)[1]	128.2	133.3	138.9

[1] For each quarter in 2014, risk-weighted assets are calculated using the general risk-based capital approach set forth in 12 CFR 225, appendix A. For each quarter in 2015 and 2016, risk-weighted assets are calculated under the Board's standardized capital risk-based approach in 12 CFR 217, subpart D, except for the risk-weighted assets used to calculate the tier 1 common ratio, which uses the general risk-based capital approach for all quarters.

Projected losses, revenue, net income and other comprehensive income through 2016:Q4

	Billions of dollars	Percent of average assets[1]
Pre-provision net revenue[2]	4.1	2.7
Other revenue[3]	0.0	
less		
Provisions	6.0	
Realized losses/gains on securities (AFS/HTM)	0.6	
Trading and counterparty losses[4]	0.0	
Other losses/gains[5]	0.0	
equals		
Net income before taxes	-2.5	-1.6
Memo items		
Other comprehensive income[6]	0.0	
Other effects on capital	*Actual 2014:Q3*	*2016:Q4*
AOCI included in capital (billions of dollars)[7]	n/a	0.0

[1] Average assets is the nine-quarter average of total assets.

[2] Pre-provision net revenue includes losses from operational-risk events, mortgage repurchase expenses, and other real estate owned (OREO) costs.

[3] Other revenue includes one-time income and (expense) items not included in pre-provision net revenue.

[4] Trading and counterparty losses include mark-to-market and credit valuation adjustments (CVA) losses and losses arising from the counterparty default scenario component applied to derivatives, securities lending, and repurchase agreement activities.

[5] Other losses/gains includes projected change in fair value of loans held for sale and loans held for investment measured under the fair-value option, and goodwill impairment losses.

[6] Other comprehensive income (OCI) is only calculated for advanced approaches BHCs, and other BHCs that opt into the advanced approaches treatment of AOCI.

[7] Certain AOCI items are subject to transition into projected regulatory capital. Those transitions are 20 percent included in projected regulatory capital for 2014, 40 percent included in projected regulatory capital for 2015, and 60 percent included in projected regulatory capital for 2016.

Table C.1.B. Ally Financial Inc.
Projected stressed capital ratios, risk-weighted assets, losses, revenues, net income before taxes, and loan losses
Federal Reserve estimates: Adverse scenario

Actual 2014:Q3 projected stressed capital ratios through 2016:Q4

	Actual 2014:Q3	Stressed capital ratios[1]	
		Ending	Minimum
Tier 1 common ratio (%)	9.7	9.5	9.3
Common equity tier 1 capital ratio (%)[2]	n/a	9.4	9.4
Tier 1 risk-based capital ratio (%)	12.7	11.6	11.6
Total risk-based capital ratio (%)	13.5	13.0	13.0
Tier 1 leverage ratio (%)	10.9	9.9	9.9

[1] The capital ratios are calculated using capital action assumptions provided within the Dodd-Frank Act stress testing rule. These projections represent hypothetical estimates that involve an economic outcome that is more adverse than expected. These estimates are not forecasts of expected losses, revenues, net income before taxes, or capital ratios. The minimum capital ratio presented is for the period 2014:Q4 to 2016:Q4.

[2] Advanced approaches bank holding companies (BHCs) are subject to the common equity tier 1 ratio for the third and fourth quarter of 2014. All bank holding companies are subject to the common equity tier 1 ratio for each quarter of 2015 and 2016. An advanced approaches BHC includes any BHC that has consolidated total assets greater than or equal to $250 billion or consolidated total on-balance sheet foreign exposure of at least $10 billion. See 12 CFR 217.100(b)(1). Other BHCs include any BHC that is subject to 12 CFR 225.8 and is not an advanced approaches BHC.

n/a Not applicable.

Projected loan losses, by type of loan, 2014:Q4–2016:Q4

	Billions of dollars	Portfolio loss rates (%)[1]
Loan losses	3.5	3.4
First-lien mortgages, domestic	0.2	4.3
Junior liens and HELOCs, domestic	0.1	5.3
Commercial and industrial[2]	1.0	2.8
Commercial real estate, domestic	0.1	2.8
Credit cards	0.0	0.0
Other consumer[3]	2.0	3.7
Other loans[4]	0.0	7.1

[1] Average loan balances used to calculate portfolio loss rates exclude loans held for sale and loans held for investment under the fair-value option and are calculated over nine quarters.

[2] Commercial and industrial loans include small- and medium-enterprise loans and corporate cards.

[3] Other consumer loans include student loans and automobile loans.

[4] Other loans include international real estate loans.

Actual 2014:Q3 and projected 2016:Q4 risk-weighted assets

	Actual 2014:Q3	Projected 2016:Q4	
		General approach	Standardized approach
Risk-weighted assets (billions of dollars)[1]	128.2	138.3	143.4

[1] For each quarter in 2014, risk-weighted assets are calculated using the general risk-based capital approach set forth in 12 CFR 225, appendix A. For each quarter in 2015 and 2016, risk-weighted assets are calculated under the Board's standardized capital risk-based approach in 12 CFR 217, subpart D, except for the risk-weighted assets used to calculate the tier 1 common ratio, which uses the general risk-based capital approach for all quarters.

Projected losses, revenue, net income and other comprehensive income through 2016:Q4

	Billions of dollars	Percent of average assets[1]
Pre-provision net revenue[2]	4.5	2.8
Other revenue[3]	0.0	
less		
Provisions	4.1	
Realized losses/gains on securities (AFS/HTM)	0.2	
Trading and counterparty losses[4]	0.0	
Other losses/gains[5]	0.0	
equals		
Net income before taxes	0.1	0.1
Memo items		
Other comprehensive income[6]	0.0	
Other effects on capital	Actual 2014:Q3	2016:Q4
AOCI included in capital (billions of dollars)[7]	n/a	0.0

[1] Average assets is the nine-quarter average of total assets.

[2] Pre-provision net revenue includes losses from operational-risk events, mortgage repurchase expenses, and other real estate owned (OREO) costs.

[3] Other revenue includes one-time income and (expense) items not included in pre-provision net revenue.

[4] Trading and counterparty losses include mark-to-market and credit valuation adjustments (CVA) losses and losses arising from the counterparty default scenario component applied to derivatives, securities lending, and repurchase agreement activities.

[5] Other losses/gains includes projected change in fair value of loans held for sale and loans held for investment measured under the fair-value option, and goodwill impairment losses.

[6] Other comprehensive income (OCI) is only calculated for advanced approaches BHCs, and other BHCs that opt into the advanced approaches treatment of AOCI.

[7] Certain AOCI items are subject to transition into projected regulatory capital. Those transitions are 20 percent included in projected regulatory capital for 2014, 40 percent included in projected regulatory capital for 2015, and 60 percent included in projected regulatory capital for 2016.

Table C.2.A. American Express Company
Projected stressed capital ratios, risk-weighted assets, losses, revenues, net income before taxes, and loan losses
Federal Reserve estimates: Severely adverse scenario

Actual 2014:Q3 projected stressed capital ratios through 2016:Q4

	Actual 2014:Q3	Stressed capital ratios[1]	
		Ending	Minimum
Tier 1 common ratio (%)	13.2	15.4	12.5
Common equity tier 1 capital ratio (%)[2]	13.6	15.1	13.0
Tier 1 risk-based capital ratio (%)	13.6	15.6	13.5
Total risk-based capital ratio (%)	15.1	17.3	15.4
Tier 1 leverage ratio (%)	11.6	13.0	11.4

[1] The capital ratios are calculated using capital action assumptions provided within the Dodd-Frank Act stress testing rule. These projections represent hypothetical estimates that involve an economic outcome that is more adverse than expected. These estimates are not forecasts of expected losses, revenues, net income before taxes, or capital ratios. The minimum capital ratio presented is for the period 2014:Q4 to 2016:Q4.

[2] Advanced approaches bank holding companies (BHCs) are subject to the common equity tier 1 ratio for the third and fourth quarter of 2014. All bank holding companies are subject to the common equity tier 1 ratio for each quarter of 2015 and 2016. An advanced approaches BHC includes any BHC that has consolidated total assets greater than or equal to $250 billion or consolidated total on-balance sheet foreign exposure of at least $10 billion. See 12 CFR 217.100(b)(1). Other BHCs include any BHC that is subject to 12 CFR 225.8 and is not an advanced approaches BHC.

Projected loan losses, by type of loan, 2014:Q4–2016:Q4

	Billions of dollars	Portfolio loss rates (%)[1]
Loan losses	10.5	9.2
First-lien mortgages, domestic	0.0	0.0
Junior liens and HELOCs, domestic	0.0	0.0
Commercial and industrial[2]	3.3	9.0
Commercial real estate, domestic	0.0	0.0
Credit cards	7.3	9.3
Other consumer[3]	0.0	14.3
Other loans[4]	0.0	0.0

[1] Average loan balances used to calculate portfolio loss rates exclude loans held for sale and loans held for investment under the fair-value option and are calculated over nine quarters.

[2] Commercial and industrial loans include small- and medium-enterprise loans and corporate cards.

[3] Other consumer loans include student loans and automobile loans.

[4] Other loans include international real estate loans.

Actual 2014:Q3 and projected 2016:Q4 risk-weighted assets

	Actual 2014:Q3	Projected 2016:Q4	
		General approach	Standardized approach
Risk-weighted assets (billions of dollars)[1]	128.9	133.2	136.7

[1] For each quarter in 2014, risk-weighted assets are calculated using the general risk-based capital approach set forth in 12 CFR 225, appendix A. For each quarter in 2015 and 2016, risk-weighted assets are calculated under the Board's standardized capital risk-based approach in 12 CFR 217, subpart D, except for the risk-weighted assets used to calculate the tier 1 common ratio, which uses the general risk-based capital approach for all quarters.

Projected losses, revenue, net income and other comprehensive income through 2016:Q4

	Billions of dollars	Percent of average assets[1]
Pre-provision net revenue[2]	23.7	14.9
Other revenue[3]	0.0	
less		
Provisions	13.7	
Realized losses/gains on securities (AFS/HTM)	0.0	
Trading and counterparty losses[4]	0.0	
Other losses/gains[5]	0.0	
equals		
Net income before taxes	10.0	6.3
Memo items		
Other comprehensive income[6]	0.0	
Other effects on capital	*Actual 2014:Q3*	*2016:Q4*
AOCI included in capital (billions of dollars)[7]	-1.3	-1.4

[1] Average assets is the nine-quarter average of total assets.

[2] Pre-provision net revenue includes losses from operational-risk events, mortgage repurchase expenses, and other real estate owned (OREO) costs.

[3] Other revenue includes one-time income and (expense) items not included in pre-provision net revenue.

[4] Trading and counterparty losses include mark-to-market and credit valuation adjustments (CVA) losses and losses arising from the counterparty default scenario component applied to derivatives, securities lending, and repurchase agreement activities.

[5] Other losses/gains includes projected change in fair value of loans held for sale and loans held for investment measured under the fair-value option and goodwill impairment losses.

[6] Other comprehensive income (OCI) is only calculated for advanced approaches BHCs, and other BHCs that opt into the advanced approaches treatment of AOCI.

[7] Certain AOCI items are subject to transition into projected regulatory capital. Those transitions are 20 percent included in projected regulatory capital for 2014, 40 percent included in projected regulatory capital for 2015, and 60 percent included in projected regulatory capital for 2016.

Table C.2.B. American Express Company

Projected stressed capital ratios, risk-weighted assets, losses, revenues, net income before taxes, and loan losses

Federal Reserve estimates: Adverse scenario

Actual 2014:Q3 projected stressed capital ratios through 2016:Q4

	Actual 2014:Q3	Stressed capital ratios[1]	
		Ending	Minimum
Tier 1 common ratio (%)	13.2	17.4	12.8
Common equity tier 1 capital ratio (%)[2]	13.6	17.1	13.4
Tier 1 risk-based capital ratio (%)	13.6	17.6	14.0
Total risk-based capital ratio (%)	15.1	19.3	15.8
Tier 1 leverage ratio (%)	11.6	14.4	11.6

[1] The capital ratios are calculated using capital action assumptions provided within the Dodd-Frank Act stress testing rule. These projections represent hypothetical estimates that involve an economic outcome that is more adverse than expected. These estimates are not forecasts of expected losses, revenues, net income before taxes, or capital ratios. The minimum capital ratio presented is for the period 2014:Q4 to 2016:Q4.

[2] Advanced approaches bank holding companies (BHCs) are subject to the common equity tier 1 ratio for the third and fourth quarter of 2014. All bank holding companies are subject to the common equity tier 1 ratio for each quarter of 2015 and 2016. An advanced approaches BHC includes any BHC that has consolidated total assets greater than or equal to $250 billion or consolidated total on-balance sheet foreign exposure of at least $10 billion. See 12 CFR 217.100(b)(1). Other BHCs include any BHC that is subject to 12 CFR 225.8 and is not an advanced approaches BHC.

Projected loan losses, by type of loan, 2014:Q4–2016:Q4

	Billions of dollars	Portfolio loss rates (%)[1]
Loan losses	8.1	7.0
First-lien mortgages, domestic	0.0	0.0
Junior liens and HELOCs, domestic	0.0	0.0
Commercial and industrial[2]	2.4	6.5
Commercial real estate, domestic	0.0	0.0
Credit cards	5.7	7.2
Other consumer[3]	0.0	12.2
Other loans[4]	0.0	0.0

[1] Average loan balances used to calculate portfolio loss rates exclude loans held for sale and loans held for investment under the fair-value option and are calculated over nine quarters.

[2] Commercial and industrial loans include small- and medium-enterprise loans and corporate cards.

[3] Other consumer loans include student loans and automobile loans.

[4] Other loans include international real estate loans.

Actual 2014:Q3 and projected 2016:Q4 risk-weighted assets

	Actual 2014:Q3	Projected 2016:Q4	
		General approach	Standardized approach
Risk-weighted assets (billions of dollars)[1]	128.9	138.0	140.5

[1] For each quarter in 2014, risk-weighted assets are calculated using the general risk-based capital approach set forth in 12 CFR 225, appendix A. For each quarter in 2015 and 2016, risk-weighted assets are calculated under the Board's standardized capital risk-based approach in 12 CFR 217, subpart D, except for the risk-weighted assets used to calculate the tier 1 common ratio, which uses the general risk-based capital approach for all quarters.

Projected losses, revenue, net income and other comprehensive income through 2016:Q4

	Billions of dollars	Percent of average assets[1]
Pre-provision net revenue[2]	25.9	15.9
Other revenue[3]	0.0	
less		
Provisions	10.8	
Realized losses/gains on securities (AFS/HTM)	0.0	
Trading and counterparty losses[4]	0.0	
Other losses/gains[5]	0.0	
equals		
Net income before taxes	15.1	9.3
Memo items		
Other comprehensive income[6]	-0.3	
Other effects on capital	*Actual 2014:Q3*	*2016:Q4*
AOCI included in capital (billions of dollars)[7]	-1.3	-1.6

[1] Average assets is the nine-quarter average of total assets.

[2] Pre-provision net revenue includes losses from operational-risk events, mortgage repurchase expenses, and other real estate owned (OREO) costs.

[3] Other revenue includes one-time income and (expense) items not included in pre-provision net revenue.

[4] Trading and counterparty losses include mark-to-market and credit valuation adjustments (CVA) losses and losses arising from the counterparty default scenario component applied to derivatives, securities lending, and repurchase agreement activities.

[5] Other losses/gains includes projected change in fair value of loans held for sale and loans held for investment measured under the fair-value option and goodwill impairment losses.

[6] Other comprehensive income (OCI) is only calculated for advanced approaches BHCs, and other BHCs that opt into the advanced approaches treatment of AOCI.

[7] Certain AOCI items are subject to transition into projected regulatory capital. Those transitions are 20 percent included in projected regulatory capital for 2014, 40 percent included in projected regulatory capital for 2015, and 60 percent included in projected regulatory capital for 2016.

Table C.3.A. Bank of America Corporation
Projected stressed capital ratios, risk-weighted assets, losses, revenues, net income before taxes, and loan losses
Federal Reserve estimates: Severely adverse scenario

Actual 2014:Q3 projected stressed capital ratios through 2016:Q4

	Actual 2014:Q3	Stressed capital ratios[1]	
		Ending	Minimum
Tier 1 common ratio (%)	11.3	7.4	7.1
Common equity tier 1 capital ratio (%)[2]	12.0	7.2	7.1
Tier 1 risk-based capital ratio (%)	12.8	7.9	7.8
Total risk-based capital ratio (%)	15.8	10.4	10.4
Tier 1 leverage ratio (%)	7.9	5.1	5.1

[1] The capital ratios are calculated using capital action assumptions provided within the Dodd-Frank Act stress testing rule. These projections represent hypothetical estimates that involve an economic outcome that is more adverse than expected. These estimates are not forecasts of expected losses, revenues, net income before taxes, or capital ratios. The minimum capital ratio presented is for the period 2014:Q4 to 2016:Q4.

[2] Advanced approaches bank holding companies (BHCs) are subject to the common equity tier 1 ratio for the third and fourth quarter of 2014. All bank holding companies are subject to the common equity tier 1 ratio for each quarter of 2015 and 2016. An advanced approaches BHC includes any BHC that has consolidated total assets greater than or equal to $250 billion or consolidated total on-balance sheet foreign exposure of at least $10 billion. See 12 CFR 217.100(b)(1). Other BHCs include any BHC that is subject to 12 CFR 225.8 and is not an advanced approaches BHC.

Projected loan losses, by type of loan, 2014:Q4–2016:Q4

	Billions of dollars	Portfolio loss rates (%)[1]
Loan losses	45.7	4.9
First-lien mortgages, domestic	7.1	3.1
Junior liens and HELOCs, domestic	8.2	9.2
Commercial and industrial[2]	8.0	3.9
Commercial real estate, domestic	5.1	8.3
Credit cards	11.7	11.4
Other consumer[3]	2.2	2.8
Other loans[4]	3.3	2.1

[1] Average loan balances used to calculate portfolio loss rates exclude loans held for sale and loans held for investment under the fair-value option and are calculated over nine quarters.

[2] Commercial and industrial loans include small- and medium-enterprise loans and corporate cards.

[3] Other consumer loans include student loans and automobile loans.

[4] Other loans include international real estate loans.

Actual 2014:Q3 and projected 2016:Q4 risk-weighted assets

	Actual 2014:Q3	Projected 2016:Q4	
		General approach	Standardized approach
Risk-weighted assets (billions of dollars)[1]	1,271.7	1,309.2	1,433.9

[1] For each quarter in 2014, risk-weighted assets are calculated using the general risk-based capital approach set forth in 12 CFR 225, appendix A. For each quarter in 2015 and 2016, risk-weighted assets are calculated under the Board's standardized capital risk-based approach in 12 CFR 217, subpart D, except for the risk-weighted assets used to calculate the tier 1 common ratio, which uses the general risk-based capital approach for all quarters.

Projected losses, revenue, net income and other comprehensive income through 2016:Q4

	Billions of dollars	Percent of average assets[1]
Pre-provision net revenue[2]	34.4	1.6
Other revenue[3]	0.0	
less		
Provisions	49.1	
Realized losses/gains on securities (AFS/HTM)	0.9	
Trading and counterparty losses[4]	17.6	
Other losses/gains[5]	4.1	
equals		
Net income before taxes	-37.3	-1.7
Memo items		
Other comprehensive income[6]	2.3	
Other effects on capital	Actual 2014:Q3	2016:Q4
AOCI included in capital (billions of dollars)[7]	-1.3	-1.1

[1] Average assets is the nine-quarter average of total assets.

[2] Pre-provision net revenue includes losses from operational-risk events, mortgage repurchase expenses, and other real estate owned (OREO) costs.

[3] Other revenue includes one-time income and (expense) items not included in pre-provision net revenue.

[4] Trading and counterparty losses include mark-to-market and credit valuation adjustments (CVA) losses and losses arising from the counterparty default scenario component applied to derivatives, securities lending, and repurchase agreement activities.

[5] Other losses/gains includes projected change in fair value of loans held for sale and loans held for investment measured under the fair-value option and goodwill impairment losses.

[6] Other comprehensive income (OCI) is only calculated for advanced approaches BHCs, and other BHCs that opt into the advanced approaches treatment of AOCI.

[7] Certain AOCI items are subject to transition into projected regulatory capital. Those transitions are 20 percent included in projected regulatory capital for 2014, 40 percent included in projected regulatory capital for 2015, and 60 percent included in projected regulatory capital for 2016.

Table C.3.B. Bank of America Corporation
Projected stressed capital ratios, risk-weighted assets, losses, revenues, net income before taxes, and loan losses
Federal Reserve estimates: Adverse scenario

Actual 2014:Q3 projected stressed capital ratios through 2016:Q4

	Actual 2014:Q3	Stressed capital ratios[1]	
		Ending	Minimum
Tier 1 common ratio (%)	11.3	11.5	10.0
Common equity tier 1 capital ratio (%)[2]	12.0	8.5	8.0
Tier 1 risk-based capital ratio (%)	12.8	9.7	9.1
Total risk-based capital ratio (%)	15.8	11.8	11.5
Tier 1 leverage ratio (%)	7.9	6.2	5.9

[1] The capital ratios are calculated using capital action assumptions provided within the Dodd-Frank Act stress testing rule. These projections represent hypothetical estimates that involve an economic outcome that is more adverse than expected. These estimates are not forecasts of expected losses, revenues, net income before taxes, or capital ratios. The minimum capital ratio presented is for the period 2014:Q4 to 2016:Q4.

[2] Advanced approaches bank holding companies (BHCs) are subject to the common equity tier 1 ratio for the third and fourth quarter of 2014. All bank holding companies are subject to the common equity tier 1 ratio for each quarter of 2015 and 2016. An advanced approaches BHC includes any BHC that has consolidated total assets greater than or equal to $250 billion or consolidated total on-balance sheet foreign exposure of at least $10 billion. See 12 CFR 217.100(b)(1). Other BHCs include any BHC that is subject to 12 CFR 225.8 and is not an advanced approaches BHC.

Projected loan losses, by type of loan, 2014:Q4–2016:Q4

	Billions of dollars	Portfolio loss rates (%)[1]
Loan losses	31.0	3.3
First-lien mortgages, domestic	4.9	2.1
Junior liens and HELOCs, domestic	5.4	5.9
Commercial and industrial[2]	4.7	2.3
Commercial real estate, domestic	2.9	4.7
Credit cards	9.4	9.0
Other consumer[3]	1.7	2.0
Other loans[4]	2.0	1.2

[1] Average loan balances used to calculate portfolio loss rates exclude loans held for sale and loans held for investment under the fair-value option and are calculated over nine quarters.

[2] Commercial and industrial loans include small- and medium-enterprise loans and corporate cards.

[3] Other consumer loans include student loans and automobile loans.

[4] Other loans include international real estate loans.

Actual 2014:Q3 and projected 2016:Q4 risk-weighted assets

	Actual 2014:Q3	Projected 2016:Q4	
		General approach	Standardized approach
Risk-weighted assets (billions of dollars)[1]	1,271.7	1,361.6	1,477.1

[1] For each quarter in 2014, risk-weighted assets are calculated using the general risk-based capital approach set forth in 12 CFR 225, appendix A. For each quarter in 2015 and 2016, risk-weighted assets are calculated under the Board's standardized capital risk-based approach in 12 CFR 217, subpart D, except for the risk-weighted assets used to calculate the tier 1 common ratio, which uses the general risk-based capital approach for all quarters.

Projected losses, revenue, net income and other comprehensive income through 2016:Q4

	Billions of dollars	Percent of average assets[1]
Pre-provision net revenue[2]	61.6	2.7
Other revenue[3]	0.0	
less		
Provisions	29.2	
Realized losses/gains on securities (AFS/HTM)	0.5	
Trading and counterparty losses[4]	9.1	
Other losses/gains[5]	2.2	
equals		
Net income before taxes	20.6	0.9
Memo items		
Other comprehensive income[6]	-26.0	
Other effects on capital	Actual 2014:Q3	2016:Q4
AOCI included in capital (billions of dollars)[7]	-1.3	-18.0

[1] Average assets is the nine-quarter average of total assets.

[2] Pre-provision net revenue includes losses from operational-risk events, mortgage repurchase expenses, and other real estate owned (OREO) costs.

[3] Other revenue includes one-time income and (expense) items not included in pre-provision net revenue.

[4] Trading and counterparty losses include mark-to-market and credit valuation adjustments (CVA) losses and losses arising from the counterparty default scenario component applied to derivatives, securities lending, and repurchase agreement activities.

[5] Other losses/gains includes projected change in fair value of loans held for sale and loans held for investment measured under the fair-value option and goodwill impairment losses.

[6] Other comprehensive income (OCI) is only calculated for advanced approaches BHCs, and other BHCs that opt into the advanced approaches treatment of AOCI.

[7] Certain AOCI items are subject to transition into projected regulatory capital. Those transitions are 20 percent included in projected regulatory capital for 2014, 40 percent included in projected regulatory capital for 2015, and 60 percent included in projected regulatory capital for 2016.

Table C.4.A. The Bank of New York Mellon Corporation
Projected stressed capital ratios, risk-weighted assets, losses, revenues, net income before taxes, and loan losses
Federal Reserve estimates: Severely adverse scenario

Actual 2014:Q3 projected stressed capital ratios through 2016:Q4

	Actual 2014:Q3	Stressed capital ratios[1]	
		Ending	Minimum
Tier 1 common ratio (%)	13.9	16.0	12.6
Common equity tier 1 capital ratio (%)[2]	15.1	15.1	12.6
Tier 1 risk-based capital ratio (%)	16.3	16.1	13.6
Total risk-based capital ratio (%)	17.0	16.5	14.2
Tier 1 leverage ratio (%)	5.8	6.0	5.2

[1] The capital ratios are calculated using capital action assumptions provided within the Dodd-Frank Act stress testing rule. These projections represent hypothetical estimates that involve an economic outcome that is more adverse than expected. These estimates are not forecasts of expected losses, revenues, net income before taxes, or capital ratios. The minimum capital ratio presented is for the period 2014:Q4 to 2016:Q4.

[2] Advanced approaches bank holding companies (BHCs) are subject to the common equity tier 1 ratio for the third and fourth quarter of 2014. All bank holding companies are subject to the common equity tier 1 ratio for each quarter of 2015 and 2016. An advanced approaches BHC includes any BHC that has consolidated total assets greater than or equal to $250 billion or consolidated total on-balance sheet foreign exposure of at least $10 billion. See 12 CFR 217.100(b)(1). Other BHCs include any BHC that is subject to 12 CFR 225.8 and is not an advanced approaches BHC.

Projected loan losses, by type of loan, 2014:Q4–2016:Q4

	Billions of dollars	Portfolio loss rates (%)[1]
Loan losses	1.4	2.3
First-lien mortgages, domestic	0.2	2.9
Junior liens and HELOCs, domestic	0.0	9.8
Commercial and industrial[2]	0.1	3.3
Commercial real estate, domestic	0.2	10.3
Credit cards	0.0	0.0
Other consumer[3]	0.3	10.6
Other loans[4]	0.6	1.4

[1] Average loan balances used to calculate portfolio loss rates exclude loans held for sale and loans held for investment under the fair-value option and are calculated over nine quarters.

[2] Commercial and industrial loans include small- and medium-enterprise loans and corporate cards.

[3] Other consumer loans include student loans and automobile loans.

[4] Other loans include international real estate loans.

Actual 2014:Q3 and projected 2016:Q4 risk-weighted assets

	Actual 2014:Q3	Projected 2016:Q4	
		General approach	Standardized approach
Risk-weighted assets (billions of dollars)[1]	128.8	130.5	142.4

[1] For each quarter in 2014, risk-weighted assets are calculated using the general risk-based capital approach set forth in 12 CFR 225, appendix A. For each quarter in 2015 and 2016, risk-weighted assets are calculated under the Board's standardized capital risk-based approach in 12 CFR 217, subpart D, except for the risk-weighted assets used to calculate the tier 1 common ratio, which uses the general risk-based capital approach for all quarters.

Projected losses, revenue, net income and other comprehensive income through 2016:Q4

	Billions of dollars	Percent of average assets[1]
Pre-provision net revenue[2]	11.8	2.9
Other revenue[3]	0.0	
less		
Provisions	1.7	
Realized losses/gains on securities (AFS/HTM)	0.2	
Trading and counterparty losses[4]	0.9	
Other losses/gains[5]	1.7	
equals		
Net income before taxes	7.2	1.8
Memo items		
Other comprehensive income[6]	-0.3	
Other effects on capital	Actual 2014:Q3	2016:Q4
AOCI included in capital (billions of dollars)[7]	-0.8	-1.0

[1] Average assets is the nine-quarter average of total assets.

[2] Pre-provision net revenue includes losses from operational-risk events, mortgage repurchase expenses, and other real estate owned (OREO) costs.

[3] Other revenue includes one-time income and (expense) items not included in pre-provision net revenue.

[4] Trading and counterparty losses include mark-to-market and credit valuation adjustments (CVA) losses and losses arising from the counterparty default scenario component applied to derivatives, securities lending, and repurchase agreement activities.

[5] Other losses/gains includes projected change in fair value of loans held for sale and loans held for investment measured under the fair-value option and goodwill impairment losses.

[6] Other comprehensive income (OCI) is only calculated for advanced approaches BHCs, and other BHCs that opt into the advanced approaches treatment of AOCI.

[7] Certain AOCI items are subject to transition into projected regulatory capital. Those transitions are 20 percent included in projected regulatory capital for 2014, 40 percent included in projected regulatory capital for 2015, and 60 percent included in projected regulatory capital for 2016.

Table C.4.B. The Bank of New York Mellon Corporation
Projected stressed capital ratios, risk-weighted assets, losses, revenues, net income before taxes, and loan losses
Federal Reserve estimates: Adverse scenario

Actual 2014:Q3 projected stressed capital ratios through 2016:Q4

	Actual 2014:Q3	Stressed capital ratios[1]	
		Ending	Minimum
Tier 1 common ratio (%)	13.9	19.6	13.3
Common equity tier 1 capital ratio (%)[2]	15.1	16.1	12.7
Tier 1 risk-based capital ratio (%)	16.3	17.1	13.9
Total risk-based capital ratio (%)	17.0	17.4	14.3
Tier 1 leverage ratio (%)	5.8	6.3	5.2

[1] The capital ratios are calculated using capital action assumptions provided within the Dodd-Frank Act stress testing rule. These projections represent hypothetical estimates that involve an economic outcome that is more adverse than expected. These estimates are not forecasts of expected losses, revenues, net income before taxes, or capital ratios. The minimum capital ratio presented is for the period 2014:Q4 to 2016:Q4.

[2] Advanced approaches bank holding companies (BHCs) are subject to the common equity tier 1 ratio for the third and fourth quarter of 2014. All bank holding companies are subject to the common equity tier 1 ratio for each quarter of 2015 and 2016. An advanced approaches BHC includes any BHC that has consolidated total assets greater than or equal to $250 billion or consolidated total on-balance sheet foreign exposure of at least $10 billion. See 12 CFR 217.100(b)(1). Other BHCs include any BHC that is subject to 12 CFR 225.8 and is not an advanced approaches BHC.

Projected loan losses, by type of loan, 2014:Q4–2016:Q4

	Billions of dollars	Portfolio loss rates (%)[1]
Loan losses	0.9	1.5
First-lien mortgages, domestic	0.1	2.1
Junior liens and HELOCs, domestic	0.0	6.3
Commercial and industrial[2]	0.0	2.0
Commercial real estate, domestic	0.1	5.9
Credit cards	0.0	0.0
Other consumer[3]	0.2	8.6
Other loans[4]	0.4	0.9

[1] Average loan balances used to calculate portfolio loss rates exclude loans held for sale and loans held for investment under the fair-value option and are calculated over nine quarters.

[2] Commercial and industrial loans include small- and medium-enterprise loans and corporate cards.

[3] Other consumer loans include student loans and automobile loans.

[4] Other loans include international real estate loans.

Actual 2014:Q3 and projected 2016:Q4 risk-weighted assets

	Actual 2014:Q3	Projected 2016:Q4	
		General approach	Standardized approach
Risk-weighted assets (billions of dollars)[1]	128.8	137.5	150.2

[1] For each quarter in 2014, risk-weighted assets are calculated using the general risk-based capital approach set forth in 12 CFR 225, appendix A. For each quarter in 2015 and 2016, risk-weighted assets are calculated under the Board's standardized capital risk-based approach in 12 CFR 217, subpart D, except for the risk-weighted assets used to calculate the tier 1 common ratio, which uses the general risk-based capital approach for all quarters.

Projected losses, revenue, net income and other comprehensive income through 2016:Q4

	Billions of dollars	Percent of average assets[1]
Pre-provision net revenue[2]	19.4	4.7
Other revenue[3]	0.0	
less		
Provisions	1.1	
Realized losses/gains on securities (AFS/HTM)	0.1	
Trading and counterparty losses[4]	0.7	
Other losses/gains[5]	0.9	
equals		
Net income before taxes	16.6	4.0
Memo items		
Other comprehensive income[6]	-6.1	
Other effects on capital	Actual 2014:Q3	2016:Q4
AOCI included in capital (billions of dollars)[7]	-0.8	-4.5

[1] Average assets is the nine-quarter average of total assets.

[2] Pre-provision net revenue includes losses from operational-risk events, mortgage repurchase expenses, and other real estate owned (OREO) costs.

[3] Other revenue includes one-time income and (expense) items not included in pre-provision net revenue.

[4] Trading and counterparty losses include mark-to-market and credit valuation adjustments (CVA) losses and losses arising from the counterparty default scenario component applied to derivatives, securities lending, and repurchase agreement activities.

[5] Other losses/gains includes projected change in fair value of loans held for sale and loans held for investment measured under the fair-value option and goodwill impairment losses.

[6] Other comprehensive income (OCI) is only calculated for advanced approaches BHCs, and other BHCs that opt into the advanced approaches treatment of AOCI.

[7] Certain AOCI items are subject to transition into projected regulatory capital. Those transitions are 20 percent included in projected regulatory capital for 2014, 40 percent included in projected regulatory capital for 2015, and 60 percent included in projected regulatory capital for 2016.

Table C.5.A. BB&T Corporation
Projected stressed capital ratios, risk-weighted assets, losses, revenues, net income before taxes, and loan losses
Federal Reserve estimates: Severely adverse scenario

Actual 2014:Q3 projected stressed capital ratios through 2016:Q4

	Actual 2014:Q3	Stressed capital ratios[1]	
		Ending	Minimum
Tier 1 common ratio (%)	10.5	8.1	8.1
Common equity tier 1 capital ratio (%)[2]	n/a	8.2	8.2
Tier 1 risk-based capital ratio (%)	12.4	9.8	9.8
Total risk-based capital ratio (%)	15.2	11.8	11.8
Tier 1 leverage ratio (%)	9.7	7.4	7.4

[1] The capital ratios are calculated using capital action assumptions provided within the Dodd-Frank Act stress testing rule. These projections represent hypothetical estimates that involve an economic outcome that is more adverse than expected. These estimates are not forecasts of expected losses, revenues, net income before taxes, or capital ratios. The minimum capital ratio presented is for the period 2014:Q4 to 2016:Q4.

[2] Advanced approaches bank holding companies (BHCs) are subject to the common equity tier 1 ratio for the third and fourth quarter of 2014. All bank holding companies are subject to the common equity tier 1 ratio for each quarter of 2015 and 2016. An advanced approaches BHC includes any BHC that has consolidated total assets greater than or equal to $250 billion or consolidated total on-balance sheet foreign exposure of at least $10 billion. See 12 CFR 217.100(b)(1). Other BHCs include any BHC that is subject to 12 CFR 225.8 and is not an advanced approaches BHC.

n/a Not applicable.

Projected loan losses, by type of loan, 2014:Q4–2016:Q4

	Billions of dollars	Portfolio loss rates (%)[1]
Loan losses	6.0	4.6
First-lien mortgages, domestic	0.9	2.7
Junior liens and HELOCs, domestic	0.3	3.6
Commercial and industrial[2]	0.8	4.1
Commercial real estate, domestic	2.4	7.0
Credit cards	0.2	13.6
Other consumer[3]	1.1	6.0
Other loans[4]	0.3	2.0

[1] Average loan balances used to calculate portfolio loss rates exclude loans held for sale and loans held for investment under the fair-value option and are calculated over nine quarters.

[2] Commercial and industrial loans include small- and medium-enterprise loans and corporate cards.

[3] Other consumer loans include student loans and automobile loans.

[4] Other loans include international real estate loans.

Actual 2014:Q3 and projected 2016:Q4 risk-weighted assets

	Actual 2014:Q3	Projected 2016:Q4	
		General approach	Standardized approach
Risk-weighted assets (billions of dollars)[1]	140.5	162.2	162.0

[1] For each quarter in 2014, risk-weighted assets are calculated using the general risk-based capital approach set forth in 12 CFR 225, appendix A. For each quarter in 2015 and 2016, risk-weighted assets are calculated under the Board's standardized capital risk-based approach in 12 CFR 217, subpart D, except for the risk-weighted assets used to calculate the tier 1 common ratio, which uses the general risk-based capital approach for all quarters.

Projected losses, revenue, net income and other comprehensive income through 2016:Q4

	Billions of dollars	Percent of average assets[1]
Pre-provision net revenue[2]	8.0	3.8
Other revenue[3]	0.0	
less		
Provisions	7.2	
Realized losses/gains on securities (AFS/HTM)	0.0	
Trading and counterparty losses[4]	0.0	
Other losses/gains[5]	0.0	
equals		
Net income before taxes	0.7	0.3
Memo items		
Other comprehensive income[6]	0.0	
Other effects on capital	*Actual 2014:Q3*	*2016:Q4*
AOCI included in capital (billions of dollars)[7]	n/a	0.0

[1] Average assets is the nine-quarter average of total assets.

[2] Pre-provision net revenue includes losses from operational-risk events, mortgage repurchase expenses, and other real estate owned (OREO) costs.

[3] Other revenue includes one-time income and (expense) items not included in pre-provision net revenue.

[4] Trading and counterparty losses include mark-to-market and credit valuation adjustments (CVA) losses and losses arising from the counterparty default scenario component applied to derivatives, securities lending, and repurchase agreement activities.

[5] Other losses/gains includes projected change in fair value of loans held for sale and loans held for investment measured under the fair-value option, and goodwill impairment losses.

[6] Other comprehensive income (OCI) is only calculated for advanced approaches BHCs, and other BHCs that opt into the advanced approaches treatment of AOCI.

[7] Certain AOCI items are subject to transition into projected regulatory capital. Those transitions are 20 percent included in projected regulatory capital for 2014, 40 percent included in projected regulatory capital for 2015, and 60 percent included in projected regulatory capital for 2016.

Table C.5.B. BB&T Corporation
Projected stressed capital ratios, risk-weighted assets, losses, revenues, net income before taxes, and loan losses
Federal Reserve estimates: Adverse scenario

Actual 2014:Q3 projected stressed capital ratios through 2016:Q4

	Actual 2014:Q3	Stressed capital ratios[1]	
		Ending	Minimum
Tier 1 common ratio (%)	10.5	9.4	8.9
Common equity tier 1 capital ratio (%)[2]	n/a	9.7	9.3
Tier 1 risk-based capital ratio (%)	12.4	11.2	10.9
Total risk-based capital ratio (%)	15.2	13.3	13.1
Tier 1 leverage ratio (%)	9.7	8.5	8.3

[1] The capital ratios are calculated using capital action assumptions provided within the Dodd-Frank Act stress testing rule. These projections represent hypothetical estimates that involve an economic outcome that is more adverse than expected. These estimates are not forecasts of expected losses, revenues, net income before taxes, or capital ratios. The minimum capital ratio presented is for the period 2014:Q4 to 2016:Q4.

[2] Advanced approaches bank holding companies (BHCs) are subject to the common equity tier 1 ratio for the third and fourth quarter of 2014. All bank holding companies are subject to the common equity tier 1 ratio for each quarter of 2015 and 2016. An advanced approaches BHC includes any BHC that has consolidated total assets greater than or equal to $250 billion or consolidated total on-balance sheet foreign exposure of at least $10 billion. See 12 CFR 217.100(b)(1). Other BHCs include any BHC that is subject to 12 CFR 225.8 and is not an advanced approaches BHC.

n/a Not applicable.

Projected loan losses, by type of loan, 2014:Q4–2016:Q4

	Billions of dollars	Portfolio loss rates (%)[1]
Loan losses	3.9	3.0
First-lien mortgages, domestic	0.7	1.9
Junior liens and HELOCs, domestic	0.2	2.3
Commercial and industrial[2]	0.5	2.6
Commercial real estate, domestic	1.4	4.2
Credit cards	0.2	10.8
Other consumer[3]	0.8	4.2
Other loans[4]	0.2	1.2

[1] Average loan balances used to calculate portfolio loss rates exclude loans held for sale and loans held for investment under the fair-value option and are calculated over nine quarters.

[2] Commercial and industrial loans include small- and medium-enterprise loans and corporate cards.

[3] Other consumer loans include student loans and automobile loans.

[4] Other loans include international real estate loans.

Actual 2014:Q3 and projected 2016:Q4 risk-weighted assets

	Actual 2014:Q3	Projected 2016:Q4	
		General approach	Standardized approach
Risk-weighted assets (billions of dollars)[1]	140.5	167.9	165.9

[1] For each quarter in 2014, risk-weighted assets are calculated using the general risk-based capital approach set forth in 12 CFR 225, appendix A. For each quarter in 2015 and 2016, risk-weighted assets are calculated under the Board's standardized capital risk-based approach in 12 CFR 217, subpart D, except for the risk-weighted assets used to calculate the tier 1 common ratio, which uses the general risk-based capital approach for all quarters.

Projected losses, revenue, net income and other comprehensive income through 2016:Q4

	Billions of dollars	Percent of average assets[1]
Pre-provision net revenue[2]	9.7	4.6
Other revenue[3]	0.0	
less		
Provisions	4.5	
Realized losses/gains on securities (AFS/HTM)	0.0	
Trading and counterparty losses[4]	0.0	
Other losses/gains[5]	0.0	
equals		
Net income before taxes	5.2	2.5
Memo items		
Other comprehensive income[6]	0.0	
Other effects on capital	*Actual 2014:Q3*	*2016:Q4*
AOCI included in capital (billions of dollars)[7]	n/a	0.0

[1] Average assets is the nine-quarter average of total assets.

[2] Pre-provision net revenue includes losses from operational-risk events, mortgage repurchase expenses, and other real estate owned (OREO) costs.

[3] Other revenue includes one-time income and (expense) items not included in pre-provision net revenue.

[4] Trading and counterparty losses include mark-to-market and credit valuation adjustments (CVA) losses and losses arising from the counterparty default scenario component applied to derivatives, securities lending, and repurchase agreement activities.

[5] Other losses/gains includes projected change in fair value of loans held for sale and loans held for investment measured under the fair-value option, and goodwill impairment losses.

[6] Other comprehensive income (OCI) is only calculated for advanced approaches BHCs, and other BHCs that opt into the advanced approaches treatment of AOCI.

[7] Certain AOCI items are subject to transition into projected regulatory capital. Those transitions are 20 percent included in projected regulatory capital for 2014, 40 percent included in projected regulatory capital for 2015, and 60 percent included in projected regulatory capital for 2016.

Table C.6.A. BBVA Compass Bancshares, Inc.

Projected stressed capital ratios, risk-weighted assets, losses, revenues, net income before taxes, and loan losses

Federal Reserve estimates: Severely adverse scenario

Actual 2014:Q3 projected stressed capital ratios through 2016:Q4

	Actual 2014:Q3	Stressed capital ratios[1]	
		Ending	Minimum
Tier 1 common ratio (%)	11.0	6.3	6.3
Common equity tier 1 capital ratio (%)[2]	n/a	6.9	6.9
Tier 1 risk-based capital ratio (%)	11.3	6.9	6.9
Total risk-based capital ratio (%)	13.3	8.7	8.7
Tier 1 leverage ratio (%)	9.6	5.5	5.5

[1] The capital ratios are calculated using capital action assumptions provided within the Dodd-Frank Act stress testing rule. These projections represent hypothetical estimates that involve an economic outcome that is more adverse than expected. These estimates are not forecasts of expected losses, revenues, net income before taxes, or capital ratios. The minimum capital ratio presented is for the period 2014:Q4 to 2016:Q4.

[2] Advanced approaches bank holding companies (BHCs) are subject to the common equity tier 1 ratio for the third and fourth quarter of 2014. All bank holding companies are subject to the common equity tier 1 ratio for each quarter of 2015 and 2016. An advanced approaches BHC includes any BHC that has consolidated total assets greater than or equal to $250 billion or consolidated total on-balance sheet foreign exposure of at least $10 billion. See 12 CFR 217.100(b)(1). Other BHCs include any BHC that is subject to 12 CFR 225.8 and is not an advanced approaches BHC.

n/a Not applicable.

Projected loan losses, by type of loan, 2014:Q4–2016:Q4

	Billions of dollars	Portfolio loss rates (%)[1]
Loan losses	3.2	5.7
First-lien mortgages, domestic	0.4	2.9
Junior liens and HELOCs, domestic	0.2	6.8
Commercial and industrial[2]	0.8	4.6
Commercial real estate, domestic	1.5	12.5
Credit cards	0.1	14.4
Other consumer[3]	0.1	4.0
Other loans[4]	0.1	1.5

[1] Average loan balances used to calculate portfolio loss rates exclude loans held for sale and loans held for investment under the fair-value option and are calculated over nine quarters.

[2] Commercial and industrial loans include small- and medium-enterprise loans and corporate cards.

[3] Other consumer loans include student loans and automobile loans.

[4] Other loans include international real estate loans.

Actual 2014:Q3 and projected 2016:Q4 risk-weighted assets

	Actual 2014:Q3	Projected 2016:Q4	
		General approach	Standardized approach
Risk-weighted assets (billions of dollars)[1]	62.0	63.7	61.5

[1] For each quarter in 2014, risk-weighted assets are calculated using the general risk-based capital approach set forth in 12 CFR 225, appendix A. For each quarter in 2015 and 2016, risk-weighted assets are calculated under the Board's standardized capital risk-based approach in 12 CFR 217, subpart D, except for the risk-weighted assets used to calculate the tier 1 common ratio, which uses the general risk-based capital approach for all quarters.

Projected losses, revenue, net income and other comprehensive income through 2016:Q4

	Billions of dollars	Percent of average assets[1]
Pre-provision net revenue[2]	1.1	1.4
Other revenue[3]	0.0	
less		
Provisions	3.8	
Realized losses/gains on securities (AFS/HTM)	0.1	
Trading and counterparty losses[4]	0.0	
Other losses/gains[5]	0.1	
equals		
Net income before taxes	-2.8	-3.4
Memo items		
Other comprehensive income[6]	0.0	
Other effects on capital	*Actual 2014:Q3*	*2016:Q4*
AOCI included in capital (billions of dollars)[7]	n/a	0.0

[1] Average assets is the nine-quarter average of total assets.

[2] Pre-provision net revenue includes losses from operational-risk events, mortgage repurchase expenses, and other real estate owned (OREO) costs.

[3] Other revenue includes one-time income and (expense) items not included in pre-provision net revenue.

[4] Trading and counterparty losses include mark-to-market and credit valuation adjustments (CVA) losses and losses arising from the counterparty default scenario component applied to derivatives, securities lending, and repurchase agreement activities.

[5] Other losses/gains includes projected change in fair value of loans held for sale and loans held for investment measured under the fair-value option, and goodwill impairment losses.

[6] Other comprehensive income (OCI) is only calculated for advanced approaches BHCs, and other BHCs that opt into the advanced approaches treatment of AOCI.

[7] Certain AOCI items are subject to transition into projected regulatory capital. Those transitions are 20 percent included in projected regulatory capital for 2014, 40 percent included in projected regulatory capital for 2015, and 60 percent included in projected regulatory capital for 2016.

Table C.6.B. BBVA Compass Bancshares, Inc.
Projected stressed capital ratios, risk-weighted assets, losses, revenues, net income before taxes, and loan losses
Federal Reserve estimates: Adverse scenario

Actual 2014:Q3 projected stressed capital ratios through 2016:Q4

	Actual 2014:Q3	Stressed capital ratios[1]	
		Ending	Minimum
Tier 1 common ratio (%)	11.0	9.5	9.5
Common equity tier 1 capital ratio (%)[2]	n/a	10.0	10.0
Tier 1 risk-based capital ratio (%)	11.3	10.0	10.0
Total risk-based capital ratio (%)	13.3	11.7	11.7
Tier 1 leverage ratio (%)	9.6	7.8	7.8

[1] The capital ratios are calculated using capital action assumptions provided within the Dodd-Frank Act stress testing rule. These projections represent hypothetical estimates that involve an economic outcome that is more adverse than expected. These estimates are not forecasts of expected losses, revenues, net income before taxes, or capital ratios. The minimum capital ratio presented is for the period 2014:Q4 to 2016:Q4.

[2] Advanced approaches bank holding companies (BHCs) are subject to the common equity tier 1 ratio for the third and fourth quarter of 2014. All bank holding companies are subject to the common equity tier 1 ratio for each quarter of 2015 and 2016. An advanced approaches BHC includes any BHC that has consolidated total assets greater than or equal to $250 billion or consolidated total on-balance sheet foreign exposure of at least $10 billion. See 12 CFR 217.100(b)(1). Other BHCs include any BHC that is subject to 12 CFR 225.8 and is not an advanced approaches BHC.

n/a Not applicable.

Projected loan losses, by type of loan, 2014:Q4–2016:Q4

	Billions of dollars	Portfolio loss rates (%)[1]
Loan losses	2.0	3.5
First-lien mortgages, domestic	0.3	2.0
Junior liens and HELOCs, domestic	0.1	5.2
Commercial and industrial[2]	0.5	2.8
Commercial real estate, domestic	0.9	7.2
Credit cards	0.1	11.9
Other consumer[3]	0.1	3.0
Other loans[4]	0.1	0.9

[1] Average loan balances used to calculate portfolio loss rates exclude loans held for sale and loans held for investment under the fair-value option and are calculated over nine quarters.

[2] Commercial and industrial loans include small- and medium-enterprise loans and corporate cards.

[3] Other consumer loans include student loans and automobile loans.

[4] Other loans include international real estate loans.

Actual 2014:Q3 and projected 2016:Q4 risk-weighted assets

	Actual 2014:Q3	Projected 2016:Q4	
		General approach	Standardized approach
Risk-weighted assets (billions of dollars)[1]	62.0	66.4	63.3

[1] For each quarter in 2014, risk-weighted assets are calculated using the general risk-based capital approach set forth in 12 CFR 225, appendix A. For each quarter in 2015 and 2016, risk-weighted assets are calculated under the Board's standardized capital risk-based approach in 12 CFR 217, subpart D, except for the risk-weighted assets used to calculate the tier 1 common ratio, which uses the general risk-based capital approach for all quarters.

Projected losses, revenue, net income and other comprehensive income through 2016:Q4

	Billions of dollars	Percent of average assets[1]
Pre-provision net revenue[2]	1.8	2.1
Other revenue[3]	0.0	
less		
Provisions	2.2	
Realized losses/gains on securities (AFS/HTM)	0.0	
Trading and counterparty losses[4]	0.0	
Other losses/gains[5]	0.0	
equals		
Net income before taxes	-0.4	-0.5
Memo items		
Other comprehensive income[6]	0.0	
Other effects on capital	Actual 2014:Q3	2016:Q4
AOCI included in capital (billions of dollars)[7]	n/a	0.0

[1] Average assets is the nine-quarter average of total assets.

[2] Pre-provision net revenue includes losses from operational-risk events, mortgage repurchase expenses, and other real estate owned (OREO) costs.

[3] Other revenue includes one-time income and (expense) items not included in pre-provision net revenue.

[4] Trading and counterparty losses include mark-to-market and credit valuation adjustments (CVA) losses and losses arising from the counterparty default scenario component applied to derivatives, securities lending, and repurchase agreement activities.

[5] Other losses/gains includes projected change in fair value of loans held for sale and loans held for investment measured under the fair-value option, and goodwill impairment losses.

[6] Other comprehensive income (OCI) is only calculated for advanced approaches BHCs, and other BHCs that opt into the advanced approaches treatment of AOCI.

[7] Certain AOCI items are subject to transition into projected regulatory capital. Those transitions are 20 percent included in projected regulatory capital for 2014, 40 percent included in projected regulatory capital for 2015, and 60 percent included in projected regulatory capital for 2016.

Table C.7.A. BMO Financial Corp.
Projected stressed capital ratios, risk-weighted assets, losses, revenues, net income before taxes, and loan losses
Federal Reserve estimates: Severely adverse scenario

Actual 2014:Q3 projected stressed capital ratios through 2016:Q4

	Actual 2014:Q3	Stressed capital ratios[1]	
		Ending	Minimum
Tier 1 common ratio (%)	11.5	9.0	9.0
Common equity tier 1 capital ratio (%)[2]	n/a	7.4	7.4
Tier 1 risk-based capital ratio (%)	11.5	7.4	7.4
Total risk-based capital ratio (%)	15.5	10.3	10.3
Tier 1 leverage ratio (%)	8.3	5.2	5.2

[1] The capital ratios are calculated using capital action assumptions provided within the Dodd-Frank Act stress testing rule. These projections represent hypothetical estimates that involve an economic outcome that is more adverse than expected. These estimates are not forecasts of expected losses, revenues, net income before taxes, or capital ratios. The minimum capital ratio presented is for the period 2014:Q4 to 2016:Q4.

[2] Advanced approaches bank holding companies (BHCs) are subject to the common equity tier 1 ratio for the third and fourth quarter of 2014. All bank holding companies are subject to the common equity tier 1 ratio for each quarter of 2015 and 2016. An advanced approaches BHC includes any BHC that has consolidated total assets greater than or equal to $250 billion or consolidated total on-balance sheet foreign exposure of at least $10 billion. See 12 CFR 217.100(b)(1). Other BHCs include any BHC that is subject to 12 CFR 225.8 and is not an advanced approaches BHC.

n/a Not applicable.

Projected loan losses, by type of loan, 2014:Q4–2016:Q4

	Billions of dollars	Portfolio loss rates (%)[1]
Loan losses	2.7	4.6
First-lien mortgages, domestic	0.3	3.5
Junior liens and HELOCs, domestic	0.3	5.0
Commercial and industrial[2]	0.8	4.8
Commercial real estate, domestic	0.7	7.9
Credit cards	0.0	10.7
Other consumer[3]	0.2	2.8
Other loans[4]	0.4	3.4

[1] Average loan balances used to calculate portfolio loss rates exclude loans held for sale and loans held for investment under the fair-value option and are calculated over nine quarters.

[2] Commercial and industrial loans include small- and medium-enterprise loans and corporate cards.

[3] Other consumer loans include student loans and automobile loans.

[4] Other loans include international real estate loans.

Actual 2014:Q3 and projected 2016:Q4 risk-weighted assets

	Actual 2014:Q3	Projected 2016:Q4	
		General approach	Standardized approach
Risk-weighted assets (billions of dollars)[1]	78.3	81.1	81.4

[1] For each quarter in 2014, risk-weighted assets are calculated using the general risk-based capital approach set forth in 12 CFR 225, appendix A. For each quarter in 2015 and 2016, risk-weighted assets are calculated under the Board's standardized capital risk-based approach in 12 CFR 217, subpart D, except for the risk-weighted assets used to calculate the tier 1 common ratio, which uses the general risk-based capital approach for all quarters.

Projected losses, revenue, net income and other comprehensive income through 2016:Q4

	Billions of dollars	Percent of average assets[1]
Pre-provision net revenue[2]	1.1	0.9
Other revenue[3]	0.0	
less		
Provisions	2.8	
Realized losses/gains on securities (AFS/HTM)	0.0	
Trading and counterparty losses[4]	0.0	
Other losses/gains[5]	0.0	
equals		
Net income before taxes	-1.7	-1.4
Memo items		
Other comprehensive income[6]	0.0	
Other effects on capital	*Actual 2014:Q3*	*2016:Q4*
AOCI included in capital (billions of dollars)[7]	n/a	0.0

[1] Average assets is the nine-quarter average of total assets.

[2] Pre-provision net revenue includes losses from operational-risk events, mortgage repurchase expenses, and other real estate owned (OREO) costs.

[3] Other revenue includes one-time income and (expense) items not included in pre-provision net revenue.

[4] Trading and counterparty losses include mark-to-market and credit valuation adjustments (CVA) losses and losses arising from the counterparty default scenario component applied to derivatives, securities lending, and repurchase agreement activities.

[5] Other losses/gains includes projected change in fair value of loans held for sale and loans held for investment measured under the fair-value option, and goodwill impairment losses.

[6] Other comprehensive income (OCI) is only calculated for advanced approaches BHCs, and other BHCs that opt into the advanced approaches treatment of AOCI.

[7] Certain AOCI items are subject to transition into projected regulatory capital. Those transitions are 20 percent included in projected regulatory capital for 2014, 40 percent included in projected regulatory capital for 2015, and 60 percent included in projected regulatory capital for 2016.

Table C.7.B. BMO Financial Corp.

Projected stressed capital ratios, risk-weighted assets, losses, revenues, net income before taxes, and loan losses

Federal Reserve estimates: Adverse scenario

Actual 2014:Q3 projected stressed capital ratios through 2016:Q4

	Actual 2014:Q3	Stressed capital ratios[1]	
		Ending	Minimum
Tier 1 common ratio (%)	11.5	12.4	11.5
Common equity tier 1 capital ratio (%)[2]	n/a	11.5	10.5
Tier 1 risk-based capital ratio (%)	11.5	11.5	10.5
Total risk-based capital ratio (%)	15.5	13.9	13.9
Tier 1 leverage ratio (%)	8.3	7.9	7.4

[1] The capital ratios are calculated using capital action assumptions provided within the Dodd-Frank Act stress testing rule. These projections represent hypothetical estimates that involve an economic outcome that is more adverse than expected. These estimates are not forecasts of expected losses, revenues, net income before taxes, or capital ratios. The minimum capital ratio presented is for the period 2014:Q4 to 2016:Q4.

[2] Advanced approaches bank holding companies (BHCs) are subject to the common equity tier 1 ratio for the third and fourth quarter of 2014. All bank holding companies are subject to the common equity tier 1 ratio for each quarter of 2015 and 2016. An advanced approaches BHC includes any BHC that has consolidated total assets greater than or equal to $250 billion or consolidated total on-balance sheet foreign exposure of at least $10 billion. See 12 CFR 217.100(b)(1). Other BHCs include any BHC that is subject to 12 CFR 225.8 and is not an advanced approaches BHC.

n/a Not applicable.

Projected loan losses, by type of loan, 2014:Q4–2016:Q4

	Billions of dollars	Portfolio loss rates (%)[1]
Loan losses	1.7	2.9
First-lien mortgages, domestic	0.2	2.7
Junior liens and HELOCs, domestic	0.2	3.0
Commercial and industrial[2]	0.5	2.8
Commercial real estate, domestic	0.4	4.9
Credit cards	0.0	8.5
Other consumer[3]	0.2	2.2
Other loans[4]	0.2	1.9

[1] Average loan balances used to calculate portfolio loss rates exclude loans held for sale and loans held for investment under the fair-value option and are calculated over nine quarters.

[2] Commercial and industrial loans include small- and medium-enterprise loans and corporate cards.

[3] Other consumer loans include student loans and automobile loans.

[4] Other loans include international real estate loans.

Actual 2014:Q3 and projected 2016:Q4 risk-weighted assets

	Actual 2014:Q3	Projected 2016:Q4	
		General approach	Standardized approach
Risk-weighted assets (billions of dollars)[1]	78.3	83.9	85.2

[1] For each quarter in 2014, risk-weighted assets are calculated using the general risk-based capital approach set forth in 12 CFR 225, appendix A. For each quarter in 2015 and 2016, risk-weighted assets are calculated under the Board's standardized capital risk-based approach in 12 CFR 217, subpart D, except for the risk-weighted assets used to calculate the tier 1 common ratio, which uses the general risk-based capital approach for all quarters.

Projected losses, revenue, net income and other comprehensive income through 2016:Q4

	Billions of dollars	Percent of average assets[1]
Pre-provision net revenue[2]	2.4	1.9
Other revenue[3]	0.0	
less		
Provisions	1.5	
Realized losses/gains on securities (AFS/HTM)	0.0	
Trading and counterparty losses[4]	0.0	
Other losses/gains[5]	0.0	
equals		
Net income before taxes	0.9	0.7
Memo items		
Other comprehensive income[6]	0.0	
Other effects on capital	Actual 2014:Q3	2016:Q4
AOCI included in capital (billions of dollars)[7]	n/a	0.0

[1] Average assets is the nine-quarter average of total assets.

[2] Pre-provision net revenue includes losses from operational-risk events, mortgage repurchase expenses, and other real estate owned (OREO) costs.

[3] Other revenue includes one-time income and (expense) items not included in pre-provision net revenue.

[4] Trading and counterparty losses include mark-to-market and credit valuation adjustments (CVA) losses and losses arising from the counterparty default scenario component applied to derivatives, securities lending, and repurchase agreement activities.

[5] Other losses/gains includes projected change in fair value of loans held for sale and loans held for investment measured under the fair-value option, and goodwill impairment losses.

[6] Other comprehensive income (OCI) is only calculated for advanced approaches BHCs, and other BHCs that opt into the advanced approaches treatment of AOCI.

[7] Certain AOCI items are subject to transition into projected regulatory capital. Those transitions are 20 percent included in projected regulatory capital for 2014, 40 percent included in projected regulatory capital for 2015, and 60 percent included in projected regulatory capital for 2016.

Table C.8.A. Capital One Financial Corporation
Projected stressed capital ratios, risk-weighted assets, losses, revenues, net income before taxes, and loan losses
Federal Reserve estimates: Severely adverse scenario

Actual 2014:Q3 projected stressed capital ratios through 2016:Q4

	Actual 2014:Q3	Stressed capital ratios[1]	
		Ending	Minimum
Tier 1 common ratio (%)	12.7	9.5	9.5
Common equity tier 1 capital ratio (%)[2]	12.7	9.4	9.4
Tier 1 risk-based capital ratio (%)	13.3	10.1	10.1
Total risk-based capital ratio (%)	15.2	11.8	11.8
Tier 1 leverage ratio (%)	10.6	7.9	7.9

[1] The capital ratios are calculated using capital action assumptions provided within the Dodd-Frank Act stress testing rule. These projections represent hypothetical estimates that involve an economic outcome that is more adverse than expected. These estimates are not forecasts of expected losses, revenues, net income before taxes, or capital ratios. The minimum capital ratio presented is for the period 2014:Q4 to 2016:Q4.

[2] Advanced approaches bank holding companies (BHCs) are subject to the common equity tier 1 ratio for the third and fourth quarter of 2014. All bank holding companies are subject to the common equity tier 1 ratio for each quarter of 2015 and 2016. An advanced approaches BHC includes any BHC that has consolidated total assets greater than or equal to $250 billion or consolidated total on-balance sheet foreign exposure of at least $10 billion. See 12 CFR 217.100(b)(1). Other BHCs include any BHC that is subject to 12 CFR 225.8 and is not an advanced approaches BHC.

Projected loan losses, by type of loan, 2014:Q4–2016:Q4

	Billions of dollars	Portfolio loss rates (%)[1]
Loan losses	22.2	10.8
First-lien mortgages, domestic	0.8	2.5
Junior liens and HELOCs, domestic	0.2	7.5
Commercial and industrial[2]	1.7	7.6
Commercial real estate, domestic	1.5	6.4
Credit cards	14.2	18.5
Other consumer[3]	3.3	8.8
Other loans[4]	0.5	3.8

[1] Average loan balances used to calculate portfolio loss rates exclude loans held for sale and loans held for investment under the fair-value option and are calculated over nine quarters.

[2] Commercial and industrial loans include small- and medium-enterprise loans and corporate cards.

[3] Other consumer loans include student loans and automobile loans.

[4] Other loans include international real estate loans.

Actual 2014:Q3 and projected 2016:Q4 risk-weighted assets

	Actual 2014:Q3	Projected 2016:Q4	
		General approach	Standardized approach
Risk-weighted assets (billions of dollars)[1]	228.8	234.6	241.9

[1] For each quarter in 2014, risk-weighted assets are calculated using the general risk-based capital approach set forth in 12 CFR 225, appendix A. For each quarter in 2015 and 2016, risk-weighted assets are calculated under the Board's standardized capital risk-based approach in 12 CFR 217, subpart D, except for the risk-weighted assets used to calculate the tier 1 common ratio, which uses the general risk-based capital approach for all quarters.

Projected losses, revenue, net income and other comprehensive income through 2016:Q4

	Billions of dollars	Percent of average assets[1]
Pre-provision net revenue[2]	21.7	7.0
Other revenue[3]	0.0	
less		
Provisions	25.9	
Realized losses/gains on securities (AFS/HTM)	0.1	
Trading and counterparty losses[4]	0.0	
Other losses/gains[5]	0.1	
equals		
Net income before taxes	-4.4	-1.4
Memo items		
Other comprehensive income[6]	-0.1	
Other effects on capital	*Actual 2014:Q3*	*2016:Q4*
AOCI included in capital (billions of dollars)[7]	-0.1	-0.3

[1] Average assets is the nine-quarter average of total assets.

[2] Pre-provision net revenue includes losses from operational-risk events, mortgage repurchase expenses, and other real estate owned (OREO) costs.

[3] Other revenue includes one-time income and (expense) items not included in pre-provision net revenue.

[4] Trading and counterparty losses include mark-to-market and credit valuation adjustments (CVA) losses and losses arising from the counterparty default scenario component applied to derivatives, securities lending, and repurchase agreement activities.

[5] Other losses/gains includes projected change in fair value of loans held for sale and loans held for investment measured under the fair-value option and goodwill impairment losses.

[6] Other comprehensive income (OCI) is only calculated for advanced approaches BHCs, and other BHCs that opt into the advanced approaches treatment of AOCI.

[7] Certain AOCI items are subject to transition into projected regulatory capital. Those transitions are 20 percent included in projected regulatory capital for 2014, 40 percent included in projected regulatory capital for 2015, and 60 percent included in projected regulatory capital for 2016.

Table C.8.B. Capital One Financial Corporation
Projected stressed capital ratios, risk-weighted assets, losses, revenues, net income before taxes, and loan losses
Federal Reserve estimates: Adverse scenario

Actual 2014:Q3 projected stressed capital ratios through 2016:Q4

	Actual 2014:Q3	Stressed capital ratios[1]	
		Ending	Minimum
Tier 1 common ratio (%)	12.7	11.5	11.5
Common equity tier 1 capital ratio (%)[2]	12.7	10.4	10.4
Tier 1 risk-based capital ratio (%)	13.3	11.1	11.1
Total risk-based capital ratio (%)	15.2	12.8	12.8
Tier 1 leverage ratio (%)	10.6	8.5	8.5

[1] The capital ratios are calculated using capital action assumptions provided within the Dodd-Frank Act stress testing rule. These projections represent hypothetical estimates that involve an economic outcome that is more adverse than expected. These estimates are not forecasts of expected losses, revenues, net income before taxes, or capital ratios. The minimum capital ratio presented is for the period 2014:Q4 to 2016:Q4.

[2] Advanced approaches bank holding companies (BHCs) are subject to the common equity tier 1 ratio for the third and fourth quarter of 2014. All bank holding companies are subject to the common equity tier 1 ratio for each quarter of 2015 and 2016. An advanced approaches BHC includes any BHC that has consolidated total assets greater than or equal to $250 billion or consolidated total on-balance sheet foreign exposure of at least $10 billion. See 12 CFR 217.100(b)(1). Other BHCs include any BHC that is subject to 12 CFR 225.8 and is not an advanced approaches BHC.

Projected loan losses, by type of loan, 2014:Q4–2016:Q4

	Billions of dollars	Portfolio loss rates (%)[1]
Loan losses	17.2	8.3
First-lien mortgages, domestic	0.5	1.5
Junior liens and HELOCs, domestic	0.1	5.6
Commercial and industrial[2]	1.1	5.0
Commercial real estate, domestic	0.9	3.9
Credit cards	11.8	15.1
Other consumer[3]	2.5	6.5
Other loans[4]	0.3	2.0

[1] Average loan balances used to calculate portfolio loss rates exclude loans held for sale and loans held for investment under the fair-value option and are calculated over nine quarters.

[2] Commercial and industrial loans include small- and medium-enterprise loans and corporate cards.

[3] Other consumer loans include student loans and automobile loans.

[4] Other loans include international real estate loans.

Actual 2014:Q3 and projected 2016:Q4 risk-weighted assets

	Actual 2014:Q3	Projected 2016:Q4	
		General approach	Standardized approach
Risk-weighted assets (billions of dollars)[1]	228.8	245.0	249.5

[1] For each quarter in 2014, risk-weighted assets are calculated using the general risk-based capital approach set forth in 12 CFR 225, appendix A. For each quarter in 2015 and 2016, risk-weighted assets are calculated under the Board's standardized capital risk-based approach in 12 CFR 217, subpart D, except for the risk-weighted assets used to calculate the tier 1 common ratio, which uses the general risk-based capital approach for all quarters.

Projected losses, revenue, net income and other comprehensive income through 2016:Q4

	Billions of dollars	Percent of average assets[1]
Pre-provision net revenue[2]	23.1	7.3
Other revenue[3]	0.0	
less		
Provisions	20.1	
Realized losses/gains on securities (AFS/HTM)	0.0	
Trading and counterparty losses[4]	0.0	
Other losses/gains[5]	0.1	
equals		
Net income before taxes	2.9	0.9
Memo items		
Other comprehensive income[6]	-2.5	
Other effects on capital	Actual 2014:Q3	2016:Q4
AOCI included in capital (billions of dollars)[7]	-0.1	-1.8

[1] Average assets is the nine-quarter average of total assets.

[2] Pre-provision net revenue includes losses from operational-risk events, mortgage repurchase expenses, and other real estate owned (OREO) costs.

[3] Other revenue includes one-time income and (expense) items not included in pre-provision net revenue.

[4] Trading and counterparty losses include mark-to-market and credit valuation adjustments (CVA) losses and losses arising from the counterparty default scenario component applied to derivatives, securities lending, and repurchase agreement activities.

[5] Other losses/gains includes projected change in fair value of loans held for sale and loans held for investment measured under the fair-value option and goodwill impairment losses.

[6] Other comprehensive income (OCI) is only calculated for advanced approaches BHCs, and other BHCs that opt into the advanced approaches treatment of AOCI.

[7] Certain AOCI items are subject to transition into projected regulatory capital. Those transitions are 20 percent included in projected regulatory capital for 2014, 40 percent included in projected regulatory capital for 2015, and 60 percent included in projected regulatory capital for 2016.

Table C.9.A. Citigroup Inc.
Projected stressed capital ratios, risk-weighted assets, losses, revenues, net income before taxes, and loan losses
Federal Reserve estimates: Severely adverse scenario

Actual 2014:Q3 projected stressed capital ratios through 2016:Q4

	Actual 2014:Q3	Stressed capital ratios[1]	
		Ending	Minimum
Tier 1 common ratio (%)	13.4	8.2	8.2
Common equity tier 1 capital ratio (%)[2]	15.1	7.1	6.8
Tier 1 risk-based capital ratio (%)	15.1	7.1	6.8
Total risk-based capital ratio (%)	17.7	9.5	9.2
Tier 1 leverage ratio (%)	9.0	4.7	4.6

[1]   The capital ratios are calculated using capital action assumptions provided within the Dodd-Frank Act stress testing rule. These projections represent hypothetical estimates that involve an economic outcome that is more adverse than expected. These estimates are not forecasts of expected losses, revenues, net income before taxes, or capital ratios. The minimum capital ratio presented is for the period 2014:Q4 to 2016:Q4.

[2]   Advanced approaches bank holding companies (BHCs) are subject to the common equity tier 1 ratio for the third and fourth quarter of 2014. All bank holding companies are subject to the common equity tier 1 ratio for each quarter of 2015 and 2016. An advanced approaches BHC includes any BHC that has consolidated total assets greater than or equal to $250 billion or consolidated total on-balance sheet foreign exposure of at least $10 billion. See 12 CFR 217.100(b)(1). Other BHCs include any BHC that is subject to 12 CFR 225.8 and is not an advanced approaches BHC.

Projected loan losses, by type of loan, 2014:Q4–2016:Q4

	Billions of dollars	Portfolio loss rates (%)[1]
Loan losses	48.3	7.2
First-lien mortgages, domestic	4.4	4.8
Junior liens and HELOCs, domestic	3.5	11.5
Commercial and industrial[2]	7.4	4.6
Commercial real estate, domestic	1.0	9.1
Credit cards	20.9	15.0
Other consumer[3]	5.9	11.9
Other loans[4]	5.1	2.7

[1]   Average loan balances used to calculate portfolio loss rates exclude loans held for sale and loans held for investment under the fair-value option and are calculated over nine quarters.

[2]   Commercial and industrial loans include small- and medium-enterprise loans and corporate cards.

[3]   Other consumer loans include student loans and automobile loans.

[4]   Other loans include international real estate loans.

Actual 2014:Q3 and projected 2016:Q4 risk-weighted assets

	Actual 2014:Q3	Projected 2016:Q4	
		General approach	Standardized approach
Risk-weighted assets (billions of dollars)[1]	1,103.6	1,136.9	1,304.2

[1]   For each quarter in 2014, risk-weighted assets are calculated using the general risk-based capital approach set forth in 12 CFR 225, appendix A. For each quarter in 2015 and 2016, risk-weighted assets are calculated under the Board's standardized capital risk-based approach in 12 CFR 217, subpart D, except for the risk-weighted assets used to calculate the tier 1 common ratio, which uses the general risk-based capital approach for all quarters.

Projected losses, revenue, net income and other comprehensive income through 2016:Q4

	Billions of dollars	Percent of average assets[1]
Pre-provision net revenue[2]	29.1	1.5
Other revenue[3]	0.0	
less		
Provisions	50.3	
Realized losses/gains on securities (AFS/HTM)	3.4	
Trading and counterparty losses[4]	18.5	
Other losses/gains[5]	5.3	
equals		
Net income before taxes	-48.4	-2.5
Memo items		
Other comprehensive income[6]	-5.6	
Other effects on capital	Actual 2014:Q3	2016:Q4
AOCI included in capital (billions of dollars)[7]	-15.4	-20.5

[1]   Average assets is the nine-quarter average of total assets.

[2]   Pre-provision net revenue includes losses from operational-risk events, mortgage repurchase expenses, and other real estate owned (OREO) costs.

[3]   Other revenue includes one-time income and (expense) items not included in pre-provision net revenue.

[4]   Trading and counterparty losses include mark-to-market and credit valuation adjustments (CVA) losses and losses arising from the counterparty default scenario component applied to derivatives, securities lending, and repurchase agreement activities.

[5]   Other losses/gains includes projected change in fair value of loans held for sale and loans held for investment measured under the fair-value option and goodwill impairment losses.

[6]   Other comprehensive income (OCI) is only calculated for advanced approaches BHCs, and other BHCs that opt into the advanced approaches treatment of AOCI.

[7]   Certain AOCI items are subject to transition into projected regulatory capital. Those transitions are 20 percent included in projected regulatory capital for 2014, 40 percent included in projected regulatory capital for 2015, and 60 percent included in projected regulatory capital for 2016.

Table C.9.B. Citigroup Inc.
Projected stressed capital ratios, risk-weighted assets, losses, revenues, net income before taxes, and loan losses
Federal Reserve estimates: Adverse scenario

Actual 2014:Q3 projected stressed capital ratios through 2016:Q4

	Actual 2014:Q3	Stressed capital ratios[1]	
		Ending	Minimum
Tier 1 common ratio (%)	13.4	12.5	11.5
Common equity tier 1 capital ratio (%)[2]	15.1	9.4	9.3
Tier 1 risk-based capital ratio (%)	15.1	9.6	9.4
Total risk-based capital ratio (%)	17.7	11.8	11.7
Tier 1 leverage ratio (%)	9.0	6.2	6.1

[1] The capital ratios are calculated using capital action assumptions provided within the Dodd-Frank Act stress testing rule. These projections represent hypothetical estimates that involve an economic outcome that is more adverse than expected. These estimates are not forecasts of expected losses, revenues, net income before taxes, or capital ratios. The minimum capital ratio presented is for the period 2014:Q4 to 2016:Q4.

[2] Advanced approaches bank holding companies (BHCs) are subject to the common equity tier 1 ratio for the third and fourth quarter of 2014. All bank holding companies are subject to the common equity tier 1 ratio for each quarter of 2015 and 2016. An advanced approaches BHC includes any BHC that has consolidated total assets greater than or equal to $250 billion or consolidated total on-balance sheet foreign exposure of at least $10 billion. See 12 CFR 217.100(b)(1). Other BHCs include any BHC that is subject to 12 CFR 225.8 and is not an advanced approaches BHC.

Projected loan losses, by type of loan, 2014:Q4–2016:Q4

	Billions of dollars	Portfolio loss rates (%)[1]
Loan losses	36.0	5.3
First-lien mortgages, domestic	3.0	3.3
Junior liens and HELOCs, domestic	2.3	7.3
Commercial and industrial[2]	4.8	3.0
Commercial real estate, domestic	0.5	5.1
Credit cards	17.0	12.1
Other consumer[3]	5.2	10.3
Other loans[4]	3.1	1.6

[1] Average loan balances used to calculate portfolio loss rates exclude loans held for sale and loans held for investment under the fair-value option and are calculated over nine quarters.

[2] Commercial and industrial loans include small- and medium-enterprise loans and corporate cards.

[3] Other consumer loans include student loans and automobile loans.

[4] Other loans include international real estate loans.

Actual 2014:Q3 and projected 2016:Q4 risk-weighted assets

	Actual 2014:Q3	Projected 2016:Q4	
		General approach	Standardized approach
Risk-weighted assets (billions of dollars)[1]	1,103.6	1,175.6	1,351.3

[1] For each quarter in 2014, risk-weighted assets are calculated using the general risk-based capital approach set forth in 12 CFR 225, appendix A. For each quarter in 2015 and 2016, risk-weighted assets are calculated under the Board's standardized capital risk-based approach in 12 CFR 217, subpart D, except for the risk-weighted assets used to calculate the tier 1 common ratio, which uses the general risk-based capital approach for all quarters.

Projected losses, revenue, net income and other comprehensive income through 2016:Q4

	Billions of dollars	Percent of average assets[1]
Pre-provision net revenue[2]	50.9	2.5
Other revenue[3]	0.0	
less		
Provisions	34.8	
Realized losses/gains on securities (AFS/HTM)	2.0	
Trading and counterparty losses[4]	10.1	
Other losses/gains[5]	3.5	
equals		
Net income before taxes	0.5	0.0
Memo items		
Other comprehensive income[6]	-20.2	
Other effects on capital	Actual 2014:Q3	2016:Q4
AOCI included in capital (billions of dollars)[7]	-15.4	-29.3

[1] Average assets is the nine-quarter average of total assets.

[2] Pre-provision net revenue includes losses from operational-risk events, mortgage repurchase expenses, and other real estate owned (OREO) costs.

[3] Other revenue includes one-time income and (expense) items not included in pre-provision net revenue.

[4] Trading and counterparty losses include mark-to-market and credit valuation adjustments (CVA) losses and losses arising from the counterparty default scenario component applied to derivatives, securities lending, and repurchase agreement activities.

[5] Other losses/gains includes projected change in fair value of loans held for sale and loans held for investment measured under the fair-value option and goodwill impairment losses.

[6] Other comprehensive income (OCI) is only calculated for advanced approaches BHCs, and other BHCs that opt into the advanced approaches treatment of AOCI.

[7] Certain AOCI items are subject to transition into projected regulatory capital. Those transitions are 20 percent included in projected regulatory capital for 2014, 40 percent included in projected regulatory capital for 2015, and 60 percent included in projected regulatory capital for 2016.

Table C.10.A. Citizens Financial Group, Inc.
Projected stressed capital ratios, risk-weighted assets, losses, revenues, net income before taxes, and loan losses
Federal Reserve estimates: Severely adverse scenario

Actual 2014:Q3 projected stressed capital ratios through 2016:Q4

	Actual 2014:Q3	Stressed capital ratios[1]	
		Ending	Minimum
Tier 1 common ratio (%)	12.9	10.7	10.7
Common equity tier 1 capital ratio (%)[2]	n/a	10.9	10.9
Tier 1 risk-based capital ratio (%)	12.9	10.9	10.9
Total risk-based capital ratio (%)	16.1	14.3	14.3
Tier 1 leverage ratio (%)	10.9	8.8	8.8

[1] The capital ratios are calculated using capital action assumptions provided within the Dodd-Frank Act stress testing rule. These projections represent hypothetical estimates that involve an economic outcome that is more adverse than expected. These estimates are not forecasts of expected losses, revenues, net income before taxes, or capital ratios. The minimum capital ratio presented is for the period 2014:Q4 to 2016:Q4.

[2] Advanced approaches bank holding companies (BHCs) are subject to the common equity tier 1 ratio for the third and fourth quarter of 2014. All bank holding companies are subject to the common equity tier 1 ratio for each quarter of 2015 and 2016. An advanced approaches BHC includes any BHC that has consolidated total assets greater than or equal to $250 billion or consolidated total on-balance sheet foreign exposure of at least $10 billion. See 12 CFR 217.100(b)(1). Other BHCs include any BHC that is subject to 12 CFR 225.8 and is not an advanced approaches BHC.

n/a Not applicable.

Projected loan losses, by type of loan, 2014:Q4–2016:Q4

	Billions of dollars	Portfolio loss rates (%)[1]
Loan losses	4.8	5.1
First-lien mortgages, domestic	0.4	2.8
Junior liens and HELOCs, domestic	1.4	7.2
Commercial and industrial[2]	1.0	3.9
Commercial real estate, domestic	1.2	11.3
Credit cards	0.2	12.5
Other consumer[3]	0.5	3.4
Other loans[4]	0.1	1.9

[1] Average loan balances used to calculate portfolio loss rates exclude loans held for sale and loans held for investment under the fair-value option and are calculated over nine quarters.

[2] Commercial and industrial loans include small- and medium-enterprise loans and corporate cards.

[3] Other consumer loans include student loans and automobile loans.

[4] Other loans include international real estate loans.

Actual 2014:Q3 and projected 2016:Q4 risk-weighted assets

	Actual 2014:Q3	Projected 2016:Q4	
		General approach	Standardized approach
Risk-weighted assets (billions of dollars)[1]	103.2	107.1	105.8

[1] For each quarter in 2014, risk-weighted assets are calculated using the general risk-based capital approach set forth in 12 CFR 225, appendix A. For each quarter in 2015 and 2016, risk-weighted assets are calculated under the Board's standardized capital risk-based approach in 12 CFR 217, subpart D, except for the risk-weighted assets used to calculate the tier 1 common ratio, which uses the general risk-based capital approach for all quarters.

Projected losses, revenue, net income and other comprehensive income through 2016:Q4

	Billions of dollars	Percent of average assets[1]
Pre-provision net revenue[2]	3.9	2.8
Other revenue[3]	0.0	
less		
Provisions	5.4	
Realized losses/gains on securities (AFS/HTM)	0.2	
Trading and counterparty losses[4]	0.0	
Other losses/gains[5]	0.1	
equals		
Net income before taxes	-1.8	-1.3
Memo items		
Other comprehensive income[6]	0.0	
Other effects on capital	*Actual 2014:Q3*	*2016:Q4*
AOCI included in capital (billions of dollars)[7]	n/a	0.0

[1] Average assets is the nine-quarter average of total assets.

[2] Pre-provision net revenue includes losses from operational-risk events, mortgage repurchase expenses, and other real estate owned (OREO) costs.

[3] Other revenue includes one-time income and (expense) items not included in pre-provision net revenue.

[4] Trading and counterparty losses include mark-to-market and credit valuation adjustments (CVA) losses and losses arising from the counterparty default scenario component applied to derivatives, securities lending, and repurchase agreement activities.

[5] Other losses/gains includes projected change in fair value of loans held for sale and loans held for investment measured under the fair-value option, and goodwill impairment losses.

[6] Other comprehensive income (OCI) is only calculated for advanced approaches BHCs, and other BHCs that opt into the advanced approaches treatment of AOCI.

[7] Certain AOCI items are subject to transition into projected regulatory capital. Those transitions are 20 percent included in projected regulatory capital for 2014, 40 percent included in projected regulatory capital for 2015, and 60 percent included in projected regulatory capital for 2016.

Table C.10.B. Citizens Financial Group, Inc.
Projected stressed capital ratios, risk-weighted assets, losses, revenues, net income before taxes, and loan losses
Federal Reserve estimates: Adverse scenario

Actual 2014:Q3 projected stressed capital ratios through 2016:Q4

	Actual 2014:Q3	Stressed capital ratios[1]	
		Ending	Minimum
Tier 1 common ratio (%)	12.9	12.3	12.1
Common equity tier 1 capital ratio (%)[2]	n/a	12.5	12.3
Tier 1 risk-based capital ratio (%)	12.9	12.5	12.3
Total risk-based capital ratio (%)	16.1	15.9	15.8
Tier 1 leverage ratio (%)	10.9	10.0	9.9

[1] The capital ratios are calculated using capital action assumptions provided within the Dodd-Frank Act stress testing rule. These projections represent hypothetical estimates that involve an economic outcome that is more adverse than expected. These estimates are not forecasts of expected losses, revenues, net income before taxes, or capital ratios. The minimum capital ratio presented is for the period 2014:Q4 to 2016:Q4.

[2] Advanced approaches bank holding companies (BHCs) are subject to the common equity tier 1 ratio for the third and fourth quarter of 2014. All bank holding companies are subject to the common equity tier 1 ratio for each quarter of 2015 and 2016. An advanced approaches BHC includes any BHC that has consolidated total assets greater than or equal to $250 billion or consolidated total on-balance sheet foreign exposure of at least $10 billion. See 12 CFR 217.100(b)(1). Other BHCs include any BHC that is subject to 12 CFR 225.8 and is not an advanced approaches BHC.

n/a Not applicable.

Projected loan losses, by type of loan, 2014:Q4–2016:Q4

	Billions of dollars	Portfolio loss rates (%)[1]
Loan losses	3.3	3.5
First-lien mortgages, domestic	0.3	1.9
Junior liens and HELOCs, domestic	1.1	5.5
Commercial and industrial[2]	0.6	2.3
Commercial real estate, domestic	0.7	6.6
Credit cards	0.2	10.3
Other consumer[3]	0.4	2.7
Other loans[4]	0.1	1.0

[1] Average loan balances used to calculate portfolio loss rates exclude loans held for sale and loans held for investment under the fair-value option and are calculated over nine quarters.

[2] Commercial and industrial loans include small- and medium-enterprise loans and corporate cards.

[3] Other consumer loans include student loans and automobile loans.

[4] Other loans include international real estate loans.

Actual 2014:Q3 and projected 2016:Q4 risk-weighted assets

	Actual 2014:Q3	Projected 2016:Q4	
		General approach	Standardized approach
Risk-weighted assets (billions of dollars)[1]	103.2	110.8	109.1

[1] For each quarter in 2014, risk-weighted assets are calculated using the general risk-based capital approach set forth in 12 CFR 225, appendix A. For each quarter in 2015 and 2016, risk-weighted assets are calculated under the Board's standardized capital risk-based approach in 12 CFR 217, subpart D, except for the risk-weighted assets used to calculate the tier 1 common ratio, which uses the general risk-based capital approach for all quarters.

Projected losses, revenue, net income and other comprehensive income through 2016:Q4

	Billions of dollars	Percent of average assets[1]
Pre-provision net revenue[2]	4.8	3.5
Other revenue[3]	0.0	
less		
Provisions	3.4	
Realized losses/gains on securities (AFS/HTM)	0.0	
Trading and counterparty losses[4]	0.0	
Other losses/gains[5]	0.0	
equals		
Net income before taxes	1.4	1.0
Memo items		
Other comprehensive income[6]	0.0	
Other effects on capital	Actual 2014:Q3	2016:Q4
AOCI included in capital (billions of dollars)[7]	n/a	0.0

[1] Average assets is the nine-quarter average of total assets.

[2] Pre-provision net revenue includes losses from operational-risk events, mortgage repurchase expenses, and other real estate owned (OREO) costs.

[3] Other revenue includes one-time income and (expense) items not included in pre-provision net revenue.

[4] Trading and counterparty losses include mark-to-market and credit valuation adjustments (CVA) losses and losses arising from the counterparty default scenario component applied to derivatives, securities lending, and repurchase agreement activities.

[5] Other losses/gains includes projected change in fair value of loans held for sale and loans held for investment measured under the fair-value option, and goodwill impairment losses.

[6] Other comprehensive income (OCI) is only calculated for advanced approaches BHCs, and other BHCs that opt into the advanced approaches treatment of AOCI.

[7] Certain AOCI items are subject to transition into projected regulatory capital. Those transitions are 20 percent included in projected regulatory capital for 2014, 40 percent included in projected regulatory capital for 2015, and 60 percent included in projected regulatory capital for 2016.

Table C.11.A. Comerica Incorporated
Projected stressed capital ratios, risk-weighted assets, losses, revenues, net income before taxes, and loan losses
Federal Reserve estimates: Severely adverse scenario

Actual 2014:Q3 projected stressed capital ratios through 2016:Q4

	Actual 2014:Q3	Stressed capital ratios[1]	
		Ending	Minimum
Tier 1 common ratio (%)	10.6	9.0	9.0
Common equity tier 1 capital ratio (%)[2]	n/a	8.7	8.7
Tier 1 risk-based capital ratio (%)	10.6	8.7	8.7
Total risk-based capital ratio (%)	12.8	10.5	10.5
Tier 1 leverage ratio (%)	10.8	8.9	8.9

[1] The capital ratios are calculated using capital action assumptions provided within the Dodd-Frank Act stress testing rule. These projections represent hypothetical estimates that involve an economic outcome that is more adverse than expected. These estimates are not forecasts of expected losses, revenues, net income before taxes, or capital ratios. The minimum capital ratio presented is for the period 2014:Q4 to 2016:Q4.

[2] Advanced approaches bank holding companies (BHCs) are subject to the common equity tier 1 ratio for the third and fourth quarter of 2014. All bank holding companies are subject to the common equity tier 1 ratio for each quarter of 2015 and 2016. An advanced approaches BHC includes any BHC that has consolidated total assets greater than or equal to $250 billion or consolidated total on-balance sheet foreign exposure of at least $10 billion. See 12 CFR 217.100(b)(1). Other BHCs include any BHC that is subject to 12 CFR 225.8 and is not an advanced approaches BHC.

n/a Not applicable.

Projected loan losses, by type of loan, 2014:Q4–2016:Q4

	Billions of dollars	Portfolio loss rates (%)[1]
Loan losses	2.2	4.5
First-lien mortgages, domestic	0.1	2.6
Junior liens and HELOCs, domestic	0.1	4.9
Commercial and industrial[2]	0.9	3.0
Commercial real estate, domestic	0.8	7.8
Credit cards	0.0	0.0
Other consumer[3]	0.0	7.8
Other loans[4]	0.4	6.6

[1] Average loan balances used to calculate portfolio loss rates exclude loans held for sale and loans held for investment under the fair-value option and are calculated over nine quarters.

[2] Commercial and industrial loans include small- and medium-enterprise loans and corporate cards.

[3] Other consumer loans include student loans and automobile loans.

[4] Other loans include international real estate loans.

Actual 2014:Q3 and projected 2016:Q4 risk-weighted assets

	Actual 2014:Q3	Projected 2016:Q4	
		General approach	Standardized approach
Risk-weighted assets (billions of dollars)[1]	67.1	69.9	71.7

[1] For each quarter in 2014, risk-weighted assets are calculated using the general risk-based capital approach set forth in 12 CFR 225, appendix A. For each quarter in 2015 and 2016, risk-weighted assets are calculated under the Board's standardized capital risk-based approach in 12 CFR 217, subpart D, except for the risk-weighted assets used to calculate the tier 1 common ratio, which uses the general risk-based capital approach for all quarters.

Projected losses, revenue, net income and other comprehensive income through 2016:Q4

	Billions of dollars	Percent of average assets[1]
Pre-provision net revenue[2]	1.7	2.4
Other revenue[3]	0.0	
less		
Provisions	2.5	
Realized losses/gains on securities (AFS/HTM)	0.0	
Trading and counterparty losses[4]	0.0	
Other losses/gains[5]	0.0	
equals		
Net income before taxes	-0.7	-1.0
Memo items		
Other comprehensive income[6]	0.0	
Other effects on capital	*Actual 2014:Q3*	*2016:Q4*
AOCI included in capital (billions of dollars)[7]	n/a	0.0

[1] Average assets is the nine-quarter average of total assets.

[2] Pre-provision net revenue includes losses from operational-risk events, mortgage repurchase expenses, and other real estate owned (OREO) costs.

[3] Other revenue includes one-time income and (expense) items not included in pre-provision net revenue.

[4] Trading and counterparty losses include mark-to-market and credit valuation adjustments (CVA) losses and losses arising from the counterparty default scenario component applied to derivatives, securities lending, and repurchase agreement activities.

[5] Other losses/gains includes projected change in fair value of loans held for sale and loans held for investment measured under the fair-value option, and goodwill impairment losses.

[6] Other comprehensive income (OCI) is only calculated for advanced approaches BHCs, and other BHCs that opt into the advanced approaches treatment of AOCI.

[7] Certain AOCI items are subject to transition into projected regulatory capital. Those transitions are 20 percent included in projected regulatory capital for 2014, 40 percent included in projected regulatory capital for 2015, and 60 percent included in projected regulatory capital for 2016.

Table C.11.B. Comerica Incorporated
Projected stressed capital ratios, risk-weighted assets, losses, revenues, net income before taxes, and loan losses
Federal Reserve estimates: Adverse scenario

Actual 2014:Q3 projected stressed capital ratios through 2016:Q4

	Actual 2014:Q3	Stressed capital ratios[1]	
		Ending	Minimum
Tier 1 common ratio (%)	10.6	10.9	10.4
Common equity tier 1 capital ratio (%)[2]	n/a	10.7	10.1
Tier 1 risk-based capital ratio (%)	10.6	10.7	10.1
Total risk-based capital ratio (%)	12.8	11.9	11.8
Tier 1 leverage ratio (%)	10.8	10.7	10.4

[1] The capital ratios are calculated using capital action assumptions provided within the Dodd-Frank Act stress testing rule. These projections represent hypothetical estimates that involve an economic outcome that is more adverse than expected. These estimates are not forecasts of expected losses, revenues, net income before taxes, or capital ratios. The minimum capital ratio presented is for the period 2014:Q4 to 2016:Q4.

[2] Advanced approaches bank holding companies (BHCs) are subject to the common equity tier 1 ratio for the third and fourth quarter of 2014. All bank holding companies are subject to the common equity tier 1 ratio for each quarter of 2015 and 2016. An advanced approaches BHC includes any BHC that has consolidated total assets greater than or equal to $250 billion or consolidated total on-balance sheet foreign exposure of at least $10 billion. See 12 CFR 217.100(b)(1). Other BHCs include any BHC that is subject to 12 CFR 225.8 and is not an advanced approaches BHC.

n/a Not applicable.

Projected loan losses, by type of loan, 2014:Q4–2016:Q4

	Billions of dollars	Portfolio loss rates (%)[1]
Loan losses	1.3	2.6
First-lien mortgages, domestic	0.0	1.8
Junior liens and HELOCs, domestic	0.1	3.1
Commercial and industrial[2]	0.5	1.7
Commercial real estate, domestic	0.5	4.4
Credit cards	0.0	0.0
Other consumer[3]	0.0	6.4
Other loans[4]	0.2	3.4

[1] Average loan balances used to calculate portfolio loss rates exclude loans held for sale and loans held for investment under the fair-value option and are calculated over nine quarters.

[2] Commercial and industrial loans include small- and medium-enterprise loans and corporate cards.

[3] Other consumer loans include student loans and automobile loans.

[4] Other loans include international real estate loans.

Actual 2014:Q3 and projected 2016:Q4 risk-weighted assets

	Actual 2014:Q3	Projected 2016:Q4	
		General approach	Standardized approach
Risk-weighted assets (billions of dollars)[1]	67.1	72.2	73.7

[1] For each quarter in 2014, risk-weighted assets are calculated using the general risk-based capital approach set forth in 12 CFR 225, appendix A. For each quarter in 2015 and 2016, risk-weighted assets are calculated under the Board's standardized capital risk-based approach in 12 CFR 217, subpart D, except for the risk-weighted assets used to calculate the tier 1 common ratio, which uses the general risk-based capital approach for all quarters.

Projected losses, revenue, net income and other comprehensive income through 2016:Q4

	Billions of dollars	Percent of average assets[1]
Pre-provision net revenue[2]	2.8	3.8
Other revenue[3]	0.0	
less		
Provisions	1.2	
Realized losses/gains on securities (AFS/HTM)	0.0	
Trading and counterparty losses[4]	0.0	
Other losses/gains[5]	0.0	
equals		
Net income before taxes	1.6	2.2
Memo items		
Other comprehensive income[6]	0.0	
Other effects on capital	*Actual 2014:Q3*	*2016:Q4*
AOCI included in capital (billions of dollars)[7]	n/a	0.0

[1] Average assets is the nine-quarter average of total assets.

[2] Pre-provision net revenue includes losses from operational-risk events, mortgage repurchase expenses, and other real estate owned (OREO) costs.

[3] Other revenue includes one-time income and (expense) items not included in pre-provision net revenue.

[4] Trading and counterparty losses include mark-to-market and credit valuation adjustments (CVA) losses and losses arising from the counterparty default scenario component applied to derivatives, securities lending, and repurchase agreement activities.

[5] Other losses/gains includes projected change in fair value of loans held for sale and loans held for investment measured under the fair-value option, and goodwill impairment losses.

[6] Other comprehensive income (OCI) is only calculated for advanced approaches BHCs, and other BHCs that opt into the advanced approaches treatment of AOCI.

[7] Certain AOCI items are subject to transition into projected regulatory capital. Those transitions are 20 percent included in projected regulatory capital for 2014, 40 percent included in projected regulatory capital for 2015, and 60 percent included in projected regulatory capital for 2016.

Table C.12.A. Deutsche Bank Trust Corporation

Projected stressed capital ratios, risk-weighted assets, losses, revenues, net income before taxes, and loan losses

Federal Reserve estimates: Severely adverse scenario

Actual 2014:Q3 projected stressed capital ratios through 2016:Q4

	Actual 2014:Q3	Stressed capital ratios[1]	
		Ending	Minimum
Tier 1 common ratio (%)	36.6	34.7	34.7
Common equity tier 1 capital ratio (%)[2]	n/a	28.6	28.6
Tier 1 risk-based capital ratio (%)	36.6	28.6	28.6
Total risk-based capital ratio (%)	37.0	29.8	29.8
Tier 1 leverage ratio (%)	11.9	11.0	11.0

[1] The capital ratios are calculated using capital action assumptions provided within the Dodd-Frank Act stress testing rule. These projections represent hypothetical estimates that involve an economic outcome that is more adverse than expected. These estimates are not forecasts of expected losses, revenues, net income before taxes, or capital ratios. The minimum capital ratio presented is for the period 2014:Q4 to 2016:Q4.

[2] Advanced approaches bank holding companies (BHCs) are subject to the common equity tier 1 ratio for the third and fourth quarter of 2014. All bank holding companies are subject to the common equity tier 1 ratio for each quarter of 2015 and 2016. An advanced approaches BHC includes any BHC that has consolidated total assets greater than or equal to $250 billion or consolidated total on-balance sheet foreign exposure of at least $10 billion. See 12 CFR 217.100(b)(1). Other BHCs include any BHC that is subject to 12 CFR 225.8 and is not an advanced approaches BHC.

n/a Not applicable.

Projected loan losses, by type of loan, 2014:Q4–2016:Q4

	Billions of dollars	Portfolio loss rates (%)[1]
Loan losses	0.8	4.5
First-lien mortgages, domestic	0.1	3.8
Junior liens and HELOCs, domestic	0.0	9.6
Commercial and industrial[2]	0.3	9.9
Commercial real estate, domestic	0.2	7.9
Credit cards	0.0	0.0
Other consumer[3]	0.0	2.3
Other loans[4]	0.1	1.4

[1] Average loan balances used to calculate portfolio loss rates exclude loans held for sale and loans held for investment under the fair-value option and are calculated over nine quarters.

[2] Commercial and industrial loans include small- and medium-enterprise loans and corporate cards.

[3] Other consumer loans include student loans and automobile loans.

[4] Other loans include international real estate loans.

Actual 2014:Q3 and projected 2016:Q4 risk-weighted assets

	Actual 2014:Q3	Projected 2016:Q4	
		General approach	Standardized approach
Risk-weighted assets (billions of dollars)[1]	19.3	20.2	24.5

[1] For each quarter in 2014, risk-weighted assets are calculated using the general risk-based capital approach set forth in 12 CFR 225, appendix A. For each quarter in 2015 and 2016, risk-weighted assets are calculated under the Board's standardized capital risk-based approach in 12 CFR 217, subpart D, except for the risk-weighted assets used to calculate the tier 1 common ratio, which uses the general risk-based capital approach for all quarters.

Projected losses, revenue, net income and other comprehensive income through 2016:Q4

	Billions of dollars	Percent of average assets[1]
Pre-provision net revenue[2]	1.0	1.6
Other revenue[3]	0.0	
less		
Provisions	1.1	
Realized losses/gains on securities (AFS/HTM)	0.0	
Trading and counterparty losses[4]	0.0	
Other losses/gains[5]	0.0	
equals		
Net income before taxes	-0.1	-0.2
Memo items		
Other comprehensive income[6]	0.0	
Other effects on capital	*Actual 2014:Q3*	*2016:Q4*
AOCI included in capital (billions of dollars)[7]	n/a	-0.1

[1] Average assets is the nine-quarter average of total assets.

[2] Pre-provision net revenue includes losses from operational-risk events, mortgage repurchase expenses, and other real estate owned (OREO) costs.

[3] Other revenue includes one-time income and (expense) items not included in pre-provision net revenue.

[4] Trading and counterparty losses include mark-to-market and credit valuation adjustments (CVA) losses and losses arising from the counterparty default scenario component applied to derivatives, securities lending, and repurchase agreement activities.

[5] Other losses/gains includes projected change in fair value of loans held for sale and loans held for investment measured under the fair-value option, and goodwill impairment losses.

[6] Other comprehensive income (OCI) is only calculated for advanced approaches BHCs, and other BHCs that opt into the advanced approaches treatment of AOCI.

[7] Certain AOCI items are subject to transition into projected regulatory capital. Those transitions are 20 percent included in projected regulatory capital for 2014, 40 percent included in projected regulatory capital for 2015, and 60 percent included in projected regulatory capital for 2016.

Table C.12.B. Deutsche Bank Trust Corporation
Projected stressed capital ratios, risk-weighted assets, losses, revenues, net income before taxes, and loan losses
Federal Reserve estimates: Adverse scenario

Actual 2014:Q3 projected stressed capital ratios through 2016:Q4

	Actual 2014:Q3	Stressed capital ratios[1]	
		Ending	Minimum
Tier 1 common ratio (%)	36.6	40.6	36.3
Common equity tier 1 capital ratio (%)[2]	n/a	33.8	30.2
Tier 1 risk-based capital ratio (%)	36.6	33.8	30.2
Total risk-based capital ratio (%)	37.0	34.6	30.6
Tier 1 leverage ratio (%)	11.9	12.8	11.8

[1] The capital ratios are calculated using capital action assumptions provided within the Dodd-Frank Act stress testing rule. These projections represent hypothetical estimates that involve an economic outcome that is more adverse than expected. These estimates are not forecasts of expected losses, revenues, net income before taxes, or capital ratios. The minimum capital ratio presented is for the period 2014:Q4 to 2016:Q4.

[2] Advanced approaches bank holding companies (BHCs) are subject to the common equity tier 1 ratio for the third and fourth quarter of 2014. All bank holding companies are subject to the common equity tier 1 ratio for each quarter of 2015 and 2016. An advanced approaches BHC includes any BHC that has consolidated total assets greater than or equal to $250 billion or consolidated total on-balance sheet foreign exposure of at least $10 billion. See 12 CFR 217.100(b)(1). Other BHCs include any BHC that is subject to 12 CFR 225.8 and is not an advanced approaches BHC.

n/a Not applicable.

Projected loan losses, by type of loan, 2014:Q4–2016:Q4

	Billions of dollars	Portfolio loss rates (%)[1]
Loan losses	0.5	2.7
First-lien mortgages, domestic	0.1	2.8
Junior liens and HELOCs, domestic	0.0	6.0
Commercial and industrial[2]	0.2	5.6
Commercial real estate, domestic	0.1	4.5
Credit cards	0.0	0.0
Other consumer[3]	0.0	2.0
Other loans[4]	0.1	0.8

[1] Average loan balances used to calculate portfolio loss rates exclude loans held for sale and loans held for investment under the fair-value option and are calculated over nine quarters.

[2] Commercial and industrial loans include small- and medium-enterprise loans and corporate cards.

[3] Other consumer loans include student loans and automobile loans.

[4] Other loans include international real estate loans.

Actual 2014:Q3 and projected 2016:Q4 risk-weighted assets

	Actual 2014:Q3	Projected 2016:Q4	
		General approach	Standardized approach
Risk-weighted assets (billions of dollars)[1]	19.3	20.9	25.2

[1] For each quarter in 2014, risk-weighted assets are calculated using the general risk-based capital approach set forth in 12 CFR 225, appendix A. For each quarter in 2015 and 2016, risk-weighted assets are calculated under the Board's standardized capital risk-based approach in 12 CFR 217, subpart D, except for the risk-weighted assets used to calculate the tier 1 common ratio, which uses the general risk-based capital approach for all quarters.

Projected losses, revenue, net income and other comprehensive income through 2016:Q4

	Billions of dollars	Percent of average assets[1]
Pre-provision net revenue[2]	2.8	4.4
Other revenue[3]	0.0	
less		
Provisions	0.7	
Realized losses/gains on securities (AFS/HTM)	0.0	
Trading and counterparty losses[4]	0.0	
Other losses/gains[5]	0.0	
equals		
Net income before taxes	2.2	3.4
Memo items		
Other comprehensive income[6]	0.0	
Other effects on capital	*Actual 2014:Q3*	*2016:Q4*
AOCI included in capital (billions of dollars)[7]	n/a	-0.1

[1] Average assets is the nine-quarter average of total assets.

[2] Pre-provision net revenue includes losses from operational-risk events, mortgage repurchase expenses, and other real estate owned (OREO) costs.

[3] Other revenue includes one-time income and (expense) items not included in pre-provision net revenue.

[4] Trading and counterparty losses include mark-to-market and credit valuation adjustments (CVA) losses and losses arising from the counterparty default scenario component applied to derivatives, securities lending, and repurchase agreement activities.

[5] Other losses/gains includes projected change in fair value of loans held for sale and loans held for investment measured under the fair-value option, and goodwill impairment losses.

[6] Other comprehensive income (OCI) is only calculated for advanced approaches BHCs, and other BHCs that opt into the advanced approaches treatment of AOCI.

[7] Certain AOCI items are subject to transition into projected regulatory capital. Those transitions are 20 percent included in projected regulatory capital for 2014, 40 percent included in projected regulatory capital for 2015, and 60 percent included in projected regulatory capital for 2016.

Table C.13.A. Discover Financial Services
Projected stressed capital ratios, risk-weighted assets, losses, revenues, net income before taxes, and loan losses
Federal Reserve estimates: Severely adverse scenario

Actual 2014:Q3 projected stressed capital ratios through 2016:Q4

	Actual 2014:Q3	Stressed capital ratios[1]	
		Ending	Minimum
Tier 1 common ratio (%)	14.8	15.3	13.9
Common equity tier 1 capital ratio (%)[2]	n/a	14.5	13.3
Tier 1 risk-based capital ratio (%)	15.6	15.2	14.1
Total risk-based capital ratio (%)	17.8	16.9	15.8
Tier 1 leverage ratio (%)	13.7	13.3	12.6

[1] The capital ratios are calculated using capital action assumptions provided within the Dodd-Frank Act stress testing rule. These projections represent hypothetical estimates that involve an economic outcome that is more adverse than expected. These estimates are not forecasts of expected losses, revenues, net income before taxes, or capital ratios. The minimum capital ratio presented is for the period 2014:Q4 to 2016:Q4.

[2] Advanced approaches bank holding companies (BHCs) are subject to the common equity tier 1 ratio for the third and fourth quarter of 2014. All bank holding companies are subject to the common equity tier 1 ratio for each quarter of 2015 and 2016. An advanced approaches BHC includes any BHC that has consolidated total assets greater than or equal to $250 billion or consolidated total on-balance sheet foreign exposure of at least $10 billion. See 12 CFR 217.100(b)(1). Other BHCs include any BHC that is subject to 12 CFR 225.8 and is not an advanced approaches BHC.

n/a   Not applicable.

Projected loan losses, by type of loan, 2014:Q4–2016:Q4

	Billions of dollars	Portfolio loss rates (%)[1]
Loan losses	8.3	12.2
First-lien mortgages, domestic	0.0	5.1
Junior liens and HELOCs, domestic	0.0	15.0
Commercial and industrial[2]	0.0	14.0
Commercial real estate, domestic	0.0	31.6
Credit cards	6.9	12.7
Other consumer[3]	1.4	10.1
Other loans[4]	0.0	4.3

[1] Average loan balances used to calculate portfolio loss rates exclude loans held for sale and loans held for investment under the fair-value option and are calculated over nine quarters.

[2] Commercial and industrial loans include small- and medium-enterprise loans and corporate cards.

[3] Other consumer loans include student loans and automobile loans.

[4] Other loans include international real estate loans.

Actual 2014:Q3 and projected 2016:Q4 risk-weighted assets

	Actual 2014:Q3	Projected 2016:Q4	
		General approach	Standardized approach
Risk-weighted assets (billions of dollars)[1]	70.1	70.9	75.4

[1] For each quarter in 2014, risk-weighted assets are calculated using the general risk-based capital approach set forth in 12 CFR 225, appendix A. For each quarter in 2015 and 2016, risk-weighted assets are calculated under the Board's standardized capital risk-based approach in 12 CFR 217, subpart D, except for the risk-weighted assets used to calculate the tier 1 common ratio, which uses the general risk-based capital approach for all quarters.

Projected losses, revenue, net income and other comprehensive income through 2016:Q4

	Billions of dollars	Percent of average assets[1]
Pre-provision net revenue[2]	12.9	15.4
Other revenue[3]	0.0	
less		
Provisions	10.1	
Realized losses/gains on securities (AFS/HTM)	0.0	
Trading and counterparty losses[4]	0.0	
Other losses/gains[5]	0.0	
equals		
Net income before taxes	2.7	3.3
Memo items		
Other comprehensive income[6]	0.0	
Other effects on capital	*Actual 2014:Q3*	*2016:Q4*
AOCI included in capital (billions of dollars)[7]	n/a	0.0

[1] Average assets is the nine-quarter average of total assets.

[2] Pre-provision net revenue includes losses from operational-risk events, mortgage repurchase expenses, and other real estate owned (OREO) costs.

[3] Other revenue includes one-time income and (expense) items not included in pre-provision net revenue.

[4] Trading and counterparty losses include mark-to-market and credit valuation adjustments (CVA) losses and losses arising from the counterparty default scenario component applied to derivatives, securities lending, and repurchase agreement activities.

[5] Other losses/gains includes projected change in fair value of loans held for sale and loans held for investment measured under the fair-value option, and goodwill impairment losses.

[6] Other comprehensive income (OCI) is only calculated for advanced approaches BHCs, and other BHCs that opt into the advanced approaches treatment of AOCI.

[7] Certain AOCI items are subject to transition into projected regulatory capital. Those transitions are 20 percent included in projected regulatory capital for 2014, 40 percent included in projected regulatory capital for 2015, and 60 percent included in projected regulatory capital for 2016.

Table C.13.B. Discover Financial Services
Projected stressed capital ratios, risk-weighted assets, losses, revenues, net income before taxes, and loan losses
Federal Reserve estimates: Adverse scenario

Actual 2014:Q3 projected stressed capital ratios through 2016:Q4

	Actual 2014:Q3	Stressed capital ratios[1]	
		Ending	Minimum
Tier 1 common ratio (%)	14.8	16.8	14.3
Common equity tier 1 capital ratio (%)[2]	n/a	16.1	14.1
Tier 1 risk-based capital ratio (%)	15.6	16.8	14.9
Total risk-based capital ratio (%)	17.8	18.4	16.7
Tier 1 leverage ratio (%)	13.7	14.4	13.0

[1] The capital ratios are calculated using capital action assumptions provided within the Dodd-Frank Act stress testing rule. These projections represent hypothetical estimates that involve an economic outcome that is more adverse than expected. These estimates are not forecasts of expected losses, revenues, net income before taxes, or capital ratios. The minimum capital ratio presented is for the period 2014:Q4 to 2016:Q4.

[2] Advanced approaches bank holding companies (BHCs) are subject to the common equity tier 1 ratio for the third and fourth quarter of 2014. All bank holding companies are subject to the common equity tier 1 ratio for each quarter of 2015 and 2016. An advanced approaches BHC includes any BHC that has consolidated total assets greater than or equal to $250 billion or consolidated total on-balance sheet foreign exposure of at least $10 billion. See 12 CFR 217.100(b)(1). Other BHCs include any BHC that is subject to 12 CFR 225.8 and is not an advanced approaches BHC.

n/a Not applicable.

Projected loan losses, by type of loan, 2014:Q4–2016:Q4

	Billions of dollars	Portfolio loss rates (%)[1]
Loan losses	6.8	9.8
First-lien mortgages, domestic	0.0	3.9
Junior liens and HELOCs, domestic	0.0	12.9
Commercial and industrial[2]	0.0	10.6
Commercial real estate, domestic	0.0	18.3
Credit cards	5.6	10.1
Other consumer[3]	1.2	8.7
Other loans[4]	0.0	2.3

[1] Average loan balances used to calculate portfolio loss rates exclude loans held for sale and loans held for investment under the fair-value option and are calculated over nine quarters.

[2] Commercial and industrial loans include small- and medium-enterprise loans and corporate cards.

[3] Other consumer loans include student loans and automobile loans.

[4] Other loans include international real estate loans.

Actual 2014:Q3 and projected 2016:Q4 risk-weighted assets

	Actual 2014:Q3	Projected 2016:Q4	
		General approach	Standardized approach
Risk-weighted assets (billions of dollars)[1]	70.1	73.1	77.3

[1] For each quarter in 2014, risk-weighted assets are calculated using the general risk-based capital approach set forth in 12 CFR 225, appendix A. For each quarter in 2015 and 2016, risk-weighted assets are calculated under the Board's standardized capital risk-based approach in 12 CFR 217, subpart D, except for the risk-weighted assets used to calculate the tier 1 common ratio, which uses the general risk-based capital approach for all quarters.

Projected losses, revenue, net income and other comprehensive income through 2016:Q4

	Billions of dollars	Percent of average assets[1]
Pre-provision net revenue[2]	13.5	15.8
Other revenue[3]	0.0	
less		
Provisions	8.5	
Realized losses/gains on securities (AFS/HTM)	0.0	
Trading and counterparty losses[4]	0.0	
Other losses/gains[5]	0.0	
equals		
Net income before taxes	5.0	5.8
Memo items		
Other comprehensive income[6]	0.0	
Other effects on capital	*Actual 2014:Q3*	*2016:Q4*
AOCI included in capital (billions of dollars)[7]	n/a	0.0

[1] Average assets is the nine-quarter average of total assets.

[2] Pre-provision net revenue includes losses from operational-risk events, mortgage repurchase expenses, and other real estate owned (OREO) costs.

[3] Other revenue includes one-time income and (expense) items not included in pre-provision net revenue.

[4] Trading and counterparty losses include mark-to-market and credit valuation adjustments (CVA) losses and losses arising from the counterparty default scenario component applied to derivatives, securities lending, and repurchase agreement activities.

[5] Other losses/gains includes projected change in fair value of loans held for sale and loans held for investment measured under the fair-value option, and goodwill impairment losses.

[6] Other comprehensive income (OCI) is only calculated for advanced approaches BHCs, and other BHCs that opt into the advanced approaches treatment of AOCI.

[7] Certain AOCI items are subject to transition into projected regulatory capital. Those transitions are 20 percent included in projected regulatory capital for 2014, 40 percent included in projected regulatory capital for 2015, and 60 percent included in projected regulatory capital for 2016.

Table C.14.A. Fifth Third Bancorp
Projected stressed capital ratios, risk-weighted assets, losses, revenues, net income before taxes, and loan losses
Federal Reserve estimates: Severely adverse scenario

Actual 2014:Q3 projected stressed capital ratios through 2016:Q4

	Actual 2014:Q3	Stressed capital ratios[1]	
		Ending	Minimum
Tier 1 common ratio (%)	9.6	7.9	7.9
Common equity tier 1 capital ratio (%)[2]	n/a	7.4	7.4
Tier 1 risk-based capital ratio (%)	10.8	8.5	8.5
Total risk-based capital ratio (%)	14.3	11.5	11.5
Tier 1 leverage ratio (%)	9.8	7.7	7.7

[1] The capital ratios are calculated using capital action assumptions provided within the Dodd-Frank Act stress testing rule. These projections represent hypothetical estimates that involve an economic outcome that is more adverse than expected. These estimates are not forecasts of expected losses, revenues, net income before taxes, or capital ratios. The minimum capital ratio presented is for the period 2014:Q4 to 2016:Q4.

[2] Advanced approaches bank holding companies (BHCs) are subject to the common equity tier 1 ratio for the third and fourth quarter of 2014. All bank holding companies are subject to the common equity tier 1 ratio for each quarter of 2015 and 2016. An advanced approaches BHC includes any BHC that has consolidated total assets greater than or equal to $250 billion or consolidated total on-balance sheet foreign exposure of at least $10 billion. See 12 CFR 217.100(b)(1). Other BHCs include any BHC that is subject to 12 CFR 225.8 and is not an advanced approaches BHC.

n/a Not applicable.

Projected loan losses, by type of loan, 2014:Q4–2016:Q4

	Billions of dollars	Portfolio loss rates (%)[1]
Loan losses	5.2	5.6
First-lien mortgages, domestic	0.6	4.4
Junior liens and HELOCs, domestic	0.5	5.7
Commercial and industrial[2]	1.8	5.0
Commercial real estate, domestic	1.3	13.2
Credit cards	0.3	14.3
Other consumer[3]	0.4	2.7
Other loans[4]	0.3	3.4

[1] Average loan balances used to calculate portfolio loss rates exclude loans held for sale and loans held for investment under the fair-value option and are calculated over nine quarters.

[2] Commercial and industrial loans include small- and medium-enterprise loans and corporate cards.

[3] Other consumer loans include student loans and automobile loans.

[4] Other loans include international real estate loans.

Actual 2014:Q3 and projected 2016:Q4 risk-weighted assets

	Actual 2014:Q3	Projected 2016:Q4	
		General approach	Standardized approach
Risk-weighted assets (billions of dollars)[1]	116.9	121.1	125.4

[1] For each quarter in 2014, risk-weighted assets are calculated using the general risk-based capital approach set forth in 12 CFR 225, appendix A. For each quarter in 2015 and 2016, risk-weighted assets are calculated under the Board's standardized capital risk-based approach in 12 CFR 217, subpart D, except for the risk-weighted assets used to calculate the tier 1 common ratio, which uses the general risk-based capital approach for all quarters.

Projected losses, revenue, net income and other comprehensive income through 2016:Q4

	Billions of dollars	Percent of average assets[1]
Pre-provision net revenue[2]	4.7	3.4
Other revenue[3]	0.0	
less		
Provisions	5.5	
Realized losses/gains on securities (AFS/HTM)	0.0	
Trading and counterparty losses[4]	0.0	
Other losses/gains[5]	0.0	
equals		
Net income before taxes	-0.8	-0.6
Memo items		
Other comprehensive income[6]	0.0	
Other effects on capital	Actual 2014:Q3	2016:Q4
AOCI included in capital (billions of dollars)[7]	n/a	0.0

[1] Average assets is the nine-quarter average of total assets.

[2] Pre-provision net revenue includes losses from operational-risk events, mortgage repurchase expenses, and other real estate owned (OREO) costs.

[3] Other revenue includes one-time income and (expense) items not included in pre-provision net revenue.

[4] Trading and counterparty losses include mark-to-market and credit valuation adjustments (CVA) losses and losses arising from the counterparty default scenario component applied to derivatives, securities lending, and repurchase agreement activities.

[5] Other losses/gains includes projected change in fair value of loans held for sale and loans held for investment measured under the fair-value option, and goodwill impairment losses.

[6] Other comprehensive income (OCI) is only calculated for advanced approaches BHCs, and other BHCs that opt into the advanced approaches treatment of AOCI.

[7] Certain AOCI items are subject to transition into projected regulatory capital. Those transitions are 20 percent included in projected regulatory capital for 2014, 40 percent included in projected regulatory capital for 2015, and 60 percent included in projected regulatory capital for 2016.

Table C.14.B. Fifth Third Bancorp
Projected stressed capital ratios, risk-weighted assets, losses, revenues, net income before taxes, and loan losses
Federal Reserve estimates: Adverse scenario

Actual 2014:Q3 projected stressed capital ratios through 2016:Q4

	Actual 2014:Q3	Stressed capital ratios[1]	
		Ending	Minimum
Tier 1 common ratio (%)	9.6	9.7	9.3
Common equity tier 1 capital ratio (%)[2]	n/a	9.3	9.0
Tier 1 risk-based capital ratio (%)	10.8	10.3	10.1
Total risk-based capital ratio (%)	14.3	12.6	12.6
Tier 1 leverage ratio (%)	9.8	9.2	9.1

[1] The capital ratios are calculated using capital action assumptions provided within the Dodd-Frank Act stress testing rule. These projections represent hypothetical estimates that involve an economic outcome that is more adverse than expected. These estimates are not forecasts of expected losses, revenues, net income before taxes, or capital ratios. The minimum capital ratio presented is for the period 2014:Q4 to 2016:Q4.

[2] Advanced approaches bank holding companies (BHCs) are subject to the common equity tier 1 ratio for the third and fourth quarter of 2014. All bank holding companies are subject to the common equity tier 1 ratio for each quarter of 2015 and 2016. An advanced approaches BHC includes any BHC that has consolidated total assets greater than or equal to $250 billion or consolidated total on-balance sheet foreign exposure of at least $10 billion. See 12 CFR 217.100(b)(1). Other BHCs include any BHC that is subject to 12 CFR 225.8 and is not an advanced approaches BHC.

n/a Not applicable.

Projected loan losses, by type of loan, 2014:Q4–2016:Q4

	Billions of dollars	Portfolio loss rates (%)[1]
Loan losses	3.4	3.7
First-lien mortgages, domestic	0.5	3.7
Junior liens and HELOCs, domestic	0.4	4.3
Commercial and industrial[2]	1.1	3.0
Commercial real estate, domestic	0.8	7.8
Credit cards	0.3	10.9
Other consumer[3]	0.3	2.0
Other loans[4]	0.2	2.2

[1] Average loan balances used to calculate portfolio loss rates exclude loans held for sale and loans held for investment under the fair-value option and are calculated over nine quarters.

[2] Commercial and industrial loans include small- and medium-enterprise loans and corporate cards.

[3] Other consumer loans include student loans and automobile loans.

[4] Other loans include international real estate loans.

Actual 2014:Q3 and projected 2016:Q4 risk-weighted assets

	Actual 2014:Q3	Projected 2016:Q4	
		General approach	Standardized approach
Risk-weighted assets (billions of dollars)[1]	116.9	125.3	128.9

[1] For each quarter in 2014, risk-weighted assets are calculated using the general risk-based capital approach set forth in 12 CFR 225, appendix A. For each quarter in 2015 and 2016, risk-weighted assets are calculated under the Board's standardized capital risk-based approach in 12 CFR 217, subpart D, except for the risk-weighted assets used to calculate the tier 1 common ratio, which uses the general risk-based capital approach for all quarters.

Projected losses, revenue, net income and other comprehensive income through 2016:Q4

	Billions of dollars	Percent of average assets[1]
Pre-provision net revenue[2]	6.3	4.4
Other revenue[3]	0.0	
less		
Provisions	3.3	
Realized losses/gains on securities (AFS/HTM)	0.0	
Trading and counterparty losses[4]	0.0	
Other losses/gains[5]	0.0	
equals		
Net income before taxes	3.0	2.1
Memo items		
Other comprehensive income[6]	0.0	
Other effects on capital	Actual 2014:Q3	2016:Q4
AOCI included in capital (billions of dollars)[7]	n/a	0.0

[1] Average assets is the nine-quarter average of total assets.

[2] Pre-provision net revenue includes losses from operational-risk events, mortgage repurchase expenses, and other real estate owned (OREO) costs.

[3] Other revenue includes one-time income and (expense) items not included in pre-provision net revenue.

[4] Trading and counterparty losses include mark-to-market and credit valuation adjustments (CVA) losses and losses arising from the counterparty default scenario component applied to derivatives, securities lending, and repurchase agreement activities.

[5] Other losses/gains includes projected change in fair value of loans held for sale and loans held for investment measured under the fair-value option, and goodwill impairment losses.

[6] Other comprehensive income (OCI) is only calculated for advanced approaches BHCs, and other BHCs that opt into the advanced approaches treatment of AOCI.

[7] Certain AOCI items are subject to transition into projected regulatory capital. Those transitions are 20 percent included in projected regulatory capital for 2014, 40 percent included in projected regulatory capital for 2015, and 60 percent included in projected regulatory capital for 2016.

Table C.15.A. The Goldman Sachs Group, Inc.
Projected stressed capital ratios, risk-weighted assets, losses, revenues, net income before taxes, and loan losses
Federal Reserve estimates: Severely adverse scenario

Actual 2014:Q3 projected stressed capital ratios through 2016:Q4

	Actual 2014:Q3	Stressed capital ratios[1]	
		Ending	Minimum
Tier 1 common ratio (%)	14.4	9.3	6.3
Common equity tier 1 capital ratio (%)[2]	15.1	7.1	5.8
Tier 1 risk-based capital ratio (%)	17.0	8.1	6.4
Total risk-based capital ratio (%)	19.8	10.0	8.1
Tier 1 leverage ratio (%)	9.0	5.9	5.4

[1] The capital ratios are calculated using capital action assumptions provided within the Dodd-Frank Act stress testing rule. These projections represent hypothetical estimates that involve an economic outcome that is more adverse than expected. These estimates are not forecasts of expected losses, revenues, net income before taxes, or capital ratios. The minimum capital ratio presented is for the period 2014:Q4 to 2016:Q4.

[2] Advanced approaches bank holding companies (BHCs) are subject to the common equity tier 1 ratio for the third and fourth quarter of 2014. All bank holding companies are subject to the common equity tier 1 ratio for each quarter of 2015 and 2016. An advanced approaches BHC includes any BHC that has consolidated total assets greater than or equal to $250 billion or consolidated total on-balance sheet foreign exposure of at least $10 billion. See 12 CFR 217.100(b)(1). Other BHCs include any BHC that is subject to 12 CFR 225.8 and is not an advanced approaches BHC.

Projected loan losses, by type of loan, 2014:Q4–2016:Q4

	Billions of dollars	Portfolio loss rates (%)[1]
Loan losses	2.2	3.2
First-lien mortgages, domestic	0.0	5.1
Junior liens and HELOCs, domestic	0.0	9.3
Commercial and industrial[2]	0.9	9.8
Commercial real estate, domestic	0.2	6.1
Credit cards	0.0	0.0
Other consumer[3]	0.0	2.7
Other loans[4]	1.1	2.0

[1] Average loan balances used to calculate portfolio loss rates exclude loans held for sale and loans held for investment under the fair-value option and are calculated over nine quarters.

[2] Commercial and industrial loans include small- and medium-enterprise loans and corporate cards.

[3] Other consumer loans include student loans and automobile loans.

[4] Other loans include international real estate loans.

Actual 2014:Q3 and projected 2016:Q4 risk-weighted assets

	Actual 2014:Q3	Projected 2016:Q4	
		General approach	Standardized approach
Risk-weighted assets (billions of dollars)[1]	456.1	489.4	665.9

[1] For each quarter in 2014, risk-weighted assets are calculated using the general risk-based capital approach set forth in 12 CFR 225, appendix A. For each quarter in 2015 and 2016, risk-weighted assets are calculated under the Board's standardized capital risk-based approach in 12 CFR 217, subpart D, except for the risk-weighted assets used to calculate the tier 1 common ratio, which uses the general risk-based capital approach for all quarters.

Projected losses, revenue, net income and other comprehensive income through 2016:Q4

	Billions of dollars	Percent of average assets[1]
Pre-provision net revenue[2]	2.4	0.3
Other revenue[3]	0.0	
less		
Provisions	2.8	
Realized losses/gains on securities (AFS/HTM)	0.0	
Trading and counterparty losses[4]	17.0	
Other losses/gains[5]	6.8	
equals		
Net income before taxes	-24.1	-2.7
Memo items		
Other comprehensive income[6]	0.0	
Other effects on capital	*Actual 2014:Q3*	*2016:Q4*
AOCI included in capital (billions of dollars)[7]	-0.5	-0.6

[1] Average assets is the nine-quarter average of total assets.

[2] Pre-provision net revenue includes losses from operational-risk events, mortgage repurchase expenses, and other real estate owned (OREO) costs.

[3] Other revenue includes one-time income and (expense) items not included in pre-provision net revenue.

[4] Trading and counterparty losses include mark-to-market and credit valuation adjustments (CVA) losses and losses arising from the counterparty default scenario component applied to derivatives, securities lending, and repurchase agreement activities.

[5] Other losses/gains includes projected change in fair value of loans held for sale and loans held for investment measured under the fair-value option and goodwill impairment losses.

[6] Other comprehensive income (OCI) is only calculated for advanced approaches BHCs, and other BHCs that opt into the advanced approaches treatment of AOCI.

[7] Certain AOCI items are subject to transition into projected regulatory capital. Those transitions are 20 percent included in projected regulatory capital for 2014, 40 percent included in projected regulatory capital for 2015, and 60 percent included in projected regulatory capital for 2016.

Table C.15.B. The Goldman Sachs Group, Inc.
Projected stressed capital ratios, risk-weighted assets, losses, revenues, net income before taxes, and loan losses
Federal Reserve estimates: Adverse scenario

Actual 2014:Q3 projected stressed capital ratios through 2016:Q4

	Actual 2014:Q3	Stressed capital ratios[1]	
		Ending	Minimum
Tier 1 common ratio (%)	14.4	13.8	12.2
Common equity tier 1 capital ratio (%)[2]	15.1	10.2	9.2
Tier 1 risk-based capital ratio (%)	17.0	11.4	10.5
Total risk-based capital ratio (%)	19.8	13.2	12.4
Tier 1 leverage ratio (%)	9.0	8.1	7.8

[1] The capital ratios are calculated using capital action assumptions provided within the Dodd-Frank Act stress testing rule. These projections represent hypothetical estimates that involve an economic outcome that is more adverse than expected. These estimates are not forecasts of expected losses, revenues, net income before taxes, or capital ratios. The minimum capital ratio presented is for the period 2014:Q4 to 2016:Q4.

[2] Advanced approaches bank holding companies (BHCs) are subject to the common equity tier 1 ratio for the third and fourth quarter of 2014. All bank holding companies are subject to the common equity tier 1 ratio for each quarter of 2015 and 2016. An advanced approaches BHC includes any BHC that has consolidated total assets greater than or equal to $250 billion or consolidated total on-balance sheet foreign exposure of at least $10 billion. See 12 CFR 217.100(b)(1). Other BHCs include any BHC that is subject to 12 CFR 225.8 and is not an advanced approaches BHC.

Actual 2014:Q3 and projected 2016:Q4 risk-weighted assets

	Actual 2014:Q3	Projected 2016:Q4	
		General approach	Standardized approach
Risk-weighted assets (billions of dollars)[1]	456.1	496.0	680.2

[1] For each quarter in 2014, risk-weighted assets are calculated using the general risk-based capital approach set forth in 12 CFR 225, appendix A. For each quarter in 2015 and 2016, risk-weighted assets are calculated under the Board's standardized capital risk-based approach in 12 CFR 217, subpart D, except for the risk-weighted assets used to calculate the tier 1 common ratio, which uses the general risk-based capital approach for all quarters.

Projected loan losses, by type of loan, 2014:Q4–2016:Q4

	Billions of dollars	Portfolio loss rates (%)[1]
Loan losses	1.4	1.9
First-lien mortgages, domestic	0.0	3.8
Junior liens and HELOCs, domestic	0.0	5.6
Commercial and industrial[2]	0.5	5.5
Commercial real estate, domestic	0.1	3.5
Credit cards	0.0	0.0
Other consumer[3]	0.0	2.3
Other loans[4]	0.7	1.3

[1] Average loan balances used to calculate portfolio loss rates exclude loans held for sale and loans held for investment under the fair-value option and are calculated over nine quarters.

[2] Commercial and industrial loans include small- and medium-enterprise loans and corporate cards.

[3] Other consumer loans include student loans and automobile loans.

[4] Other loans include international real estate loans.

Projected losses, revenue, net income and other comprehensive income through 2016:Q4

	Billions of dollars	Percent of average assets[1]
Pre-provision net revenue[2]	19.0	2.1
Other revenue[3]	0.0	
less		
Provisions	1.7	
Realized losses/gains on securities (AFS/HTM)	0.0	
Trading and counterparty losses[4]	9.9	
Other losses/gains[5]	3.4	
equals		
Net income before taxes	4.1	0.4
Memo items		
Other comprehensive income[6]	0.0	
Other effects on capital	Actual 2014:Q3	2016:Q4
AOCI included in capital (billions of dollars)[7]	-0.5	-0.6

[1] Average assets is the nine-quarter average of total assets.

[2] Pre-provision net revenue includes losses from operational-risk events, mortgage repurchase expenses, and other real estate owned (OREO) costs.

[3] Other revenue includes one-time income and (expense) items not included in pre-provision net revenue.

[4] Trading and counterparty losses include mark-to-market and credit valuation adjustments (CVA) losses and losses arising from the counterparty default scenario component applied to derivatives, securities lending, and repurchase agreement activities.

[5] Other losses/gains includes projected change in fair value of loans held for sale and loans held for investment measured under the fair-value option and goodwill impairment losses.

[6] Other comprehensive income (OCI) is only calculated for advanced approaches BHCs, and other BHCs that opt into the advanced approaches treatment of AOCI.

[7] Certain AOCI items are subject to transition into projected regulatory capital. Those transitions are 20 percent included in projected regulatory capital for 2014, 40 percent included in projected regulatory capital for 2015, and 60 percent included in projected regulatory capital for 2016.

Table C.16.A. HSBC North America Holdings Inc.
Projected stressed capital ratios, risk-weighted assets, losses, revenues, net income before taxes, and loan losses
Federal Reserve estimates: Severely adverse scenario

Actual 2014:Q3 projected stressed capital ratios through 2016:Q4

	Actual 2014:Q3	Stressed capital ratios[1]	
		Ending	Minimum
Tier 1 common ratio (%)	14.0	8.9	8.9
Common equity tier 1 capital ratio (%)[2]	16.3	8.9	8.9
Tier 1 risk-based capital ratio (%)	17.3	10.0	10.0
Total risk-based capital ratio (%)	26.1	14.8	14.8
Tier 1 leverage ratio (%)	9.4	6.0	6.0

[1] The capital ratios are calculated using capital action assumptions provided within the Dodd-Frank Act stress testing rule. These projections represent hypothetical estimates that involve an economic outcome that is more adverse than expected. These estimates are not forecasts of expected losses, revenues, net income before taxes, or capital ratios. The minimum capital ratio presented is for the period 2014:Q4 to 2016:Q4.

[2] Advanced approaches bank holding companies (BHCs) are subject to the common equity tier 1 ratio for the third and fourth quarter of 2014. All bank holding companies are subject to the common equity tier 1 ratio for each quarter of 2015 and 2016. An advanced approaches BHC includes any BHC that has consolidated total assets greater than or equal to $250 billion or consolidated total on-balance sheet foreign exposure of at least $10 billion. See 12 CFR 217.100(b)(1). Other BHCs include any BHC that is subject to 12 CFR 225.8 and is not an advanced approaches BHC.

Projected loan losses, by type of loan, 2014:Q4–2016:Q4

	Billions of dollars	Portfolio loss rates (%)[1]
Loan losses	8.2	8.6
First-lien mortgages, domestic	4.7	12.5
Junior liens and HELOCs, domestic	1.1	22.3
Commercial and industrial[2]	1.1	3.5
Commercial real estate, domestic	0.9	9.6
Credit cards	0.1	14.7
Other consumer[3]	0.0	7.4
Other loans[4]	0.3	2.7

[1] Average loan balances used to calculate portfolio loss rates exclude loans held for sale and loans held for investment under the fair-value option and are calculated over nine quarters.

[2] Commercial and industrial loans include small- and medium-enterprise loans and corporate cards.

[3] Other consumer loans include student loans and automobile loans.

[4] Other loans include international real estate loans.

Actual 2014:Q3 and projected 2016:Q4 risk-weighted assets

	Actual 2014:Q3	Projected 2016:Q4	
		General approach	Standardized approach
Risk-weighted assets (billions of dollars)[1]	159.3	161.5	187.0

[1] For each quarter in 2014, risk-weighted assets are calculated using the general risk-based capital approach set forth in 12 CFR 225, appendix A. For each quarter in 2015 and 2016, risk-weighted assets are calculated under the Board's standardized capital risk-based approach in 12 CFR 217, subpart D, except for the risk-weighted assets used to calculate the tier 1 common ratio, which uses the general risk-based capital approach for all quarters.

Projected losses, revenue, net income and other comprehensive income through 2016:Q4

	Billions of dollars	Percent of average assets[1]
Pre-provision net revenue[2]	-0.7	-0.3
Other revenue[3]	0.0	
less		
Provisions	7.6	
Realized losses/gains on securities (AFS/HTM)	0.1	
Trading and counterparty losses[4]	0.0	
Other losses/gains[5]	0.7	
equals		
Net income before taxes	-9.1	-3.1
Memo items		
Other comprehensive income[6]	0.8	
Other effects on capital	*Actual 2014:Q3*	*2016:Q4*
AOCI included in capital (billions of dollars)[7]	-0.1	0.2

[1] Average assets is the nine-quarter average of total assets.

[2] Pre-provision net revenue includes losses from operational-risk events, mortgage repurchase expenses, and other real estate owned (OREO) costs.

[3] Other revenue includes one-time income and (expense) items not included in pre-provision net revenue.

[4] Trading and counterparty losses include mark-to-market and credit valuation adjustments (CVA) losses and losses arising from the counterparty default scenario component applied to derivatives, securities lending, and repurchase agreement activities.

[5] Other losses/gains includes projected change in fair value of loans held for sale and loans held for investment measured under the fair-value option and goodwill impairment losses.

[6] Other comprehensive income (OCI) is only calculated for advanced approaches BHCs, and other BHCs that opt into the advanced approaches treatment of AOCI.

[7] Certain AOCI items are subject to transition into projected regulatory capital. Those transitions are 20 percent included in projected regulatory capital for 2014, 40 percent included in projected regulatory capital for 2015, and 60 percent included in projected regulatory capital for 2016.

Table C.16.B. HSBC North America Holdings Inc.
Projected stressed capital ratios, risk-weighted assets, losses, revenues, net income before taxes, and loan losses
Federal Reserve estimates: Adverse scenario

Actual 2014:Q3 projected stressed capital ratios through 2016:Q4

	Actual 2014:Q3	Stressed capital ratios[1]	
		Ending	Minimum
Tier 1 common ratio (%)	14.0	14.4	13.9
Common equity tier 1 capital ratio (%)[2]	16.3	11.3	11.1
Tier 1 risk-based capital ratio (%)	17.3	12.7	12.5
Total risk-based capital ratio (%)	26.1	16.6	16.6
Tier 1 leverage ratio (%)	9.4	7.6	7.5

[1] The capital ratios are calculated using capital action assumptions provided within the Dodd-Frank Act stress testing rule. These projections represent hypothetical estimates that involve an economic outcome that is more adverse than expected. These estimates are not forecasts of expected losses, revenues, net income before taxes, or capital ratios. The minimum capital ratio presented is for the period 2014:Q4 to 2016:Q4.

[2] Advanced approaches bank holding companies (BHCs) are subject to the common equity tier 1 ratio for the third and fourth quarter of 2014. All bank holding companies are subject to the common equity tier 1 ratio for each quarter of 2015 and 2016. An advanced approaches BHC includes any BHC that has consolidated total assets greater than or equal to $250 billion or consolidated total on-balance sheet foreign exposure of at least $10 billion. See 12 CFR 217.100(b)(1). Other BHCs include any BHC that is subject to 12 CFR 225.8 and is not an advanced approaches BHC.

Projected loan losses, by type of loan, 2014:Q4–2016:Q4

	Billions of dollars	Portfolio loss rates (%)[1]
Loan losses	6.1	6.4
First-lien mortgages, domestic	3.8	10.0
Junior liens and HELOCs, domestic	0.9	19.2
Commercial and industrial[2]	0.6	1.9
Commercial real estate, domestic	0.5	5.3
Credit cards	0.1	11.9
Other consumer[3]	0.0	6.4
Other loans[4]	0.2	1.5

[1] Average loan balances used to calculate portfolio loss rates exclude loans held for sale and loans held for investment under the fair-value option and are calculated over nine quarters.

[2] Commercial and industrial loans include small- and medium-enterprise loans and corporate cards.

[3] Other consumer loans include student loans and automobile loans.

[4] Other loans include international real estate loans.

Actual 2014:Q3 and projected 2016:Q4 risk-weighted assets

	Actual 2014:Q3	Projected 2016:Q4	
		General approach	Standardized approach
Risk-weighted assets (billions of dollars)[1]	159.3	168.2	194.6

[1] For each quarter in 2014, risk-weighted assets are calculated using the general risk-based capital approach set forth in 12 CFR 225, appendix A. For each quarter in 2015 and 2016, risk-weighted assets are calculated under the Board's standardized capital risk-based approach in 12 CFR 217, subpart D, except for the risk-weighted assets used to calculate the tier 1 common ratio, which uses the general risk-based capital approach for all quarters.

Projected losses, revenue, net income and other comprehensive income through 2016:Q4

	Billions of dollars	Percent of average assets[1]
Pre-provision net revenue[2]	4.5	1.5
Other revenue[3]	0.0	
less		
Provisions	4.9	
Realized losses/gains on securities (AFS/HTM)	0.0	
Trading and counterparty losses[4]	0.0	
Other losses/gains[5]	0.3	
equals		
Net income before taxes	-0.7	-0.2
Memo items		
Other comprehensive income[6]	-2.3	
Other effects on capital	*Actual 2014:Q3*	*2016:Q4*
AOCI included in capital (billions of dollars)[7]	-0.1	-1.7

[1] Average assets is the nine-quarter average of total assets.

[2] Pre-provision net revenue includes losses from operational-risk events, mortgage repurchase expenses, and other real estate owned (OREO) costs.

[3] Other revenue includes one-time income and (expense) items not included in pre-provision net revenue.

[4] Trading and counterparty losses include mark-to-market and credit valuation adjustments (CVA) losses and losses arising from the counterparty default scenario component applied to derivatives, securities lending, and repurchase agreement activities.

[5] Other losses/gains includes projected change in fair value of loans held for sale and loans held for investment measured under the fair-value option and goodwill impairment losses.

[6] Other comprehensive income (OCI) is only calculated for advanced approaches BHCs, and other BHCs that opt into the advanced approaches treatment of AOCI.

[7] Certain AOCI items are subject to transition into projected regulatory capital. Those transitions are 20 percent included in projected regulatory capital for 2014, 40 percent included in projected regulatory capital for 2015, and 60 percent included in projected regulatory capital for 2016.

Table C.17.A. Huntington Bancshares Incorporated
Projected stressed capital ratios, risk-weighted assets, losses, revenues, net income before taxes, and loan losses
Federal Reserve estimates: Severely adverse scenario

Actual 2014:Q3 projected stressed capital ratios through 2016:Q4

	Actual 2014:Q3	Stressed capital ratios[1]	
		Ending	Minimum
Tier 1 common ratio (%)	10.3	9.0	9.0
Common equity tier 1 capital ratio (%)[2]	n/a	8.7	8.7
Tier 1 risk-based capital ratio (%)	11.6	9.4	9.4
Total risk-based capital ratio (%)	13.7	11.6	11.6
Tier 1 leverage ratio (%)	9.8	8.0	8.0

[1] The capital ratios are calculated using capital action assumptions provided within the Dodd-Frank Act stress testing rule. These projections represent hypothetical estimates that involve an economic outcome that is more adverse than expected. These estimates are not forecasts of expected losses, revenues, net income before taxes, or capital ratios. The minimum capital ratio presented is for the period 2014:Q4 to 2016:Q4.

[2] Advanced approaches bank holding companies (BHCs) are subject to the common equity tier 1 ratio for the third and fourth quarter of 2014. All bank holding companies are subject to the common equity tier 1 ratio for each quarter of 2015 and 2016. An advanced approaches BHC includes any BHC that has consolidated total assets greater than or equal to $250 billion or consolidated total on-balance sheet foreign exposure of at least $10 billion. See 12 CFR 217.100(b)(1). Other BHCs include any BHC that is subject to 12 CFR 225.8 and is not an advanced approaches BHC.

n/a   Not applicable.

Projected loan losses, by type of loan, 2014:Q4–2016:Q4

	Billions of dollars	Portfolio loss rates (%)[1]
Loan losses	2.0	4.2
First-lien mortgages, domestic	0.2	2.8
Junior liens and HELOCs, domestic	0.3	4.5
Commercial and industrial[2]	0.5	4.0
Commercial real estate, domestic	0.6	7.2
Credit cards	0.0	14.7
Other consumer[3]	0.3	3.2
Other loans[4]	0.1	2.1

[1] Average loan balances used to calculate portfolio loss rates exclude loans held for sale and loans held for investment under the fair-value option and are calculated over nine quarters.

[2] Commercial and industrial loans include small- and medium-enterprise loans and corporate cards.

[3] Other consumer loans include student loans and automobile loans.

[4] Other loans include international real estate loans.

Actual 2014:Q3 and projected 2016:Q4 risk-weighted assets

	Actual 2014:Q3	Projected 2016:Q4	
		General approach	Standardized approach
Risk-weighted assets (billions of dollars)[1]	53.2	55.0	57.3

[1] For each quarter in 2014, risk-weighted assets are calculated using the general risk-based capital approach set forth in 12 CFR 225, appendix A. For each quarter in 2015 and 2016, risk-weighted assets are calculated under the Board's standardized capital risk-based approach in 12 CFR 217, subpart D, except for the risk-weighted assets used to calculate the tier 1 common ratio, which uses the general risk-based capital approach for all quarters.

Projected losses, revenue, net income and other comprehensive income through 2016:Q4

	Billions of dollars	Percent of average assets[1]
Pre-provision net revenue[2]	2.2	3.3
Other revenue[3]	0.0	
less		
Provisions	2.1	
Realized losses/gains on securities (AFS/HTM)	0.2	
Trading and counterparty losses[4]	0.0	
Other losses/gains[5]	0.0	
equals		
Net income before taxes	-0.1	-0.2
Memo items		
Other comprehensive income[6]	0.0	
Other effects on capital	*Actual 2014:Q3*	*2016:Q4*
AOCI included in capital (billions of dollars)[7]	n/a	0.0

[1] Average assets is the nine-quarter average of total assets.

[2] Pre-provision net revenue includes losses from operational-risk events, mortgage repurchase expenses, and other real estate owned (OREO) costs.

[3] Other revenue includes one-time income and (expense) items not included in pre-provision net revenue.

[4] Trading and counterparty losses include mark-to-market and credit valuation adjustments (CVA) losses and losses arising from the counterparty default scenario component applied to derivatives, securities lending, and repurchase agreement activities.

[5] Other losses/gains includes projected change in fair value of loans held for sale and loans held for investment measured under the fair-value option, and goodwill impairment losses.

[6] Other comprehensive income (OCI) is only calculated for advanced approaches BHCs, and other BHCs that opt into the advanced approaches treatment of AOCI.

[7] Certain AOCI items are subject to transition into projected regulatory capital. Those transitions are 20 percent included in projected regulatory capital for 2014, 40 percent included in projected regulatory capital for 2015, and 60 percent included in projected regulatory capital for 2016.

Table C.17.B. Huntington Bancshares Incorporated
Projected stressed capital ratios, risk-weighted assets, losses, revenues, net income before taxes, and loan losses
Federal Reserve estimates: Adverse scenario

Actual 2014:Q3 projected stressed capital ratios through 2016:Q4

	Actual 2014:Q3	Stressed capital ratios[1]	
		Ending	Minimum
Tier 1 common ratio (%)	10.3	10.1	10.0
Common equity tier 1 capital ratio (%)[2]	n/a	9.8	9.7
Tier 1 risk-based capital ratio (%)	11.6	10.5	10.4
Total risk-based capital ratio (%)	13.7	12.4	12.4
Tier 1 leverage ratio (%)	9.8	8.8	8.8

[1] The capital ratios are calculated using capital action assumptions provided within the Dodd-Frank Act stress testing rule. These projections represent hypothetical estimates that involve an economic outcome that is more adverse than expected. These estimates are not forecasts of expected losses, revenues, net income before taxes, or capital ratios. The minimum capital ratio presented is for the period 2014:Q4 to 2016:Q4.

[2] Advanced approaches bank holding companies (BHCs) are subject to the common equity tier 1 ratio for the third and fourth quarter of 2014. All bank holding companies are subject to the common equity tier 1 ratio for each quarter of 2015 and 2016. An advanced approaches BHC includes any BHC that has consolidated total assets greater than or equal to $250 billion or consolidated total on-balance sheet foreign exposure of at least $10 billion. See 12 CFR 217.100(b)(1). Other BHCs include any BHC that is subject to 12 CFR 225.8 and is not an advanced approaches BHC.

n/a Not applicable.

Projected loan losses, by type of loan, 2014:Q4–2016:Q4

	Billions of dollars	Portfolio loss rates (%)[1]
Loan losses	1.4	2.8
First-lien mortgages, domestic	0.2	2.2
Junior liens and HELOCs, domestic	0.2	3.4
Commercial and industrial[2]	0.3	2.5
Commercial real estate, domestic	0.4	4.5
Credit cards	0.0	11.9
Other consumer[3]	0.2	2.4
Other loans[4]	0.0	1.2

[1] Average loan balances used to calculate portfolio loss rates exclude loans held for sale and loans held for investment under the fair-value option and are calculated over nine quarters.

[2] Commercial and industrial loans include small- and medium-enterprise loans and corporate cards.

[3] Other consumer loans include student loans and automobile loans.

[4] Other loans include international real estate loans.

Actual 2014:Q3 and projected 2016:Q4 risk-weighted assets

	Actual 2014:Q3	Projected 2016:Q4	
		General approach	Standardized approach
Risk-weighted assets (billions of dollars)[1]	53.2	56.8	58.8

[1] For each quarter in 2014, risk-weighted assets are calculated using the general risk-based capital approach set forth in 12 CFR 225, appendix A. For each quarter in 2015 and 2016, risk-weighted assets are calculated under the Board's standardized capital risk-based approach in 12 CFR 217, subpart D, except for the risk-weighted assets used to calculate the tier 1 common ratio, which uses the general risk-based capital approach for all quarters.

Projected losses, revenue, net income and other comprehensive income through 2016:Q4

	Billions of dollars	Percent of average assets[1]
Pre-provision net revenue[2]	2.5	3.6
Other revenue[3]	0.0	
less		
Provisions	1.4	
Realized losses/gains on securities (AFS/HTM)	0.1	
Trading and counterparty losses[4]	0.0	
Other losses/gains[5]	0.0	
equals		
Net income before taxes	1.0	1.5
Memo items		
Other comprehensive income[6]	0.0	
Other effects on capital	Actual 2014:Q3	2016:Q4
AOCI included in capital (billions of dollars)[7]	n/a	0.0

[1] Average assets is the nine-quarter average of total assets.

[2] Pre-provision net revenue includes losses from operational-risk events, mortgage repurchase expenses, and other real estate owned (OREO) costs.

[3] Other revenue includes one-time income and (expense) items not included in pre-provision net revenue.

[4] Trading and counterparty losses include mark-to-market and credit valuation adjustments (CVA) losses and losses arising from the counterparty default scenario component applied to derivatives, securities lending, and repurchase agreement activities.

[5] Other losses/gains includes projected change in fair value of loans held for sale and loans held for investment measured under the fair-value option, and goodwill impairment losses.

[6] Other comprehensive income (OCI) is only calculated for advanced approaches BHCs, and other BHCs that opt into the advanced approaches treatment of AOCI.

[7] Certain AOCI items are subject to transition into projected regulatory capital. Those transitions are 20 percent included in projected regulatory capital for 2014, 40 percent included in projected regulatory capital for 2015, and 60 percent included in projected regulatory capital for 2016.

Table C.18.A. JPMorgan Chase & Co.
Projected stressed capital ratios, risk-weighted assets, losses, revenues, net income before taxes, and loan losses
Federal Reserve estimates: Severely adverse scenario

Actual 2014:Q3 projected stressed capital ratios through 2016:Q4

	Actual 2014:Q3	Stressed capital ratios[1]	
		Ending	Minimum
Tier 1 common ratio (%)	10.9	6.5	6.5
Common equity tier 1 capital ratio (%)[2]	11.1	6.4	6.3
Tier 1 risk-based capital ratio (%)	12.6	7.3	7.3
Total risk-based capital ratio (%)	15.0	9.6	9.6
Tier 1 leverage ratio (%)	7.6	4.6	4.6

[1]   The capital ratios are calculated using capital action assumptions provided within the Dodd-Frank Act stress testing rule. These projections represent hypothetical estimates that involve an economic outcome that is more adverse than expected. These estimates are not forecasts of expected losses, revenues, net income before taxes, or capital ratios. The minimum capital ratio presented is for the period 2014:Q4 to 2016:Q4.

[2]   Advanced approaches bank holding companies (BHCs) are subject to the common equity tier 1 ratio for the third and fourth quarter of 2014. All bank holding companies are subject to the common equity tier 1 ratio for each quarter of 2015 and 2016. An advanced approaches BHC includes any BHC that has consolidated total assets greater than or equal to $250 billion or consolidated total on-balance sheet foreign exposure of at least $10 billion. See 12 CFR 217.100(b)(1). Other BHCs include any BHC that is subject to 12 CFR 225.8 and is not an advanced approaches BHC.

Projected loan losses, by type of loan, 2014:Q4–2016:Q4

	Billions of dollars	Portfolio loss rates (%)[1]
Loan losses	49.7	6.4
First-lien mortgages, domestic	5.4	3.8
Junior liens and HELOCs, domestic	6.7	9.7
Commercial and industrial[2]	9.6	7.5
Commercial real estate, domestic	5.4	6.7
Credit cards	12.9	11.0
Other consumer[3]	2.5	3.7
Other loans[4]	7.1	4.1

[1]   Average loan balances used to calculate portfolio loss rates exclude loans held for sale and loans held for investment under the fair-value option and are calculated over nine quarters.

[2]   Commercial and industrial loans include small- and medium-enterprise loans and corporate cards.

[3]   Other consumer loans include student loans and automobile loans.

[4]   Other loans include international real estate loans.

Actual 2014:Q3 and projected 2016:Q4 risk-weighted assets

	Actual 2014:Q3	Projected 2016:Q4	
		General approach	Standardized approach
Risk-weighted assets (billions of dollars)[1]	1,462.2	1,525.7	1,608.4

[1]   For each quarter in 2014, risk-weighted assets are calculated using the general risk-based capital approach set forth in 12 CFR 225, appendix A. For each quarter in 2015 and 2016, risk-weighted assets are calculated under the Board's standardized capital risk-based approach in 12 CFR 217, subpart D, except for the risk-weighted assets used to calculate the tier 1 common ratio, which uses the general risk-based capital approach for all quarters.

Projected losses, revenue, net income and other comprehensive income through 2016:Q4

	Billions of dollars	Percent of average assets[1]
Pre-provision net revenue[2]	30.4	1.2
Other revenue[3]	0.0	
less		
Provisions	55.5	
Realized losses/gains on securities (AFS/HTM)	4.1	
Trading and counterparty losses[4]	23.6	
Other losses/gains[5]	2.1	
equals		
Net income before taxes	-54.8	-2.1
Memo items		
Other comprehensive income[6]	-5.4	
Other effects on capital	*Actual 2014:Q3*	*2016:Q4*
AOCI included in capital (billions of dollars)[7]	0.6	-1.3

[1]   Average assets is the nine-quarter average of total assets.

[2]   Pre-provision net revenue includes losses from operational-risk events, mortgage repurchase expenses, and other real estate owned (OREO) costs.

[3]   Other revenue includes one-time income and (expense) items not included in pre-provision net revenue.

[4]   Trading and counterparty losses include mark-to-market and credit valuation adjustments (CVA) losses and losses arising from the counterparty default scenario component applied to derivatives, securities lending, and repurchase agreement activities.

[5]   Other losses/gains includes projected change in fair value of loans held for sale and loans held for investment measured under the fair-value option and goodwill impairment losses.

[6]   Other comprehensive income (OCI) is only calculated for advanced approaches BHCs, and other BHCs that opt into the advanced approaches treatment of AOCI.

[7]   Certain AOCI items are subject to transition into projected regulatory capital. Those transitions are 20 percent included in projected regulatory capital for 2014, 40 percent included in projected regulatory capital for 2015, and 60 percent included in projected regulatory capital for 2016.

Table C.18.B. JPMorgan Chase & Co.
Projected stressed capital ratios, risk-weighted assets, losses, revenues, net income before taxes, and loan losses
Federal Reserve estimates: Adverse scenario

Actual 2014:Q3 projected stressed capital ratios through 2016:Q4

	Actual 2014:Q3	Stressed capital ratios[1]	
		Ending	Minimum
Tier 1 common ratio (%)	10.9	10.1	9.6
Common equity tier 1 capital ratio (%)[2]	11.1	9.1	8.8
Tier 1 risk-based capital ratio (%)	12.6	10.3	10.0
Total risk-based capital ratio (%)	15.0	12.1	12.1
Tier 1 leverage ratio (%)	7.6	6.3	6.3

[1] The capital ratios are calculated using capital action assumptions provided within the Dodd-Frank Act stress testing rule. These projections represent hypothetical estimates that involve an economic outcome that is more adverse than expected. These estimates are not forecasts of expected losses, revenues, net income before taxes, or capital ratios. The minimum capital ratio presented is for the period 2014:Q4 to 2016:Q4.

[2] Advanced approaches bank holding companies (BHCs) are subject to the common equity tier 1 ratio for the third and fourth quarter of 2014. All bank holding companies are subject to the common equity tier 1 ratio for each quarter of 2015 and 2016. An advanced approaches BHC includes any BHC that has consolidated total assets greater than or equal to $250 billion or consolidated total on-balance sheet foreign exposure of at least $10 billion. See 12 CFR 217.100(b)(1). Other BHCs include any BHC that is subject to 12 CFR 225.8 and is not an advanced approaches BHC.

Projected loan losses, by type of loan, 2014:Q4–2016:Q4

	Billions of dollars	Portfolio loss rates (%)[1]
Loan losses	33.1	4.2
First-lien mortgages, domestic	3.6	2.5
Junior liens and HELOCs, domestic	4.2	6.0
Commercial and industrial[2]	5.9	4.6
Commercial real estate, domestic	3.0	3.6
Credit cards	10.3	8.7
Other consumer[3]	2.0	3.0
Other loans[4]	4.0	2.3

[1] Average loan balances used to calculate portfolio loss rates exclude loans held for sale and loans held for investment under the fair-value option and are calculated over nine quarters.

[2] Commercial and industrial loans include small- and medium-enterprise loans and corporate cards.

[3] Other consumer loans include student loans and automobile loans.

[4] Other loans include international real estate loans.

Actual 2014:Q3 and projected 2016:Q4 risk-weighted assets

	Actual 2014:Q3	Projected 2016:Q4	
		General approach	Standardized approach
Risk-weighted assets (billions of dollars)[1]	1,462.2	1,577.7	1,658.4

[1] For each quarter in 2014, risk-weighted assets are calculated using the general risk-based capital approach set forth in 12 CFR 225, appendix A. For each quarter in 2015 and 2016, risk-weighted assets are calculated under the Board's standardized capital risk-based approach in 12 CFR 217, subpart D, except for the risk-weighted assets used to calculate the tier 1 common ratio, which uses the general risk-based capital approach for all quarters.

Projected losses, revenue, net income and other comprehensive income through 2016:Q4

	Billions of dollars	Percent of average assets[1]
Pre-provision net revenue[2]	70.5	2.6
Other revenue[3]	0.0	
less		
Provisions	33.7	
Realized losses/gains on securities (AFS/HTM)	2.3	
Trading and counterparty losses[4]	12.2	
Other losses/gains[5]	1.1	
equals		
Net income before taxes	21.2	0.8
Memo items		
Other comprehensive income[6]	-22.8	
Other effects on capital	*Actual 2014:Q3*	*2016:Q4*
AOCI included in capital (billions of dollars)[7]	0.6	-11.7

[1] Average assets is the nine-quarter average of total assets.

[2] Pre-provision net revenue includes losses from operational-risk events, mortgage repurchase expenses, and other real estate owned (OREO) costs.

[3] Other revenue includes one-time income and (expense) items not included in pre-provision net revenue.

[4] Trading and counterparty losses include mark-to-market and credit valuation adjustments (CVA) losses and losses arising from the counterparty default scenario component applied to derivatives, securities lending, and repurchase agreement activities.

[5] Other losses/gains includes projected change in fair value of loans held for sale and loans held for investment measured under the fair-value option and goodwill impairment losses.

[6] Other comprehensive income (OCI) is only calculated for advanced approaches BHCs, and other BHCs that opt into the advanced approaches treatment of AOCI.

[7] Certain AOCI items are subject to transition into projected regulatory capital. Those transitions are 20 percent included in projected regulatory capital for 2014, 40 percent included in projected regulatory capital for 2015, and 60 percent included in projected regulatory capital for 2016.

Table C.19.A. KeyCorp
Projected stressed capital ratios, risk-weighted assets, losses, revenues, net income before taxes, and loan losses
Federal Reserve estimates: Severely adverse scenario

Actual 2014:Q3 projected stressed capital ratios through 2016:Q4

	Actual 2014:Q3	Stressed capital ratios[1]	
		Ending	Minimum
Tier 1 common ratio (%)	11.3	9.9	9.9
Common equity tier 1 capital ratio (%)[2]	n/a	9.6	9.6
Tier 1 risk-based capital ratio (%)	12.0	9.9	9.9
Total risk-based capital ratio (%)	14.1	12.1	12.1
Tier 1 leverage ratio (%)	11.2	9.3	9.3

[1] The capital ratios are calculated using capital action assumptions provided within the Dodd-Frank Act stress testing rule. These projections represent hypothetical estimates that involve an economic outcome that is more adverse than expected. These estimates are not forecasts of expected losses, revenues, net income before taxes, or capital ratios. The minimum capital ratio presented is for the period 2014:Q4 to 2016:Q4.

[2] Advanced approaches bank holding companies (BHCs) are subject to the common equity tier 1 ratio for the third and fourth quarter of 2014. All bank holding companies are subject to the common equity tier 1 ratio for each quarter of 2015 and 2016. An advanced approaches BHC includes any BHC that has consolidated total assets greater than or equal to $250 billion or consolidated total on-balance sheet foreign exposure of at least $10 billion. See 12 CFR 217.100(b)(1). Other BHCs include any BHC that is subject to 12 CFR 225.8 and is not an advanced approaches BHC.

n/a Not applicable.

Projected loan losses, by type of loan, 2014:Q4–2016:Q4

	Billions of dollars	Portfolio loss rates (%)[1]
Loan losses	3.0	5.0
First-lien mortgages, domestic	0.2	4.3
Junior liens and HELOCs, domestic	0.4	4.5
Commercial and industrial[2]	0.9	4.0
Commercial real estate, domestic	0.7	8.0
Credit cards	0.1	12.8
Other consumer[3]	0.4	8.8
Other loans[4]	0.3	2.5

[1] Average loan balances used to calculate portfolio loss rates exclude loans held for sale and loans held for investment under the fair-value option and are calculated over nine quarters.

[2] Commercial and industrial loans include small- and medium-enterprise loans and corporate cards.

[3] Other consumer loans include student loans and automobile loans.

[4] Other loans include international real estate loans.

Actual 2014:Q3 and projected 2016:Q4 risk-weighted assets

	Actual 2014:Q3	Projected 2016:Q4	
		General approach	Standardized approach
Risk-weighted assets (billions of dollars)[1]	83.5	87.0	90.8

[1] For each quarter in 2014, risk-weighted assets are calculated using the general risk-based capital approach set forth in 12 CFR 225, appendix A. For each quarter in 2015 and 2016, risk-weighted assets are calculated under the Board's standardized capital risk-based approach in 12 CFR 217, subpart D, except for the risk-weighted assets used to calculate the tier 1 common ratio, which uses the general risk-based capital approach for all quarters.

Projected losses, revenue, net income and other comprehensive income through 2016:Q4

	Billions of dollars	Percent of average assets[1]
Pre-provision net revenue[2]	3.1	3.3
Other revenue[3]	0.0	
less		
Provisions	3.3	
Realized losses/gains on securities (AFS/HTM)	0.0	
Trading and counterparty losses[4]	0.0	
Other losses/gains[5]	0.2	
equals		
Net income before taxes	-0.4	-0.4
Memo items		
Other comprehensive income[6]	0.0	
Other effects on capital	*Actual 2014:Q3*	*2016:Q4*
AOCI included in capital (billions of dollars)[7]	n/a	0.0

[1] Average assets is the nine-quarter average of total assets.

[2] Pre-provision net revenue includes losses from operational-risk events, mortgage repurchase expenses, and other real estate owned (OREO) costs.

[3] Other revenue includes one-time income and (expense) items not included in pre-provision net revenue.

[4] Trading and counterparty losses include mark-to-market and credit valuation adjustments (CVA) losses and losses arising from the counterparty default scenario component applied to derivatives, securities lending, and repurchase agreement activities.

[5] Other losses/gains includes projected change in fair value of loans held for sale and loans held for investment measured under the fair-value option, and goodwill impairment losses.

[6] Other comprehensive income (OCI) is only calculated for advanced approaches BHCs, and other BHCs that opt into the advanced approaches treatment of AOCI.

[7] Certain AOCI items are subject to transition into projected regulatory capital. Those transitions are 20 percent included in projected regulatory capital for 2014, 40 percent included in projected regulatory capital for 2015, and 60 percent included in projected regulatory capital for 2016.

Table C.19.B. KeyCorp
Projected stressed capital ratios, risk-weighted assets, losses, revenues, net income before taxes, and loan losses
Federal Reserve estimates: Adverse scenario

Actual 2014:Q3 projected stressed capital ratios through 2016:Q4

	Actual 2014:Q3	Stressed capital ratios[1]	
		Ending	Minimum
Tier 1 common ratio (%)	11.3	11.3	10.8
Common equity tier 1 capital ratio (%)[2]	n/a	10.9	10.5
Tier 1 risk-based capital ratio (%)	12.0	11.2	10.9
Total risk-based capital ratio (%)	14.1	13.1	12.9
Tier 1 leverage ratio (%)	11.2	10.4	10.2

[1] The capital ratios are calculated using capital action assumptions provided within the Dodd-Frank Act stress testing rule. These projections represent hypothetical estimates that involve an economic outcome that is more adverse than expected. These estimates are not forecasts of expected losses, revenues, net income before taxes, or capital ratios. The minimum capital ratio presented is for the period 2014:Q4 to 2016:Q4.

[2] Advanced approaches bank holding companies (BHCs) are subject to the common equity tier 1 ratio for the third and fourth quarter of 2014. All bank holding companies are subject to the common equity tier 1 ratio for each quarter of 2015 and 2016. An advanced approaches BHC includes any BHC that has consolidated total assets greater than or equal to $250 billion or consolidated total on-balance sheet foreign exposure of at least $10 billion. See 12 CFR 217.100(b)(1). Other BHCs include any BHC that is subject to 12 CFR 225.8 and is not an advanced approaches BHC.

n/a Not applicable.

Projected loan losses, by type of loan, 2014:Q4–2016:Q4

	Billions of dollars	Portfolio loss rates (%)[1]
Loan losses	2.0	3.2
First-lien mortgages, domestic	0.2	3.4
Junior liens and HELOCs, domestic	0.3	3.3
Commercial and industrial[2]	0.5	2.2
Commercial real estate, domestic	0.5	4.8
Credit cards	0.1	10.1
Other consumer[3]	0.3	7.1
Other loans[4]	0.2	1.5

[1] Average loan balances used to calculate portfolio loss rates exclude loans held for sale and loans held for investment under the fair-value option and are calculated over nine quarters.

[2] Commercial and industrial loans include small- and medium-enterprise loans and corporate cards.

[3] Other consumer loans include student loans and automobile loans.

[4] Other loans include international real estate loans.

Actual 2014:Q3 and projected 2016:Q4 risk-weighted assets

	Actual 2014:Q3	Projected 2016:Q4	
		General approach	Standardized approach
Risk-weighted assets (billions of dollars)[1]	83.5	90.0	93.4

[1] For each quarter in 2014, risk-weighted assets are calculated using the general risk-based capital approach set forth in 12 CFR 225, appendix A. For each quarter in 2015 and 2016, risk-weighted assets are calculated under the Board's standardized capital risk-based approach in 12 CFR 217, subpart D, except for the risk-weighted assets used to calculate the tier 1 common ratio, which uses the general risk-based capital approach for all quarters.

Projected losses, revenue, net income and other comprehensive income through 2016:Q4

	Billions of dollars	Percent of average assets[1]
Pre-provision net revenue[2]	4.1	4.3
Other revenue[3]	0.0	
less		
Provisions	2.0	
Realized losses/gains on securities (AFS/HTM)	0.0	
Trading and counterparty losses[4]	0.0	
Other losses/gains[5]	0.2	
equals		
Net income before taxes	2.0	2.1
Memo items		
Other comprehensive income[6]	0.0	
Other effects on capital	*Actual 2014:Q3*	*2016:Q4*
AOCI included in capital (billions of dollars)[7]	n/a	0.0

[1] Average assets is the nine-quarter average of total assets.

[2] Pre-provision net revenue includes losses from operational-risk events, mortgage repurchase expenses, and other real estate owned (OREO) costs.

[3] Other revenue includes one-time income and (expense) items not included in pre-provision net revenue.

[4] Trading and counterparty losses include mark-to-market and credit valuation adjustments (CVA) losses and losses arising from the counterparty default scenario component applied to derivatives, securities lending, and repurchase agreement activities.

[5] Other losses/gains includes projected change in fair value of loans held for sale and loans held for investment measured under the fair-value option, and goodwill impairment losses.

[6] Other comprehensive income (OCI) is only calculated for advanced approaches BHCs, and other BHCs that opt into the advanced approaches treatment of AOCI.

[7] Certain AOCI items are subject to transition into projected regulatory capital. Those transitions are 20 percent included in projected regulatory capital for 2014, 40 percent included in projected regulatory capital for 2015, and 60 percent included in projected regulatory capital for 2016.

Table C.20.A. M&T Bank Corporation
Projected stressed capital ratios, risk-weighted assets, losses, revenues, net income before taxes, and loan losses
Federal Reserve estimates: Severely adverse scenario

Actual 2014:Q3 projected stressed capital ratios through 2016:Q4

	Actual 2014:Q3	Stressed capital ratios[1]	
		Ending	Minimum
Tier 1 common ratio (%)	9.8	7.3	7.3
Common equity tier 1 capital ratio (%)[2]	n/a	7.5	7.5
Tier 1 risk-based capital ratio (%)	12.5	8.8	8.8
Total risk-based capital ratio (%)	15.4	11.6	11.6
Tier 1 leverage ratio (%)	10.6	6.8	6.8

[1] The capital ratios are calculated using capital action assumptions provided within the Dodd-Frank Act stress testing rule. These projections represent hypothetical estimates that involve an economic outcome that is more adverse than expected. These estimates are not forecasts of expected losses, revenues, net income before taxes, or capital ratios. The minimum capital ratio presented is for the period 2014:Q4 to 2016:Q4.

[2] Advanced approaches bank holding companies (BHCs) are subject to the common equity tier 1 ratio for the third and fourth quarter of 2014. All bank holding companies are subject to the common equity tier 1 ratio for each quarter of 2015 and 2016. An advanced approaches BHC includes any BHC that has consolidated total assets greater than or equal to $250 billion or consolidated total on-balance sheet foreign exposure of at least $10 billion. See 12 CFR 217.100(b)(1). Other BHCs include any BHC that is subject to 12 CFR 225.8 and is not an advanced approaches BHC.

n/a Not applicable.

Projected loan losses, by type of loan, 2014:Q4–2016:Q4

	Billions of dollars	Portfolio loss rates (%)[1]
Loan losses	4.4	5.2
First-lien mortgages, domestic	1.0	3.7
Junior liens and HELOCs, domestic	0.4	6.1
Commercial and industrial[2]	0.6	3.8
Commercial real estate, domestic	2.0	7.5
Credit cards	0.0	14.7
Other consumer[3]	0.3	6.2
Other loans[4]	0.1	2.5

[1] Average loan balances used to calculate portfolio loss rates exclude loans held for sale and loans held for investment under the fair-value option and are calculated over nine quarters.

[2] Commercial and industrial loans include small- and medium-enterprise loans and corporate cards.

[3] Other consumer loans include student loans and automobile loans.

[4] Other loans include international real estate loans.

Actual 2014:Q3 and projected 2016:Q4 risk-weighted assets

	Actual 2014:Q3	Projected 2016:Q4	
		General approach	Standardized approach
Risk-weighted assets (billions of dollars)[1]	75.8	93.1	93.1

[1] For each quarter in 2014, risk-weighted assets are calculated using the general risk-based capital approach set forth in 12 CFR 225, appendix A. For each quarter in 2015 and 2016, risk-weighted assets are calculated under the Board's standardized capital risk-based approach in 12 CFR 217, subpart D, except for the risk-weighted assets used to calculate the tier 1 common ratio, which uses the general risk-based capital approach for all quarters.

Projected losses, revenue, net income and other comprehensive income through 2016:Q4

	Billions of dollars	Percent of average assets[1]
Pre-provision net revenue[2]	4.1	3.3
Other revenue[3]	0.0	
less		
Provisions	5.4	
Realized losses/gains on securities (AFS/HTM)	0.0	
Trading and counterparty losses[4]	0.0	
Other losses/gains[5]	0.1	
equals		
Net income before taxes	-1.4	-1.1
Memo items		
Other comprehensive income[6]	0.0	
Other effects on capital	Actual 2014:Q3	2016:Q4
AOCI included in capital (billions of dollars)[7]	n/a	0.0

[1] Average assets is the nine-quarter average of total assets.

[2] Pre-provision net revenue includes losses from operational-risk events, mortgage repurchase expenses, and other real estate owned (OREO) costs.

[3] Other revenue includes one-time income and (expense) items not included in pre-provision net revenue.

[4] Trading and counterparty losses include mark-to-market and credit valuation adjustments (CVA) losses and losses arising from the counterparty default scenario component applied to derivatives, securities lending, and repurchase agreement activities.

[5] Other losses/gains includes projected change in fair value of loans held for sale and loans held for investment measured under the fair-value option, and goodwill impairment losses.

[6] Other comprehensive income (OCI) is only calculated for advanced approaches BHCs, and other BHCs that opt into the advanced approaches treatment of AOCI.

[7] Certain AOCI items are subject to transition into projected regulatory capital. Those transitions are 20 percent included in projected regulatory capital for 2014, 40 percent included in projected regulatory capital for 2015, and 60 percent included in projected regulatory capital for 2016.

Table C.20.B. M&T Bank Corporation
Projected stressed capital ratios, risk-weighted assets, losses, revenues, net income before taxes, and loan losses
Federal Reserve estimates: Adverse scenario

Actual 2014:Q3 projected stressed capital ratios through 2016:Q4

	Actual 2014:Q3	Stressed capital ratios[1]	
		Ending	Minimum
Tier 1 common ratio (%)	9.8	9.4	9.3
Common equity tier 1 capital ratio (%)[2]	n/a	9.7	9.5
Tier 1 risk-based capital ratio (%)	12.5	11.0	10.9
Total risk-based capital ratio (%)	15.4	13.7	13.7
Tier 1 leverage ratio (%)	10.6	8.3	8.3

[1] The capital ratios are calculated using capital action assumptions provided within the Dodd-Frank Act stress testing rule. These projections represent hypothetical estimates that involve an economic outcome that is more adverse than expected. These estimates are not forecasts of expected losses, revenues, net income before taxes, or capital ratios. The minimum capital ratio presented is for the period 2014:Q4 to 2016:Q4.

[2] Advanced approaches bank holding companies (BHCs) are subject to the common equity tier 1 ratio for the third and fourth quarter of 2014. All bank holding companies are subject to the common equity tier 1 ratio for each quarter of 2015 and 2016. An advanced approaches BHC includes any BHC that has consolidated total assets greater than or equal to $250 billion or consolidated total on-balance sheet foreign exposure of at least $10 billion. See 12 CFR 217.100(b)(1). Other BHCs include any BHC that is subject to 12 CFR 225.8 and is not an advanced approaches BHC.

n/a Not applicable.

Projected loan losses, by type of loan, 2014:Q4–2016:Q4

	Billions of dollars	Portfolio loss rates (%)[1]
Loan losses	3.0	3.6
First-lien mortgages, domestic	0.8	2.8
Junior liens and HELOCs, domestic	0.3	4.7
Commercial and industrial[2]	0.4	2.5
Commercial real estate, domestic	1.3	4.6
Credit cards	0.0	11.9
Other consumer[3]	0.2	4.3
Other loans[4]	0.0	1.4

[1] Average loan balances used to calculate portfolio loss rates exclude loans held for sale and loans held for investment under the fair-value option and are calculated over nine quarters.

[2] Commercial and industrial loans include small- and medium-enterprise loans and corporate cards.

[3] Other consumer loans include student loans and automobile loans.

[4] Other loans include international real estate loans.

Actual 2014:Q3 and projected 2016:Q4 risk-weighted assets

	Actual 2014:Q3	Projected 2016:Q4	
		General approach	Standardized approach
Risk-weighted assets (billions of dollars)[1]	75.8	96.4	95.2

[1] For each quarter in 2014, risk-weighted assets are calculated using the general risk-based capital approach set forth in 12 CFR 225, appendix A. For each quarter in 2015 and 2016, risk-weighted assets are calculated under the Board's standardized capital risk-based approach in 12 CFR 217, subpart D, except for the risk-weighted assets used to calculate the tier 1 common ratio, which uses the general risk-based capital approach for all quarters.

Projected losses, revenue, net income and other comprehensive income through 2016:Q4

	Billions of dollars	Percent of average assets[1]
Pre-provision net revenue[2]	5.3	4.2
Other revenue[3]	0.0	
less		
Provisions	3.5	
Realized losses/gains on securities (AFS/HTM)	0.0	
Trading and counterparty losses[4]	0.0	
Other losses/gains[5]	0.0	
equals		
Net income before taxes	1.8	1.4
Memo items		
Other comprehensive income[6]	0.0	
Other effects on capital	*Actual 2014:Q3*	*2016:Q4*
AOCI included in capital (billions of dollars)[7]	n/a	0.0

[1] Average assets is the nine-quarter average of total assets.

[2] Pre-provision net revenue includes losses from operational-risk events, mortgage repurchase expenses, and other real estate owned (OREO) costs.

[3] Other revenue includes one-time income and (expense) items not included in pre-provision net revenue.

[4] Trading and counterparty losses include mark-to-market and credit valuation adjustments (CVA) losses and losses arising from the counterparty default scenario component applied to derivatives, securities lending, and repurchase agreement activities.

[5] Other losses/gains includes projected change in fair value of loans held for sale and loans held for investment measured under the fair-value option, and goodwill impairment losses.

[6] Other comprehensive income (OCI) is only calculated for advanced approaches BHCs, and other BHCs that opt into the advanced approaches treatment of AOCI.

[7] Certain AOCI items are subject to transition into projected regulatory capital. Those transitions are 20 percent included in projected regulatory capital for 2014, 40 percent included in projected regulatory capital for 2015, and 60 percent included in projected regulatory capital for 2016.

Table C.21.A. Morgan Stanley
Projected stressed capital ratios, risk-weighted assets, losses, revenues, net income before taxes, and loan losses
Federal Reserve estimates: Severely adverse scenario

Actual 2014:Q3 projected stressed capital ratios through 2016:Q4

	Actual 2014:Q3	Stressed capital ratios[1]	
		Ending	Minimum
Tier 1 common ratio (%)	15.0	8.8	6.2
Common equity tier 1 capital ratio (%)[2]	15.2	8.3	6.3
Tier 1 risk-based capital ratio (%)	17.1	8.8	6.5
Total risk-based capital ratio (%)	19.8	11.3	8.6
Tier 1 leverage ratio (%)	8.2	4.9	4.5

[1]   The capital ratios are calculated using capital action assumptions provided within the Dodd-Frank Act stress testing rule. These projections represent hypothetical estimates that involve an economic outcome that is more adverse than expected. These estimates are not forecasts of expected losses, revenues, net income before taxes, or capital ratios. The minimum capital ratio presented is for the period 2014:Q4 to 2016:Q4.

[2]   Advanced approaches bank holding companies (BHCs) are subject to the common equity tier 1 ratio for the third and fourth quarter of 2014. All bank holding companies are subject to the common equity tier 1 ratio for each quarter of 2015 and 2016. An advanced approaches BHC includes any BHC that has consolidated total assets greater than or equal to $250 billion or consolidated total on-balance sheet foreign exposure of at least $10 billion. See 12 CFR 217.100(b)(1). Other BHCs include any BHC that is subject to 12 CFR 225.8 and is not an advanced approaches BHC.

Projected loan losses, by type of loan, 2014:Q4–2016:Q4

	Billions of dollars	Portfolio loss rates (%)[1]
Loan losses	2.6	4.0
First-lien mortgages, domestic	0.2	1.6
Junior liens and HELOCs, domestic	0.0	9.3
Commercial and industrial[2]	0.6	8.0
Commercial real estate, domestic	0.9	19.7
Credit cards	0.0	0.0
Other consumer[3]	0.2	0.7
Other loans[4]	0.6	4.1

[1]   Average loan balances used to calculate portfolio loss rates exclude loans held for sale and loans held for investment under the fair-value option and are calculated over nine quarters.

[2]   Commercial and industrial loans include small- and medium-enterprise loans and corporate cards.

[3]   Other consumer loans include student loans and automobile loans.

[4]   Other loans include international real estate loans.

Actual 2014:Q3 and projected 2016:Q4 risk-weighted assets

	Actual 2014:Q3	Projected 2016:Q4	
		General approach	Standardized approach
Risk-weighted assets (billions of dollars)[1]	390.6	409.8	482.2

[1]   For each quarter in 2014, risk-weighted assets are calculated using the general risk-based capital approach set forth in 12 CFR 225, appendix A. For each quarter in 2015 and 2016, risk-weighted assets are calculated under the Board's standardized capital risk-based approach in 12 CFR 217, subpart D, except for the risk-weighted assets used to calculate the tier 1 common ratio, which uses the general risk-based capital approach for all quarters.

Projected losses, revenue, net income and other comprehensive income through 2016:Q4

	Billions of dollars	Percent of average assets[1]
Pre-provision net revenue[2]	4.1	0.5
Other revenue[3]	0.0	
less		
Provisions	3.5	
Realized losses/gains on securities (AFS/HTM)	0.2	
Trading and counterparty losses[4]	15.8	
Other losses/gains[5]	3.6	
equals		
Net income before taxes	-19.0	-2.2
Memo items		
Other comprehensive income[6]	0.0	
Other effects on capital	*Actual 2014:Q3*	*2016:Q4*
AOCI included in capital (billions of dollars)[7]	-0.6	-0.8

[1]   Average assets is the nine-quarter average of total assets.

[2]   Pre-provision net revenue includes losses from operational-risk events, mortgage repurchase expenses, and other real estate owned (OREO) costs.

[3]   Other revenue includes one-time income and (expense) items not included in pre-provision net revenue.

[4]   Trading and counterparty losses include mark-to-market and credit valuation adjustments (CVA) losses and losses arising from the counterparty default scenario component applied to derivatives, securities lending, and repurchase agreement activities.

[5]   Other losses/gains includes projected change in fair value of loans held for sale and loans held for investment measured under the fair-value option and goodwill impairment losses.

[6]   Other comprehensive income (OCI) is only calculated for advanced approaches BHCs, and other BHCs that opt into the advanced approaches treatment of AOCI.

[7]   Certain AOCI items are subject to transition into projected regulatory capital. Those transitions are 20 percent included in projected regulatory capital for 2014, 40 percent included in projected regulatory capital for 2015, and 60 percent included in projected regulatory capital for 2016.

Table C.21.B. Morgan Stanley
Projected stressed capital ratios, risk-weighted assets, losses, revenues, net income before taxes, and loan losses
Federal Reserve estimates: Adverse scenario

Actual 2014:Q3 projected stressed capital ratios through 2016:Q4

	Actual 2014:Q3	Stressed capital ratios[1]	
		Ending	Minimum
Tier 1 common ratio (%)	15.0	14.0	12.2
Common equity tier 1 capital ratio (%)[2]	15.2	11.9	10.7
Tier 1 risk-based capital ratio (%)	17.1	13.1	11.9
Total risk-based capital ratio (%)	19.8	15.5	14.4
Tier 1 leverage ratio (%)	8.2	7.0	6.7

[1] The capital ratios are calculated using capital action assumptions provided within the Dodd-Frank Act stress testing rule. These projections represent hypothetical estimates that involve an economic outcome that is more adverse than expected. These estimates are not forecasts of expected losses, revenues, net income before taxes, or capital ratios. The minimum capital ratio presented is for the period 2014:Q4 to 2016:Q4.

[2] Advanced approaches bank holding companies (BHCs) are subject to the common equity tier 1 ratio for the third and fourth quarter of 2014. All bank holding companies are subject to the common equity tier 1 ratio for each quarter of 2015 and 2016. An advanced approaches BHC includes any BHC that has consolidated total assets greater than or equal to $250 billion or consolidated total on-balance sheet foreign exposure of at least $10 billion. See 12 CFR 217.100(b)(1). Other BHCs include any BHC that is subject to 12 CFR 225.8 and is not an advanced approaches BHC.

Projected loan losses, by type of loan, 2014:Q4–2016:Q4

	Billions of dollars	Portfolio loss rates (%)[1]
Loan losses	1.5	2.3
First-lien mortgages, domestic	0.2	1.0
Junior liens and HELOCs, domestic	0.0	5.6
Commercial and industrial[2]	0.4	4.4
Commercial real estate, domestic	0.5	10.8
Credit cards	0.0	0.0
Other consumer[3]	0.1	0.7
Other loans[4]	0.4	2.4

[1] Average loan balances used to calculate portfolio loss rates exclude loans held for sale and loans held for investment under the fair-value option and are calculated over nine quarters.

[2] Commercial and industrial loans include small- and medium-enterprise loans and corporate cards.

[3] Other consumer loans include student loans and automobile loans.

[4] Other loans include international real estate loans.

Actual 2014:Q3 and projected 2016:Q4 risk-weighted assets

	Actual 2014:Q3	Projected 2016:Q4	
		General approach	Standardized approach
Risk-weighted assets (billions of dollars)[1]	390.6	416.5	489.3

[1] For each quarter in 2014, risk-weighted assets are calculated using the general risk-based capital approach set forth in 12 CFR 225, appendix A. For each quarter in 2015 and 2016, risk-weighted assets are calculated under the Board's standardized capital risk-based approach in 12 CFR 217, subpart D, except for the risk-weighted assets used to calculate the tier 1 common ratio, which uses the general risk-based capital approach for all quarters.

Projected losses, revenue, net income and other comprehensive income through 2016:Q4

	Billions of dollars	Percent of average assets[1]
Pre-provision net revenue[2]	16.6	1.9
Other revenue[3]	0.0	
less		
Provisions	2.0	
Realized losses/gains on securities (AFS/HTM)	0.1	
Trading and counterparty losses[4]	8.1	
Other losses/gains[5]	1.7	
equals		
Net income before taxes	4.7	0.5
Memo items		
Other comprehensive income[6]	-3.7	
Other effects on capital	Actual 2014:Q3	2016:Q4
AOCI included in capital (billions of dollars)[7]	-0.6	-3.1

[1] Average assets is the nine-quarter average of total assets.

[2] Pre-provision net revenue includes losses from operational-risk events, mortgage repurchase expenses, and other real estate owned (OREO) costs.

[3] Other revenue includes one-time income and (expense) items not included in pre-provision net revenue.

[4] Trading and counterparty losses include mark-to-market and credit valuation adjustments (CVA) losses and losses arising from the counterparty default scenario component applied to derivatives, securities lending, and repurchase agreement activities.

[5] Other losses/gains includes projected change in fair value of loans held for sale and loans held for investment measured under the fair-value option and goodwill impairment losses.

[6] Other comprehensive income (OCI) is only calculated for advanced approaches BHCs, and other BHCs that opt into the advanced approaches treatment of AOCI.

[7] Certain AOCI items are subject to transition into projected regulatory capital. Those transitions are 20 percent included in projected regulatory capital for 2014, 40 percent included in projected regulatory capital for 2015, and 60 percent included in projected regulatory capital for 2016.

Table C.22.A. MUFG Americas Holdings Corporation
Projected stressed capital ratios, risk-weighted assets, losses, revenues, net income before taxes, and loan losses
Federal Reserve estimates: Severely adverse scenario

Actual 2014:Q3 projected stressed capital ratios through 2016:Q4

	Actual 2014:Q3	Stressed capital ratios[1]	
		Ending	Minimum
Tier 1 common ratio (%)	12.7	8.0	8.0
Common equity tier 1 capital ratio (%)[2]	12.7	8.0	8.0
Tier 1 risk-based capital ratio (%)	12.7	8.0	8.0
Total risk-based capital ratio (%)	14.6	10.2	10.2
Tier 1 leverage ratio (%)	11.4	7.1	7.1

[1] The capital ratios are calculated using capital action assumptions provided within the Dodd-Frank Act stress testing rule. These projections represent hypothetical estimates that involve an economic outcome that is more adverse than expected. These estimates are not forecasts of expected losses, revenues, net income before taxes, or capital ratios. The minimum capital ratio presented is for the period 2014:Q4 to 2016:Q4.

[2] Advanced approaches bank holding companies (BHCs) are subject to the common equity tier 1 ratio for the third and fourth quarter of 2014. All bank holding companies are subject to the common equity tier 1 ratio for each quarter of 2015 and 2016. An advanced approaches BHC includes any BHC that has consolidated total assets greater than or equal to $250 billion or consolidated total on-balance sheet foreign exposure of at least $10 billion. See 12 CFR 217.100(b)(1). Other BHCs include any BHC that is subject to 12 CFR 225.8 and is not an advanced approaches BHC.

Projected loan losses, by type of loan, 2014:Q4–2016:Q4

	Billions of dollars	Portfolio loss rates (%)[1]
Loan losses	3.8	5.0
First-lien mortgages, domestic	0.9	3.1
Junior liens and HELOCs, domestic	0.1	4.2
Commercial and industrial[2]	0.9	4.8
Commercial real estate, domestic	1.4	9.0
Credit cards	0.0	0.0
Other consumer[3]	0.0	14.7
Other loans[4]	0.3	4.1

[1] Average loan balances used to calculate portfolio loss rates exclude loans held for sale and loans held for investment under the fair-value option and are calculated over nine quarters.

[2] Commercial and industrial loans include small- and medium-enterprise loans and corporate cards.

[3] Other consumer loans include student loans and automobile loans.

[4] Other loans include international real estate loans.

Actual 2014:Q3 and projected 2016:Q4 risk-weighted assets

	Actual 2014:Q3	Projected 2016:Q4	
		General approach	Standardized approach
Risk-weighted assets (billions of dollars)[1]	96.2	99.3	99.7

[1] For each quarter in 2014, risk-weighted assets are calculated using the general risk-based capital approach set forth in 12 CFR 225, appendix A. For each quarter in 2015 and 2016, risk-weighted assets are calculated under the Board's standardized capital risk-based approach in 12 CFR 217, subpart D, except for the risk-weighted assets used to calculate the tier 1 common ratio, which uses the general risk-based capital approach for all quarters.

Projected losses, revenue, net income and other comprehensive income through 2016:Q4

	Billions of dollars	Percent of average assets[1]
Pre-provision net revenue[2]	1.1	1.0
Other revenue[3]	0.0	
less		
Provisions	4.9	
Realized losses/gains on securities (AFS/HTM)	0.6	
Trading and counterparty losses[4]	0.0	
Other losses/gains[5]	0.0	
equals		
Net income before taxes	-4.4	-3.8
Memo items		
Other comprehensive income[6]	0.0	
Other effects on capital	*Actual 2014:Q3*	*2016:Q4*
AOCI included in capital (billions of dollars)[7]	0.4	0.0

[1] Average assets is the nine-quarter average of total assets.

[2] Pre-provision net revenue includes losses from operational-risk events, mortgage repurchase expenses, and other real estate owned (OREO) costs.

[3] Other revenue includes one-time income and (expense) items not included in pre-provision net revenue.

[4] Trading and counterparty losses include mark-to-market and credit valuation adjustments (CVA) losses and losses arising from the counterparty default scenario component applied to derivatives, securities lending, and repurchase agreement activities.

[5] Other losses/gains includes projected change in fair value of loans held for sale and loans held for investment measured under the fair-value option and goodwill impairment losses.

[6] Other comprehensive income (OCI) is only calculated for advanced approaches BHCs, and other BHCs that opt into the advanced approaches treatment of AOCI.

[7] Certain AOCI items are subject to transition into projected regulatory capital. Those transitions are 20 percent included in projected regulatory capital for 2014, 40 percent included in projected regulatory capital for 2015, and 60 percent included in projected regulatory capital for 2016.

Table C.22.B. MUFG Americas Holdings Corporation
Projected stressed capital ratios, risk-weighted assets, losses, revenues, net income before taxes, and loan losses
Federal Reserve estimates: Adverse scenario

Actual 2014:Q3 projected stressed capital ratios through 2016:Q4

	Actual 2014:Q3	Stressed capital ratios[1]	
		Ending	Minimum
Tier 1 common ratio (%)	12.7	11.3	11.3
Common equity tier 1 capital ratio (%)[2]	12.7	11.4	11.4
Tier 1 risk-based capital ratio (%)	12.7	11.4	11.4
Total risk-based capital ratio (%)	14.6	13.3	13.3
Tier 1 leverage ratio (%)	11.4	9.8	9.8

[1] The capital ratios are calculated using capital action assumptions provided within the Dodd-Frank Act stress testing rule. These projections represent hypothetical estimates that involve an economic outcome that is more adverse than expected. These estimates are not forecasts of expected losses, revenues, net income before taxes, or capital ratios. The minimum capital ratio presented is for the period 2014:Q4 to 2016:Q4.

[2] Advanced approaches bank holding companies (BHCs) are subject to the common equity tier 1 ratio for the third and fourth quarter of 2014. All bank holding companies are subject to the common equity tier 1 ratio for each quarter of 2015 and 2016. An advanced approaches BHC includes any BHC that has consolidated total assets greater than or equal to $250 billion or consolidated total on-balance sheet foreign exposure of at least $10 billion. See 12 CFR 217.100(b)(1). Other BHCs include any BHC that is subject to 12 CFR 225.8 and is not an advanced approaches BHC.

Projected loan losses, by type of loan, 2014:Q4–2016:Q4

	Billions of dollars	Portfolio loss rates (%)[1]
Loan losses	2.1	2.8
First-lien mortgages, domestic	0.6	1.9
Junior liens and HELOCs, domestic	0.1	1.8
Commercial and industrial[2]	0.5	2.7
Commercial real estate, domestic	0.8	4.9
Credit cards	0.0	0.0
Other consumer[3]	0.0	11.9
Other loans[4]	0.2	2.2

[1] Average loan balances used to calculate portfolio loss rates exclude loans held for sale and loans held for investment under the fair-value option and are calculated over nine quarters.

[2] Commercial and industrial loans include small- and medium-enterprise loans and corporate cards.

[3] Other consumer loans include student loans and automobile loans.

[4] Other loans include international real estate loans.

Actual 2014:Q3 and projected 2016:Q4 risk-weighted assets

	Actual 2014:Q3	Projected 2016:Q4	
		General approach	Standardized approach
Risk-weighted assets (billions of dollars)[1]	96.2	103.3	103.1

[1] For each quarter in 2014, risk-weighted assets are calculated using the general risk-based capital approach set forth in 12 CFR 225, appendix A. For each quarter in 2015 and 2016, risk-weighted assets are calculated under the Board's standardized capital risk-based approach in 12 CFR 217, subpart D, except for the risk-weighted assets used to calculate the tier 1 common ratio, which uses the general risk-based capital approach for all quarters.

Projected losses, revenue, net income and other comprehensive income through 2016:Q4

	Billions of dollars	Percent of average assets[1]
Pre-provision net revenue[2]	2.2	1.9
Other revenue[3]	0.0	
less		
Provisions	2.6	
Realized losses/gains on securities (AFS/HTM)	0.3	
Trading and counterparty losses[4]	0.0	
Other losses/gains[5]	0.0	
equals		
Net income before taxes	-0.7	-0.6
Memo items		
Other comprehensive income[6]	0.0	
Other effects on capital	*Actual 2014:Q3*	*2016:Q4*
AOCI included in capital (billions of dollars)[7]	0.4	0.0

[1] Average assets is the nine-quarter average of total assets.

[2] Pre-provision net revenue includes losses from operational-risk events, mortgage repurchase expenses, and other real estate owned (OREO) costs.

[3] Other revenue includes one-time income and (expense) items not included in pre-provision net revenue.

[4] Trading and counterparty losses include mark-to-market and credit valuation adjustments (CVA) losses and losses arising from the counterparty default scenario component applied to derivatives, securities lending, and repurchase agreement activities.

[5] Other losses/gains includes projected change in fair value of loans held for sale and loans held for investment measured under the fair-value option and goodwill impairment losses.

[6] Other comprehensive income (OCI) is only calculated for advanced approaches BHCs, and other BHCs that opt into the advanced approaches treatment of AOCI.

[7] Certain AOCI items are subject to transition into projected regulatory capital. Those transitions are 20 percent included in projected regulatory capital for 2014, 40 percent included in projected regulatory capital for 2015, and 60 percent included in projected regulatory capital for 2016.

Table C.23.A. Northern Trust Corporation
Projected stressed capital ratios, risk-weighted assets, losses, revenues, net income before taxes, and loan losses
Federal Reserve estimates: Severely adverse scenario

Actual 2014:Q3 projected stressed capital ratios through 2016:Q4

	Actual 2014:Q3	Stressed capital ratios[1]	
		Ending	Minimum
Tier 1 common ratio (%)	12.8	12.4	12.3
Common equity tier 1 capital ratio (%)[2]	12.8	10.9	10.8
Tier 1 risk-based capital ratio (%)	13.6	11.4	11.3
Total risk-based capital ratio (%)	16.0	13.6	13.6
Tier 1 leverage ratio (%)	7.9	7.4	7.4

[1] The capital ratios are calculated using capital action assumptions provided within the Dodd-Frank Act stress testing rule. These projections represent hypothetical estimates that involve an economic outcome that is more adverse than expected. These estimates are not forecasts of expected losses, revenues, net income before taxes, or capital ratios. The minimum capital ratio presented is for the period 2014:Q4 to 2016:Q4.

[2] Advanced approaches bank holding companies (BHCs) are subject to the common equity tier 1 ratio for the third and fourth quarter of 2014. All bank holding companies are subject to the common equity tier 1 ratio for each quarter of 2015 and 2016. An advanced approaches BHC includes any BHC that has consolidated total assets greater than or equal to $250 billion or consolidated total on-balance sheet foreign exposure of at least $10 billion. See 12 CFR 217.100(b)(1). Other BHCs include any BHC that is subject to 12 CFR 225.8 and is not an advanced approaches BHC.

Projected loan losses, by type of loan, 2014:Q4–2016:Q4

	Billions of dollars	Portfolio loss rates (%)[1]
Loan losses	1.5	4.9
First-lien mortgages, domestic	0.3	3.5
Junior liens and HELOCs, domestic	0.3	13.0
Commercial and industrial[2]	0.2	4.0
Commercial real estate, domestic	0.3	8.5
Credit cards	0.0	0.0
Other consumer[3]	0.0	13.1
Other loans[4]	0.4	3.7

[1] Average loan balances used to calculate portfolio loss rates exclude loans held for sale and loans held for investment under the fair-value option and are calculated over nine quarters.

[2] Commercial and industrial loans include small- and medium-enterprise loans and corporate cards.

[3] Other consumer loans include student loans and automobile loans.

[4] Other loans include international real estate loans.

Actual 2014:Q3 and projected 2016:Q4 risk-weighted assets

	Actual 2014:Q3	Projected 2016:Q4	
		General approach	Standardized approach
Risk-weighted assets (billions of dollars)[1]	61.0	63.5	72.0

[1] For each quarter in 2014, risk-weighted assets are calculated using the general risk-based capital approach set forth in 12 CFR 225, appendix A. For each quarter in 2015 and 2016, risk-weighted assets are calculated under the Board's standardized capital risk-based approach in 12 CFR 217, subpart D, except for the risk-weighted assets used to calculate the tier 1 common ratio, which uses the general risk-based capital approach for all quarters.

Projected losses, revenue, net income and other comprehensive income through 2016:Q4

	Billions of dollars	Percent of average assets[1]
Pre-provision net revenue[2]	3.2	2.8
Other revenue[3]	0.0	
less		
Provisions	1.9	
Realized losses/gains on securities (AFS/HTM)	0.0	
Trading and counterparty losses[4]	0.0	
Other losses/gains[5]	0.0	
equals		
Net income before taxes	1.3	1.1
Memo items		
Other comprehensive income[6]	0.1	
Other effects on capital	Actual 2014:Q3	2016:Q4
AOCI included in capital (billions of dollars)[7]	0.0	-0.1

[1] Average assets is the nine-quarter average of total assets.

[2] Pre-provision net revenue includes losses from operational-risk events, mortgage repurchase expenses, and other real estate owned (OREO) costs.

[3] Other revenue includes one-time income and (expense) items not included in pre-provision net revenue.

[4] Trading and counterparty losses include mark-to-market and credit valuation adjustments (CVA) losses and losses arising from the counterparty default scenario component applied to derivatives, securities lending, and repurchase agreement activities.

[5] Other losses/gains includes projected change in fair value of loans held for sale and loans held for investment measured under the fair-value option and goodwill impairment losses.

[6] Other comprehensive income (OCI) is only calculated for advanced approaches BHCs, and other BHCs that opt into the advanced approaches treatment of AOCI.

[7] Certain AOCI items are subject to transition into projected regulatory capital. Those transitions are 20 percent included in projected regulatory capital for 2014, 40 percent included in projected regulatory capital for 2015, and 60 percent included in projected regulatory capital for 2016.

Table C.23.B. Northern Trust Corporation
Projected stressed capital ratios, risk-weighted assets, losses, revenues, net income before taxes, and loan losses
Federal Reserve estimates: Adverse scenario

Actual 2014:Q3 projected stressed capital ratios through 2016:Q4

	Actual 2014:Q3	Stressed capital ratios[1]	
		Ending	Minimum
Tier 1 common ratio (%)	12.8	14.3	12.5
Common equity tier 1 capital ratio (%)[2]	12.8	11.7	10.9
Tier 1 risk-based capital ratio (%)	13.6	12.2	11.5
Total risk-based capital ratio (%)	16.0	14.0	13.5
Tier 1 leverage ratio (%)	7.9	7.8	7.4

[1] The capital ratios are calculated using capital action assumptions provided within the Dodd-Frank Act stress testing rule. These projections represent hypothetical estimates that involve an economic outcome that is more adverse than expected. These estimates are not forecasts of expected losses, revenues, net income before taxes, or capital ratios. The minimum capital ratio presented is for the period 2014:Q4 to 2016:Q4.

[2] Advanced approaches bank holding companies (BHCs) are subject to the common equity tier 1 ratio for the third and fourth quarter of 2014. All bank holding companies are subject to the common equity tier 1 ratio for each quarter of 2015 and 2016. An advanced approaches BHC includes any BHC that has consolidated total assets greater than or equal to $250 billion or consolidated total on-balance sheet foreign exposure of at least $10 billion. See 12 CFR 217.100(b)(1). Other BHCs include any BHC that is subject to 12 CFR 225.8 and is not an advanced approaches BHC.

Projected loan losses, by type of loan, 2014:Q4–2016:Q4

	Billions of dollars	Portfolio loss rates (%)[1]
Loan losses	1.0	3.1
First-lien mortgages, domestic	0.2	2.6
Junior liens and HELOCs, domestic	0.2	9.1
Commercial and industrial[2]	0.1	2.2
Commercial real estate, domestic	0.2	5.0
Credit cards	0.0	0.0
Other consumer[3]	0.0	10.4
Other loans[4]	0.2	2.0

[1] Average loan balances used to calculate portfolio loss rates exclude loans held for sale and loans held for investment under the fair-value option and are calculated over nine quarters.

[2] Commercial and industrial loans include small- and medium-enterprise loans and corporate cards.

[3] Other consumer loans include student loans and automobile loans.

[4] Other loans include international real estate loans.

Actual 2014:Q3 and projected 2016:Q4 risk-weighted assets

	Actual 2014:Q3	Projected 2016:Q4	
		General approach	Standardized approach
Risk-weighted assets (billions of dollars)[1]	61.0	66.2	74.7

[1] For each quarter in 2014, risk-weighted assets are calculated using the general risk-based capital approach set forth in 12 CFR 225, appendix A. For each quarter in 2015 and 2016, risk-weighted assets are calculated under the Board's standardized capital risk-based approach in 12 CFR 217, subpart D, except for the risk-weighted assets used to calculate the tier 1 common ratio, which uses the general risk-based capital approach for all quarters.

Projected losses, revenue, net income and other comprehensive income through 2016:Q4

	Billions of dollars	Percent of average assets[1]
Pre-provision net revenue[2]	4.8	4.1
Other revenue[3]	0.0	
less		
Provisions	1.1	
Realized losses/gains on securities (AFS/HTM)	0.0	
Trading and counterparty losses[4]	0.0	
Other losses/gains[5]	0.0	
equals		
Net income before taxes	3.7	3.1
Memo items		
Other comprehensive income[6]	-1.0	
Other effects on capital	*Actual 2014:Q3*	*2016:Q4*
AOCI included in capital (billions of dollars)[7]	0.0	-0.8

[1] Average assets is the nine-quarter average of total assets.

[2] Pre-provision net revenue includes losses from operational-risk events, mortgage repurchase expenses, and other real estate owned (OREO) costs.

[3] Other revenue includes one-time income and (expense) items not included in pre-provision net revenue.

[4] Trading and counterparty losses include mark-to-market and credit valuation adjustments (CVA) losses and losses arising from the counterparty default scenario component applied to derivatives, securities lending, and repurchase agreement activities.

[5] Other losses/gains includes projected change in fair value of loans held for sale and loans held for investment measured under the fair-value option and goodwill impairment losses.

[6] Other comprehensive income (OCI) is only calculated for advanced approaches BHCs, and other BHCs that opt into the advanced approaches treatment of AOCI.

[7] Certain AOCI items are subject to transition into projected regulatory capital. Those transitions are 20 percent included in projected regulatory capital for 2014, 40 percent included in projected regulatory capital for 2015, and 60 percent included in projected regulatory capital for 2016.

Table C.24.A. The PNC Financial Services Group, Inc.
Projected stressed capital ratios, risk-weighted assets, losses, revenues, net income before taxes, and loan losses
Federal Reserve estimates: Severely adverse scenario

Actual 2014:Q3 projected stressed capital ratios through 2016:Q4

	Actual 2014:Q3	Stressed capital ratios[1]	
		Ending	Minimum
Tier 1 common ratio (%)	11.0	9.5	9.5
Common equity tier 1 capital ratio (%)[2]	11.1	8.4	8.4
Tier 1 risk-based capital ratio (%)	12.8	9.9	9.9
Total risk-based capital ratio (%)	16.1	12.5	12.5
Tier 1 leverage ratio (%)	11.1	8.7	8.7

[1] The capital ratios are calculated using capital action assumptions provided within the Dodd-Frank Act stress testing rule. These projections represent hypothetical estimates that involve an economic outcome that is more adverse than expected. These estimates are not forecasts of expected losses, revenues, net income before taxes, or capital ratios. The minimum capital ratio presented is for the period 2014:Q4 to 2016:Q4.

[2] Advanced approaches bank holding companies (BHCs) are subject to the common equity tier 1 ratio for the third and fourth quarter of 2014. All bank holding companies are subject to the common equity tier 1 ratio for each quarter of 2015 and 2016. An advanced approaches BHC includes any BHC that has consolidated total assets greater than or equal to $250 billion or consolidated total on-balance sheet foreign exposure of at least $10 billion. See 12 CFR 217.100(b)(1). Other BHCs include any BHC that is subject to 12 CFR 225.8 and is not an advanced approaches BHC.

Projected loan losses, by type of loan, 2014:Q4–2016:Q4

	Billions of dollars	Portfolio loss rates (%)[1]
Loan losses	9.6	4.7
First-lien mortgages, domestic	0.4	1.7
Junior liens and HELOCs, domestic	0.7	3.0
Commercial and industrial[2]	3.7	5.7
Commercial real estate, domestic	3.1	9.3
Credit cards	0.5	12.1
Other consumer[3]	0.8	3.2
Other loans[4]	0.4	1.5

[1] Average loan balances used to calculate portfolio loss rates exclude loans held for sale and loans held for investment under the fair-value option and are calculated over nine quarters.

[2] Commercial and industrial loans include small- and medium-enterprise loans and corporate cards.

[3] Other consumer loans include student loans and automobile loans.

[4] Other loans include international real estate loans.

Actual 2014:Q3 and projected 2016:Q4 risk-weighted assets

	Actual 2014:Q3	Projected 2016:Q4	
		General approach	Standardized approach
Risk-weighted assets (billions of dollars)[1]	277.3	287.3	301.1

[1] For each quarter in 2014, risk-weighted assets are calculated using the general risk-based capital approach set forth in 12 CFR 225, appendix A. For each quarter in 2015 and 2016, risk-weighted assets are calculated under the Board's standardized capital risk-based approach in 12 CFR 217, subpart D, except for the risk-weighted assets used to calculate the tier 1 common ratio, which uses the general risk-based capital approach for all quarters.

Projected losses, revenue, net income and other comprehensive income through 2016:Q4

	Billions of dollars	Percent of average assets[1]
Pre-provision net revenue[2]	11.5	3.3
Other revenue[3]	0.0	
less		
Provisions	10.8	
Realized losses/gains on securities (AFS/HTM)	0.5	
Trading and counterparty losses[4]	0.0	
Other losses/gains[5]	0.4	
equals		
Net income before taxes	-0.2	-0.1
Memo items		
Other comprehensive income[6]	-0.9	
Other effects on capital	*Actual 2014:Q3*	*2016:Q4*
AOCI included in capital (billions of dollars)[7]	0.1	-0.3

[1] Average assets is the nine-quarter average of total assets.

[2] Pre-provision net revenue includes losses from operational-risk events, mortgage repurchase expenses, and other real estate owned (OREO) costs.

[3] Other revenue includes one-time income and (expense) items not included in pre-provision net revenue.

[4] Trading and counterparty losses include mark-to-market and credit valuation adjustments (CVA) losses and losses arising from the counterparty default scenario component applied to derivatives, securities lending, and repurchase agreement activities.

[5] Other losses/gains includes projected change in fair value of loans held for sale and loans held for investment measured under the fair-value option and goodwill impairment losses.

[6] Other comprehensive income (OCI) is only calculated for advanced approaches BHCs, and other BHCs that opt into the advanced approaches treatment of AOCI.

[7] Certain AOCI items are subject to transition into projected regulatory capital. Those transitions are 20 percent included in projected regulatory capital for 2014, 40 percent included in projected regulatory capital for 2015, and 60 percent included in projected regulatory capital for 2016.

Table C.24.B. The PNC Financial Services Group, Inc.
Projected stressed capital ratios, risk-weighted assets, losses, revenues, net income before taxes, and loan losses
Federal Reserve estimates: Adverse scenario

Actual 2014:Q3 projected stressed capital ratios through 2016:Q4

	Actual 2014:Q3	Stressed capital ratios[1]	
		Ending	Minimum
Tier 1 common ratio (%)	11.0	11.2	10.7
Common equity tier 1 capital ratio (%)[2]	11.1	9.8	9.5
Tier 1 risk-based capital ratio (%)	12.8	11.1	10.9
Total risk-based capital ratio (%)	16.1	13.5	13.5
Tier 1 leverage ratio (%)	11.1	9.7	9.6

[1] The capital ratios are calculated using capital action assumptions provided within the Dodd-Frank Act stress testing rule. These projections represent hypothetical estimates that involve an economic outcome that is more adverse than expected. These estimates are not forecasts of expected losses, revenues, net income before taxes, or capital ratios. The minimum capital ratio presented is for the period 2014:Q4 to 2016:Q4.

[2] Advanced approaches bank holding companies (BHCs) are subject to the common equity tier 1 ratio for the third and fourth quarter of 2014. All bank holding companies are subject to the common equity tier 1 ratio for each quarter of 2015 and 2016. An advanced approaches BHC includes any BHC that has consolidated total assets greater than or equal to $250 billion or consolidated total on-balance sheet foreign exposure of at least $10 billion. See 12 CFR 217.100(b)(1). Other BHCs include any BHC that is subject to 12 CFR 225.8 and is not an advanced approaches BHC.

Projected loan losses, by type of loan, 2014:Q4–2016:Q4

	Billions of dollars	Portfolio loss rates (%)[1]
Loan losses	6.1	2.9
First-lien mortgages, domestic	0.3	1.0
Junior liens and HELOCs, domestic	0.4	1.8
Commercial and industrial[2]	2.3	3.4
Commercial real estate, domestic	1.8	5.5
Credit cards	0.4	9.5
Other consumer[3]	0.6	2.6
Other loans[4]	0.3	0.9

[1] Average loan balances used to calculate portfolio loss rates exclude loans held for sale and loans held for investment under the fair-value option and are calculated over nine quarters.

[2] Commercial and industrial loans include small- and medium-enterprise loans and corporate cards.

[3] Other consumer loans include student loans and automobile loans.

[4] Other loans include international real estate loans.

Actual 2014:Q3 and projected 2016:Q4 risk-weighted assets

	Actual 2014:Q3	Projected 2016:Q4	
		General approach	Standardized approach
Risk-weighted assets (billions of dollars)[1]	277.3	298.9	311.6

[1] For each quarter in 2014, risk-weighted assets are calculated using the general risk-based capital approach set forth in 12 CFR 225, appendix A. For each quarter in 2015 and 2016, risk-weighted assets are calculated under the Board's standardized capital risk-based approach in 12 CFR 217, subpart D, except for the risk-weighted assets used to calculate the tier 1 common ratio, which uses the general risk-based capital approach for all quarters.

Projected losses, revenue, net income and other comprehensive income through 2016:Q4

	Billions of dollars	Percent of average assets[1]
Pre-provision net revenue[2]	15.8	4.5
Other revenue[3]	0.0	
less		
Provisions	6.0	
Realized losses/gains on securities (AFS/HTM)	0.2	
Trading and counterparty losses[4]	0.0	
Other losses/gains[5]	0.3	
equals		
Net income before taxes	9.3	2.6
Memo items		
Other comprehensive income[6]	-3.4	
Other effects on capital	*Actual 2014:Q3*	*2016:Q4*
AOCI included in capital (billions of dollars)[7]	0.1	-1.8

[1] Average assets is the nine-quarter average of total assets.

[2] Pre-provision net revenue includes losses from operational-risk events, mortgage repurchase expenses, and other real estate owned (OREO) costs.

[3] Other revenue includes one-time income and (expense) items not included in pre-provision net revenue.

[4] Trading and counterparty losses include mark-to-market and credit valuation adjustments (CVA) losses and losses arising from the counterparty default scenario component applied to derivatives, securities lending, and repurchase agreement activities.

[5] Other losses/gains includes projected change in fair value of loans held for sale and loans held for investment measured under the fair-value option and goodwill impairment losses.

[6] Other comprehensive income (OCI) is only calculated for advanced approaches BHCs, and other BHCs that opt into the advanced approaches treatment of AOCI.

[7] Certain AOCI items are subject to transition into projected regulatory capital. Those transitions are 20 percent included in projected regulatory capital for 2014, 40 percent included in projected regulatory capital for 2015, and 60 percent included in projected regulatory capital for 2016.

Table C.25.A. Regions Financial Corporation
Projected stressed capital ratios, risk-weighted assets, losses, revenues, net income before taxes, and loan losses
Federal Reserve estimates: Severely adverse scenario

Actual 2014:Q3 projected stressed capital ratios through 2016:Q4

	Actual 2014:Q3	Stressed capital ratios[1]	
		Ending	Minimum
Tier 1 common ratio (%)	11.8	8.3	8.3
Common equity tier 1 capital ratio (%)[2]	n/a	8.5	8.5
Tier 1 risk-based capital ratio (%)	12.7	9.0	9.0
Total risk-based capital ratio (%)	15.5	11.4	11.4
Tier 1 leverage ratio (%)	11.0	7.6	7.6

[1] The capital ratios are calculated using capital action assumptions provided within the Dodd-Frank Act stress testing rule. These projections represent hypothetical estimates that involve an economic outcome that is more adverse than expected. These estimates are not forecasts of expected losses, revenues, net income before taxes, or capital ratios. The minimum capital ratio presented is for the period 2014:Q4 to 2016:Q4.

[2] Advanced approaches bank holding companies (BHCs) are subject to the common equity tier 1 ratio for the third and fourth quarter of 2014. All bank holding companies are subject to the common equity tier 1 ratio for each quarter of 2015 and 2016. An advanced approaches BHC includes any BHC that has consolidated total assets greater than or equal to $250 billion or consolidated total on-balance sheet foreign exposure of at least $10 billion. See 12 CFR 217.100(b)(1). Other BHCs include any BHC that is subject to 12 CFR 225.8 and is not an advanced approaches BHC.

n/a   Not applicable.

Projected loan losses, by type of loan, 2014:Q4–2016:Q4

	Billions of dollars	Portfolio loss rates (%)[1]
Loan losses	5.4	6.9
First-lien mortgages, domestic	0.7	4.7
Junior liens and HELOCs, domestic	0.6	6.5
Commercial and industrial[2]	1.1	4.8
Commercial real estate, domestic	2.3	14.7
Credit cards	0.1	13.9
Other consumer[3]	0.3	5.8
Other loans[4]	0.3	2.8

[1] Average loan balances used to calculate portfolio loss rates exclude loans held for sale and loans held for investment under the fair-value option and are calculated over nine quarters.

[2] Commercial and industrial loans include small- and medium-enterprise loans and corporate cards.

[3] Other consumer loans include student loans and automobile loans.

[4] Other loans include international real estate loans.

Actual 2014:Q3 and projected 2016:Q4 risk-weighted assets

	Actual 2014:Q3	Projected 2016:Q4	
		General approach	Standardized approach
Risk-weighted assets (billions of dollars)[1]	98.4	101.7	102.5

[1] For each quarter in 2014, risk-weighted assets are calculated using the general risk-based capital approach set forth in 12 CFR 225, appendix A. For each quarter in 2015 and 2016, risk-weighted assets are calculated under the Board's standardized capital risk-based approach in 12 CFR 217, subpart D, except for the risk-weighted assets used to calculate the tier 1 common ratio, which uses the general risk-based capital approach for all quarters.

Projected losses, revenue, net income and other comprehensive income through 2016:Q4

	Billions of dollars	Percent of average assets[1]
Pre-provision net revenue[2]	3.7	3.0
Other revenue[3]	0.0	
less		
Provisions	6.2	
Realized losses/gains on securities (AFS/HTM)	0.0	
Trading and counterparty losses[4]	0.0	
Other losses/gains[5]	0.0	
equals		
Net income before taxes	-2.6	-2.1
Memo items		
Other comprehensive income[6]	0.0	
Other effects on capital	*Actual 2014:Q3*	*2016:Q4*
AOCI included in capital (billions of dollars)[7]	n/a	0.0

[1] Average assets is the nine-quarter average of total assets.

[2] Pre-provision net revenue includes losses from operational-risk events, mortgage repurchase expenses, and other real estate owned (OREO) costs.

[3] Other revenue includes one-time income and (expense) items not included in pre-provision net revenue.

[4] Trading and counterparty losses include mark-to-market and credit valuation adjustments (CVA) losses and losses arising from the counterparty default scenario component applied to derivatives, securities lending, and repurchase agreement activities.

[5] Other losses/gains includes projected change in fair value of loans held for sale and loans held for investment measured under the fair-value option, and goodwill impairment losses.

[6] Other comprehensive income (OCI) is only calculated for advanced approaches BHCs, and other BHCs that opt into the advanced approaches treatment of AOCI.

[7] Certain AOCI items are subject to transition into projected regulatory capital. Those transitions are 20 percent included in projected regulatory capital for 2014, 40 percent included in projected regulatory capital for 2015, and 60 percent included in projected regulatory capital for 2016.

Table C.25.B. Regions Financial Corporation
Projected stressed capital ratios, risk-weighted assets, losses, revenues, net income before taxes, and loan losses
Federal Reserve estimates: Adverse scenario

Actual 2014:Q3 projected stressed capital ratios through 2016:Q4

	Actual 2014:Q3	Stressed capital ratios[1]	
		Ending	Minimum
Tier 1 common ratio (%)	11.8	10.7	10.6
Common equity tier 1 capital ratio (%)[2]	n/a	10.7	10.7
Tier 1 risk-based capital ratio (%)	12.7	11.4	11.4
Total risk-based capital ratio (%)	15.5	13.8	13.7
Tier 1 leverage ratio (%)	11.0	9.5	9.5

[1] The capital ratios are calculated using capital action assumptions provided within the Dodd-Frank Act stress testing rule. These projections represent hypothetical estimates that involve an economic outcome that is more adverse than expected. These estimates are not forecasts of expected losses, revenues, net income before taxes, or capital ratios. The minimum capital ratio presented is for the period 2014:Q4 to 2016:Q4.

[2] Advanced approaches bank holding companies (BHCs) are subject to the common equity tier 1 ratio for the third and fourth quarter of 2014. All bank holding companies are subject to the common equity tier 1 ratio for each quarter of 2015 and 2016. An advanced approaches BHC includes any BHC that has consolidated total assets greater than or equal to $250 billion or consolidated total on-balance sheet foreign exposure of at least $10 billion. See 12 CFR 217.100(b)(1). Other BHCs include any BHC that is subject to 12 CFR 225.8 and is not an advanced approaches BHC.

n/a Not applicable.

Projected loan losses, by type of loan, 2014:Q4–2016:Q4

	Billions of dollars	Portfolio loss rates (%)[1]
Loan losses	3.6	4.5
First-lien mortgages, domestic	0.6	4.0
Junior liens and HELOCs, domestic	0.4	4.8
Commercial and industrial[2]	0.6	2.8
Commercial real estate, domestic	1.4	8.9
Credit cards	0.1	11.0
Other consumer[3]	0.2	4.4
Other loans[4]	0.2	1.7

[1] Average loan balances used to calculate portfolio loss rates exclude loans held for sale and loans held for investment under the fair-value option and are calculated over nine quarters.

[2] Commercial and industrial loans include small- and medium-enterprise loans and corporate cards.

[3] Other consumer loans include student loans and automobile loans.

[4] Other loans include international real estate loans.

Actual 2014:Q3 and projected 2016:Q4 risk-weighted assets

	Actual 2014:Q3	Projected 2016:Q4	
		General approach	Standardized approach
Risk-weighted assets (billions of dollars)[1]	98.4	105.4	105.4

[1] For each quarter in 2014, risk-weighted assets are calculated using the general risk-based capital approach set forth in 12 CFR 225, appendix A. For each quarter in 2015 and 2016, risk-weighted assets are calculated under the Board's standardized capital risk-based approach in 12 CFR 217, subpart D, except for the risk-weighted assets used to calculate the tier 1 common ratio, which uses the general risk-based capital approach for all quarters.

Projected losses, revenue, net income and other comprehensive income through 2016:Q4

	Billions of dollars	Percent of average assets[1]
Pre-provision net revenue[2]	4.9	3.9
Other revenue[3]	0.0	
less		
Provisions	3.9	
Realized losses/gains on securities (AFS/HTM)	0.0	
Trading and counterparty losses[4]	0.0	
Other losses/gains[5]	0.0	
equals		
Net income before taxes	1.0	0.8
Memo items		
Other comprehensive income[6]	0.0	
Other effects on capital	*Actual 2014:Q3*	*2016:Q4*
AOCI included in capital (billions of dollars)[7]	n/a	0.0

[1] Average assets is the nine-quarter average of total assets.

[2] Pre-provision net revenue includes losses from operational-risk events, mortgage repurchase expenses, and other real estate owned (OREO) costs.

[3] Other revenue includes one-time income and (expense) items not included in pre-provision net revenue.

[4] Trading and counterparty losses include mark-to-market and credit valuation adjustments (CVA) losses and losses arising from the counterparty default scenario component applied to derivatives, securities lending, and repurchase agreement activities.

[5] Other losses/gains includes projected change in fair value of loans held for sale and loans held for investment measured under the fair-value option, and goodwill impairment losses.

[6] Other comprehensive income (OCI) is only calculated for advanced approaches BHCs, and other BHCs that opt into the advanced approaches treatment of AOCI.

[7] Certain AOCI items are subject to transition into projected regulatory capital. Those transitions are 20 percent included in projected regulatory capital for 2014, 40 percent included in projected regulatory capital for 2015, and 60 percent included in projected regulatory capital for 2016.

Table C.26.A. Santander Holdings USA, Inc.
Projected stressed capital ratios, risk-weighted assets, losses, revenues, net income before taxes, and loan losses
Federal Reserve estimates: Severely adverse scenario

Actual 2014:Q3 projected stressed capital ratios through 2016:Q4

	Actual 2014:Q3	Stressed capital ratios[1]	
		Ending	Minimum
Tier 1 common ratio (%)	11.0	9.4	9.4
Common equity tier 1 capital ratio (%)[2]	n/a	10.3	10.3
Tier 1 risk-based capital ratio (%)	13.1	10.7	10.7
Total risk-based capital ratio (%)	15.0	12.5	12.5
Tier 1 leverage ratio (%)	12.3	9.6	9.6

[1]   The capital ratios are calculated using capital action assumptions provided within the Dodd-Frank Act stress testing rule. These projections represent hypothetical estimates that involve an economic outcome that is more adverse than expected. These estimates are not forecasts of expected losses, revenues, net income before taxes, or capital ratios. The minimum capital ratio presented is for the period 2014:Q4 to 2016:Q4.

[2]   Advanced approaches bank holding companies (BHCs) are subject to the common equity tier 1 ratio for the third and fourth quarter of 2014. All bank holding companies are subject to the common equity tier 1 ratio for each quarter of 2015 and 2016. An advanced approaches BHC includes any BHC that has consolidated total assets greater than or equal to $250 billion or consolidated total on-balance sheet foreign exposure of at least $10 billion. See 12 CFR 217.100(b)(1). Other BHCs include any BHC that is subject to 12 CFR 225.8 and is not an advanced approaches BHC.

n/a   Not applicable.

Projected loan losses, by type of loan, 2014:Q4–2016:Q4

	Billions of dollars	Portfolio loss rates (%)[1]
Loan losses	7.2	9.6
First-lien mortgages, domestic	0.4	4.5
Junior liens and HELOCs, domestic	0.3	4.5
Commercial and industrial[2]	0.6	3.6
Commercial real estate, domestic	1.6	9.0
Credit cards	0.0	14.7
Other consumer[3]	4.2	17.2
Other loans[4]	0.1	3.8

[1]   Average loan balances used to calculate portfolio loss rates exclude loans held for sale and loans held for investment under the fair-value option and are calculated over nine quarters.

[2]   Commercial and industrial loans include small- and medium-enterprise loans and corporate cards.

[3]   Other consumer loans include student loans and automobile loans.

[4]   Other loans include international real estate loans.

Actual 2014:Q3 and projected 2016:Q4 risk-weighted assets

	Actual 2014:Q3	Projected 2016:Q4	
		General approach	Standardized approach
Risk-weighted assets (billions of dollars)[1]	97.0	99.2	102.2

[1]   For each quarter in 2014, risk-weighted assets are calculated using the general risk-based capital approach set forth in 12 CFR 225, appendix A. For each quarter in 2015 and 2016, risk-weighted assets are calculated under the Board's standardized capital risk-based approach in 12 CFR 217, subpart D, except for the risk-weighted assets used to calculate the tier 1 common ratio, which uses the general risk-based capital approach for all quarters.

Projected losses, revenue, net income and other comprehensive income through 2016:Q4

	Billions of dollars	Percent of average assets[1]
Pre-provision net revenue[2]	6.2	5.2
Other revenue[3]	0.0	
less		
Provisions	8.1	
Realized losses/gains on securities (AFS/HTM)	0.1	
Trading and counterparty losses[4]	0.0	
Other losses/gains[5]	0.1	
equals		
Net income before taxes	-2.1	-1.8
Memo items		
Other comprehensive income[6]	0.0	
Other effects on capital	*Actual 2014:Q3*	*2016:Q4*
AOCI included in capital (billions of dollars)[7]	n/a	0.0

[1]   Average assets is the nine-quarter average of total assets.

[2]   Pre-provision net revenue includes losses from operational-risk events, mortgage repurchase expenses, and other real estate owned (OREO) costs.

[3]   Other revenue includes one-time income and (expense) items not included in pre-provision net revenue.

[4]   Trading and counterparty losses include mark-to-market and credit valuation adjustments (CVA) losses and losses arising from the counterparty default scenario component applied to derivatives, securities lending, and repurchase agreement activities.

[5]   Other losses/gains includes projected change in fair value of loans held for sale and loans held for investment measured under the fair-value option, and goodwill impairment losses.

[6]   Other comprehensive income (OCI) is only calculated for advanced approaches BHCs, and other BHCs that opt into the advanced approaches treatment of AOCI.

[7]   Certain AOCI items are subject to transition into projected regulatory capital. Those transitions are 20 percent included in projected regulatory capital for 2014, 40 percent included in projected regulatory capital for 2015, and 60 percent included in projected regulatory capital for 2016.

Table C.26.B. Santander Holdings USA, Inc.
Projected stressed capital ratios, risk-weighted assets, losses, revenues, net income before taxes, and loan losses
Federal Reserve estimates: Adverse scenario

Actual 2014:Q3 projected stressed capital ratios through 2016:Q4

	Actual 2014:Q3	Stressed capital ratios[1]	
		Ending	Minimum
Tier 1 common ratio (%)	11.0	11.5	11.5
Common equity tier 1 capital ratio (%)[2]	n/a	12.2	12.2
Tier 1 risk-based capital ratio (%)	13.1	13.0	13.0
Total risk-based capital ratio (%)	15.0	14.9	14.9
Tier 1 leverage ratio (%)	12.3	11.5	11.5

[1] The capital ratios are calculated using capital action assumptions provided within the Dodd-Frank Act stress testing rule. These projections represent hypothetical estimates that involve an economic outcome that is more adverse than expected. These estimates are not forecasts of expected losses, revenues, net income before taxes, or capital ratios. The minimum capital ratio presented is for the period 2014:Q4 to 2016:Q4.

[2] Advanced approaches bank holding companies (BHCs) are subject to the common equity tier 1 ratio for the third and fourth quarter of 2014. All bank holding companies are subject to the common equity tier 1 ratio for each quarter of 2015 and 2016. An advanced approaches BHC includes any BHC that has consolidated total assets greater than or equal to $250 billion or consolidated total on-balance sheet foreign exposure of at least $10 billion. See 12 CFR 217.100(b)(1). Other BHCs include any BHC that is subject to 12 CFR 225.8 and is not an advanced approaches BHC.

n/a Not applicable.

Projected loan losses, by type of loan, 2014:Q4–2016:Q4

	Billions of dollars	Portfolio loss rates (%)[1]
Loan losses	5.1	6.8
First-lien mortgages, domestic	0.3	3.6
Junior liens and HELOCs, domestic	0.2	3.2
Commercial and industrial[2]	0.4	2.2
Commercial real estate, domestic	1.0	5.3
Credit cards	0.0	11.9
Other consumer[3]	3.3	13.2
Other loans[4]	0.0	2.2

[1] Average loan balances used to calculate portfolio loss rates exclude loans held for sale and loans held for investment under the fair-value option and are calculated over nine quarters.

[2] Commercial and industrial loans include small- and medium-enterprise loans and corporate cards.

[3] Other consumer loans include student loans and automobile loans.

[4] Other loans include international real estate loans.

Actual 2014:Q3 and projected 2016:Q4 risk-weighted assets

	Actual 2014:Q3	Projected 2016:Q4	
		General approach	Standardized approach
Risk-weighted assets (billions of dollars)[1]	97.0	103.2	105.2

[1] For each quarter in 2014, risk-weighted assets are calculated using the general risk-based capital approach set forth in 12 CFR 225, appendix A. For each quarter in 2015 and 2016, risk-weighted assets are calculated under the Board's standardized capital risk-based approach in 12 CFR 217, subpart D, except for the risk-weighted assets used to calculate the tier 1 common ratio, which uses the general risk-based capital approach for all quarters.

Projected losses, revenue, net income and other comprehensive income through 2016:Q4

	Billions of dollars	Percent of average assets[1]
Pre-provision net revenue[2]	6.6	5.5
Other revenue[3]	0.0	
less		
Provisions	5.4	
Realized losses/gains on securities (AFS/HTM)	0.1	
Trading and counterparty losses[4]	0.0	
Other losses/gains[5]	0.0	
equals		
Net income before taxes	1.1	0.9
Memo items		
Other comprehensive income[6]	0.0	
Other effects on capital	Actual 2014:Q3	2016:Q4
AOCI included in capital (billions of dollars)[7]	n/a	0.0

[1] Average assets is the nine-quarter average of total assets.

[2] Pre-provision net revenue includes losses from operational-risk events, mortgage repurchase expenses, and other real estate owned (OREO) costs.

[3] Other revenue includes one-time income and (expense) items not included in pre-provision net revenue.

[4] Trading and counterparty losses include mark-to-market and credit valuation adjustments (CVA) losses and losses arising from the counterparty default scenario component applied to derivatives, securities lending, and repurchase agreement activities.

[5] Other losses/gains includes projected change in fair value of loans held for sale and loans held for investment measured under the fair-value option, and goodwill impairment losses.

[6] Other comprehensive income (OCI) is only calculated for advanced approaches BHCs, and other BHCs that opt into the advanced approaches treatment of AOCI.

[7] Certain AOCI items are subject to transition into projected regulatory capital. Those transitions are 20 percent included in projected regulatory capital for 2014, 40 percent included in projected regulatory capital for 2015, and 60 percent included in projected regulatory capital for 2016.

Table C.27.A. State Street Corporation
Projected stressed capital ratios, risk-weighted assets, losses, revenues, net income before taxes, and loan losses
Federal Reserve estimates: Severely adverse scenario

Actual 2014:Q3 projected stressed capital ratios through 2016:Q4

	Actual 2014:Q3	Stressed capital ratios[1]	
		Ending	Minimum
Tier 1 common ratio (%)	13.7	14.1	11.8
Common equity tier 1 capital ratio (%)[2]	15.0	9.7	8.1
Tier 1 risk-based capital ratio (%)	16.7	11.2	9.7
Total risk-based capital ratio (%)	19.1	13.1	11.6
Tier 1 leverage ratio (%)	6.4	5.4	4.8

[1]   The capital ratios are calculated using capital action assumptions provided within the Dodd-Frank Act stress testing rule. These projections represent hypothetical estimates that involve an economic outcome that is more adverse than expected. These estimates are not forecasts of expected losses, revenues, net income before taxes, or capital ratios. The minimum capital ratio presented is for the period 2014:Q4 to 2016:Q4.

[2]   Advanced approaches bank holding companies (BHCs) are subject to the common equity tier 1 ratio for the third and fourth quarter of 2014. All bank holding companies are subject to the common equity tier 1 ratio for each quarter of 2015 and 2016. An advanced approaches BHC includes any BHC that has consolidated total assets greater than or equal to $250 billion or consolidated total on-balance sheet foreign exposure of at least $10 billion. See 12 CFR 217.100(b)(1). Other BHCs include any BHC that is subject to 12 CFR 225.8 and is not an advanced approaches BHC.

Projected loan losses, by type of loan, 2014:Q4–2016:Q4

	Billions of dollars	Portfolio loss rates (%)[1]
Loan losses	0.6	3.3
First-lien mortgages, domestic	0.0	0.0
Junior liens and HELOCs, domestic	0.0	0.0
Commercial and industrial[2]	0.1	4.8
Commercial real estate, domestic	0.1	29.4
Credit cards	0.0	0.0
Other consumer[3]	0.0	0.6
Other loans[4]	0.5	2.7

[1]   Average loan balances used to calculate portfolio loss rates exclude loans held for sale and loans held for investment under the fair-value option and are calculated over nine quarters.

[2]   Commercial and industrial loans include small- and medium-enterprise loans and corporate cards.

[3]   Other consumer loans include student loans and automobile loans.

[4]   Other loans include international real estate loans.

Actual 2014:Q3 and projected 2016:Q4 risk-weighted assets

	Actual 2014:Q3	Projected 2016:Q4	
		General approach	Standardized approach
Risk-weighted assets (billions of dollars)[1]	91.8	96.4	124.8

[1]   For each quarter in 2014, risk-weighted assets are calculated using the general risk-based capital approach set forth in 12 CFR 225, appendix A. For each quarter in 2015 and 2016, risk-weighted assets are calculated under the Board's standardized capital risk-based approach in 12 CFR 217, subpart D, except for the risk-weighted assets used to calculate the tier 1 common ratio, which uses the general risk-based capital approach for all quarters.

Projected losses, revenue, net income and other comprehensive income through 2016:Q4

	Billions of dollars	Percent of average assets[1]
Pre-provision net revenue[2]	7.0	2.5
Other revenue[3]	0.0	
less		
Provisions	0.8	
Realized losses/gains on securities (AFS/HTM)	0.9	
Trading and counterparty losses[4]	2.0	
Other losses/gains[5]	0.0	
equals		
Net income before taxes	3.3	1.2
Memo items		
Other comprehensive income[6]	-2.8	
Other effects on capital	Actual 2014:Q3	2016:Q4
AOCI included in capital (billions of dollars)[7]	-0.3	-1.8

[1]   Average assets is the nine-quarter average of total assets.

[2]   Pre-provision net revenue includes losses from operational-risk events, mortgage repurchase expenses, and other real estate owned (OREO) costs.

[3]   Other revenue includes one-time income and (expense) items not included in pre-provision net revenue.

[4]   Trading and counterparty losses include mark-to-market and credit valuation adjustments (CVA) losses and losses arising from the counterparty default scenario component applied to derivatives, securities lending, and repurchase agreement activities.

[5]   Other losses/gains includes projected change in fair value of loans held for sale and loans held for investment measured under the fair-value option and goodwill impairment losses.

[6]   Other comprehensive income (OCI) is only calculated for advanced approaches BHCs, and other BHCs that opt into the advanced approaches treatment of AOCI.

[7]   Certain AOCI items are subject to transition into projected regulatory capital. Those transitions are 20 percent included in projected regulatory capital for 2014, 40 percent included in projected regulatory capital for 2015, and 60 percent included in projected regulatory capital for 2016.

Table C.27.B. State Street Corporation
Projected stressed capital ratios, risk-weighted assets, losses, revenues, net income before taxes, and loan losses
Federal Reserve estimates: Adverse scenario

Actual 2014:Q3 projected stressed capital ratios through 2016:Q4

	Actual 2014:Q3	Stressed capital ratios[1]	
		Ending	Minimum
Tier 1 common ratio (%)	13.7	17.3	12.7
Common equity tier 1 capital ratio (%)[2]	15.0	10.0	8.7
Tier 1 risk-based capital ratio (%)	16.7	11.5	10.3
Total risk-based capital ratio (%)	19.1	13.3	12.0
Tier 1 leverage ratio (%)	6.4	5.5	5.0

[1] The capital ratios are calculated using capital action assumptions provided within the Dodd-Frank Act stress testing rule. These projections represent hypothetical estimates that involve an economic outcome that is more adverse than expected. These estimates are not forecasts of expected losses, revenues, net income before taxes, or capital ratios. The minimum capital ratio presented is for the period 2014:Q4 to 2016:Q4.

[2] Advanced approaches bank holding companies (BHCs) are subject to the common equity tier 1 ratio for the third and fourth quarter of 2014. All bank holding companies are subject to the common equity tier 1 ratio for each quarter of 2015 and 2016. An advanced approaches BHC includes any BHC that has consolidated total assets greater than or equal to $250 billion or consolidated total on-balance sheet foreign exposure of at least $10 billion. See 12 CFR 217.100(b)(1). Other BHCs include any BHC that is subject to 12 CFR 225.8 and is not an advanced approaches BHC.

Actual 2014:Q3 and projected 2016:Q4 risk-weighted assets

	Actual 2014:Q3	Projected 2016:Q4	
		General approach	Standardized approach
Risk-weighted assets (billions of dollars)[1]	91.8	100.4	129.7

[1] For each quarter in 2014, risk-weighted assets are calculated using the general risk-based capital approach set forth in 12 CFR 225, appendix A. For each quarter in 2015 and 2016, risk-weighted assets are calculated under the Board's standardized capital risk-based approach in 12 CFR 217, subpart D, except for the risk-weighted assets used to calculate the tier 1 common ratio, which uses the general risk-based capital approach for all quarters.

Projected losses, revenue, net income and other comprehensive income through 2016:Q4

	Billions of dollars	Percent of average assets[1]
Pre-provision net revenue[2]	10.9	3.7
Other revenue[3]	0.0	
less		
Provisions	0.5	
Realized losses/gains on securities (AFS/HTM)	0.4	
Trading and counterparty losses[4]	0.8	
Other losses/gains[5]	0.0	
equals		
Net income before taxes	9.2	3.2
Memo items		
Other comprehensive income[6]	-6.5	
Other effects on capital	*Actual 2014:Q3*	*2016:Q4*
AOCI included in capital (billions of dollars)[7]	-0.3	-4.1

[1] Average assets is the nine-quarter average of total assets.

[2] Pre-provision net revenue includes losses from operational-risk events, mortgage repurchase expenses, and other real estate owned (OREO) costs.

[3] Other revenue includes one-time income and (expense) items not included in pre-provision net revenue.

[4] Trading and counterparty losses include mark-to-market and credit valuation adjustments (CVA) losses and losses arising from the counterparty default scenario component applied to derivatives, securities lending, and repurchase agreement activities.

[5] Other losses/gains includes projected change in fair value of loans held for sale and loans held for investment measured under the fair-value option and goodwill impairment losses.

[6] Other comprehensive income (OCI) is only calculated for advanced approaches BHCs, and other BHCs that opt into the advanced approaches treatment of AOCI.

[7] Certain AOCI items are subject to transition into projected regulatory capital. Those transitions are 20 percent included in projected regulatory capital for 2014, 40 percent included in projected regulatory capital for 2015, and 60 percent included in projected regulatory capital for 2016.

Projected loan losses, by type of loan, 2014:Q4–2016:Q4

	Billions of dollars	Portfolio loss rates (%)[1]
Loan losses	0.4	2.0
First-lien mortgages, domestic	0.0	0.0
Junior liens and HELOCs, domestic	0.0	0.0
Commercial and industrial[2]	0.0	2.6
Commercial real estate, domestic	0.1	17.0
Credit cards	0.0	0.0
Other consumer[3]	0.0	0.6
Other loans[4]	0.3	1.7

[1] Average loan balances used to calculate portfolio loss rates exclude loans held for sale and loans held for investment under the fair-value option and are calculated over nine quarters.

[2] Commercial and industrial loans include small- and medium-enterprise loans and corporate cards.

[3] Other consumer loans include student loans and automobile loans.

[4] Other loans include international real estate loans.

Table C.28.A. SunTrust Banks, Inc.
Projected stressed capital ratios, risk-weighted assets, losses, revenues, net income before taxes, and loan losses
Federal Reserve estimates: Severely adverse scenario

Actual 2014:Q3 projected stressed capital ratios through 2016:Q4

	Actual 2014:Q3	Stressed capital ratios[1]	
		Ending	Minimum
Tier 1 common ratio (%)	9.6	8.2	8.2
Common equity tier 1 capital ratio (%)[2]	n/a	8.2	8.2
Tier 1 risk-based capital ratio (%)	10.5	9.0	9.0
Total risk-based capital ratio (%)	12.3	10.8	10.8
Tier 1 leverage ratio (%)	9.5	7.6	7.6

[1]   The capital ratios are calculated using capital action assumptions provided within the Dodd-Frank Act stress testing rule. These projections represent hypothetical estimates that involve an economic outcome that is more adverse than expected. These estimates are not forecasts of expected losses, revenues, net income before taxes, or capital ratios. The minimum capital ratio presented is for the period 2014:Q4 to 2016:Q4.

[2]   Advanced approaches bank holding companies (BHCs) are subject to the common equity tier 1 ratio for the third and fourth quarter of 2014. All bank holding companies are subject to the common equity tier 1 ratio for each quarter of 2015 and 2016. An advanced approaches BHC includes any BHC that has consolidated total assets greater than or equal to $250 billion or consolidated total on-balance sheet foreign exposure of at least $10 billion. See 12 CFR 217.100(b)(1). Other BHCs include any BHC that is subject to 12 CFR 225.8 and is not an advanced approaches BHC.

n/a   Not applicable.

Projected loan losses, by type of loan, 2014:Q4–2016:Q4

	Billions of dollars	Portfolio loss rates (%)[1]
Loan losses	6.1	4.5
First-lien mortgages, domestic	1.0	4.0
Junior liens and HELOCs, domestic	1.0	7.1
Commercial and industrial[2]	1.8	4.5
Commercial real estate, domestic	1.2	6.9
Credit cards	0.1	13.9
Other consumer[3]	0.7	3.4
Other loans[4]	0.2	1.5

[1]   Average loan balances used to calculate portfolio loss rates exclude loans held for sale and loans held for investment under the fair-value option and are calculated over nine quarters.

[2]   Commercial and industrial loans include small- and medium-enterprise loans and corporate cards.

[3]   Other consumer loans include student loans and automobile loans.

[4]   Other loans include international real estate loans.

Actual 2014:Q3 and projected 2016:Q4 risk-weighted assets

	Actual 2014:Q3	Projected 2016:Q4	
		General approach	Standardized approach
Risk-weighted assets (billions of dollars)[1]	160.0	165.5	159.2

[1]   For each quarter in 2014, risk-weighted assets are calculated using the general risk-based capital approach set forth in 12 CFR 225, appendix A. For each quarter in 2015 and 2016, risk-weighted assets are calculated under the Board's standardized capital risk-based approach in 12 CFR 217, subpart D, except for the risk-weighted assets used to calculate the tier 1 common ratio, which uses the general risk-based capital approach for all quarters.

Projected losses, revenue, net income and other comprehensive income through 2016:Q4

	Billions of dollars	Percent of average assets[1]
Pre-provision net revenue[2]	6.2	3.2
Other revenue[3]	0.0	
less		
Provisions	6.6	
Realized losses/gains on securities (AFS/HTM)	0.0	
Trading and counterparty losses[4]	0.0	
Other losses/gains[5]	0.7	
equals		
Net income before taxes	-1.0	-0.5
Memo items		
Other comprehensive income[6]	0.0	
Other effects on capital	Actual 2014:Q3	2016:Q4
AOCI included in capital (billions of dollars)[7]	n/a	0.0

[1]   Average assets is the nine-quarter average of total assets.

[2]   Pre-provision net revenue includes losses from operational-risk events, mortgage repurchase expenses, and other real estate owned (OREO) costs.

[3]   Other revenue includes one-time income and (expense) items not included in pre-provision net revenue.

[4]   Trading and counterparty losses include mark-to-market and credit valuation adjustments (CVA) losses and losses arising from the counterparty default scenario component applied to derivatives, securities lending, and repurchase agreement activities.

[5]   Other losses/gains includes projected change in fair value of loans held for sale and loans held for investment measured under the fair-value option, and goodwill impairment losses.

[6]   Other comprehensive income (OCI) is only calculated for advanced approaches BHCs, and other BHCs that opt into the advanced approaches treatment of AOCI.

[7]   Certain AOCI items are subject to transition into projected regulatory capital. Those transitions are 20 percent included in projected regulatory capital for 2014, 40 percent included in projected regulatory capital for 2015, and 60 percent included in projected regulatory capital for 2016.

Table C.28.B. SunTrust Banks, Inc.
Projected stressed capital ratios, risk-weighted assets, losses, revenues, net income before taxes, and loan losses
Federal Reserve estimates: Adverse scenario

Actual 2014:Q3 projected stressed capital ratios through 2016:Q4

	Actual 2014:Q3	Stressed capital ratios[1]	
		Ending	Minimum
Tier 1 common ratio (%)	9.6	10.0	9.4
Common equity tier 1 capital ratio (%)[2]	n/a	10.3	9.8
Tier 1 risk-based capital ratio (%)	10.5	11.1	10.7
Total risk-based capital ratio (%)	12.3	12.8	12.4
Tier 1 leverage ratio (%)	9.5	9.2	9.0

[1] The capital ratios are calculated using capital action assumptions provided within the Dodd-Frank Act stress testing rule. These projections represent hypothetical estimates that involve an economic outcome that is more adverse than expected. These estimates are not forecasts of expected losses, revenues, net income before taxes, or capital ratios. The minimum capital ratio presented is for the period 2014:Q4 to 2016:Q4.

[2] Advanced approaches bank holding companies (BHCs) are subject to the common equity tier 1 ratio for the third and fourth quarter of 2014. All bank holding companies are subject to the common equity tier 1 ratio for each quarter of 2015 and 2016. An advanced approaches BHC includes any BHC that has consolidated total assets greater than or equal to $250 billion or consolidated total on-balance sheet foreign exposure of at least $10 billion. See 12 CFR 217.100(b)(1). Other BHCs include any BHC that is subject to 12 CFR 225.8 and is not an advanced approaches BHC.

n/a Not applicable.

Projected loan losses, by type of loan, 2014:Q4–2016:Q4

	Billions of dollars	Portfolio loss rates (%)[1]
Loan losses	4.2	3.1
First-lien mortgages, domestic	0.8	3.3
Junior liens and HELOCs, domestic	0.8	5.5
Commercial and industrial[2]	1.1	2.5
Commercial real estate, domestic	0.7	4.1
Credit cards	0.1	10.7
Other consumer[3]	0.5	2.5
Other loans[4]	0.1	0.9

[1] Average loan balances used to calculate portfolio loss rates exclude loans held for sale and loans held for investment under the fair-value option and are calculated over nine quarters.

[2] Commercial and industrial loans include small- and medium-enterprise loans and corporate cards.

[3] Other consumer loans include student loans and automobile loans.

[4] Other loans include international real estate loans.

Actual 2014:Q3 and projected 2016:Q4 risk-weighted assets

	Actual 2014:Q3	Projected 2016:Q4	
		General approach	Standardized approach
Risk-weighted assets (billions of dollars)[1]	160.0	171.0	164.1

[1] For each quarter in 2014, risk-weighted assets are calculated using the general risk-based capital approach set forth in 12 CFR 225, appendix A. For each quarter in 2015 and 2016, risk-weighted assets are calculated under the Board's standardized capital risk-based approach in 12 CFR 217, subpart D, except for the risk-weighted assets used to calculate the tier 1 common ratio, which uses the general risk-based capital approach for all quarters.

Projected losses, revenue, net income and other comprehensive income through 2016:Q4

	Billions of dollars	Percent of average assets[1]
Pre-provision net revenue[2]	8.7	4.4
Other revenue[3]	0.0	
less		
Provisions	4.1	
Realized losses/gains on securities (AFS/HTM)	0.0	
Trading and counterparty losses[4]	0.0	
Other losses/gains[5]	0.3	
equals		
Net income before taxes	4.4	2.2
Memo items		
Other comprehensive income[6]	0.0	
Other effects on capital	Actual 2014:Q3	2016:Q4
AOCI included in capital (billions of dollars)[7]	n/a	0.0

[1] Average assets is the nine-quarter average of total assets.

[2] Pre-provision net revenue includes losses from operational-risk events, mortgage repurchase expenses, and other real estate owned (OREO) costs.

[3] Other revenue includes one-time income and (expense) items not included in pre-provision net revenue.

[4] Trading and counterparty losses include mark-to-market and credit valuation adjustments (CVA) losses and losses arising from the counterparty default scenario component applied to derivatives, securities lending, and repurchase agreement activities.

[5] Other losses/gains includes projected change in fair value of loans held for sale and loans held for investment measured under the fair-value option, and goodwill impairment losses.

[6] Other comprehensive income (OCI) is only calculated for advanced approaches BHCs, and other BHCs that opt into the advanced approaches treatment of AOCI.

[7] Certain AOCI items are subject to transition into projected regulatory capital. Those transitions are 20 percent included in projected regulatory capital for 2014, 40 percent included in projected regulatory capital for 2015, and 60 percent included in projected regulatory capital for 2016.

Table C.29.A. U.S. Bancorp
Projected stressed capital ratios, risk-weighted assets, losses, revenues, net income before taxes, and loan losses
Federal Reserve estimates: Severely adverse scenario

Actual 2014:Q3 projected stressed capital ratios through 2016:Q4

	Actual 2014:Q3	Stressed capital ratios[1]	
		Ending	Minimum
Tier 1 common ratio (%)	9.5	8.6	8.5
Common equity tier 1 capital ratio (%)[2]	9.7	8.2	8.1
Tier 1 risk-based capital ratio (%)	11.3	9.6	9.6
Total risk-based capital ratio (%)	13.6	11.7	11.7
Tier 1 leverage ratio (%)	9.4	8.1	8.0

[1]   The capital ratios are calculated using capital action assumptions provided within the Dodd-Frank Act stress testing rule. These projections represent hypothetical estimates that involve an economic outcome that is more adverse than expected. These estimates are not forecasts of expected losses, revenues, net income before taxes, or capital ratios. The minimum capital ratio presented is for the period 2014:Q4 to 2016:Q4.

[2]   Advanced approaches bank holding companies (BHCs) are subject to the common equity tier 1 ratio for the third and fourth quarter of 2014. All bank holding companies are subject to the common equity tier 1 ratio for each quarter of 2015 and 2016. An advanced approaches BHC includes any BHC that has consolidated total assets greater than or equal to $250 billion or consolidated total on-balance sheet foreign exposure of at least $10 billion. See 12 CFR 217.100(b)(1). Other BHCs include any BHC that is subject to 12 CFR 225.8 and is not an advanced approaches BHC.

Projected loan losses, by type of loan, 2014:Q4–2016:Q4

	Billions of dollars	Portfolio loss rates (%)[1]
Loan losses	16.2	6.5
First-lien mortgages, domestic	1.4	2.4
Junior liens and HELOCs, domestic	0.9	5.3
Commercial and industrial[2]	4.9	7.8
Commercial real estate, domestic	4.4	11.0
Credit cards	2.7	14.7
Other consumer[3]	1.2	3.4
Other loans[4]	0.8	3.7

[1]   Average loan balances used to calculate portfolio loss rates exclude loans held for sale and loans held for investment under the fair-value option and are calculated over nine quarters.

[2]   Commercial and industrial loans include small- and medium-enterprise loans and corporate cards.

[3]   Other consumer loans include student loans and automobile loans.

[4]   Other loans include international real estate loans.

Actual 2014:Q3 and projected 2016:Q4 risk-weighted assets

	Actual 2014:Q3	Projected 2016:Q4	
		General approach	Standardized approach
Risk-weighted assets (billions of dollars)[1]	311.9	321.0	335.1

[1]   For each quarter in 2014, risk-weighted assets are calculated using the general risk-based capital approach set forth in 12 CFR 225, appendix A. For each quarter in 2015 and 2016, risk-weighted assets are calculated under the Board's standardized capital risk-based approach in 12 CFR 217, subpart D, except for the risk-weighted assets used to calculate the tier 1 common ratio, which uses the general risk-based capital approach for all quarters.

Projected losses, revenue, net income and other comprehensive income through 2016:Q4

	Billions of dollars	Percent of average assets[1]
Pre-provision net revenue[2]	22.8	5.6
Other revenue[3]	0.0	
less		
Provisions	18.1	
Realized losses/gains on securities (AFS/HTM)	0.1	
Trading and counterparty losses[4]	0.0	
Other losses/gains[5]	0.0	
equals		
Net income before taxes	4.7	1.2
Memo items		
Other comprehensive income[6]	0.2	
Other effects on capital	Actual 2014:Q3	2016:Q4
AOCI included in capital (billions of dollars)[7]	-0.1	-0.2

[1]   Average assets is the nine-quarter average of total assets.

[2]   Pre-provision net revenue includes losses from operational-risk events, mortgage repurchase expenses, and other real estate owned (OREO) costs.

[3]   Other revenue includes one-time income and (expense) items not included in pre-provision net revenue.

[4]   Trading and counterparty losses include mark-to-market and credit valuation adjustments (CVA) losses and losses arising from the counterparty default scenario component applied to derivatives, securities lending, and repurchase agreement activities.

[5]   Other losses/gains includes projected change in fair value of loans held for sale and loans held for investment measured under the fair-value option and goodwill impairment losses.

[6]   Other comprehensive income (OCI) is only calculated for advanced approaches BHCs, and other BHCs that opt into the advanced approaches treatment of AOCI.

[7]   Certain AOCI items are subject to transition into projected regulatory capital. Those transitions are 20 percent included in projected regulatory capital for 2014, 40 percent included in projected regulatory capital for 2015, and 60 percent included in projected regulatory capital for 2016.

Table C.29.B. U.S. Bancorp
Projected stressed capital ratios, risk-weighted assets, losses, revenues, net income before taxes, and loan losses
Federal Reserve estimates: Adverse scenario

Actual 2014:Q3 projected stressed capital ratios through 2016:Q4

	Actual 2014:Q3	Stressed capital ratios[1]	
		Ending	Minimum
Tier 1 common ratio (%)	9.5	10.5	9.3
Common equity tier 1 capital ratio (%)[2]	9.7	9.4	8.8
Tier 1 risk-based capital ratio (%)	11.3	10.8	10.3
Total risk-based capital ratio (%)	13.6	12.9	12.4
Tier 1 leverage ratio (%)	9.4	8.9	8.6

[1] The capital ratios are calculated using capital action assumptions provided within the Dodd-Frank Act stress testing rule. These projections represent hypothetical estimates that involve an economic outcome that is more adverse than expected. These estimates are not forecasts of expected losses, revenues, net income before taxes, or capital ratios. The minimum capital ratio presented is for the period 2014:Q4 to 2016:Q4.

[2] Advanced approaches bank holding companies (BHCs) are subject to the common equity tier 1 ratio for the third and fourth quarter of 2014. All bank holding companies are subject to the common equity tier 1 ratio for each quarter of 2015 and 2016. An advanced approaches BHC includes any BHC that has consolidated total assets greater than or equal to $250 billion or consolidated total on-balance sheet foreign exposure of at least $10 billion. See 12 CFR 217.100(b)(1). Other BHCs include any BHC that is subject to 12 CFR 225.8 and is not an advanced approaches BHC.

Projected loan losses, by type of loan, 2014:Q4–2016:Q4

	Billions of dollars	Portfolio loss rates (%)[1]
Loan losses	10.8	4.3
First-lien mortgages, domestic	1.0	1.8
Junior liens and HELOCs, domestic	0.6	3.5
Commercial and industrial[2]	3.2	5.0
Commercial real estate, domestic	2.5	6.4
Credit cards	2.2	11.8
Other consumer[3]	0.8	2.5
Other loans[4]	0.5	2.2

[1] Average loan balances used to calculate portfolio loss rates exclude loans held for sale and loans held for investment under the fair-value option and are calculated over nine quarters.

[2] Commercial and industrial loans include small- and medium-enterprise loans and corporate cards.

[3] Other consumer loans include student loans and automobile loans.

[4] Other loans include international real estate loans.

Actual 2014:Q3 and projected 2016:Q4 risk-weighted assets

	Actual 2014:Q3	Projected 2016:Q4	
		General approach	Standardized approach
Risk-weighted assets (billions of dollars)[1]	311.9	335.0	347.0

[1] For each quarter in 2014, risk-weighted assets are calculated using the general risk-based capital approach set forth in 12 CFR 225, appendix A. For each quarter in 2015 and 2016, risk-weighted assets are calculated under the Board's standardized capital risk-based approach in 12 CFR 217, subpart D, except for the risk-weighted assets used to calculate the tier 1 common ratio, which uses the general risk-based capital approach for all quarters.

Projected losses, revenue, net income and other comprehensive income through 2016:Q4

	Billions of dollars	Percent of average assets[1]
Pre-provision net revenue[2]	27.1	6.5
Other revenue[3]	0.0	
less		
Provisions	11.3	
Realized losses/gains on securities (AFS/HTM)	0.0	
Trading and counterparty losses[4]	0.0	
Other losses/gains[5]	0.0	
equals		
Net income before taxes	15.8	3.8
Memo items		
Other comprehensive income[6]	-3.7	
Other effects on capital	Actual 2014:Q3	2016:Q4
AOCI included in capital (billions of dollars)[7]	-0.1	-2.5

[1] Average assets is the nine-quarter average of total assets.

[2] Pre-provision net revenue includes losses from operational-risk events, mortgage repurchase expenses, and other real estate owned (OREO) costs.

[3] Other revenue includes one-time income and (expense) items not included in pre-provision net revenue.

[4] Trading and counterparty losses include mark-to-market and credit valuation adjustments (CVA) losses and losses arising from the counterparty default scenario component applied to derivatives, securities lending, and repurchase agreement activities.

[5] Other losses/gains includes projected change in fair value of loans held for sale and loans held for investment measured under the fair-value option and goodwill impairment losses.

[6] Other comprehensive income (OCI) is only calculated for advanced approaches BHCs, and other BHCs that opt into the advanced approaches treatment of AOCI.

[7] Certain AOCI items are subject to transition into projected regulatory capital. Those transitions are 20 percent included in projected regulatory capital for 2014, 40 percent included in projected regulatory capital for 2015, and 60 percent included in projected regulatory capital for 2016.

Table C.30.A. Wells Fargo & Company
Projected stressed capital ratios, risk-weighted assets, losses, revenues, net income before taxes, and loan losses
Federal Reserve estimates: Severely adverse scenario

Actual 2014:Q3 projected stressed capital ratios through 2016:Q4

	Actual 2014:Q3	Stressed capital ratios[1]	
		Ending	Minimum
Tier 1 common ratio (%)	10.8	7.5	7.5
Common equity tier 1 capital ratio (%)[2]	11.1	6.9	6.9
Tier 1 risk-based capital ratio (%)	12.6	8.2	8.2
Total risk-based capital ratio (%)	15.6	11.1	11.1
Tier 1 leverage ratio (%)	9.6	6.4	6.4

[1] The capital ratios are calculated using capital action assumptions provided within the Dodd-Frank Act stress testing rule. These projections represent hypothetical estimates that involve an economic outcome that is more adverse than expected. These estimates are not forecasts of expected losses, revenues, net income before taxes, or capital ratios. The minimum capital ratio presented is for the period 2014:Q4 to 2016:Q4.

[2] Advanced approaches bank holding companies (BHCs) are subject to the common equity tier 1 ratio for the third and fourth quarter of 2014. All bank holding companies are subject to the common equity tier 1 ratio for each quarter of 2015 and 2016. An advanced approaches BHC includes any BHC that has consolidated total assets greater than or equal to $250 billion or consolidated total on-balance sheet foreign exposure of at least $10 billion. See 12 CFR 217.100(b)(1). Other BHCs include any BHC that is subject to 12 CFR 225.8 and is not an advanced approaches BHC.

Projected loan losses, by type of loan, 2014:Q4–2016:Q4

	Billions of dollars	Portfolio loss rates (%)[1]
Loan losses	48.8	5.8
First-lien mortgages, domestic	7.3	2.9
Junior liens and HELOCs, domestic	6.3	7.9
Commercial and industrial[2]	10.9	6.7
Commercial real estate, domestic	10.3	8.3
Credit cards	4.3	14.8
Other consumer[3]	5.7	6.6
Other loans[4]	4.0	3.4

[1] Average loan balances used to calculate portfolio loss rates exclude loans held for sale and loans held for investment under the fair-value option and are calculated over nine quarters.

[2] Commercial and industrial loans include small- and medium-enterprise loans and corporate cards.

[3] Other consumer loans include student loans and automobile loans.

[4] Other loans include international real estate loans.

Actual 2014:Q3 and projected 2016:Q4 risk-weighted assets

	Actual 2014:Q3	Projected 2016:Q4	
		General approach	Standardized approach
Risk-weighted assets (billions of dollars)[1]	1,222.9	1,265.8	1,313.6

[1] For each quarter in 2014, risk-weighted assets are calculated using the general risk-based capital approach set forth in 12 CFR 225, appendix A. For each quarter in 2015 and 2016, risk-weighted assets are calculated under the Board's standardized capital risk-based approach in 12 CFR 217, subpart D, except for the risk-weighted assets used to calculate the tier 1 common ratio, which uses the general risk-based capital approach for all quarters.

Projected losses, revenue, net income and other comprehensive income through 2016:Q4

	Billions of dollars	Percent of average assets[1]
Pre-provision net revenue[2]	42.7	2.5
Other revenue[3]	0.0	
less		
Provisions	56.4	
Realized losses/gains on securities (AFS/HTM)	5.0	
Trading and counterparty losses[4]	7.3	
Other losses/gains[5]	3.2	
equals		
Net income before taxes	-29.3	-1.7
Memo items		
Other comprehensive income[6]	-0.7	
Other effects on capital	*Actual 2014:Q3*	*2016:Q4*
AOCI included in capital (billions of dollars)[7]	0.6	1.4

[1] Average assets is the nine-quarter average of total assets.

[2] Pre-provision net revenue includes losses from operational-risk events, mortgage repurchase expenses, and other real estate owned (OREO) costs.

[3] Other revenue includes one-time income and (expense) items not included in pre-provision net revenue.

[4] Trading and counterparty losses include mark-to-market and credit valuation adjustments (CVA) losses and losses arising from the counterparty default scenario component applied to derivatives, securities lending, and repurchase agreement activities.

[5] Other losses/gains includes projected change in fair value of loans held for sale and loans held for investment measured under the fair-value option and goodwill impairment losses.

[6] Other comprehensive income (OCI) is only calculated for advanced approaches BHCs, and other BHCs that opt into the advanced approaches treatment of AOCI.

[7] Certain AOCI items are subject to transition into projected regulatory capital. Those transitions are 20 percent included in projected regulatory capital for 2014, 40 percent included in projected regulatory capital for 2015, and 60 percent included in projected regulatory capital for 2016.

Table C.30.B. Wells Fargo & Company
Projected stressed capital ratios, risk-weighted assets, losses, revenues, net income before taxes, and loan losses
Federal Reserve estimates: Adverse scenario

Actual 2014:Q3 projected stressed capital ratios through 2016:Q4

	Actual 2014:Q3	Stressed capital ratios[1]	
		Ending	Minimum
Tier 1 common ratio (%)	10.8	9.9	9.7
Common equity tier 1 capital ratio (%)[2]	11.1	8.4	8.4
Tier 1 risk-based capital ratio (%)	12.6	9.7	9.6
Total risk-based capital ratio (%)	15.6	12.3	12.3
Tier 1 leverage ratio (%)	9.6	7.4	7.4

[1] The capital ratios are calculated using capital action assumptions provided within the Dodd-Frank Act stress testing rule. These projections represent hypothetical estimates that involve an economic outcome that is more adverse than expected. These estimates are not forecasts of expected losses, revenues, net income before taxes, or capital ratios. The minimum capital ratio presented is for the period 2014:Q4 to 2016:Q4.

[2] Advanced approaches bank holding companies (BHCs) are subject to the common equity tier 1 ratio for the third and fourth quarter of 2014. All bank holding companies are subject to the common equity tier 1 ratio for each quarter of 2015 and 2016. An advanced approaches BHC includes any BHC that has consolidated total assets greater than or equal to $250 billion or consolidated total on-balance sheet foreign exposure of at least $10 billion. See 12 CFR 217.100(b)(1). Other BHCs include any BHC that is subject to 12 CFR 225.8 and is not an advanced approaches BHC.

Projected loan losses, by type of loan, 2014:Q4–2016:Q4

	Billions of dollars	Portfolio loss rates (%)[1]
Loan losses	32.0	3.7
First-lien mortgages, domestic	4.5	1.8
Junior liens and HELOCs, domestic	4.0	5.0
Commercial and industrial[2]	7.2	4.3
Commercial real estate, domestic	6.0	4.8
Credit cards	3.5	12.0
Other consumer[3]	4.5	5.1
Other loans[4]	2.3	1.9

[1] Average loan balances used to calculate portfolio loss rates exclude loans held for sale and loans held for investment under the fair-value option and are calculated over nine quarters.

[2] Commercial and industrial loans include small- and medium-enterprise loans and corporate cards.

[3] Other consumer loans include student loans and automobile loans.

[4] Other loans include international real estate loans.

Actual 2014:Q3 and projected 2016:Q4 risk-weighted assets

	Actual 2014:Q3	Projected 2016:Q4	
		General approach	Standardized approach
Risk-weighted assets (billions of dollars)[1]	1,222.9	1,319.2	1,361.7

[1] For each quarter in 2014, risk-weighted assets are calculated using the general risk-based capital approach set forth in 12 CFR 225, appendix A. For each quarter in 2015 and 2016, risk-weighted assets are calculated under the Board's standardized capital risk-based approach in 12 CFR 217, subpart D, except for the risk-weighted assets used to calculate the tier 1 common ratio, which uses the general risk-based capital approach for all quarters.

Projected losses, revenue, net income and other comprehensive income through 2016:Q4

	Billions of dollars	Percent of average assets[1]
Pre-provision net revenue[2]	66.5	3.8
Other revenue[3]	0.0	
less		
Provisions	33.2	
Realized losses/gains on securities (AFS/HTM)	2.1	
Trading and counterparty losses[4]	4.0	
Other losses/gains[5]	1.7	
equals		
Net income before taxes	25.5	1.5
Memo items		
Other comprehensive income[6]	-21.9	
Other effects on capital	Actual 2014:Q3	2016:Q4
AOCI included in capital (billions of dollars)[7]	0.6	-11.3

[1] Average assets is the nine-quarter average of total assets.

[2] Pre-provision net revenue includes losses from operational-risk events, mortgage repurchase expenses, and other real estate owned (OREO) costs.

[3] Other revenue includes one-time income and (expense) items not included in pre-provision net revenue.

[4] Trading and counterparty losses include mark-to-market and credit valuation adjustments (CVA) losses and losses arising from the counterparty default scenario component applied to derivatives, securities lending, and repurchase agreement activities.

[5] Other losses/gains includes projected change in fair value of loans held for sale and loans held for investment measured under the fair-value option and goodwill impairment losses.

[6] Other comprehensive income (OCI) is only calculated for advanced approaches BHCs, and other BHCs that opt into the advanced approaches treatment of AOCI.

[7] Certain AOCI items are subject to transition into projected regulatory capital. Those transitions are 20 percent included in projected regulatory capital for 2014, 40 percent included in projected regulatory capital for 2015, and 60 percent included in projected regulatory capital for 2016.

Table C.31.A. Zions Bancorporation
Projected stressed capital ratios, risk-weighted assets, losses, revenues, net income before taxes, and loan losses
Federal Reserve estimates: Severely adverse scenario

Actual 2014:Q3 projected stressed capital ratios through 2016:Q4

	Actual 2014:Q3	Stressed capital ratios[1]	
		Ending	Minimum
Tier 1 common ratio (%)	11.9	5.1	5.1
Common equity tier 1 capital ratio (%)[2]	n/a	6.0	6.0
Tier 1 risk-based capital ratio (%)	14.4	7.3	7.3
Total risk-based capital ratio (%)	16.3	9.4	9.4
Tier 1 leverage ratio (%)	11.9	5.9	5.9

[1]   The capital ratios are calculated using capital action assumptions provided within the Dodd-Frank Act stress testing rule. These projections represent hypothetical estimates that involve an economic outcome that is more adverse than expected. These estimates are not forecasts of expected losses, revenues, net income before taxes, or capital ratios. The minimum capital ratio presented is for the period 2014:Q4 to 2016:Q4.

[2]   Advanced approaches bank holding companies (BHCs) are subject to the common equity tier 1 ratio for the third and fourth quarter of 2014. All bank holding companies are subject to the common equity tier 1 ratio for each quarter of 2015 and 2016. An advanced approaches BHC includes any BHC that has consolidated total assets greater than or equal to $250 billion or consolidated total on-balance sheet foreign exposure of at least $10 billion. See 12 CFR 217.100(b)(1). Other BHCs include any BHC that is subject to 12 CFR 225.8 and is not an advanced approaches BHC.

n/a   Not applicable.

Projected loan losses, by type of loan, 2014:Q4–2016:Q4

	Billions of dollars	Portfolio loss rates (%)[1]
Loan losses	2.6	6.5
First-lien mortgages, domestic	0.0	0.9
Junior liens and HELOCs, domestic	0.1	4.2
Commercial and industrial[2]	0.8	6.8
Commercial real estate, domestic	1.5	8.2
Credit cards	0.0	14.7
Other consumer[3]	0.1	11.6
Other loans[4]	0.1	4.6

[1]   Average loan balances used to calculate portfolio loss rates exclude loans held for sale and loans held for investment under the fair-value option and are calculated over nine quarters.

[2]   Commercial and industrial loans include small- and medium-enterprise loans and corporate cards.

[3]   Other consumer loans include student loans and automobile loans.

[4]   Other loans include international real estate loans.

Actual 2014:Q3 and projected 2016:Q4 risk-weighted assets

	Actual 2014:Q3	Projected 2016:Q4	
		General approach	Standardized approach
Risk-weighted assets (billions of dollars)[1]	45.4	46.2	48.0

[1]   For each quarter in 2014, risk-weighted assets are calculated using the general risk-based capital approach set forth in 12 CFR 225, appendix A. For each quarter in 2015 and 2016, risk-weighted assets are calculated under the Board's standardized capital risk-based approach in 12 CFR 217, subpart D, except for the risk-weighted assets used to calculate the tier 1 common ratio, which uses the general risk-based capital approach for all quarters.

Projected losses, revenue, net income and other comprehensive income through 2016:Q4

	Billions of dollars	Percent of average assets[1]
Pre-provision net revenue[2]	0.6	1.1
Other revenue[3]	0.0	
less		
Provisions	3.0	
Realized losses/gains on securities (AFS/HTM)	0.4	
Trading and counterparty losses[4]	0.0	
Other losses/gains[5]	0.0	
equals		
Net income before taxes	-2.9	-5.0
Memo items		
Other comprehensive income[6]	0.0	
Other effects on capital	*Actual 2014:Q3*	*2016:Q4*
AOCI included in capital (billions of dollars)[7]	n/a	0.0

[1]   Average assets is the nine-quarter average of total assets.

[2]   Pre-provision net revenue includes losses from operational-risk events, mortgage repurchase expenses, and other real estate owned (OREO) costs.

[3]   Other revenue includes one-time income and (expense) items not included in pre-provision net revenue.

[4]   Trading and counterparty losses include mark-to-market and credit valuation adjustments (CVA) losses and losses arising from the counterparty default scenario component applied to derivatives, securities lending, and repurchase agreement activities.

[5]   Other losses/gains includes projected change in fair value of loans held for sale and loans held for investment measured under the fair-value option, and goodwill impairment losses.

[6]   Other comprehensive income (OCI) is only calculated for advanced approaches BHCs, and other BHCs that opt into the advanced approaches treatment of AOCI.

[7]   Certain AOCI items are subject to transition into projected regulatory capital. Those transitions are 20 percent included in projected regulatory capital for 2014, 40 percent included in projected regulatory capital for 2015, and 60 percent included in projected regulatory capital for 2016.

Table C.31.B. Zions Bancorporation
Projected stressed capital ratios, risk-weighted assets, losses, revenues, net income before taxes, and loan losses
Federal Reserve estimates: Adverse scenario

Actual 2014:Q3 projected stressed capital ratios through 2016:Q4

	Actual 2014:Q3	Stressed capital ratios[1]	
		Ending	Minimum
Tier 1 common ratio (%)	11.9	10.4	10.4
Common equity tier 1 capital ratio (%)[2]	n/a	10.3	10.3
Tier 1 risk-based capital ratio (%)	14.4	12.3	12.3
Total risk-based capital ratio (%)	16.3	14.4	14.4
Tier 1 leverage ratio (%)	11.9	9.8	9.8

[1] The capital ratios are calculated using capital action assumptions provided within the Dodd-Frank Act stress testing rule. These projections represent hypothetical estimates that involve an economic outcome that is more adverse than expected. These estimates are not forecasts of expected losses, revenues, net income before taxes, or capital ratios. The minimum capital ratio presented is for the period 2014:Q4 to 2016:Q4.

[2] Advanced approaches bank holding companies (BHCs) are subject to the common equity tier 1 ratio for the third and fourth quarter of 2014. All bank holding companies are subject to the common equity tier 1 ratio for each quarter of 2015 and 2016. An advanced approaches BHC includes any BHC that has consolidated total assets greater than or equal to $250 billion or consolidated total on-balance sheet foreign exposure of at least $10 billion. See 12 CFR 217.100(b)(1). Other BHCs include any BHC that is subject to 12 CFR 225.8 and is not an advanced approaches BHC.

n/a Not applicable.

Projected loan losses, by type of loan, 2014:Q4–2016:Q4

	Billions of dollars	Portfolio loss rates (%)[1]
Loan losses	1.6	3.8
First-lien mortgages, domestic	0.0	0.4
Junior liens and HELOCs, domestic	0.1	2.6
Commercial and industrial[2]	0.5	4.2
Commercial real estate, domestic	0.8	4.7
Credit cards	0.0	11.9
Other consumer[3]	0.0	9.3
Other loans[4]	0.1	2.7

[1] Average loan balances used to calculate portfolio loss rates exclude loans held for sale and loans held for investment under the fair-value option and are calculated over nine quarters.

[2] Commercial and industrial loans include small- and medium-enterprise loans and corporate cards.

[3] Other consumer loans include student loans and automobile loans.

[4] Other loans include international real estate loans.

Actual 2014:Q3 and projected 2016:Q4 risk-weighted assets

	Actual 2014:Q3	Projected 2016:Q4	
		General approach	Standardized approach
Risk-weighted assets (billions of dollars)[1]	45.4	48.3	49.2

[1] For each quarter in 2014, risk-weighted assets are calculated using the general risk-based capital approach set forth in 12 CFR 225, appendix A. For each quarter in 2015 and 2016, risk-weighted assets are calculated under the Board's standardized capital risk-based approach in 12 CFR 217, subpart D, except for the risk-weighted assets used to calculate the tier 1 common ratio, which uses the general risk-based capital approach for all quarters.

Projected losses, revenue, net income and other comprehensive income through 2016:Q4

	Billions of dollars	Percent of average assets[1]
Pre-provision net revenue[2]	1.5	2.6
Other revenue[3]	0.0	
less		
Provisions	1.6	
Realized losses/gains on securities (AFS/HTM)	0.1	
Trading and counterparty losses[4]	0.0	
Other losses/gains[5]	0.0	
equals		
Net income before taxes	-0.2	-0.4
Memo items		
Other comprehensive income[6]	0.0	
Other effects on capital	Actual 2014:Q3	2016:Q4
AOCI included in capital (billions of dollars)[7]	n/a	0.0

[1] Average assets is the nine-quarter average of total assets.

[2] Pre-provision net revenue includes losses from operational-risk events, mortgage repurchase expenses, and other real estate owned (OREO) costs.

[3] Other revenue includes one-time income and (expense) items not included in pre-provision net revenue.

[4] Trading and counterparty losses include mark-to-market and credit valuation adjustments (CVA) losses and losses arising from the counterparty default scenario component applied to derivatives, securities lending, and repurchase agreement activities.

[5] Other losses/gains includes projected change in fair value of loans held for sale and loans held for investment measured under the fair-value option, and goodwill impairment losses.

[6] Other comprehensive income (OCI) is only calculated for advanced approaches BHCs, and other BHCs that opt into the advanced approaches treatment of AOCI.

[7] Certain AOCI items are subject to transition into projected regulatory capital. Those transitions are 20 percent included in projected regulatory capital for 2014, 40 percent included in projected regulatory capital for 2015, and 60 percent included in projected regulatory capital for 2016.

Appendix D: Additional Aggregate Results

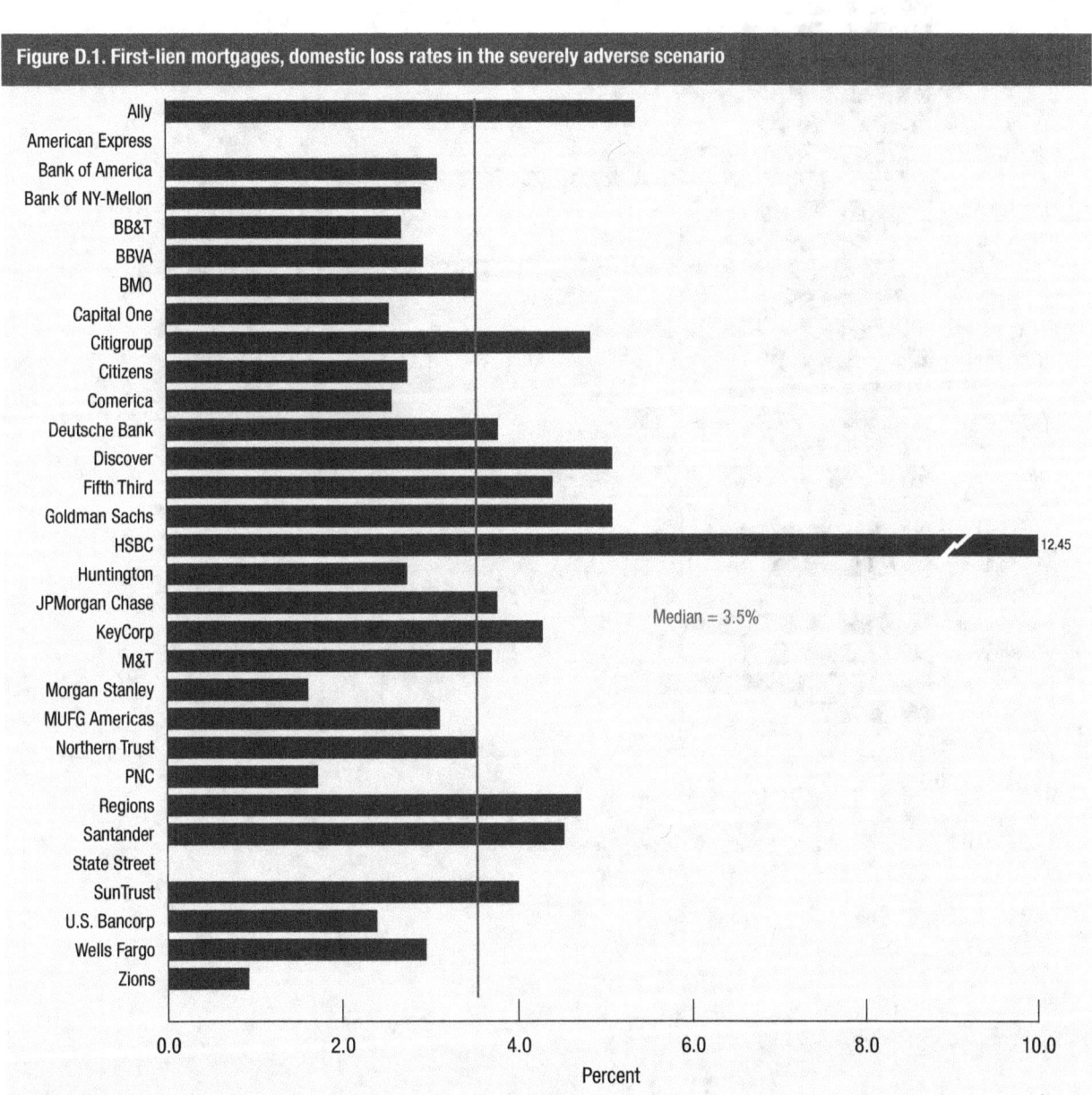

Figure D.1. First-lien mortgages, domestic loss rates in the severely adverse scenario

Estimates are for nine-quarter period from 2014:Q4–2016:Q4 as a percent of average balances.

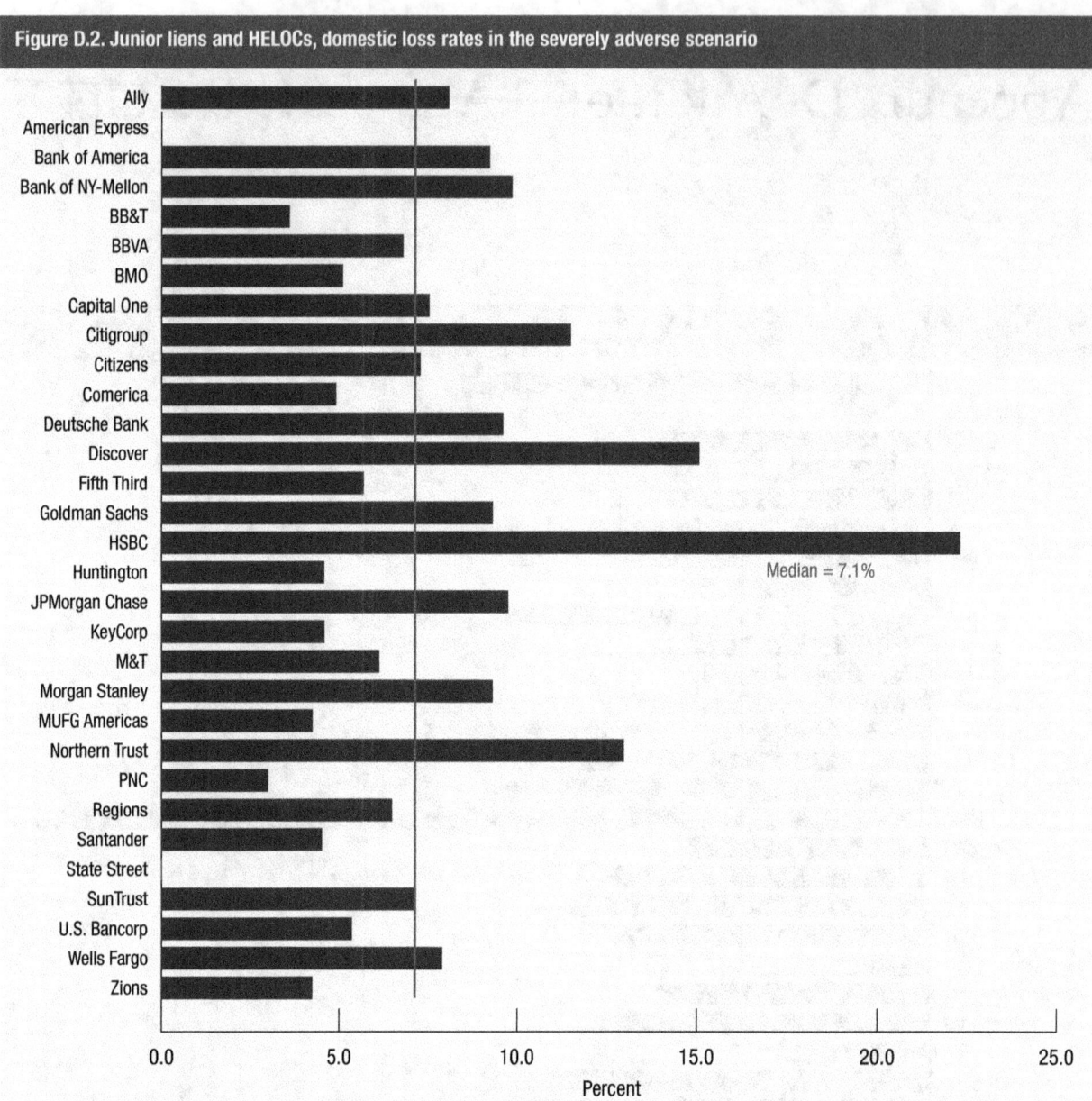

Figure D.2. Junior liens and HELOCs, domestic loss rates in the severely adverse scenario

Median = 7.1%

Percent

Estimates are for nine-quarter period from 2014:Q4–2016:Q4 as a percent of average balances.

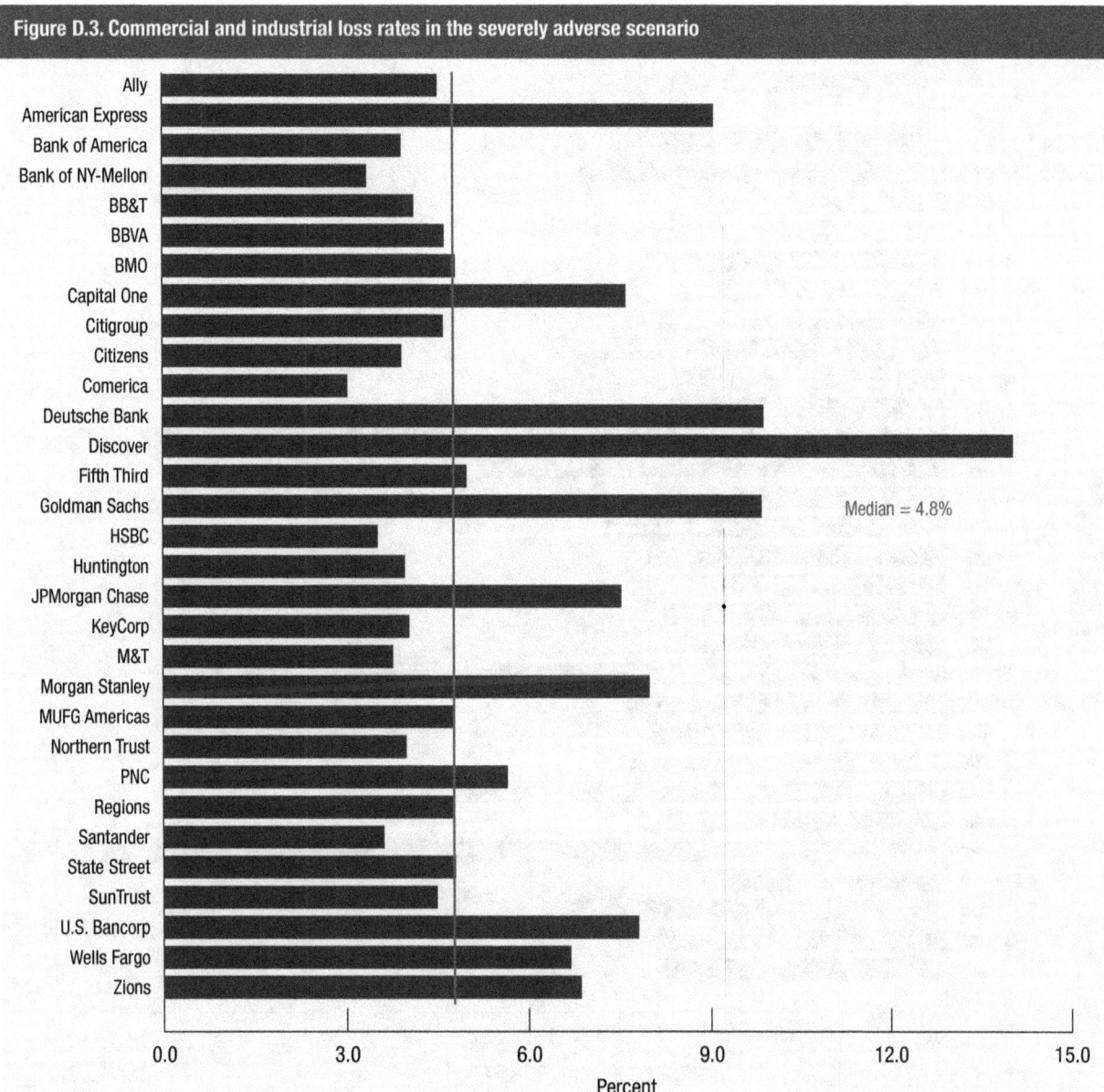

Figure D.3. Commercial and industrial loss rates in the severely adverse scenario

Median = 4.8%

Percent

Note: Estimates are for the nine-quarter period from 2014:Q4–2016:Q4 as a percent of average balances. Losses are calculated based on the exposure at default, which includes both outstanding balances and any additional drawdown of the credit line that occurs prior to default, while loss rates are calculated as a percent of outstanding balances.

Figure D.4. Commercial real estate, domestic loss rates in the severely adverse scenario

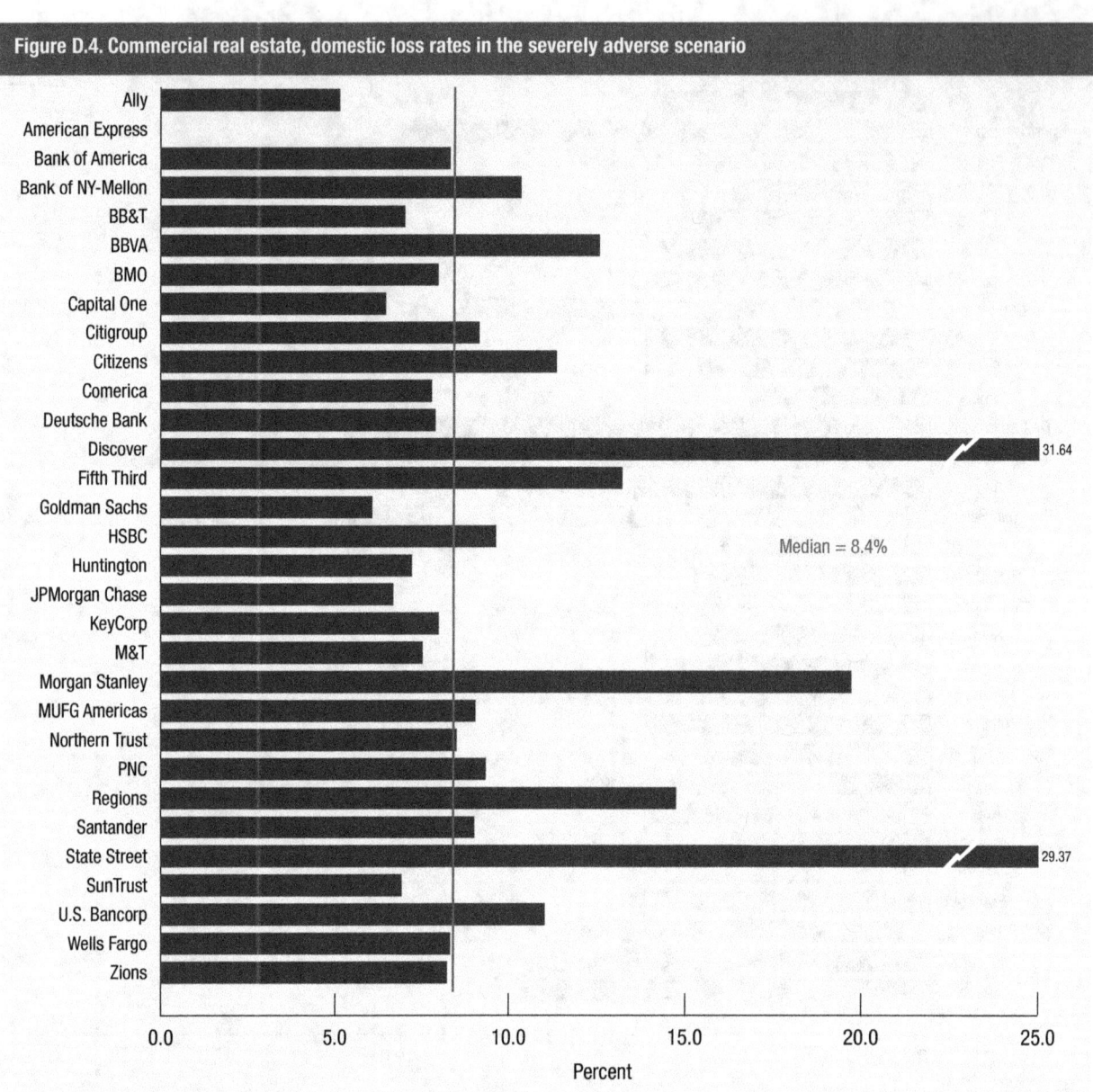

Note: Estimates are for the nine-quarter period from 2014:Q4–2016:Q4 as a percent of average balances.

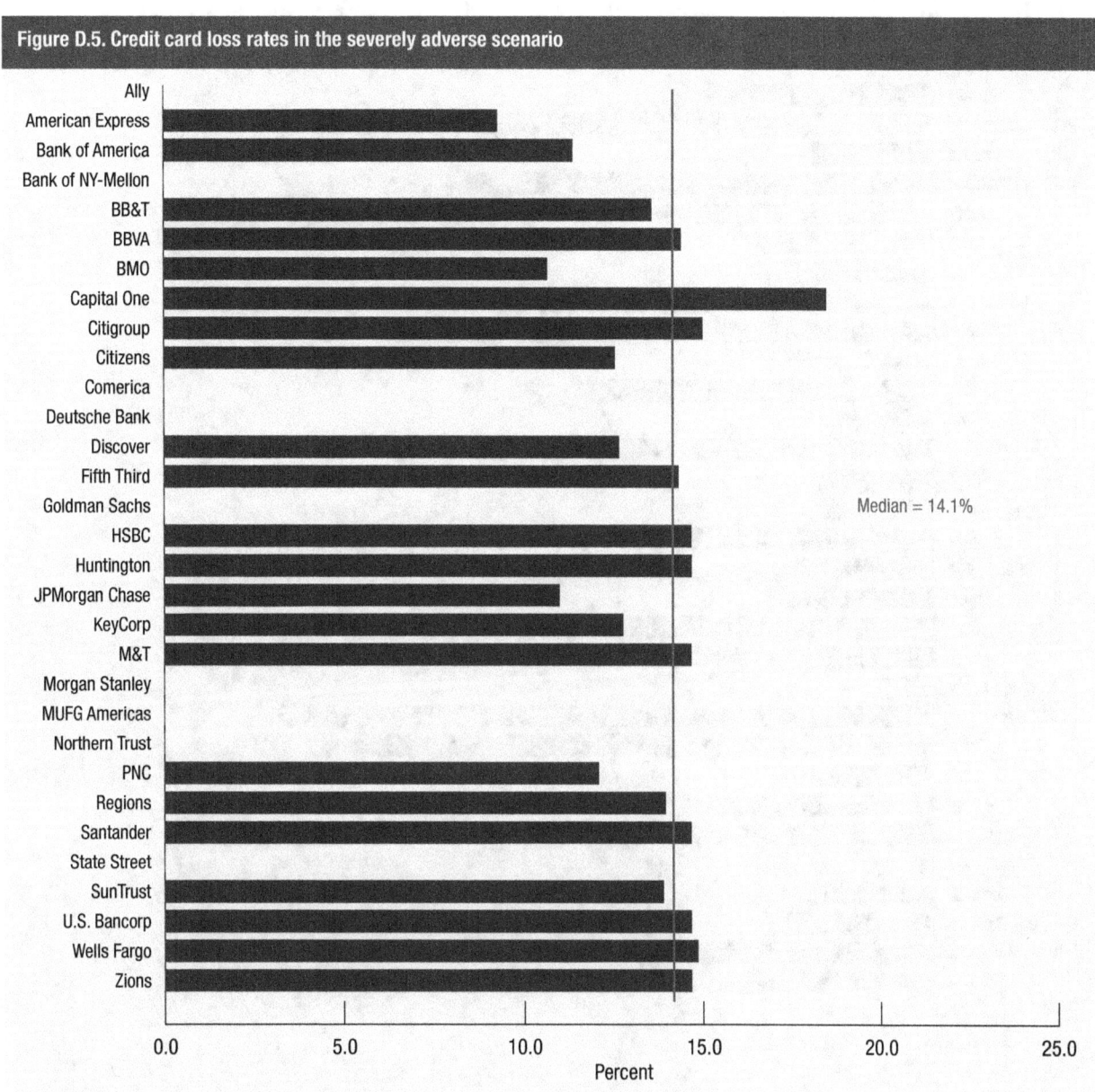

Figure D.5. Credit card loss rates in the severely adverse scenario

Note: Estimates are for the nine-quarter period from 2014:Q4–2016:Q4 as a percent of average balances.

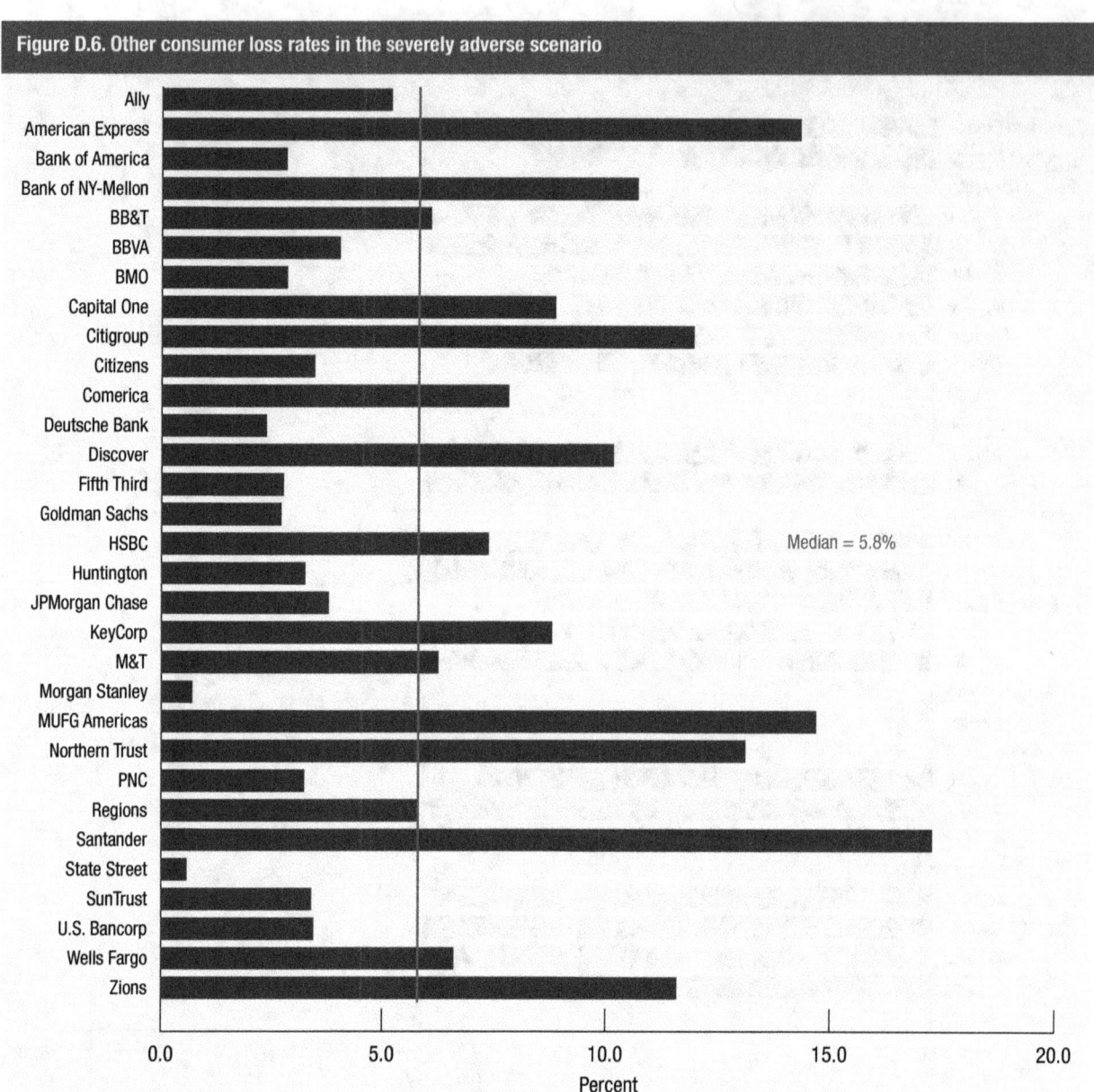

Figure D.6. Other consumer loss rates in the severely adverse scenario

Note: Estimates are for the nine-quarter period from 2014:Q4–2016:Q4 as a percent of average balances.

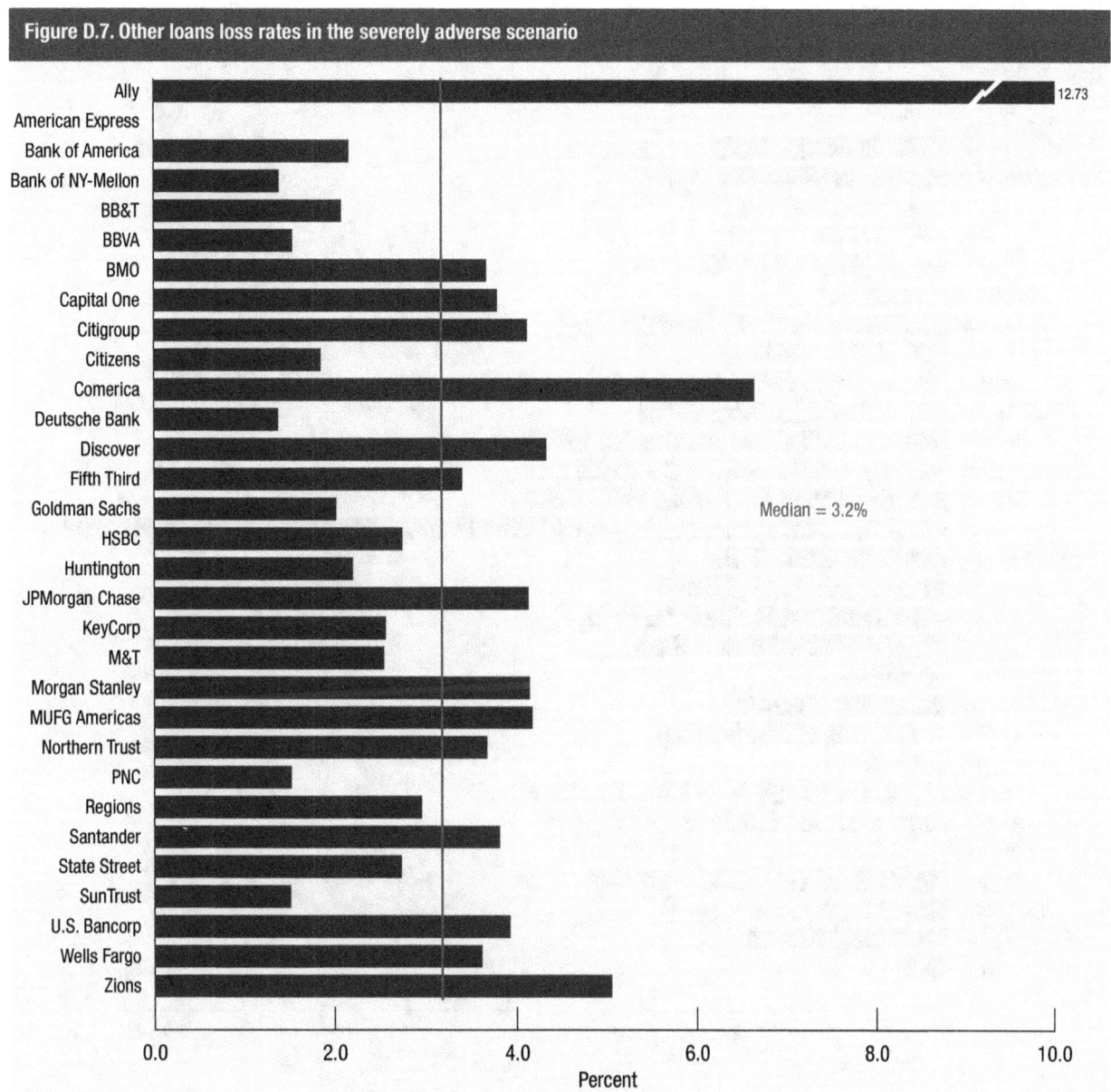

Figure D.7. Other loans loss rates in the severely adverse scenario

Note: Estimates are for the nine-quarter period from 2014:Q4–2016:Q4 as a percent of average balances.

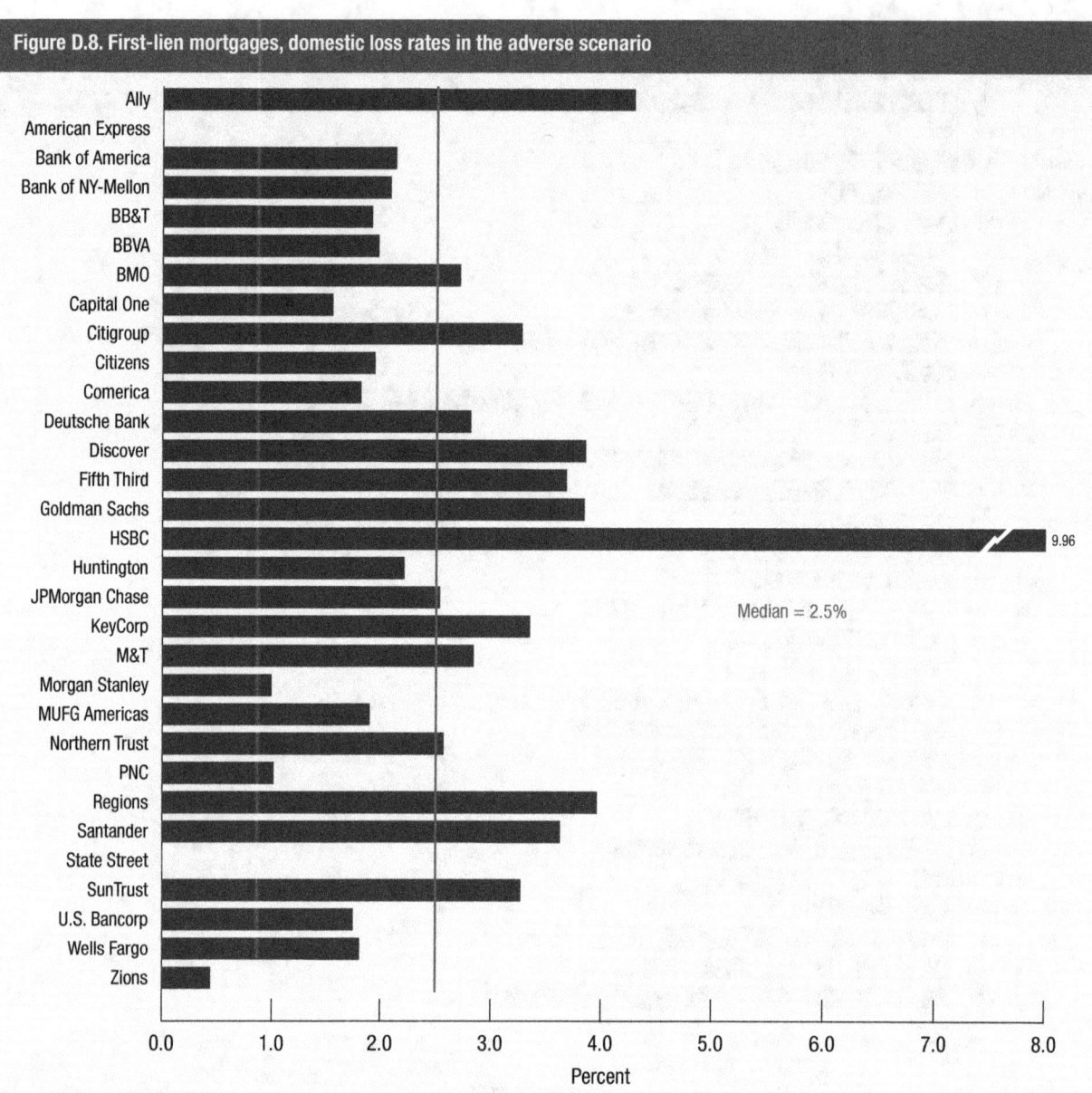

Figure D.8. First-lien mortgages, domestic loss rates in the adverse scenario

Estimates are for nine-quarter period from 2014:Q4–2016:Q4 as a percent of average balances.

Figure D.9. Junior liens and HELOCs, domestic loss rates in the adverse scenario

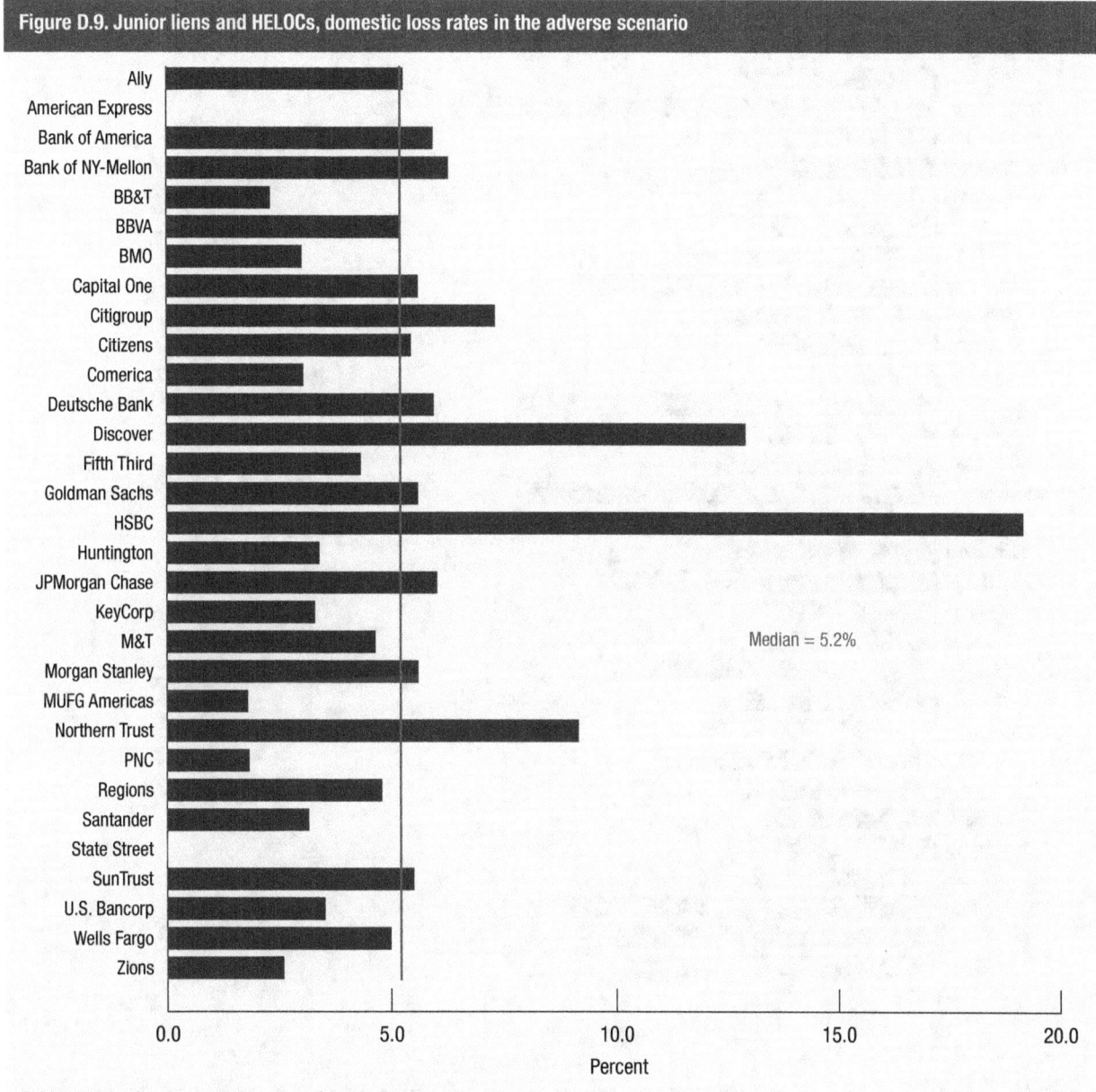

Median = 5.2%

Estimates are for nine-quarter period from 2014:Q4–2016:Q4 as a percent of average balances.

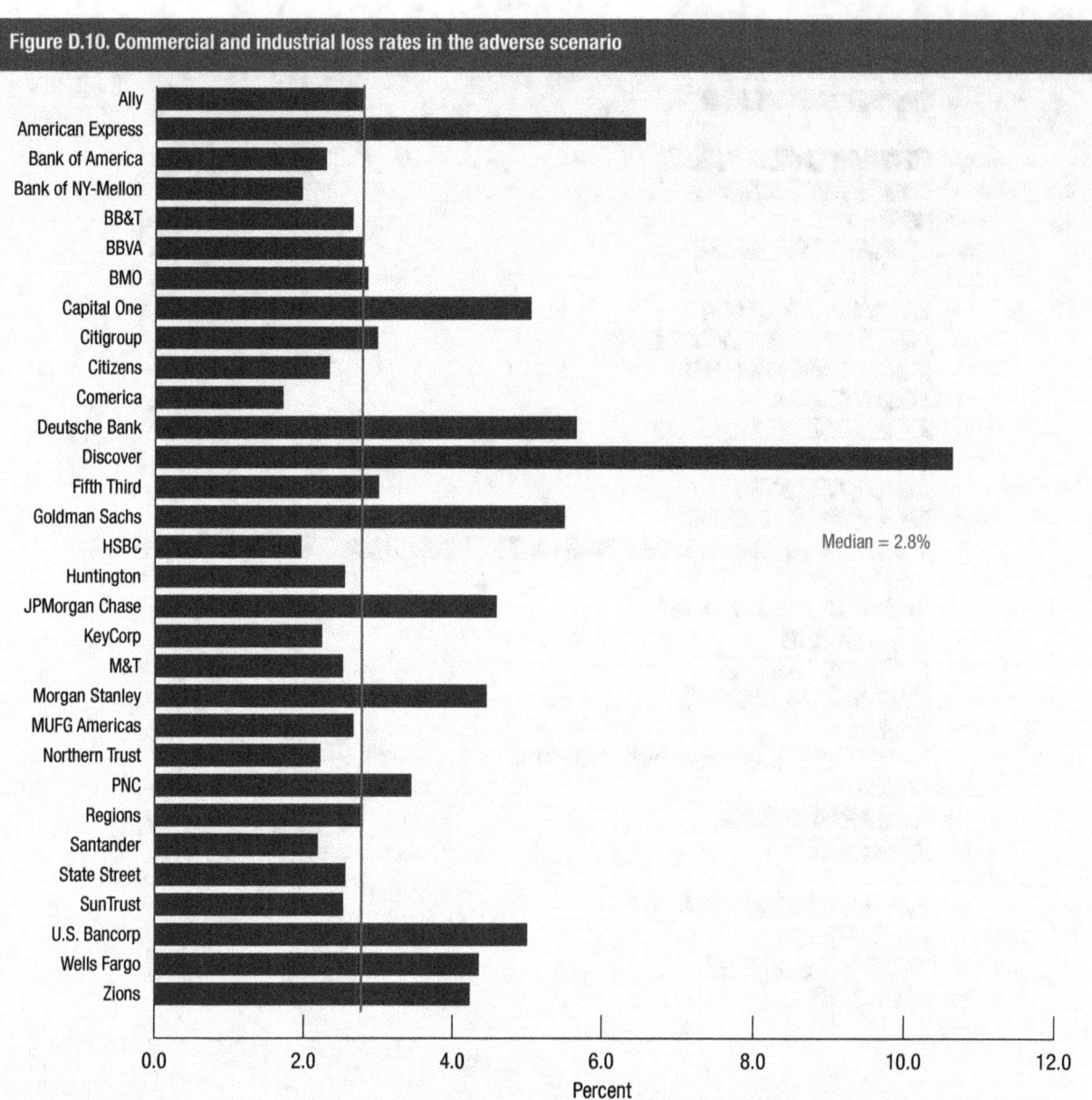

Figure D.10. Commercial and industrial loss rates in the adverse scenario

Median = 2.8%

Percent

Note: Estimates are for the nine-quarter period from 2014:Q4–2016:Q4 as a percent of average balances. Losses are calculated based on the exposure at default, which includes both outstanding balances and any additional drawdown of the credit line that occurs prior to default, while loss rates are calculated as a percent of outstanding balances.

Figure D.11. Commercial real estate, domestic loss rates in the adverse scenario

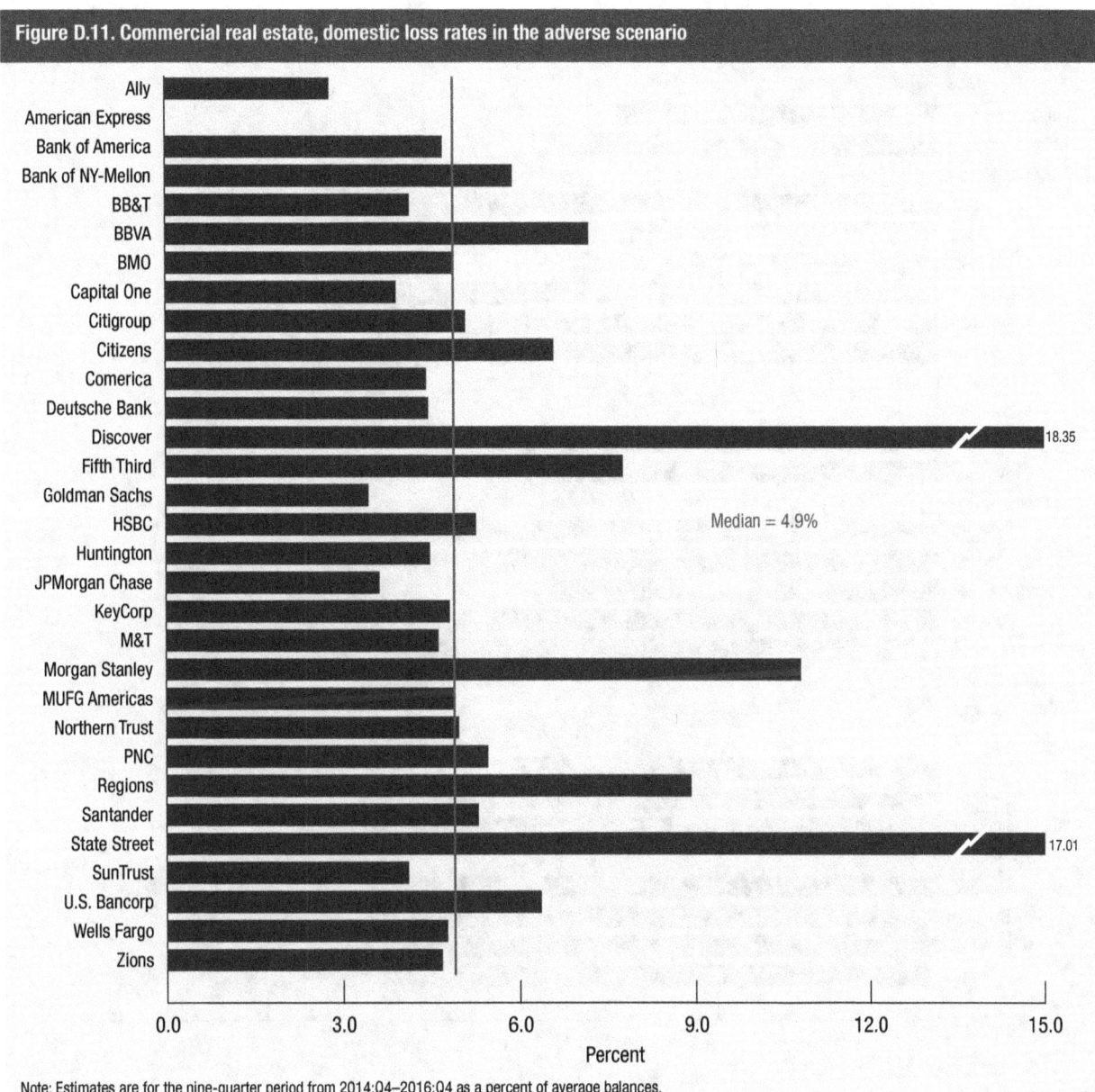

Note: Estimates are for the nine-quarter period from 2014:Q4–2016:Q4 as a percent of average balances.

Figure D.12. Credit card loss rates in the adverse scenario

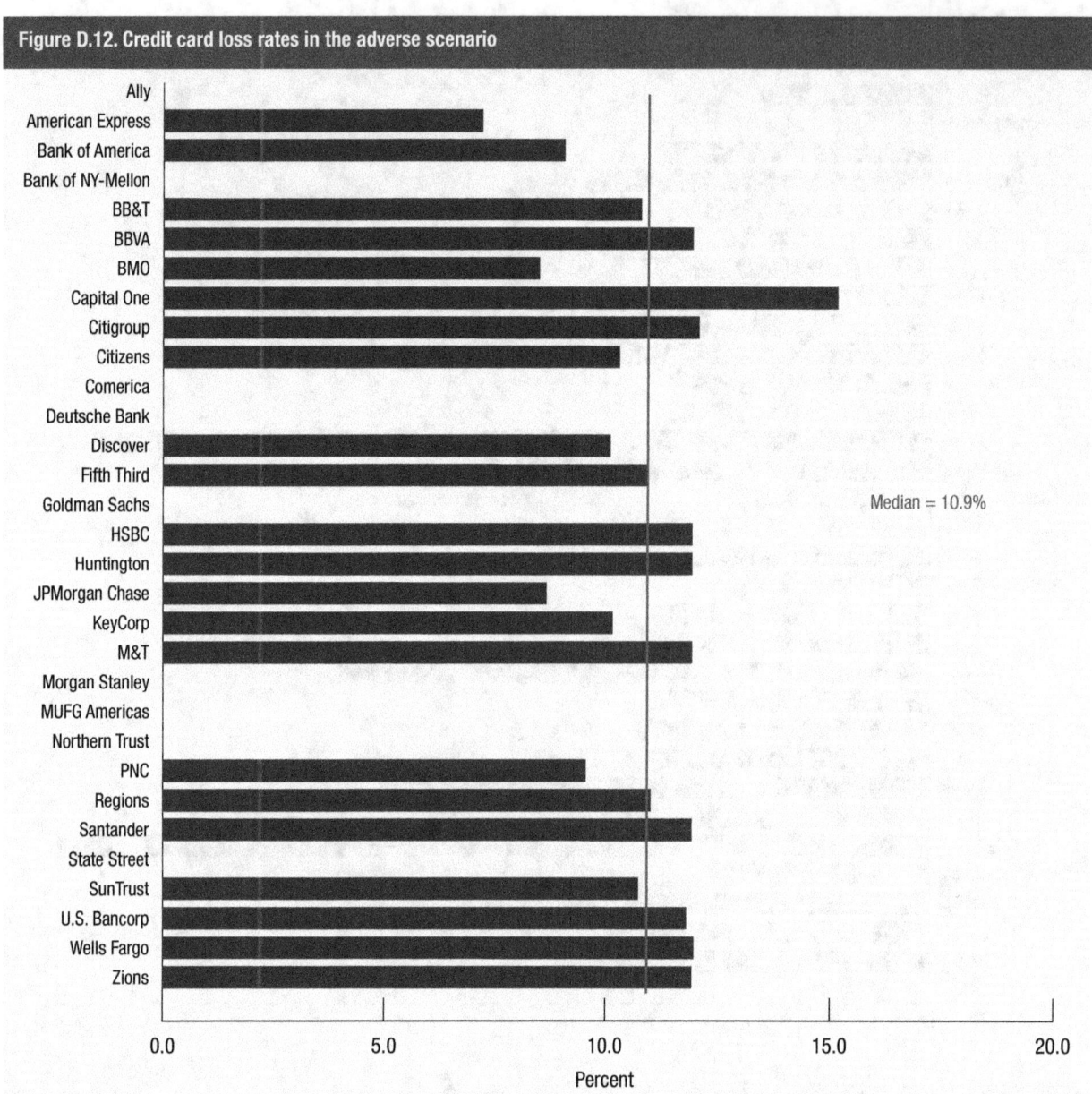

Note: Estimates are for the nine-quarter period from 2014:Q4–2016:Q4 as a percent of average balances.

Figure D.13. Other consumer loss rates in the adverse scenario

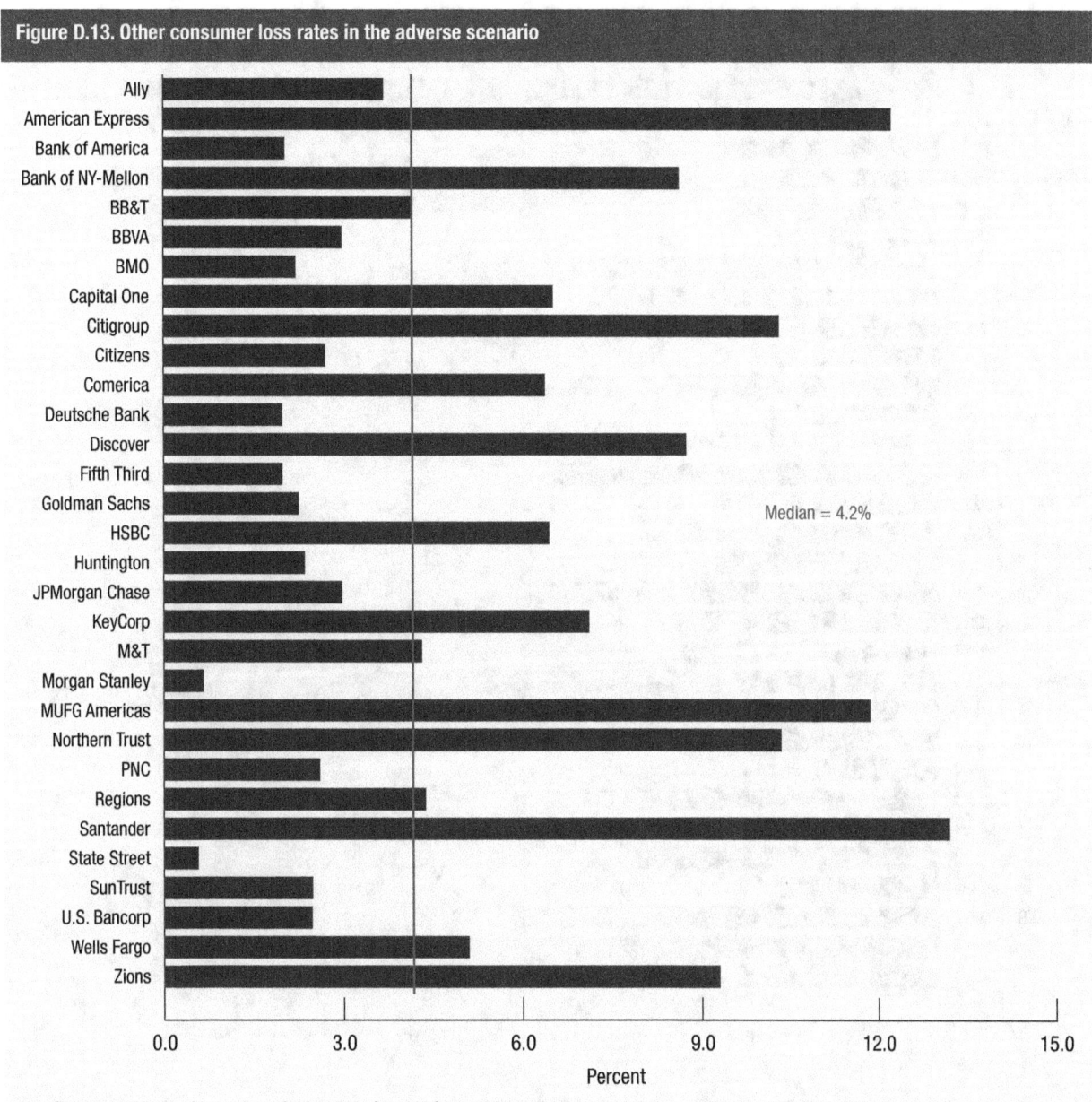

Note: Estimates are for the nine-quarter period from 2014:Q4–2016:Q4 as a percent of average balances.

Figure D.14. Other loans loss rates in the adverse scenario

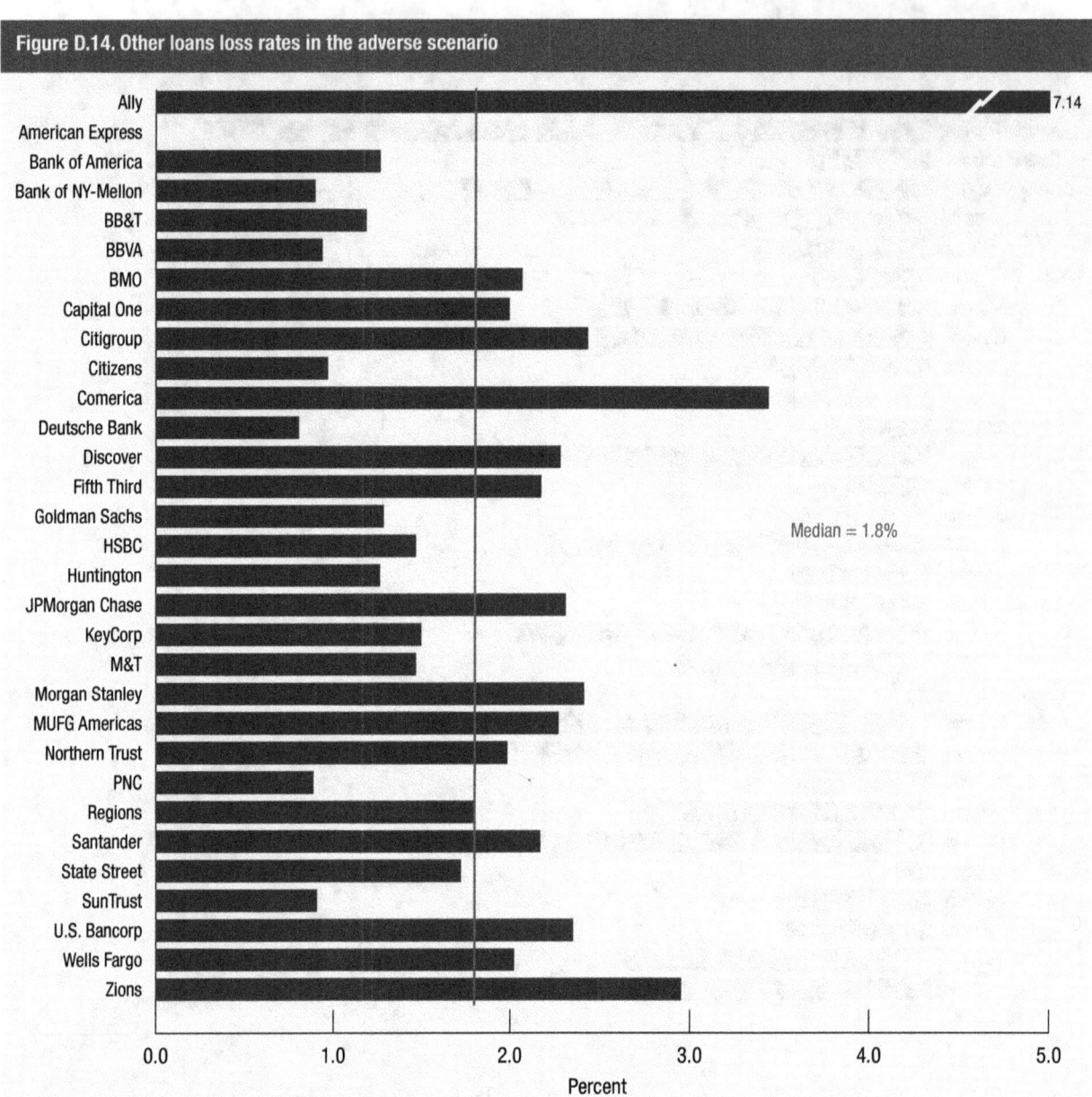

Note: Estimates are for the nine-quarter period from 2014:Q4–2016:Q4 as a percent of average balances.

www.ingramcontent.com/pod-product-compliance
Lightning Source LLC
Chambersburg PA
CBHW080253290526
45790CB00005B/1791